D1710529

"What a wonderful man in his physical conformation is Andrew Jackson! . . . the iron man of his age—the incarnation of American courage."

Mississippi Free Trader and Natchez Weekly Gazette
January 16, 1840

National Portrait Gallery
Tennessee State Museum

Andrew Jackson
A Portrait Study

James G. Barber

Published by the

National Portrait Gallery, Smithsonian Institution, Washington, D.C.

and by the

Tennessee State Museum, Nashville

in association with the

University of Washington Press, Seattle and London

1991

This book has been sponsored in part through the support of the Tennessee General Assembly.

Library of Congress Cataloging-in-Publication Data
Barber, James, 1952-
   Andrew Jackson: a portrait study/ James G. Barber
      p. cm.
   Includes bibliographical references and index.
   ISBN 0-295-97082-0: $29.95
   1. Jackson, Andrew, 1767–1845—Portraits. 2. Presidents—United States—Portraits.
   I. National Portrait Gallery (Smithsonian Institution) II. Tennessee State Museum. III.
   Title.
E382.B25 1991
973.5'6—dc20
                                            90-15517
                                            CIP

Frontispiece:
The "National Picture" of Andrew Jackson. Oil on canvas by Ralph E. W. Earl
(circa 1788–1838), 1836–1837. National Museum of American Art, Smithsonian Institution,
Washington, D.C.; transfer from United States District Court for the District of Columbia

Contents

Foreword

Andrew Jackson, thin and tall (though not as tall as George Washington), erect of carriage, with angular features and a penetrating gaze, presented an unforgettable appearance to all who saw him. Neither conventionally handsome nor elegant in his dress, he was characterized by an anonymous English journalist as "the model of republican simplicity and straightforwardness," and appeared to actress Fanny Kemble as "a good specimen of a fine old, well-battered soldier." Another traveler from abroad thought Jackson "at first sight not altogether unlike Shakespeare's starved apothecary."[1]

His striking appearance by itself might have been an attraction to artists, but coupled with Jackson's military and political victories in fierce contests, and his enormous popular appeal as the first national leader to emerge from a modest background, he was an irresistible magnet for portraitists. As Jackson became more prominent—and the demand for his portraits increased—he became a favored subject; indeed, he was probably the most painted of all the American Presidents, with Ralph E. W. Earl alone accounting for more than thirty likenesses.

As Arthur Schlesinger, Jr., has observed in *The Age of Jackson,* "a flowering of American arts and letters occurred during the Jacksonian age."[2] By the time of Jackson's presidency, the European-trained artists who had set the early standards in American portraiture had given way to a new generation of accomplished native-born painters and sculptors. By 1845, the year of Jackson's death, the new art of photography had come to America and, though the former President was old and ill, he yielded to the daguerreotypists' pleadings and was recorded by the lens as well as the brush.

Unlike the previous Presidents, Jackson had grown up in humble circumstances, and (based on the extant record) seems never to have had a portrait done before his forty-eighth year. Because he was the quintessential man of the people, one does not think of Jackson portrayed in the "grand manner," as George Washington was depicted in Gilbert Stuart's "Lansdowne" portrait. Yet, while Washington kept his distance from artists as much as he was able, Jackson actually had a painter-in-residence during his presidency. Like Washington, Jackson is reported to have been impatient with the demands of artists for likenesses, and was ill at ease in sittings, but the presence of his friend and protégé, the painter Ralph E. W. Earl, as a member of his family circle in the White House may have helped him to understand something of the artist's requirements and to yield with more kindness than Washington did to their importunities.

Jackson was fundamentally a simple man of conventional tastes. His patronage of Earl may have sprung more from his affection for the man than from a conscious desire to support the arts. His fostering of other humanistic pursuits may have emerged from a similarly intuitive or instinctive sense of what might be appropriate for the nation. For example, John S. Meehan, Jackson's appointee as Librarian of Congress, presided over the expansion and democratization of the Library and set it on its course as America's national library. The acquisition and cataloging of collections was improved, the space allotted to the Library was expanded, and the premises were opened to admit readers who were not members of Congress. And, in a sense, Jackson was instrumental in establishing the Institution within which the National Portrait Gallery exists.

In 1826, shortly before Jackson became President, James Smithson—the illegitimate son of a prominent nobleman—died. In 1835 his one remaining residuary legatee passed away; Smithson's will provided that if this occurred his estate would pass to "the United States of America, to found at Washington . . . an Establishment for the increase and diffusion of knowledge among men." Jackson appointed Richard Rush as a special agent in 1836 to prosecute America's claim to the Smithson bequest in the British Courts of Chancery; only two years later—a remarkably short time, given the usual course of actions in the Chancery Courts—the bequest was allowed. John Quincy Adams, Jackson's predecessor in the White House, was now a member of the House of Representatives, and was appointed chairman of a select committee which would determine how to use the funds. In Adams's speeches during the deliberations about the Smithson bequest, he alluded to the recent bitterness of the presidential election, clearly signifying his distance from Jackson's populist supporters, but he also paid tribute to the negotiating skill of Jackson's agent, and to the President for bringing the matter to such a promising conclusion. The Smithson bequest—the curious combination of an unexpected windfall from a formerly unfriendly land, the determined action of a rough-hewn President, and the intellectual guidance of one of America's principal aristocrats—was, of course, the foundation of the Smithsonian Institution. Thus, the National Portrait Gallery—a bureau of the Smithsonian—owes a special debt to President Jackson, which, we hope, is partially repaid in this celebration of the record of his life in portraiture.

In 1990, having previously explored in exhibitions the legislative and judicial branches of the federal government of the United States of America as part of the bicentennial commemoration of the American Constitution, the National Portrait Gallery turned at last to the executive branch. James G. Barber, one of the Gallery's historians, has concentrated on a single President, instead of attempting a survey of presidential or cabinet likenesses; the exhibition he organized, and the catalogue he wrote, sketched the career of Jackson using as landmarks a succession of selected portraits done at various stages of Jackson's life, augmented with likenesses of friends, family, and contemporaries, as well as documents and artifacts that illuminated them. What could not be attempted in the exhibition was a survey of all the significant portraits of "Old Hickory," so this book has been prepared to bring between covers the extraordinary pictorial record of a remarkable man.

Alan Fern
Director
National Portrait Gallery

1. These quotations are from Reda C. Goff, "A Physical Profile of Andrew Jackson," *Tennessee Historical Quarterly* 28 (Fall 1969): 302.

2. Arthur Schlesinger, Jr., *The Age of Jackson* (Boston, 1953), p. 5.

Preface

In celebration of the bicentennial of the American presidency, the Tennessee State Museum and the National Portrait Gallery co-produced "Old Hickory: A Life Sketch of Andrew Jackson" in 1990. In conjunction with the exhibition, the two institutions have produced this comprehensive volume on the life images of Andrew Jackson. This fully illustrated reference will be of great value for years to come.

Andrew Jackson became an icon in his own lifetime, one that spanned from the Revolutionary period to the dawn of photography. Naturally, the major portraitists of his day vied to preserve his likeness for future generations. These artists—painters, sculptors, engravers, and caricaturists—included Rembrandt Peale, William Rush, John Vanderlyn, Asher B. Durand, Edward Williams Clay, Hiram Powers, George P. A. Healy, Clark Mills, and Ralph E. W. Earl. Earl, in fact, dubbed himself the "King's Painter" and produced more than thirty portraits of his patron-hero.

Both museums have worked closely together to bring the Jackson exhibition and this portrait study to fruition. The two venues for our joint efforts are each uniquely appropriate. The National Portrait Gallery, where the exhibition will commence, is housed in the former United States Patent Office building in Washington, D.C. President Jackson himself laid its cornerstone in 1836. The other venue, the Tennessee State Museum, is located in Nashville, Andrew Jackson's hometown. It stands within a few blocks of the location of his former law office. We are very pleased to co-publish this unique and important study of Andrew Jackson portraits, and are gratified to thus honor both the office of the President of the United States and Tennessean Andrew Jackson. We trust that the public will be as happy with it as we are.

Lois Riggins Ezzell
Executive Director
Tennessee State Museum

Acknowledgments

The iconography of Andrew Jackson begins in the Catalog of American Portraits, a research facility within the National Portrait Gallery. Established in 1966, the CAP, as it is commonly called, is a national reference center containing photographs and documentation for more than 80,000 likenesses of historically important Americans. Essentially consisting of cabinet files, an automated database of indices—and a dedicated staff—the CAP is capable of providing detailed information about portraits and artists represented in public and private collections throughout the country. In 1966, historian Virginia Purdy began the systematic compilation of the Andrew Jackson file. Quite by accident, she was aided by art historian Anna Wells Rutledge, who in the early 1940s had begun a thorough portrait study of Andrew Jackson. Except for a brief article by Charles Henry Hart in *McClure's Magazine* in 1897, no such survey had ever been published. Although the domestic exigencies of World War II prevented Miss Rutledge from completing her work, she eventually deposited her research notes with Mrs. Purdy and the CAP. By 1967, the file on Jackson was substantial enough to interest Susan Clover Symonds, a graduate student in art history at the University of Delaware, who incorporated much of it in a master's thesis. Although her "Portraits of Andrew Jackson: 1815–1845" discusses a selection of paintings only, this much-consulted work has been the single source on Jackson portraits until now. In the subsequent score of years, the CAP has significantly bolstered its Jackson file, making feasible for the first time a comprehensive study of his life portraits.

For their untiring assistance throughout this project, I am especially grateful to Linda Thrift, current keeper of the CAP; staff members Deborah Sisum, Patricia Svoboda, Ann Wagner, and Ellen Collison; and former keepers Mona Dearborn and Richard Doud.

Long before this study was undertaken, the Jackson Papers Project had the foresight to keep its own portrait file on Old Hickory. For access to it, I am indebted to the project's editor-director Harold Moser, and to his former associate, Sharon Macpherson, now the historian at the Hermitage, Jackson's preserved home near Nashville. During a period of several years, each of them generously forwarded information that significantly facilitated the completion of this manuscript, which they in turn critiqued, as did associate editors George Hoemann and David Hoth.

I must extend similar gratitude to Marsha Mullin, curator of the Hermitage collection, and to her assistant, Brenda Abernathy, for promptly fielding many and oftentimes cumbersome requests for information and photographs. At the Tennessee State Museum, former curator James Kelly aptly handled similar requests with interest and enthusiasm. Dr. Kelly and Donna Frost were also instrumental in helping to find funding for this project, for which the National Portrait Gallery and I are most appreciative.

At other locales and institutions, I received much-needed help from curators and historians alike, most especially Robert Cason of the Alabama Department of Archives and History; Georgia Barnhill of the American Antiquarian Society; Lynda Heffley of City Hall, Charleston, South Carolina; David Cassidy and Linda Stanley of the Historical Society of Pennsylvania; Kathleen Johnson of Historic Hudson Valley; John Mahe of the Historic New Orleans Collection; Kenneth Finkel of the Library Company of Philadelphia; John McDonough of the Library of Congress; John B. Harter of the Louisiana State Museum; Martha A. Sandweiss of the Mead Art Museum, Amherst College; William Lind of the National Archives; Wendy Shadwell of the New-York Historical Society; and Betty Monkman at the White House. At the Smithsonian's National Museum of American History, Larry Bird, James Bruns, Donald Kloster, Anne Serio, and Butch Vosloh all gave timely assistance, as did Leah Akbar at the Bureau of Engraving and Printing.

For sharing their insights into certain aspects of Jackson's portraiture, I must also thank George Jordan of New Orleans and Gary Stradling of New York. Along similar lines, William Cook greatly expanded my knowledge of early Jackson iconography. I am especially grateful to him and his wife Jean for their hospitality and interest in the work of the National Portrait Gallery.

Within the Gallery itself, I am indebted to many staff members who contributed their special expertise in one way or another: Beverly Cox, Claire Kelly, Vandy Cook, Cheryl Anderson, Frederick Voss, Daphne Greene, Wendy Reaves, Bridget Barber, Ann Shumard, William Stapp, Margaret Dwyer, Martin Kalfatovic, Rolland White, Mary Blair Dunton, and Barbara Day, a former Smithsonian fellow. No individual logged more hours over this manuscript than editor Dru Dowdy. Her improvements have been inestimable, and I am most grateful. As on former occasions, I am indebted to publications officer Frances Stevenson for her own suggestions and for overseeing the many details of production. I must also thank Director Alan Fern, Carolyn Carr, Marc Pachter, Robert Stewart, Ellen Miles, and Margaret Christman for their critical review of the manuscript.

During the course of this study, Merl Moore contributed pertinent information from his personal research files. In the past he has generously assisted many other researchers, and I am fortunate to have been one of them. Likewise, my former intern, Cheryl Kramer, proved indispensable in researching details for this study, and I sincerely appreciate her expeditious and scholarly efforts.

James G. Barber

List of Portraits

Dates listed here indicate when individual portraits were executed and do not necessarily reflect times of sittings. For instance, Jackson was sitting to sculptor Hiram Powers in about December 1834 and perhaps even January 1835. Yet Powers did not begin his marble bust until 1838 and did not finish it until 1839. Consequently, Powers's marble *Jackson* has been dated later than his plaster model. If the execution of a portrait cannot be positively ascertained within a reasonable time frame, it has been designated as "not dated." With sculpted works, only the height dimension has been given. Dimensions of prints and drawings are of the images only.

For further details about the portraits listed here, the text should be consulted. The page number on which the portrait is illustrated follows each entry, in italics. Likenesses referred to as replicas are close facsimiles by the original artist; those listed as copies are not necessarily exact reproductions and may be by different artists. For additional information concerning provenances and condition reports, consult the Catalog of American Portraits at the National Portrait Gallery, Smithsonian Institution, or the accession records of the respective owners.

Introduction

Figure 1. Andrew Jackson. Watercolor on ivory by S. M. Charles (active 1830s), 4.9 x 4 cm. (1¹⁵⁄₁₆ x 1⁹⁄₁₆ in.), 1835. Signed right margin: "Painted by S. M. Charles 1835." The White House Collection, Washington, D.C.; gift of Mr. and Mrs. Ronald Tree. *Page 26*

Figure 2. *General Jackson Hero of New Orleans.* Aquatint engraving by William Strickland (1788–1854), 22.7 x 16.8 cm. (8¹⁵⁄₁₆ x 6⅝ in.), circa 1815. The New-York Historical Society, New York City. *Page 28*

Figure 3. Andrew Jackson. Oil on panel by unidentified artist, 58.7 x 47.6 cm. (23⅛ x 18¾ in.), circa 1822. The Hermitage: Home of President Andrew Jackson, Hermitage, Tennessee. *Page 30*

Chapter One

Figure 4. *A Correct View of the Battle Near the City of New Orleans, on the Eighth of January 1815. . . .* Etching, engraving, aquatint, and soft ground on paper by Francisco Scacki (active circa 1815–1816), 40.6 x 60.5 cm. (16 x 23¹³⁄₁₆ in.), circa 1816 (second state, containing identification key). National Portrait Gallery, Smithsonian Institution, Washington, D.C. *Page 35*

Figure 5. *Battle of New Orleans and Death of Major General Packenham.* Engraving by Joseph Yeager (circa 1792–1859), after West, 38.9 x 49.5 cm. (15⁵⁄₁₆ x 19½ in.), circa 1817 (third state, containing identification key). National Portrait Gallery, Smithsonian Institution, Washington, D.C. *Page 35*

Figure 6. Andrew Jackson. Watercolor on ivory by Jean François de Vallée (active in New Orleans 1808–1818), 7.6 x 6.4 cm. (3 x 2½ in.), 1815. Accompanying inscription on paper in Jackson's hand: "Mr. E. Livingston is requested to accept this picture as a mark of the sense I entertain of his public services, and a token of my private friendship and Esteem. Headquarters N. Orleans. May 1st. 1815. *Andrew Jackson.*" Historic Hudson Valley, Tarrytown, New York. *Page 36*

Figure 7. *Majr. Gal. Andrew Jackson.* Engraving attributed to Arsène Lacarrière Latour (circa 1770–1839), after Jean François de Vallée, 10.8 x 9.2 cm. (4¼ x 3⅝ in.), 1816. Published as frontispiece in Latour's *Historical Memoir of the War in West Florida and Louisiana in 1814–15,* Philadelphia, 1816. Historic New Orleans Collection, Louisiana; Museum/Research Center, Acc. No. 73-12-L. *Page 37*

Figure 8. Andrew Jackson. Engraving by Alexander Hay Ritchie (1822–1895), after Jean François de Vallée, 7.6 x 6.2 cm. (3 x 2⁷⁄₁₆ in.), circa 1864. Published in Charles Havens Hunt, *The Life of Edward Livingston,* New York, 1864. National Portrait Gallery, Smithsonian Institution, Washington, D.C. *Page 38*

Figure 9. *General Jackson.* Engraving by David Edwin (1776–1841), after Nathan W. Wheeler, 12.7 x 10.2 cm. (5 x 4 in.), circa 1816. Published as frontispiece in John Reid and John Henry Eaton, *The Life of Andrew Jackson,* Philadelphia, 1817. Prints and Photographs Division, Library of Congress, Washington, D.C. *Page 39*

Figure 10. Andrew Jackson. Oil on canvas by Nathan W. Wheeler (circa 1789–1849), 76.2 x 65.4 cm. (30 x 25¾ in.), 1815. The Historical Society of Pennsylvania, Philadelphia. *Page 39*

Figure 11. *Major Genl. Andrew Jackson Of the United States Army.* Engraving by Thomas Gimbrede (1781–1832), after Nathan W. Wheeler, 26.7 x 19.7 cm. (10½ x 7¾ in.), 1816. The New-York Historical Society, New York City. *Page 39*

Figure 12. Andrew Jackson. Oil on panel by John Wesley Jarvis (1780–1840), after Nathan W. Wheeler, 64.8 x 53 cm. (25½ x 20⅞ in.), circa 1817. The White House Collection, Washington, D.C.; gift of Mr. and Mrs. Gerard B. Lambert. *Page 40*

Figure 13. Andrew Jackson. Red wax bas-relief on dark blue glass by Giuseppe Valaperta (died circa 1817), 9.5 cm. (3¾ in.) diameter, circa 1815. The New-York Historical Society, New York City. *Page 42*

Figure 14. Andrew Jackson. Oil on canvas by Ralph E. W. Earl (circa 1788–1838), 240 x 146.7 cm. (94 ½ x 57¾ in.), 1818. Tennessee State Museum, Nashville. *Page 44*

Figure 15. Andrew Jackson. Oil on canvas by Ralph E. W. Earl, 74.9 x 62.2 cm. (29½ x 24½ in.), circa 1817–1818. The Hermitage: Home of President Andrew Jackson, Hermitage, Tennessee. *Page 45*

Figure 16. Andrew Jackson. Oil on panel attributed to Nathan W. Wheeler, 42.5 x 35.6 cm. (16¾ x 14 in.), not dated. Hurja Collection, Tennessee State Museum, Nashville. *Page 47*

Figure 17. *Andrew Jackson.* Engraving by Charles Phillips (lifedates unknown), after John Wesley Jarvis, 9.8 x 9.2 cm. (3⅞ x 3⅝ in.), circa 1841. Published in *United States Magazine, and Democratic Review,* January 1842. Private collection. *Page 47*

Figure 18. Andrew Jackson. Oil on canvas attributed to Ralph E. W. Earl, 76.2 x 63.5 cm. (30 x 25 in.), circa 1817. Camden District Heritage Foundation, Camden, South Carolina. *Page 48*

Chapter Two

Figure 19. Andrew Jackson. Oil on canvas by Charles Willson Peale (1741–1827), 71.1 x 56.8 cm. (28 x 22⅜ in.), 1819. The Masonic Library and Museum of Pennsylvania, Philadelphia. *Page 52*

Figure 20. Andrew Jackson. Watercolor on ivory by Anna Claypoole Peale (1791–1878), 7.6 x 6.4 cm. (3 x 2½ in.), 1819. Signed lower right: "Anna C. Peale 1819." Mabel Brady Garvan Collection, Yale University Art Gallery, New Haven, Connecticut. *Page 53*

Figure 21. Andrew Jackson. Oil on canvas by Thomas Sully (1783–1872), 118.1 x 93.9 cm. (46½ x 37 in.), 1819. Signed on bridle: "TS 1819." New York State Office of Parks, Recreation, and Historic Preservation, Clermont State Historic Site. *Page 55*

Figure 22. Andrew Jackson. Stipple engraving, proof, by James Barton Longacre (1794–1864), after Thomas Sully, 37.5 x 30 cm. (14¾ x 11¹³⁄₁₆ in.), 1819–1820. Sully's penciled instructions appear in bottom margin: *I have put the Hair in better Keeping; and* attempted *to touch the face but the paper would not bear the Crayon: I would therefore refer you to the* Sketch *on Canvass. Lighten the Iris close to the pupil in both Eyes on the right side; it will give more animation. The Cheek close to the nose on the right side wants alteration—see sketch. Some slight indications of wrinkles on the forehead & corners of the Eyes—but the mouth requires most attention: the under lip is too light. Face made narrow near to the Chin. Whole back ground & Horse kept down—especially near the figures.* National Portrait Gallery, Smithsonian Institution, Washington, D.C. *Page 56*

Figure 23. *Major General Andrew Jackson.* Hand-colored stipple engraving by James Barton Longacre, after Thomas Sully, 37.1 x 30 cm. (14⅝ x 11¹³⁄₁₆ in.), 1820. National Portrait Gallery, Smithsonian Institution, Washington, D.C. *Page 57*

Figure 24. Andrew Jackson. Charcoal on paper by Thomas Sully, 41.9 x 33.7 cm. (16½ x 13¼ in.), circa 1824. Inscribed lower right: "Original sketch of Genl Jackson, taken immediately after the battle of New Orleans. T Sully." The Detroit Institute of Arts, Michigan; gift of Mrs. Walter O. Briggs. *Page 57*

Figure 25. Andrew Jackson. Terra-cotta by William Rush (1756–1833), 50.5 cm. (19⅞ in.), 1819. The Art Institute of Chicago, Illinois; Bessie Bennett Fund, W. G. Field Fund, Ada Turnbull Hertle Fund, Laura T. Magnusson Fund, Major Acquisition Fund, and restricted gifts of Jamee J. and Marshall Field, and the Brooks and Hope B. McCormick Foundation, 1985.251. *Page 58*

Figure 26. Back of Jackson sculpture by Rush. *Page 58*

Figure 27. *The Long Room.* Watercolor by Charles Willson Peale and Titian Ramsey Peale (1799–1885), 35.6 x 52.7 cm. (14 x 20¾ in.), 1822. The Detroit Institute of Arts, Michigan; Founders Society Purchase, Director's Discretionary Fund. *Page 59*

Figure 28. Andrew Jackson. Oil on canvas by Samuel Lovett Waldo (1783–1861), 65.4 x 53.3 cm. (25¾ x 21 in.), study, circa 1819. The Metropolitan Museum of Art, New York City; Rogers Fund, 1906. *Page 60*

Figure 29. Andrew Jackson. Oil on canvas by Samuel Lovett Waldo, 84.8 x 67.3 cm. (33⅜ x 26½ in.), circa 1819. Historic New Orleans Collection, Louisiana; Museum/Research Center, Acc. No. 1979.112. *Page 60*

Figure 30. Andrew Jackson. Oil on canvas by Samuel Lovett Waldo, 90.5 x 69.9 cm. (35⅝ x 27½ in.), circa 1819. State of Tennessee, Governor's Residence, Nashville. *Page 61*

Figure 31. Andrew Jackson. Oil on canvas by Samuel Lovett Waldo, 83.5 x 64.2 cm. (32⅞ x 25¼ in.), circa 1819. Addison Gallery of American Art, Phillips Academy, Andover, Massachusetts; gift of The Alfred and Margaret Caspary Foundation, Inc., in memory of Thomas Cochran. *Page 61*

Figure 32. *Maj. Gen. Andrew Jackson.* Engraving by Peter Maverick (1780–1831), after Samuel Lovett Waldo, 21 x 16.4 cm. (8¼ x 6 ⅞ in.), circa 1819. National Portrait Gallery, Smithsonian Institution, Washington, D.C. *Page 61*

Figure 33. Andrew Jackson. Oil on canvas by John Wesley Jarvis, 123.2 x 91.4 cm. (48½ x 36 in.), 1819. The Metropolitan Museum of Art, New York City; Harris Brisbane Dick Fund, 1964. *Page 63*

Figure 34. Detail of Jarvis's *Jackson. Page 63*

Figure 35. Andrew Jackson. Oil on canvas by John Vanderlyn (1775–1852), 243.8 x 162.6 cm. (96 x 64 in.), 1819–1820. The Art Commission of the City of New York. *Page 65*

Figure 36. Andrew Jackson. Oil on canvas by John Vanderlyn, 68.6 x 57.2 cm. (27 x 22½ in.), circa 1819. City Hall Collection, Charleston, South Carolina. *Page 66*

Figure 37. French-made porcelain vase with a portrait of Andrew Jackson, after John Vanderlyn, 32.5 cm. (12¹³⁄₁₆ in.), circa 1825–1830. The White House Collection, Washington, D.C. *Page 67*

Figure 38. *General Andrew Jackson. New Orleans Jany. 8th. 1815.* Engraving by Asher B. Durand (1796–1886), after John Vanderlyn, 52.1 x 37.5 cm. (20½ x 14¾ in.), 1828. The New-York Historical Society, New York City. *Page 67*

Figure 39. Andrew Jackson. Oil on canvas by Rembrandt Peale (1778–1860), 95.3 x 77.5 cm. (37½ x 30½ in.), 1819. Baltimore City Life Museums, Maryland. *Page 68*

Figure 40. Andrew Jackson. Marble by unidentified artist after William Rush, 67.3 cm. (26½ in.), not dated. The Hermitage: Home of President Andrew Jackson, Hermitage, Tennessee. *Page 71*

Chapter Three

Figure 41. Andrew Jackson. Gold medal engraved by Moritz Fürst (born 1782), 6.4 cm. (2½ in.) diameter, 1824. The American Numismatic Society, New York City. *Page 77*

Figure 42. Andrew Jackson. Oil on canvas by John Vanderlyn, 248.9 x 158.8 cm. (98 x 62½ in.), 1824. City Hall Collection, Charleston, South Carolina. *Page 80*

Figure 43. Andrew Jackson. Oil on canvas by Robert Street (1796–1865), 92.1 x 76.2 cm. (36¼ x 30 in.), 1824. Signed lower left: "R Street. 1824." Sedalia Public Library, Sedalia, Missouri. *Page 81*

Figure 44. *Andrew Jackson.* Engraving by James Barton Longacre, after Joseph Wood, 15.4 x 12.2 cm. (6¹⁄₁₆ x 4¹³⁄₁₆ in.), 1824. Published in *Casket,* January 1828. National Portrait Gallery, Smithsonian Institution, Washington, D.C. *Page 83*

Figure 45. *Maj. Gen. Andrew Jackson.* Stipple engraving by Peter Maverick, after Joseph Wood, 8.6 x 7.3 cm. (3⅜ x 2⅞ in.), 1825. Published as frontispiece in Samuel Putnam Waldo, *Civil and Military History of Andrew Jackson,* New York, 1825. National Portrait Gallery, Smithsonian Institution, Washington, D.C. *Page 83*

Figure 46. *Andrew Jackson, President Elect of the United States of N.A.* Engraving by James W. Steel (1799–1879), after Joseph Wood, 8.1 x 6.8 cm. (3³⁄₁₆ x 2¹¹⁄₁₆ in.), 1829. Published as frontispiece in *The Jackson Wreath, or National Souvenir,* Philadelphia, 1829. Private collection. *Page 84*

Figure 47. *John Quincy Adams./Genl. Andrew Jackson.* Hand-colored engraving by W. Harrison (lifedates unknown), after Thomas Sully and Joseph Wood, 7.6 cm. (3 in.) diameter, circa 1828. Private collection. *Page 84*

Figure 48. Andrew Jackson. Oil on panel attributed to Franklin Witcher (lifedates unknown), after Joseph Wood, 26.7 x 20.5 cm. (10½ x 8¹⁄₁₆ in.), circa 1828. The Hermitage: Home of President Andrew Jackson, Hermitage, Tennessee. *Page 85*

Figure 49. Lusterware plate with image of General Jackson, after Joseph Wood,

22.2 cm. (8¾ in.) diameter, circa 1828. Inscribed: "General Jackson The Hero of New Orleans." National Museum of American History, Smithsonian Institution, Washington, D.C. *Page 85*

Figure 50. Copper lusterware pitcher with image of General Jackson, after Joseph Wood, 20.9 cm. (8¼ in.), circa 1828. Inscribed: "General Jackson The Hero of New Orleans." National Museum of American History, Smithsonian Institution, Washington, D.C. *Page 85*

Figure 51. Andrew Jackson. Oil on canvas by Aaron H. Corwine (1802–1830), 69.9 x 55.9 cm. (27½ x 22 in.), 1825. Mr. and Mrs. Jackson P. Ravenscroft. *Page 86*

Figure 52. *Andrew Jackson.* Engraving by Charles Cutler Torrey (1799–1827), after Ralph E. W. Earl, 41.6 x 36.2 cm. (16⅜ x 14¼ in.), 1826. National Portrait Gallery, Smithsonian Institution, Washington, D.C. *Page 88*

Figure 53. Andrew Jackson. Oil on canvas by Ralph E. W. Earl, 76.2 x 63.5 cm. (30 x 25 in.), 1817 or after. Alabama Department of Archives and History, Montgomery. *Page 88*

Figure 54. Andrew Jackson. Oil on canvas by Ralph E. W. Earl, 73.7 x 63.5 cm. (29 x 25 in.), circa 1817 or after. The Hermitage: Home of President Andrew Jackson, Hermitage, Tennessee. *Page 89*

Figure 55. Andrew Jackson. Oil on canvas by Ralph E. W. Earl, 76.2 x 64.8 cm. (30 x 25½ in.), circa 1817 or after. National Portrait Gallery, Smithsonian Institution, Washington, D.C.; transfer from the National Gallery of Art, gift of Andrew W. Mellon, 1942. *Page 89*

Figure 56. Andrew Jackson. Oil on canvas by Ralph E. W. Earl, 74.9 x 62.2 cm. (29½ x 24½ in.), circa 1826. The Hermitage: Home of President Andrew Jackson, Hermitage, Tennessee. *Page 90*

Figure 57. *Andrew Jackson.* Engraving by James Barton Longacre, after Ralph E. W. Earl, 12.4 x 10.5 cm. (4⅞ x 4⅛ in.), 1828. Prints Collection, Miriam and Ira D. Wallach Division of Art, Prints and Photographs, The New York Public Library, New York; Astor, Lenox and Tilden Foundations. *Page 91*

Figure 58. Snuff box with portrait of Andrew Jackson. Oil on lacquered wood by unidentified artist, possibly Ralph E. W. Earl, 5.1 cm. (2 in.) diameter, circa 1829. The White House Collection, Washington, D.C.; gift of Hays Rittenhouse Browning. *Page 93*

Figure 59. Andrew Jackson. Silhouette on paper attributed to William James Hubard (1809–1862), 8.9 x 6.4 cm. (3½ x 2½ in.), 1828. Printed label on reverse: "Cut with Scissors by Master Hubard without Drawing or Machine," and inscribed: "To my friend Edward Livingston Charleston S.C. 1828." Tennessee State Museum, Nashville. *Page 94*

Figure 60. Rachel Donelson Jackson? (1767–1828). Silhouette on paper attributed to William James Hubard, 8.9 x 6.4 cm. (3½ x 2½ in.), 1828. Inscribed on reverse: "Profiles of Mr & Mrs. Andrew Jackson done at Charleston S. C 1828. January. Given to Hon. Edward Livingston of Rhin[e]beck N.Y. Later property of sister Mrs. R. Montgomery Rhinebeck N.Y. done by Master Hubard." Tennessee State Museum, Nashville. *Page 94*

Figure 61. *Andrew Jackson.* Engraving by Orramel Hinckley Throop (born 1798), 43.8 x 36.8 cm. (17¼ x 14½ in.), 1828. The Baltimore Museum of Art, Maryland; gift of Aaron Strauss and Lillie Strauss Foundation, Inc., BMA 1958.184.5. *Page 95*

Figure 62. Andrew Jackson. Oil on canvas by unidentified artist, after Aaron Corwine, 73.7 x 61 cm. (29 x 24 in.), not dated. Tennessee Botanical Gardens and Fine Arts Center, Inc., at Cheekwood, Nashville. *Page 98*

Chapter Four

Figure 63. Andrew Jackson peace medal with beadwork necklace and eagle claw ornament. Silver, engraved by Moritz Fürst, 7.6 cm. (3 in.) diameter, circa 1832. National Museum of the American Indian, Smithsonian Institution, Washington, D.C. *Page 103*

Figure 64. Andrew Jackson. Silver Indian peace medal, engraved by Moritz Fürst, 5.1 cm. (2 in.) diameter, circa 1832. The Hermitage: Home of President Andrew Jackson, Hermitage, Tennessee. *Page 104*

Figure 65. Reverse of Jackson Indian peace medal. *Page 104*

Figure 66. Andrew Jackson. Oil on canvas by Auguste Hervieu (born 1794), 245.1 x 154.3 cm. (96½ x 60¾ in.), 1830. Signed lower left: "Aug Hervieu 1830." Redwood Library and Athenaeum, Newport, Rhode Island. *Page 105*

Figure 67. Andrew Jackson. Lithograph after Auguste Hervieu, 17.3 x 11.9 cm. (6¹³⁄₁₆ x 4¹¹⁄₁₆ in.), 1832. Published in volume 2 of Frances Trollope, *Domestic Manners of the Americans,* London, 1832. The New-York Historical Society, New York City. *Page 106*

Figure 68. Andrew Jackson. Marble by E. Luigi Persico (1791–1860), 77.5 cm. (30½ in.), 1829–1834. Inscribed on reverse: "Persico." The Hermitage: Home of President Andrew Jackson, Hermitage, Tennessee. *Page 107*

Figure 69. *Andrew Jackson of Tennessee. President of the United-States.* Stipple engraving by James Barton Longacre, 9.5 x 7.9 cm. (3¾ x 3⅛ in.), 1829. Print Collection, Miriam and Ira D. Wallach Division of Art, Prints and Photographs, The New York Public Library, New York; Astor, Lenox and Tilden Foundations. *Page 108*

Figure 70. Andrew Jackson. Sepia watercolor on artist board by James Barton Longacre, 25.6 x 20.2 cm. (10¹⁄₁₆ x 7¹⁵⁄₁₆ in.), 1829. National Portrait Gallery, Smithsonian Institution, Washington, D.C. *Page 108*

Figure 71. Andrew Jackson. Sepia watercolor on artist board by James Barton Longacre, 21.6 x 18.9 cm. (8½ x 7 ⁷⁄₁₆ in.), 1829. National Portrait Gallery, Smithsonian Institution, Washington, D.C.; gift of the Swedish Colonial Society through Mrs. William Hacker. *Page 109*

Figure 72. Andrew Jackson. Watercolor on ivory by James Barton Longacre, 8.3 x 6.7 cm. (3¼ x 2⅝ in.), circa 1829. Mr. and Mrs. Mack A. Lewis, Jr. *Page 109*

Figure 73. Andrew Jackson. Oil on panel by Francis Alexander (1800–1880), 75.6 x 62.9 cm. (29¾ x 24¾ in.), 1830. Private collection. *Page 110*

Figure 74. *Andrew Jackson, President of the United States.* Lithograph by Albert Newsam (1809–1864), after William James Hubard, published by Cephas G. Childs lithography company, 49.8 x 35.6 cm. (19⅝ x 14 in.), 1830. National Portrait Gallery, Smithsonian Institution, Washington, D.C. *Page 112*

Figure 75. *Andrew Jackson. President of the United States.* Lithograph by Albert Newsam, after William James Hubard, published by Childs and Lehman lithography company, 48.6 x 34.4 cm. (19⅛ x 13³⁄₁₆ in.), 1834. National Portrait Gallery, Smithsonian Institution, Washington, D.C. *Page 113*

Figure 76. Andrew Jackson, Jr. (1808–1865). Oil on canvas by Ralph E. W. Earl, 74.9 x 59.7 cm. (29½ x 23½ in.), circa 1833. The Hermitage: Home of President Andrew Jackson, Hermitage, Tennessee. *Page 114*

Figure 77. Sarah Yorke Jackson (1805–1887). Oil on canvas by Ralph E. W. Earl, 74.9 x 62.2 cm. (29½ x 24½ in.), circa 1833. The Hermitage: Home of President Andrew Jackson, Hermitage, Tennessee. *Page 114*

Figure 78. *Andrew Jackson.* Stipple engraving by Thomas Illman (died circa 1859–1860), after Henry Hoppner Meyer, 7.6 x 7 cm. (3 x 2¾ in.), circa 1833. National Portrait Gallery, Smithsonian Institution, Washington, D.C. *Page 115*

Figure 79. Andrew Jackson. Oil on canvas by Philip Hewins (1806–1850), 69.5 x 56.5 cm. (27⅜ x 22¼ in.), 1833. Signed inside hat brim: "P. Hewins." The Connecticut Historical Society, Hartford. *Page 116*

Figure 80. Andrew Jackson. Plaster by John Frazee (1790–1852), 33 cm. (13 in.), 1834. The Art Museum, Princeton University; Museum purchase, John Maclean Magie and Gertrude Magie Fund. *Page 118*

Figure 81. Andrew Jackson. Marble begun by John Frazee and thought to have been completed by Nelson Swezey, approximately 61 cm. (24 in.), begun circa 1850. Shelby County Courthouse, Memphis, Tennessee. *Page 119*

Figure 82. *Andrew Jackson.* Engraving by Waterman Lilly Ormsby (1809–1883), after a model of John Frazee's bust made by his partner Robert E. Launitz, 31.8 x 25.4 cm. (12½ x 10 in.), not dated. The New-York Historical Society, New York City. *Page 119*

Figure 83. Andrew Jackson. Marble by Hiram Powers (1805–1873), 87.6 cm. (34½ in.), 1838–1839. Inscribed on reverse: "Hiram Powers Sculp." The Metropolitan Museum of Art, New York City; gift of Mrs. Francis V. Nash, 1894. *Page 121*

Figure 84. Andrew Jackson. Plaster by Hiram Powers, 72.1 cm. (28⅜ in.), 1835. National Museum of American Art, Smithsonian Institution, Washington, D.C.; Museum purchase in memory of Ralph Cross Johnson. *Page 122*

Figure 85. Andrew Jackson. Oil on canvas by Asher B. Durand, 81.3 x 66 cm. (32 x 26 in.), 1835. United States Naval Academy Museum, Annapolis, Maryland. *Page 124*

Figure 86. Andrew Jackson. Oil on canvas by Asher B. Durand, 76.2 x 63.5 cm. (30 x 25 in.), 1835. The New-York Historical Society, New York City. *Page 125*

Figure 87. Andrew Jackson. Oil on canvas by David Rent Etter (1807–1881), 126.5 x 100.5 cm. (49¹³⁄₁₆ x 39 ⁷⁄₁₆ in.), 1835. Signed lower left: "D. Etter Pinx 1835." Independence National Historical Park, Philadelphia. *Page 125*

Figure 88. Andrew Jackson. Watercolor on ivory by unidentified artist, 2.2 x 1.7 cm. (⅞ x ¹¹⁄₁₆ in.), 1835. Inscribed on reverse: "Jno. D. Coffee—from—Genl. Andrew Jackson—1835." The Hermitage: Home of President Andrew Jackson, Hermitage, Tennessee. *Page 126*

Figure 89. Andrew Jackson. Marble by Ferdinand Pettrich (1798–1872), 61 cm. (24 in.), 1836. Ursuline Convent Archives and Museum, New Orleans. *Page 126*

Figure 90. Andrew Jackson. Marble by Ferdinand Pettrich, 63.5 cm. (25 in.), 1836 or after. The Chrysler Museum, Norfolk, Virginia; gift of James H. Ricau and Museum purchase. *Page 127*

Figure 91. Andrew Jackson. Marble by Ferdinand Pettrich, 62.2 cm. (24½ in.), 1836 or after. The Historical Society of Pennsylvania, Philadelphia. *Page 127*

Figure 92. Andrew Jackson. Oil on canvas by John P. Merrill (active 1836–1847), 60.3 x 45.1 cm. (23¾ x 17¾ in.), 1836. Signed lower left: "J. P. Merrill, Wash 1836." Mr. and Mrs. John R. Neal. *Page 128*

Chapter Five

Figure 93. Andrew Jackson. Oil on panel by Ralph E. W. Earl, 78.7 x 66 cm. (31 x 26 in.), 1834. Inscribed on reverse: "R. E. W. Earl 1834." Mr. R. Gwin Follis. *Page 136*

Figure 94. Andrew Jackson. "Farmer Jackson." Oil on canvas by Ralph E. W. Earl, 74.9 x 62.2 cm. (29½ x 24 ½ in.), 1830. Private collection. *Page 137*

Figure 95. *Andrew Jackson at the Hermitage. 1830.* Lithograph by John Henry Bufford (1810–1870), after Ralph E. W. Earl, published by Pendleton lithography company, 53.3 x 43.2 cm. (21 x 17 in.), 1832. National Portrait Gallery, Smithsonian Institution, Washington, D.C.; gift of Mrs. Katie Louchheim. *Page 139*

Figure 96. Andrew Jackson. Oil on canvas by Ralph E. W. Earl, 61 x 50.8 cm. (24 x 20 in.), circa 1833. Private collection. *Page 139*

Figure 97. Andrew Jackson. Oil on canvas by Ralph E. W. Earl, 76.5 x 64 cm. (30⅛ x 25⁵⁄₁₆ in.), circa 1830. The Daughters of the American Revolution Museum, Washington, D.C.; Friends of the Museum purchase. *Page 140*

Figure 98. Andrew Jackson. "Tennessee Gentleman." Oil on canvas by Ralph E. W. Earl, 71.1 x 53.3 cm. (28 x 21 in.), not dated. The Hermitage: Home of President Andrew Jackson, Hermitage, Tennessee. *Page 140*

Figure 99. *Andrew Jackson.* Engraving by Henry B. Hall (1808–1884), after Ralph E. W. Earl, 12.7 x 7.6 cm. (5 x 3 in.), circa 1860. Published as frontispiece in volume 3 of James Parton, *Life of Andrew Jackson,* New York, 1861. National Portrait Gallery, Smithsonian Institution, Washington, D.C. *Page 141*

Figure 100. Andrew Jackson. Oil on canvas by Ralph E. W. Earl, 91.4 x 73.7 cm. (36 x 29 in.), 1833. Signed lower right: "R. E. W. Earl Pinxt 1833." Memphis Brooks Museum of Art, Tennessee; Memphis Park Commission purchase, 46.2. *Page 142*

Figure 101. Andrew Jackson. Oil on canvas by Ralph E. W. Earl, 91.1 x 70.8 cm. (35⅞ x 27⅞ in.), 1835. Signed lower right: "R. E. W. Earl Pinxt. 1835." National Museum of American Art, Smithsonian Institution, Washington, D.C.; transfer from the National Institute. *Page 143*

Figure 102. Andrew Jackson. Oil on canvas by Ralph E. W. Earl, 74.9 x 62.2 cm. (29½ x 24½ in.), circa 1835. The Hermitage: Home of President Andrew Jackson, Hermitage, Tennessee. *Page 143*

Figure 103. Andrew Jackson astride Sam Patch. Oil on canvas by Ralph E. W. Earl, 77.5 x 53.3 cm. (30½ x 21 in.), circa 1833. The Hermitage: Home of President Andrew Jackson, Hermitage, Tennessee. *Page 144*

Figure 104. Andrew Jackson. Oil on canvas by Ralph E. W. Earl, 57.5 x 45.1 cm. (22⅝ x 17¾ in.), 1836. Inscribed on reverse: "Original Portrait of General Jackson, painted for me, from life, by Col. Earl, at the President's house, Washington, 1836, J. K. Kane." Columbia Museum of Art, Columbia, South Carolina; gift of Mrs. Ben C. Hough, #1958.28. *Page 144*

Figure 105. Andrew Jackson. Oil on canvas by Ralph E. W. Earl, 58.4 x 40.6 cm. (23 x 16 in.), study, 1836. The Hermitage: Home of President Andrew Jackson, Hermitage, Tennessee. *Page 145*

Figure 106. The "National Picture" of Andrew Jackson. Oil on canvas by Ralph E. W. Earl, 320 x 236.2 cm. (126 x 93 in.), 1836–1837. National Museum of American Art, Smithsonian Institution, Washington, D.C.; transfer from United States District Court for the District of Columbia. *Page 145*

Figure 107. Andrew Jackson. Painted poplar carving by William Rumney (active 1860s), 198.8 cm. (78¼ in.), circa 1860. The Metropolitan Museum of Art, New York City; purchase, Rogers Fund, The J. M. Kaplan Fund, Inc., and Mrs. Frederick A. Stoughton Gifts, Harris Brisbane Dick and Louis V. Bell Funds, 1978. *Page 148*

Chapter Six

Figure 108. *American Justice!! or The Ferocious Yankee Genl. Jack's Reward for Butchering Two British Subjects!!!* Hand-colored engraving published by J. Sidebetham (active 1819), 24.8 x 34.9 cm. (9¾ x 13¾ in.), 1819. Tennessee State Museum, Nashville. *Page 151*

Figure 109. *Caucus Curs in full Yell, or a War-Whoop to saddle on the People, a Pappoose President.* Aquatint by James Akin (circa 1773–1846), 45.6 x 51.4 cm.

($17^{15}/_{16}$ x 20¼ in.), 1824. Prints and Photographs Division, Library of Congress, Washington, D.C. *Page 152*

Figure 110. *The Man! The Jack Ass.* Lithograph by James Akin, 27.3 x 12.1 cm. (10¾ x 4¾ in.), not dated. American Antiquarian Society, Worcester, Massachusetts. *Page 152*

Figure 111. *Office Hunters for the Year 1834.* Lithograph attributed to James Akin, 25.1 x 38.7 cm. (9⅞ x 15¼ in.), 1834. Peters Collection, National Museum of American History, Smithsonian Institution, Washington, D.C. *Page 153*

Figure 112. *A Brief Account of some of the Bloody Deeds of General Jackson.* Handbill, 55.2 x 39.1 cm. (21¾ x 15⅜ in.), 1828. Private collection. *Page 154*

Figure 113. *A Grand Functionary. "The Lord High Keeper."* Lithograph by Edward Williams Clay (1799–1857), 21.4 x 14.8 cm. ($8^{7}/_{16}$ x $5^{13}/_{16}$ in.), 1829. National Portrait Gallery, Smithsonian Institution, Washington, D.C. *Page 154*

Figure 114. Andrew Jackson. Pencil on paper by Edward Williams Clay, 20.3 x 8.3 cm. (8 x 3¼ in.), 1831. National Portrait Gallery, Smithsonian Institution, Washington, D.C.; gift of J. William Middendorf II. *Page 155*

Figure 115. *The Rats leaving a Falling House.* Lithograph by Edward Williams Clay, 26.4 x 19.7 cm. (10⅜ x 7¾ in.), 1831. Annotated in bottom margin by Samuel Breck: *I know all the heads represented here, and can vouch for their perfect resemblance. Jackson's, the President is a very stricking [sic] likeness, and so is Ingham's. W. Clay—the Caricaturist of Philadelphia, has seldom been so happy in design and execution. The worn hickory broom, in the hands of the Imp, is a severe hit, at Old hickory, as the President is sometimes called; and so is the foot upon Van beuren's [sic] tail; indicating his well known wish to retain him. S. Breck.* The Library Company of Philadelphia, Pennsylvania. *Page 156*

Figure 116. *,00001—The value of a unit with four cyphers going before it.* Lithograph by Edward Williams Clay, 39.4 x 29.2 cm. (15½ x 11½ in.), 1831. Annotated in bottom margin by Samuel Breck: *These portraits are admirable likenesses. I know personally every one. The President (Jackson) in the chair—Jno. Randolph at the door. Webster at the window, and Clay on his left. Calhoun as the Dog—Van Bueren [sic] at the foot of the ladder. Lewis snug in the lap. Eaton, Ingham—Branch and Berrien as Rats. S. Breck.* The Library Company of Philadelphia, Pennsylvania. *Page 156*

Figure 117. *"The Government." "[I] Take the Responsibility."* Hand-colored lithograph published by George Endicott and Moses Swett lithography company (active 1830–1834), 21.6 x 33.7 cm. (8½ x 13¼ in.), 1834. Prints and Photographs Division, Library of Congress, Washington, D.C. *Page 157*

Figure 118. *King Andrew the First, "Born to Command."* Lithograph by Edward Williams Clay, 70.5 x 29.8 cm. (27¾ x 11¾ in.), circa 1834. Tennessee Historical Society Collection, Tennessee State Museum, Nashville. *Page 157*

Figure 119. *A Political Game of Bragg. Or the best hand out of four.* Hand-colored lithograph by Edward Williams Clay, 20 x 28.9 cm. (7⅞ x 11⅜ in.), 1832. The Library Company of Philadelphia, Pennsylvania. *Page 158*

Figure 120. *I Take It on My Responsibility.* Lithograph by unidentified artist, 36.8 x 47.3 cm. (14½ x 18⅝ in.), circa 1834. The Library Company of Philadelphia, Pennsylvania. *Page 159*

Figure 121. *The Downfall of Mother Bank.* Lithograph by Edward Williams Clay, 23.5 x 33.7 cm. (9¼ x 13¼ in.), 1833. American Antiquarian Society, Worcester, Massachusetts. *Page 160*

Figure 122. *Set to Between Old Hickory and Bully Nick.* Lithograph attributed to Edward Williams Clay, 32.4 x 32.5 cm. (12¾ x $12^{13}/_{16}$ in.), 1834. Prints and Photographs Division, Library of Congress, Washington, D.C. *Page 160*

Figure 123. *General Jackson Slaying the Many Headed Monster.* Lithograph by Alfred

M. Hoffy (active 1835–1860), 30.5 x 36.5 cm. (12 x 14⅜ in.), circa 1836. Prints and Photographs Division, Library of Congress, Washington, D.C. *Page 160*

Figure 124. *On the Way to Araby!* Lithograph by Edward Williams Clay, 27.6 x 37.1 cm. (10⅞ x 14⅝ in.), 1836. Prints and Photographs Division, Library of Congress, Washington, D.C. *Page 160*

Figure 125. *The Model of a Republican President.* Hand-colored lithograph attributed to Edward Williams Clay, 25.7 x 43.2 cm. (10⅛ x 17 in.), 1834. The Library Company of Philadelphia, Pennsylvania. *Page 160*

Figure 126. *Symptoms of a Locked Jaw.* Lithograph by David Claypoole Johnston (1799–1865), 24.1 x 20.2 cm. (9½ x 7¹⁵⁄₁₆ in.), 1827. American Antiquarian Society, Worcester, Massachusetts. *Page 162*

Figure 127. *Richard III.* Engraving and stipple by David Claypoole Johnston, 16.8 x 11.4 cm. (6⅝ x 4½ in.), circa 1828. The New-York Historical Society, New York City. *Page 162*

Figure 128. *The Grand National Caravan Moving East.* Lithograph published by George Endicott and Moses Swett lithography company, 22.9 x 36.5 cm. (9 x 14⅜ in.), 1833. Prints and Photographs Division, Library of Congress, Washington, D.C. *Page 163*

Figure 129. Andrew Jackson as the Great Father. Lithograph by unidentified artist, 31.8 x 23.3 cm. (12½ x 9³⁄₁₆ in.), not dated. William L. Clements Library, University of Michigan, Ann Arbor. *Page 165*

Figure 130. Andrew Jackson. Wooden figurehead by Laban S. Beecher (born circa 1805), carved for frigate *Constitution,* 274.3 cm. (108 in.), 1834. Replacement head carved in 1835 by [Jeremiah] Dodge and Son [Charles J.] (active 1828–1838). Museum of the City of New York, New York; gift of the Seawanhaka Corinthian Yacht Club. *Page 165*

Figure 131. *The Decapitation of a great Blockhead by the Mysterious agency of the Claret coloured Coat.* Lithograph by unidentified artist, 31 x 45.1 cm. (12³⁄₁₆ x 17¾ in.), 1834. Prints and Photographs Division, Library of Congress, Washington, D.C. *Page 167*

Figure 132. *Fixing a block-head to the Constitution or putting a wart on the nose of old Ironsides.* Lithograph published by Anthony Imbert (died circa 1835), 30.5 x 47.3 cm. (12 x 18⅝ in.), 1834. The Library Company of Philadelphia, Pennsylvania. *Page 167*

Figure 133. *The Attempted Assassination, of the President of the United States, Jan. 30. 1835.* Lithograph published by George Endicott (1802–1848), 33.9 x 42.9 cm. (13⅜ x 16⅞ in.), 1835. Prints and Photographs Division, Library of Congress, Washington, D.C. *Page 167*

Figure 134. *The Old Lion, and the Cock What Won't Fight.* Hand-colored lithograph by unidentified artist, 26 x 33 cm. (10¼ x 13 in.), 1835. Tennessee State Library and Archives, Nashville. *Page 168*

Figure 135. *Grand Virginia Reel and Scamperdown at the White House Washington. All the World completely Discumgalligumfricated.* Lithograph by Edward Williams Clay, 28.6 x 47.1 cm. (11¼ x 18⁹⁄₁₆ in.), 1836. Prints and Photographs Division, Library of Congress, Washington, D.C. *Page 169*

Figure 136. Andrew Jackson and Louis-Philippe. Wood carving by Pierre Joseph Landry (1770–1843), 64.8 cm. (25½ in.), 1836. Inscribed on reverse: "Sculpte. Par. P. J. Landry." The Hermitage: Home of President Andrew Jackson, Hermitage, Tennessee. *Page 169*

Figure 137. *Caucus on the Surplus Bill.* Lithograph by Edward Williams Clay, 21.9 x 34 cm. (8⅝ x 13⅜ in.), 1836. Prints and Photographs Division, Library of Congress, Washington, D.C. *Page 170*

Figure 138. *Grand Match Between the Kinderhook Poney and the Ohio Ploughman.*

Lithograph by Edward Williams Clay, 27.6 x 44.1 cm. (10⅞ x 17⅜ in.), 1836. Prints and Photographs Division, Library of Congress, Washington, D.C. *Page 170*

Figure 139. *The Modern Balaam and His Ass.* Hand-colored lithograph by unidentified artist, 31.4 x 41.4 cm. (12⅜ x 16 5/16 in.), 1837. Prints and Photographs Division, Library of Congress, Washington, D.C. *Page 171*

Figure 140. *Fifty Cents Shin Plaster.* Lithograph attributed to Edward Williams Clay, 26.7 x 44.3 cm. (10½ x 17 7/16 in.), 1837. Prints and Photographs Division, Library of Congress, Washington, D.C. *Page 172*

Figure 141. *Treasury Note 75 cents.* Hand-colored lithograph by Napoleon Sarony (1821–1896), 24.8 x 44.1 cm. (9¾ x 17⅜ in.), 1837. American Antiquarian Society, Worcester, Massachusetts. *Page 172*

Figure 142. *The Times.* Lithograph by Edward Williams Clay, 32.7 x 48.3 cm. (12⅞ x 19 in.), 1837. Peters Collection, National Museum of American History, Smithsonian Institution, Washington, D.C. *Page 173*

Figure 143. *Weighed & Found Wanting, or the Effects of a Summer's Ramble.* Hand-colored lithograph by Henry Dacre (active 1840–1850), 27 x 37.8 cm. (10⅝ x 14⅞ in.), circa 1840. Prints and Photographs Division, Library of Congress, Washington, D.C. *Page 173*

Chapter Seven

Figure 144. Andrew Jackson. Oil on canvas by Thomas J. Jackson (1815–1894), 25.4 x 20.3 cm. (10 x 8 in.), 1838. Inscribed on reverse: "Painted by Thos. J. Jackson Hermitage June 1838." The Hermitage: Home of President Andrew Jackson, Hermitage, Tennessee. *Page 177*

Figure 145. Andrew Jackson. Marble by Joel Tanner Hart (1810–1877), 64.8 cm. (25½ in.), circa 1850. Inscribed (incorrectly) on reverse: "The original; modeled at the Hermitage, U. S. A. in Dec. 1838. by J. T. Hart Sclt." Kentucky Historical Society, Frankfort. *Page 178*

Figure 146. Andrew Jackson. Plaster by Joel Tanner Hart, 69.9 cm. (27½ in.), 1838 or after. Inscribed on reverse: "J. T. Hart, Sculpt. 1838." The Stradlings, New York City. *Page 178*

Figure 147. Andrew Jackson. Crayon on paper by R. Brand (lifedates unknown), 22.5 x 18.4 cm. (8⅞ x 7¼ in.), 1840. Inscribed in bottom margin: "New Orleans the 8th January 1840 A sketch from recollection by R Brand." Louisiana State Museum, New Orleans. *Page 179*

Figure 148. Andrew Jackson. Oil on canvas by Jacques Guillaume Lucien Amans (1801–1888), 153.7 x 125.7 cm. (60½ x 49½ in.), 1840. Signed: "Amans 8 Janvier 1840." Historic New Orleans Collection, Louisiana; Museum/Research Center, Acc. No. 1982.11. *Page 181*

Figure 149. Andrew Jackson. Oil on canvas by Jacques Guillaume Lucien Amans, 145.7 x 114.3 cm. (57⅜ x 45 in.), 1840. Signed: "Amans Janvier 1840." The Chicago Historical Society, Illinois, 1920.54. *Page 182*

Figure 150. Andrew Jackson. Oil on canvas by Jacques Guillaume Lucien Amans, 182.9 x 121.9 cm. (72 x 48 in.), not dated. Tennessee State Museum, Nashville. *Page 182*

Figure 151. Andrew Jackson. Oil on canvas by Edward Dalton Marchant (1806–1887), 76.2 x 63.5 cm. (30 x 25 in.), 1840. The Union League of Philadelphia, Pennsylvania. *Page 183*

Figure 152. Andrew Jackson. Watercolor on ivory by James Tooley, Jr. (1816–1844), after Edward Dalton Marchant, 10.8 x 8.6 cm. (4¼ x 3⅜ in.), 1840. Inscribed on reverse: "Andrew Jackson painted by Jas. Tooley, Jr. 1840." National Portrait

Gallery, Smithsonian Institution, Washington, D.C.; gift of Mr. William H. Lively, Mrs. Mary Lively Hoffman, and Dr. Charles J. Lively. *Page 183*

Figure 153. Andrew Jackson. Oil on canvas by Trevor Thomas Fowler (active 1829–1869), 76.5 x 63.8 cm. (30⅛ x 25⅛ in.), 1840. Inscribed on replacement liner: "Trevor Tho. Fowler New Orleans *19 Camp St.*" Manuscript on reverse of canvas: "I certify that this portrait is the Original picture for which Genl Jackson sat to me while on board the Steamer Vicksburg on her return to Nashville from this City in Jany 1840." The Chicago Historical Society, Illinois, 1947.8. *Page 185*

Figure 154. Andrew Jackson. Oil on canvas by Trevor Thomas Fowler, 76.8 x 63.5 cm. (30¼ x 25 in.), 1840. National Portrait Gallery, Smithsonian Institution, Washington, D.C. *Page 185*

Figure 155. Andrew Jackson. Oil on canvas by Miner Kilbourne Kellogg (1814–1889), 76 x 63.3 cm. (29¹⁵⁄₁₆ x 24¹⁵⁄₁₆ in.), circa 1840. National Museum of American Art, Smithsonian Institution, Washington, D.C.; transfer from the United States Navy Department. *Page 187*

Figure 156. Andrew Jackson. Oil on canvas by Miner Kilbourne Kellogg, 74.9 x 62.5 cm. (29½ x 24⅝ in.), circa 1840. The White House Collection, Washington, D.C. *Page 187*

Figure 157. Andrew Jackson. Oil on canvas by Miner Kilbourne Kellogg, 76.2 x 63.5 cm. (30 x 25 in.), 1840. Cincinnati Art Museum, Ohio; gift of Charles H. Kellogg, Sr., 1888. *Page 187*

Figure 158. *The Last Likeness Taken of Andrew Jackson Painted on Ivory by John W. Dodge and Engraved on Steel by M. I. Danforth.* Engraving by Moseley Isaac Danforth (1800–1862), after John Wood Dodge, 26.4 x 20.6 cm. (10⅜ x 8⅛ in.), 1843. National Portrait Gallery, Smithsonian Institution, Washington, D.C. *Page 189*

Figure 159. Andrew Jackson. Watercolor on ivory by John Wood Dodge (1807–1893), 5.7 x 4.8 cm. (2¼ x 1⅞ in.), 1842. Inscribed on reverse: "Copied by John W. Dodge from his original miniature of General Andrew Jackson April 22nd 1842 for Gen. Armstrong." Tennessee State Museum, Nashville. *Page 190*

Figure 160. Five-dollar note with image of Andrew Jackson after John Wood Dodge, issued by the Farmers and Merchants Bank of Cecil County, Maryland, 1863. National Numismatic Collection, National Museum of American History, Smithsonian Institution, Washington, D.C. *Page 190*

Figure 161. Two-cent "Black Jack" postage stamp, with image of Andrew Jackson after John Wood Dodge, 1863. National Philatelic Collection, National Museum of American History, Smithsonian Institution, Washington, D.C. *Page 190*

Figure 162. *Andrew Jackson.* Lithograph by E. B. and E. C. Kellogg lithography company (active circa 1842–1867), after William Henry Brown, 34.3 x 25.4 cm. (13½ x 10 in.), 1843. Published in William Henry Brown, *Portrait Gallery of Distinguished American Citizens,* Hartford, 1845. National Portrait Gallery, Smithsonian Institution, Washington, D.C.; gift of Wilmarth Sheldon Lewis. *Page 191*

Figure 163. Andrew Jackson. Oil on canvas by Jacques Amans and Theodore Sidney Moise (1808–1885), 304.8 x 228.6 cm. (120 x 90 in.), 1844. Gallier Hall, City of New Orleans, Louisiana. *Page 192*

Figure 164. *Andrew Jackson In His Last Days.* Engraving by Thomas Doney (active 1844–1849), 13.7 x 10.5 cm. (5⅜ x 4⅛ in.), 1845. Published in the *United States Magazine, and Democratic Review,* September 1845. National Portrait Gallery, Smithsonian Institution, Washington, D.C. *Page 194*

Figure 165. *Andrew Jackson.* Lithograph with tintstone by Jean-Baptiste Adolphe Lafosse (circa 1810–1879), 54.5 x 43.5 cm. (21⁷⁄₁₆ x 17⅛ in.), 1856. National Portrait Gallery, Smithsonian Institution, Washington, D.C. *Page 194*

Figure 166. Andrew Jackson. Daguerreotype attributed to Anthony, Edwards & Co.

(active 1842–1847), 13.9 x 10.9 cm. (5½ x 4⁵⁄₁₆ in.), 1845. Mead Art Museum, Amherst College, Amherst, Massachusetts; gift of William Macbeth, Inc. *Page 195*

Figure 167. Andrew Jackson. Daguerreotype attributed to Anthony, Edwards & Co., 13.8 x 10.8 cm. (5⁷⁄₁₆ x 4¼ in.), 1845. Prints and Photographs Division, Library of Congress, Washington, D.C. *Page 195*

Figure 168. Andrew Jackson. Daguerreotype attributed to Anthony, Edwards & Co., or remotely Langenheim Brothers, Philadelphia, 13.8 x 10.8 cm. (5⁷⁄₁₆ x 4¼ in.), 1845. Private collection. *Page 196*

Figure 169. Andrew Jackson. Daguerreotype attributed to Daniel Adams (1810–1885), 8.3 x 7 cm. (3¼ x 2¾ in.), circa 1845. George Eastman House, Rochester, New York; gift of A. Conger Goodyear. *Page 196*

Figure 170. Andrew Jackson. Oil on canvas by George P. A. Healy (1813–1894), 74.3 x 56.5 cm. (29¼ x 22¼ in.), 1845. Musée National de la Coopération Franco-Américaine, Blérancourt, Cliché Réunion des Musées Nationaux. *Page 198*

Figure 171. Andrew Jackson. Oil on canvas by George P. A. Healy, 61 x 50.8 cm. (24 x 20 in.), 1845. Signed center right: "G. P. A. Healy May 29th, 1845." The Hermitage: Home of President Andrew Jackson, Hermitage, Tennessee. *Page 198*

Figure 172. Andrew Jackson. Oil on canvas by George P. A. Healy, 76.5 x 63.8 cm. (30⅛ x 25⅛ in.), 1845. Signed lower right: "Healy. 1845." Cummer Gallery of Art, Jacksonville, Florida; gift of Mr. and Mrs. Algur H. Meadows, 1972. *Page 199*

Chapter Eight

Figure 173. *In Memory of Andrew Jackson, The Illustrious Patriot, Statesman and Hero.* Silk memorial ribbon, after Ralph E. W. Earl, 1845. Private collection. *Page 206*

Figure 174. *To Commemorate the Death of General Andrew Jackson.* Silk memorial ribbon, after James B. Longacre, 1845. Private collection. *Page 206*

Figure 175. *To The Memory of Andrew Jackson, The Soldier, Patriot & Statesman.* Silk memorial ribbon, after William James Hubard, 1845. Private collection. *Page 206*

Figure 176. *Death of Genl. Andrew Jackson.* Hand-colored lithograph by Nathaniel Currier (1813–1888), 30 x 21.7 cm. (11¹³⁄₁₆ x 8⁹⁄₁₆ in.), 1845. National Portrait Gallery, Smithsonian Institution, Washington, D.C. *Page 207*

Figure 177. Andrew Jackson. Oil on canvas by Thomas Sully, 51.8 x 43.8 cm. (20⅜ x 17¼ in.), circa 1824. National Gallery of Art, Washington, D.C.; Andrew W. Mellon Collection. *Page 208*

Figure 178. *Jackson.* Engraving by Thomas B. Welch (1814–1874), after Thomas Sully, 56.8 x 44.5 cm. (22⅜ x 17½ in.), 1852. Prints and Photographs Division, Library of Congress, Washington, D.C. *Page 209*

Figure 179. Andrew Jackson. Oil on canvas by Thomas Sully, 59 x 49.5 cm. (23¼ x 19½ in.), 1845. Mrs. Arnold A. Willcox. *Page 209*

Figure 180. Andrew Jackson. Oil on canvas by Thomas Sully, 59.7 x 49.5 cm. (23½ x 19½ in.), 1845. Inscribed on liner: "From a study made in 1824 from Genl. Jackson. TS 1845." The R. W. Norton Art Gallery, Shreveport, Louisiana. *Page 209*

Figure 181. Andrew Jackson. Oil on canvas by Thomas Sully, 247 x 156.2 cm. (97¼ x 61½ in.), 1845. Signed lower left: "TS 1845." The Corcoran Gallery of Art, Washington, D.C.; gift of William Wilson Corcoran, 1869. *Page 210*

Figure 182. Five-dollar United States Treasury note with image of Andrew Jackson after Thomas Sully, engraved by Alfred Sealey, "rainbow series" of 1869. National Numismatic Collection, National Museum of American History, Smithsonian Institution, Washington, D.C. *Page 211*

Figure 183. Andrew Jackson. Bronze by Clark Mills (1815–1883), dedicated January 8, 1853, in Lafayette Square, Washington, D.C. *Page 215*

Figure 184. *Mill's Colossean Equestrian Statue of General Andrew Jackson.* Lithograph with tintstone by Wagner and McGuigan lithography company (active 1846–1858), 47.6 x 41.6 cm. (18¾ x 16⅜ in.), 1853. Prints and Photographs Division, Library of Congress, Washington, D.C. *Page 216*

Figure 185. Andrew Jackson. Pot metal statuette cast by Cornelius and Baker of Philadelphia, after Clark Mills, 66 cm. (26 in.), patented 1855. National Portrait Gallery, Smithsonian Institution, Washington, D.C.; gift of Mr. and Mrs. John L. Sanders in memory of William Monroe Geer. *Page 216*

Figure 186. *General Andrew Jackson Before Judge Hall.* Oil on canvas by Christian Schussele (1824–1879), 108 x 152.4 cm. (42½ x 60 in.), 1859. Signed lower right: "C. Schusselle [*sic*] 1859." The Thomas Gilcrease Institute of American History and Art, Tulsa, Oklahoma. *Page 217*

Figure 187. *General Andrew Jackson Before Judge Hall.* Charcoal and pencil on paper by Christian Schussele, 50.2 x 75.6 cm. (19¾ x 29¾ in.), study, 1858. Signed lower right: "C Sch. June 1858." Pennsylvania Academy of the Fine Arts, Philadelphia; gift of Mrs. Francis P. Garvan. *Page 221*

Figure 188. *General Andrew Jackson Before Judge Hall.* Oil on canvas by Christian Schussele, 52.1 x 76.2 cm. (20½ x 30 in.), study, circa 1858. Pennsylvania Academy of the Fine Arts, Philadelphia; Collections Fund purchase. *Page 221*

Chapter Nine

Figure 189. Andrew Jackson. Oil on canvas by Ralph E. W. Earl, 74.9 x 62.2 cm. (29½ x 24½ in.), circa 1825. The Hermitage: Home of President Andrew Jackson, Hermitage, Tennessee. *Page 222*

Figure 190. Rachel Jackson. Oil on canvas by Ralph E. W. Earl, 73.7 x 61 cm. (29 x 24 in.), circa 1825. The Hermitage: Home of President Andrew Jackson, Hermitage, Tennessee. *Page 222*

Figure 191. Rachel Jackson. Oil on canvas by Ralph E. W. Earl, 73.7 x 60.9 cm. (29 x 24 in.), circa 1827. The Hermitage: Home of President Andrew Jackson, Hermitage, Tennessee. *Page 224*

Figure 192. Rachel Jackson. Oil on canvas attributed to Washington Bogart Cooper (1802–1888), after Ralph E. W. Earl, 74.9 x 62.2 cm. (29½ x 24½ in.), circa 1830. Tennessee State Museum, Nashville. *Page 225*

Figure 193. Rachel Jackson. Oil on canvas by Ralph E. W. Earl, 75.6 x 62.2 cm. (29¾ x 24½ in.), circa 1831. The Hermitage: Home of President Andrew Jackson, Hermitage, Tennessee. *Page 226*

Figure 194. Rachel Jackson. Oil on canvas by Howard Chandler Christy (1873–1952), after Ralph E. W. Earl, 104.1 x 79.1 cm. (41 x 31⅛ in.), 1941. Signed lower left: "Howard Chandler Christy." The White House Collection, Washington, D.C.; gift of the State of Tennessee. *Page 226*

Figure 195. Rachel Jackson. Watercolor on ivory by Louisa Catherine Strobel (1803–1883), after Ralph E. W. Earl, 6.4 x 5.1 cm. (2½ x 2 in.), circa 1831. The Hermitage: Home of President Andrew Jackson, Hermitage, Tennessee. *Page 227*

Figure 196. *Mrs. Andrew Jackson.* Engraving by John Chester Buttre (1821–1893), after Louisa Catherine Strobel, after Ralph E. W. Earl, 10.2 x 9.2 cm. (4 x 3⅝ in.), not dated. National Portrait Gallery, Smithsonian Institution, Washington, D.C. *Page 227*

Appendix

Figure 197. Andrew Jackson. Oil on canvas by Ralph E. W. Earl, 76.4 x 63.7 cm. (30⅟₁₆ x 25⅟₁₆ in.), circa 1830–1832. The Daughters of the American Revolution Museum, Washington, D.C.; gift of Mrs. Cyrus Griffith Martin. *Page 230*

Figure 198. Andrew Jackson. Oil on panel by Ralph E. W. Earl, 76.2 x 62.9 cm. (30 x 24¾ in.), circa 1830–1832. North Carolina Museum of Art, Raleigh; purchased with funds from the state of North Carolina. *Page 230*

Figure 199. *The Presidents of the United States.* Engraving by John W. Casilear (1811–1893), 26.4 x 21 cm. (10⅜ x 8¼ in.), 1834. The Historical Society of Pennsylvania, Philadelphia. *Page 230*

Figure 200. Andrew Jackson. Oil on canvas by Ralph E. W. Earl, 77.5 x 63.5 cm. (30½ x 25 in.), circa 1833. Private collection. *Page 231*

Figure 201. Andrew Jackson. Oil on canvas attributed to Ralph E. W. Earl, 74.9 x 61 cm. (29½ x 24 in.), circa 1833. The Hermitage: Home of President Andrew Jackson, Hermitage, Tennessee. *Page 231*

Figure 202. Andrew Jackson. Oil on canvas by Ralph E. W. Earl, 72.4 x 62.2 cm. (28½ x 24½ in.), not dated. Washington County Museum of Fine Arts, Hagerstown, Maryland. *Page 231*

Figure 203. Andrew Jackson. Oil on canvas by Ralph E. W. Earl, 72.7 x 56.5 cm. (28⅝ x 22¼ in.), circa 1834 or after. The Museum of Fine Arts, Houston, the Bayou Bend Collection; gift of Miss Ima Hogg. *Page 231*

Figure 204. Andrew Jackson. Oil on canvas by Ralph E. W. Earl, 76.2 x 63.5 cm. (30 x 25 in.), circa 1834 or after. Pennsylvania Academy of the Fine Arts, Philadelphia; John Frederick Lewis Memorial Collection. *Page 231*

Figure 205. Andrew Jackson. Oil on canvas by Ralph E. W. Earl, 73.8 x 60.6 cm. (29⅟₁₆ x 23⅞ in.), circa 1834 or after. Friends of Linden Place, Bristol, Rhode Island. *Page 231*

Figure 206. Andrew Jackson. Oil on canvas by Ralph E. W. Earl, 76.2 x 63.5 cm. (30 x 25 in.), circa 1834 or after. The Hermitage: Home of President Andrew Jackson, Hermitage, Tennessee. *Page 232*

Figure 207. Andrew Jackson. Oil on canvas by Ralph E. W. Earl, 73.7 x 62.2 cm. (29 x 24½ in.), circa 1834 or after. Tennessee Historical Society Collection, Tennessee State Museum, Nashville. *Page 232*

Figure 208. Andrew Jackson. Oil on canvas by Ralph E. W. Earl, 75.7 x 61.9 cm. (29¹³⁄₁₆ x 24⅜ in.), circa 1834 or after. The White House Collection, Washington, D.C.; gift of the White House Historical Association, 1977. *Page 232*

Figure 209. Andrew Jackson. Oil on canvas by Ralph E. W. Earl, 76.5 x 63.8 cm. (30⅛ x 25⅛ in.), circa 1834 or after. Mabel Brady Garvan Collection, Yale University Art Gallery, New Haven, Connecticut. *Page 232*

Introduction

Figure 1.
Watercolor on ivory by S. M. Charles,
1835. The White House Collection; gift of
Mr. and Mrs. Ronald Tree

Sometime in 1835, a little-known portraitist who signed his works "S. M. Charles" painted a miniature of Andrew Jackson. Now in the collection of the White House, this homely likeness is what one might expect of an obscure amateur artist, though the piece exudes its own charm and realism [Fig. 1]. Judging from the melancholy eyes and the pursed lips, both traits described by contemporaries, the portrait was probably painted from life while Jackson occupied the presidential mansion. Typically, he left no detailed account of it for posterity.[1] The miniature itself must tell its own story.

How different Jackson was from his predecessor, John Quincy Adams of Massachusetts, the nation's sixth President! Between April 1 and April 20, 1839, Adams's diary mentions seven sittings with Mr. Charles for a portrait that he considered to be really a "caricature." Moreover, the occasion prompted Adams, then in his seventy-first year, to reflect back upon the thirty-four previous times when he had sat for a painting, sculpted bust, or commemorative medal. On a piece of paper he listed these, giving the artist, the place, and the year of each sitting as best he could remember back to 1783.[2]

Jackson was never the contemplative type, disposed to assess his past through portraiture or any other medium. His life was an extraordinary one, too. As a frontier lawyer and judge, Indian fighter and military hero, and ultimately as President of the United States, Jackson was perhaps the best example of the self-made American in the first half of the nineteenth century. Seemingly every schoolboy in the country knew of his humble beginnings in the Carolina backcountry, of his political rise in Tennessee, and most especially of his battlefield exploits against superior British forces at New Orleans in 1815. When he occupied the White House, most adults capable of reading a newspaper followed his democratic reforms with keen interest.

Indeed, Jackson's celebrity status rivaled that of the immortal George Washington. In the 1830s his levees in the presidential mansion attracted unprecedented mobs eager to shake his hand, and whenever he traveled, crowds of cheering spectators lined his route. Cities, steamboats, and favorite sons were all named after him. In the opinion of New York diarist Philip Hone, Jackson stood supreme in the affections of the American people. "Talk of him as the second Washington!" wrote Hone in 1833. "It won't do now; Washington was only the first Jackson."[3]

Indicative of his widespread popularity, portrait likenesses of Jackson adorned tavern signs and parlor mantels alike. Engravings and cartoon lithographs abounded. After his victory at New Orleans, Jackson was almost constantly in demand by painters and sculptors; and the art that survives is in itself a sweeping survey of American portraiture before the Civil War.

Invariably, after much coaxing, Jackson would sit to artists, some of whom made special and long, arduous journeys solely to get a firsthand look at him. Because his personality was devoid of narcissistic traits, he almost never mentioned these sittings in his voluminous correspondence. Fortunately, there were others like Adams who were verbose in speaking of the fine arts and human nature, and in fact his diary reveals significantly more about Jackson's portraits than Jackson ever revealed.

Born on March 15, 1767, almost four months before his Yankee countryman John Quincy Adams, Jackson lived his first years in the Waxhaw settlement in South Carolina. There, paints and canvases were used principally to construct covered wagons, and clay to chink drafty log cabins. In 1765 his parents had emigrated from Carrickfergus, Ireland; the death of his father in 1767 and his mother in 1781 left the young lad of fourteen to explore for himself the advantages America had to offer. Jackson made the most of a rowdy youth, surviving capture and injury during the American Revolution to settle down to the study and practice of law in North Carolina and then in Tennessee. An appointment to the bench of the Tennessee Superior Court in 1798 and a commission as major general of the state militia in 1802 counterbalanced the privations and perils of the frontier.

Indians were always a preoccupation for settler and nation alike. In 1814 Jackson's volunteer army defeated the Creek at Horseshoe Bend, Mississippi Territory. The Treaty of Fort Jackson, which he negotiated for the United States, removed the Creek Nation from their ancestral lands in southern Georgia and what is now Alabama. This was the beginning of a brutal, long-standing policy of removal that would ultimately drive America's natives west of the Mississippi River and beyond. Old "Sharp Knife," or "Pointed Arrow" as the Indians called him, once again proved as tough as hickory, the more familiar sobriquet favored by his troops.[4]

Jackson's victory over the British at New Orleans the following year ended the War of 1812 and reasserted the sovereignty of the young nation. It was this battlefield triumph and not the Treaty of Ghent, coincidentally signed in the midst of the campaign, that kindled a new sense of nationalism. Meanwhile in Belgium, John Quincy Adams, one of five American peace commissioners, was having his portrait painted (as were his American colleagues) to mark the treaty's signing. He was no more deserving than Jackson, but because of his cultured upbringing, he was more inclined to take advantage of such opportunities.[5] In one sense, portraiture personified social prestige and diplomatic privilege.

Jackson's family background, education, and early career were vastly different from Adams's social milieu. The circles he moved in around Nashville were primitive by comparison. In 1797, when he lived briefly in the culturally forward city of Philadelphia as a freshman congressman from the new state of Tennessee, he probably did not sit for his portrait; at least no such likeness survives. Albert Gallatin, himself a leading member of Congress and later one of Adams's fellow commissioners at Ghent, partially filled the void years later. He remembered Jackson as "a tall, lank, uncouth-looking personage, with long locks of hair hanging over his face, and a queue down his back tied in an eel skin; his dress singular, his manners and deportment those of a rough backwoodsman."[6]

Still, it is unlikely that a man of Jackson's social standing did not own some likeness of himself before the Battle of New Orleans. In January 1813 he mentioned having a miniature of his wife Rachel, which he promised to wear next to his heart.[7] No doubt Rachel had her own likeness of Mr. Jackson, as she was wont to call him. Perhaps these were among the family keepsakes lost in the fire that destroyed the Hermitage, Jackson's home near Nashville, in 1834.

What might be the earliest documented attempt to portray Jackson occurred in 1814. The legislature of the Mississippi Territory voted a resolution of gratitude to Jackson for his victory over the Creek Indians, thus saving a great portion of the country "from savage cruelty and devastation." It authorized Governor David Holmes to procure an appropriate presentation sword, costing no more than five hundred dollars. Holmes in turn sought the aid of Robert Patterson, director of the United States Mint, specifying that the hilt and scabbard should be of gold. With regard to suitable emblems to be engraved on it, Patterson may have suggested a likeness of Jackson. In any event, Holmes mailed the following description in July: "Genl Jackson is about five feet eleven inches high, has large bones, but thin of flesh. His face is rather narrow than otherwise. Cheek bones prominent his nose tolerably large but not aquiline. Countenance open, intelligent and determined."[8]

The splendid sword and scabbard, lost long ago, were presented to Jackson by Tennessee Governor Willie Blount at a grand banquet in Nashville honoring his triumphant return from New Orleans in May 1815.

Figure 2.
Aquatint engraving by William Strickland, circa 1815. The New-York Historical Society

❧

Predictably, fame and glory were inducements enough for the hero finally to pause and remove his chapeau for an artist or two. What survive are a miniature by a Frenchman, Jean François de Vallée, and a crude oil on canvas by an American, Nathan W. Wheeler, painted in New Orleans after the battle of January 8, 1815. As likenesses they are not much better than the fabrications of numerous engravers, who seemingly used imagination alone to produce illustrations of the nation's newest celebrity. Typical was an aquatint by the young Philadelphia architect William Strickland [Fig. 2]. In 1809 Strickland temporarily took up portrait painting and engraving, producing a number of illustrations related to the War of 1812.

Surprisingly, in the four years following Jackson's New Orleans victory, his life portraiture still proved meager and unsatisfying, with the exception of a charming small bas-relief profile worked in red wax by Giuseppe Valaperta in Washington about 1815. Jackson's military preoccupation with chastising the Indians, especially the Seminole, during the war of 1818 in Spanish-held West Florida, had much to do with his unavailability for portrait sittings. The highlight of this period, however, was the arrival of Ralph Eleaser Whiteside Earl in Nashville in the winter of 1817. Earl became a lifelong friend and lived in the White House during Jackson's eight-year presidency. His story will unfold in detail; he painted approximately three dozen portraits of Jackson that can be documented and must have produced many more that are now lost. The supreme irony is that, for a President who was ridiculed for ignoring the advancement of the arts in America, Jackson had in Earl what many considered a court painter. It was not until 1819, when Jackson toured the Northeast's major cities, from Washington to New York, that a number of the country's finest portraitists—Charles Willson Peale, Thomas Sully, and John Wesley Jarvis—painted reputable likenesses, thus revealing the real man for the first time. The portrait record from this period until the very eve of Jackson's death on June 8, 1845, is an extraordinary chronicle of an American hero and statesman who was the premier icon of his age.

A concluding note about the methodology employed in this portrait study may be useful in evaluating the contents. In a span of approximately thirty-five years, nearly fifty different artists produced, in various mediums, more than a hundred likenesses of Andrew Jackson. Countless variations and copy images appeared more casually in such disparate forms as political broadsides, snuffboxes, glass and chinaware, postage stamps, and currency. A complete iconographic study would have been unwieldy for a single volume. Further, the inclusion of the many peripheral images would have been the equivalent of looking at Jackson through a hall of mirrors. In effect, the real man represented by the life portraits would have become diffused, distorted, and confused.

The images discussed herein represent principally life sittings, replicas, and portraits of historical or artistic significance. Because Ralph E. W. Earl was extraordinarily prolific, as many likenesses by him as practical have been included. In addition, a selection of caricatures and cartoons—subject matter worthy of a study in itself—has been inserted so as not to ignore this significant facet of Jackson's portrait record.

With regard to the selection process, works that have historical documentation, provenance, integrity as a likeness, and signatures and dates have been given high priority.[9] A brief mention of four pieces of sculpture will illustrate this process. In 1968 the Smithsonian Institution's National Museum of American Art purchased a plaster of Hiram Powers's 1834–1835 likeness from the Powers studio collection. The provenance here is as true as the likeness itself, not to mention the lengthy record of this life sitting in Powers's correspondence. In another case, William Rush's original 1819 terra-cotta lay for decades unidentified in the Burlington County (New Jersey) Historical Society.[10] Absolutely nothing was known of its early provenance. Although the identities of the sitter and artist were not discovered until 1982, the likeness had been amply documented in newspapers and letters of the period. How different was the fate of a marble bust of Jackson by Ferdinand Pettrich, of which four copies are extant. For more than a century, the sculptor of this remarkably detailed and vigorous bust remained a mystery. Because of its integrity as a likeness, it was indeed probable that it was based on a life sitting. Yet scarcely a shred of historical documentation existed to corroborate this view. Only the discovery that Pettrich was in Washington to see Jackson in 1836 led to the otherwise remote chance of comparing his work with the heretofore unattributed bust. The riddle solved itself almost immediately. Finally, in the Hermitage stands a marble bust of Jackson that formerly had been regarded as the work of Hiram Powers. Then someone discovered the chiseled inscription "Persico" on the back.

Still other portraits lie beyond the reach of this study. For instance, the Washington *Globe* reported on August 18, 1832, that Nicholas Gevelot, a sculptor formerly employed at the United States Capitol, had modeled a likeness of President Jackson from life. The artist, the paper claimed, "preserves the features with the most striking accuracy."[11] Regrettably, Gevelot's *Jackson* has proven no more physically durable than the living model. Nor is it possible to know precisely what other works may have been lost over the years. What survives is what follows.

Notes

1. Jackson, however, did leave a record of having reimbursed his artist-friend Ralph E. W. Earl with a check for forty-two dollars for a miniature portrait by Charles. See entry of June 22,

1836, in Check Register, Bank of the Metropolis, 1835–1837, Andrew Jackson Papers, Library of Congress, Washington, D.C.

The miniature was presented to the White House as a gift in 1961 by Mr. and Mrs. Ronald Tree. Before that, it belonged to Colonel John C. Rives's descendants, some of whom lived near Bladensburg, Maryland. See records of the Catalog of American Portraits.

2. It is fortunate that Adams left a record of his sittings to Mr. Charles, because the portrait is now lost. See Andrew Oliver, *Portraits of John Quincy Adams and His Wife* (Cambridge, Mass., 1970), pp. 1–3, 202–3.

3. Philip Hone, *The Diary of Philip Hone, 1828–1851,* ed. Allan Nevins (New York, 1927), vol. 1, pp. 96–97.

4. Robert V. Remini, *Andrew Jackson* (New York, 1977–1981), vol. 1, pp. 180, 227.

5. Oliver, *Portraits of Adams,* pp. 50–57.

6. James Parton, *Life of Andrew Jackson* (New York, 1861), vol. 1, p. 196.

7. Andrew Jackson, *The Papers of Andrew Jackson,* Volume 2: *1804–1813,* ed. Harold D. Moser *et al.* (Knoxville, Tenn., 1984), p. 353.

8. David Holmes to Robert Patterson, July 13, 1814, Territorial Papers: Mississippi, Records of the Department of State, Record Group 59, National Archives, Washington, D.C.

9. An especially intriguing profile likeness has all but eluded historical documentation and artistic verification. Five versions are extant, all but one painted in oils on wood panels, measuring approximately 22   x 18   inches. Two versions are now in the collection of the Ladies' Hermitage Association. The one hanging in Tulip Grove—the house adjacent to the Hermitage and once the home of Jackson's former ward, Andrew Jackson Donelson— descended from the Donelson family to the Ladies' Hermitage Association in 1959. A card attached to the back of the portrait bears the inscription "J. C. Wilson, Portrait Painter and Gilder, Nashville, Tennessee, June 15th, 1822." Although the likeness seems to corroborate this date, it has always been assumed that Wilson was merely the framemaker. A second profile, now in storage, was presented to the Ladies' Hermitage Association in 1980 by Mrs. John S. Fletcher [Fig. 3]. A third, less finished version is in the Historic New Orleans Collection; still another is in private hands. Yet a fifth and larger version, an oil on canvas, is in the Tennessee State Museum in Nashville.

These likenesses have been attributed to John Wesley Jarvis, Ralph E. W. Earl, and Matthew Harris Jouett. Of these artists, Jouett may be the most likely, since he painted many portraits on wood panels the same size as these. Yet he left no record of ever having painted Jackson, and neither did his grandson, Richard Jouett Menefee, who compiled an extensive catalogue of the artist's work. This catalogue has been published in Samuel Woodson Price, *The Old Masters of the Bluegrass: Jouett, Bush, Grimes, Frazer, Morgan, Hart* (Louisville, Ky., 1902), pp. 51–67. For additional references to these profile images, see George E. Jordan, "New Orleans Masterpieces: The Jackson Portraits," *New Orleans Art Review* 2 (January–February 1983): 14; National Society of the Colonial Dames of America in the State of Alabama, *Alabama Portraits Prior to 1870* (Mobile, Ala., 1969), p. 185.

10. Milo M. Naeve, "William Rush's Terracotta and Plaster Busts of General Andrew Jackson," *American Art Journal* 21 (1989): 35.

11. Washington *Globe,* August 18, 1832. For a statue of Jackson that Enrico Causici proposed sculpting, but never accomplished, see Washington *Globe,* November 20, 1832.

Figure 3.
Oil on panel by unidentified artist, circa 1822. The Hermitage: Home of President Andrew Jackson

Andrew Jackson: A Portrait Study

1767
March 15: Born, Waxhaw settlement, South Carolina

1780–1781
Participates in American Revolution; is captured and suffers head wound

1787–1788
Practices law in North Carolina

1788
October: Arrives in Nashville, Tennessee

Circa 1791
Marries Rachel Donelson Robards

1794
January 18: Remarries Rachel in legal ceremony

1795
December 19: Is elected delegate to Tennessee Constitutional Convention

1796
October 22: Is elected to United States House of Representatives

1797
September: Is elected to United States Senate; resigns seat in 1798

1798
December 20: Is elected judge of Superior Court of Tennessee

1802
April 1: Is commissioned major general of Tennessee militia

1804
August 4: Purchases Hermitage property, near Nashville

1806
May 30: Kills Charles Dickinson in duel

1814
March 27: Defeats Creek Indians at Horseshoe Bend, Mississippi Territory

May 28: Is commissioned major general in United States Army

August 9: Imposes Treaty of Fort Jackson on Creek Nation, ending Creek War

1815
January 8: Defeats British in battle of New Orleans, ending War of 1812

February 27: Is voted a gold medal by United States Congress in honor of his victory

March 31: Is fined one thousand dollars by Judge Dominick A. Hall for contempt of court

Miniature painted by Jean François de Vallée

Oil portrait painted by Nathan W. Wheeler in New Orleans

1818
Full-length life-size portrait painted by Ralph E. W. Earl in Nashville

Assumes command of Seminole War in Spanish Florida

Chapter 1

Hero of New Orleans, 1815–1818

By noon of January 8, 1815, with the guns of battle mercifully quiet on the plain of Chalmette, some five miles from the city of New Orleans, Major General Andrew Jackson stood triumphant over a cane field, silver with frost that morning but now littered with the dead and wounded of George III's red-coated army. Among the fallen, and symbolic of the British defeat, lay the commanding general, Sir Edward Michael Pakenham, who had been killed while leading a futile advance against the American line. The month-long campaign had taken its toll on the forty-seven-year-old Jackson as well. For nights he could not sleep. Chronic illness wasted his already lean, tall frame. He was existing on only a few tablespoons of rice each day; his system could bear no more. Even his uniform fatigued him; the weight of the left epaulet inflamed his shoulder, where a pistol bullet still lodged, a painful souvenir of a former personal dispute.[1] Yet that day's action lifted his spirits, if not entirely freeing his mind about the ultimate outcome of the battle, for the enemy refused to strike camp in retreat. Its eventual departure from Lake Borgne, however, signaled victory for the Americans and brought to a close the protracted War of 1812. Jackson returned to the city a savior and a hero. In the days and weeks that followed, news of his stunning triumph spread throughout the country, and the name of Andrew Jackson became known to all.

Rough sketches of his life appeared in the newspapers and sparked the imagination of individuals, such as the man from Delaware who wrote to Jackson suggesting that they might be relatives. A year after the battle, Jackson received a letter from New Orleans informing him that the children of the La Ronde family "never went to sleep without calling on God to bless their Father and Mother and Genl. Jackson."[2]

The nation wanted a look at this American Napoleon, the reincarnation of the immortal Washington, whose own full-length portrait after Gilbert Stuart had been whisked out of the presidential mansion to safety by the indomitable first lady, Dolley Madison, when the British had burned the capital city five months earlier. But unlike Washington, Jackson remained a stranger to most Americans. Scarcely a crude portrait or an engraving of him was known to exist at the time of the battle. This dearth of imagery would not persist, as artists, sculptors, friends, and admirers began asking Jackson for his likeness, which today is as common as a twenty-dollar bill.

I

Two of the first attempts to artistically venerate Jackson and his victory at New Orleans were markedly different. On February 27, 1815, the United States Congress unanimously voted its thanks to Major General Jackson and resolved that the President should have struck a gold medal with emblems of the splendid achievement.[3] The resolution did not specify that the medal bear a portrait of Jackson; this decision was made later. However eager Congress was to extend its thanks, nine years passed before Jackson's medal was finished and presented to him.

Meanwhile, on March 25, 1815, Joseph Delaplaine, a Philadelphia publisher and print dealer, wrote to Jackson about a grand idea of his own. Best remembered for his two-volume illustrated work, *Repository of the Lives and Portraits of Distinguished American Characters* (1815-1816), Delaplaine proposed to publish a print of the Battle of New Orleans. He arranged with Charles R. Leslie in London to paint the picture, and with Alexander Lawson of Philadelphia to engrave it.[4]

Delaplaine carefully explained the procedure to Jackson. He requested the general to furnish him with "a ground plan of the fortifications" and "a sketch of the appearance of the country taken from within our lines looking down the road towards the British as they were advancing." Delaplaine also wanted *a description of the times of the Battle that will be the most favourable and interesting to make the picture from and the situations you were in at those times—what officers stood near you, their names, Rank etc—what was the general uniform of the Tennessee & Kentucky Troops—uniform of the New Orleans Volunteers—whether you & your officers near you wore rounded or cocked hats.*[5]

Delaplaine explained further that he would forward this information to Mr. Leslie, who would then finish the picture and send it back to Philadelphia. Upon its return, he added, "the engraver commences *his* work & when he comes to your portrait in the picture & also those of your officers who were near you in battle, he will want likenesses, or portraits of each." Delaplaine inquired of Jackson if "there is a portrait of yourself, *by whom painted,* & whether I can be permitted at the time it will be wanted, to have it here for the use of the engraver."[6] He suggested that if Jackson intended to visit Philadelphia, he would engage the city's finest portrait painter—undoubtedly Thomas Sully—to take his likeness. Apparently nothing came of this venture, because no such print or painting has been discovered.

෴

Public fascination with Jackson's victory at New Orleans inspired other artists and engravers. Hyacinthe Laclotte, an architect and assistant engineer in the Louisiana militia, made a panoramic drawing of the battle from the field, which proved to be the only historically accurate depiction. In 1817 he returned to France and had the scene engraved in Paris by Philibert-Louis Debucourt, a great master of colored aquatint.[7] The following year it was published in Philadelphia.

Another contemporary battle scene was engraved, this one bearing an image of Jackson in the bottom margin. *A Correct View of the Battle Near the City of New Orleans* was the work of Francisco Scacki. This crude production was said to have been his first and last attempt at engraving. Scacki experimented with a variety of techniques—etching, stipple and line engraving, roulette, and aquatint—much "as a schoolboy uses white chalk on large expanses of smooth brick wall." But not even a barrage of methods could satisfy him with the first strike. Not wishing to waste precious paper, he printed a second state on the reverse [Fig. 4].[8] This time, however, he added five figures, which are all the more evident because of the surrounding patches of white, the result of his first having to burnish the plate smooth before reengraving it. In addition, Scacki enhanced the appearance of the battle smoke over the American rampart at the

Figure 4.
Etching, engraving, aquatint, and soft ground on paper by Francisco Scacki, circa 1816 (second state, containing identification key). National Portrait Gallery, Smithsonian Institution

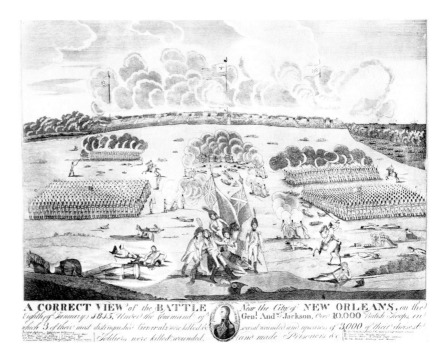

Figure 5.
Engraving by Joseph Yeager, after West, circa 1817 (third state, containing identification key). National Portrait Gallery, Smithsonian Institution

top. He also introduced an identification key on either side in the bottom margin.

In about 1816 or 1817, Joseph Yeager of Philadelphia published a better engraving, entitled *Battle of New Orleans and Death of Major General Packenham* [Fig. 5].[9] The composition may have been inspired by Benjamin West's 1770 painting of the death of General Wolfe. For instance, the soldiers attending the dying Pakenham are suggestive of those attending Wolfe. Yeager inserted a likeness of Jackson in the bottom margin that is scarcely better than

Scacki's; it was probably copied from a contemporary print after an 1815 oil painting by Nathan W. Wheeler of New Orleans.[10]

None of these battle scenes came close to revealing the state of the arts in early nineteenth-century America, though they did reflect the popularity of the historical genre. For example, in 1827 Cincinnati's Western Museum exhibited a large transparency of the Battle of New Orleans, and from time to time other cities displayed similar battle art, always with Old Hickory in the limelight. In January 1844, for instance, it was suggested that a monumental painting of the battle be placed in the Capitol rotunda on a large vacant panel facing the surrender of Cornwallis at Yorktown.[11] Nothing, however, came of this suggestion.

II

After Jackson's victory of January 8, Jean François de Vallée, a French artist living in New Orleans, painted an ivory miniature of the hero [Fig. 6]. This likeness and an oil on canvas executed by Nathan Wheeler at about the same time are the two earliest extant portraits of Andrew Jackson. Vallée left Paris about 1785 and immigrated to Alexandria, Virginia, where he planned to enter the cotton trade. This venture failed, and by 1794 Vallée was in Philadelphia, listed as a boarding-house keeper. He eventually moved south, living for a time in Charleston, South Carolina, before reaching New Orleans.

How Vallée came to paint Jackson's likeness is not known. The image itself is unique, as stated by one of Jackson's early biographers, James Parton: *It is so unlike the portraits familiar to the public, that not a man in the United States would recognize in it the features of General Jackson. Abundant, reddish-sandy hair falls low over the high, narrow forehead, and almost hides it from view. . . . Eyes of a remarkably bright blue. Complexion fair, fresh and ruddy. . . . The miniature reminds you of a good country deacon out for a day's soldiering.*[12]

Vallée also made Jackson appear younger and healthier than he actually was. His face shows none of the lines of the sickness and turmoil that had beset him. As Parton noted, the most discordant feature is Jackson's hair, which lies limp on his forehead. Jackson was always known for his bristling locks. Vallée's treatment of them appears to be his own nationalistic formula and is characteristic of the Empire style prevalent in France at the time of Napoleon.[13]

Before Jackson left New Orleans for his home in Tennessee in that spring of 1815, he presented his miniature by Vallée to Edward Livingston, the best legal authority in the city.[14] Livingston was a man of talent and diplomacy and was just the type of confidant Jackson wanted around him. Their relationship dated to 1796, when they had both served in Congress. In time, he became Jackson's military secretary, aide-de-camp, interpreter, and confidential and legal adviser.

Upon Jackson's arrival in New Orleans in early December of 1814, Livingston was one of the first to welcome him. He invited the general to a dinner party, and the occasion provided an amusing insight into the preconceived notions held by fashionable New Orleans toward this relatively unknown frontiersman. Mrs. Livingston, initially annoyed at having to seat another guest, prepared her friends for what was to come; all expected to greet some sort of wild Indian fighter in buckskins. Great was their surprise when General Jackson entered the room. A true gentleman and soldier stood before them, tall, erect, and perfectly composed in his dark blue uniform. Jackson graciously bowed to the ladies, offered his arm to the hostess, and made agreeable conversation throughout the meal. Afterward, the bevy of ladies looked with wonder. "Is this your backwoodsman?" they exclaimed. "He is a prince!"[15]

The Livingston family always treasured Vallée's miniature of Jackson. In 1816 Edward Livingston wrote to Jackson and explained that his son had taken the image to New York, but lost the little note of appreciation that Jackson had written to accompany it. He enclosed the contents of the message and requested Jackson to write it once more for him.

Livingston also mentioned "a vile Caricature" of Jackson that had appeared as the frontispiece of a newly published book, *Historical Memoir of the War in West Florida and Louisiana in 1814-15,* by Major Arsène Lacarrière Latour [Fig. 7].[16] The illustration was a primitive copy of the Vallée miniature. Latour probably made the copy himself.

In New Orleans, Latour advertised himself as an engineer and architect. For a time he formed a partnership with Hyacinthe Laclotte, and together they opened a school for instruction in a wide variety of skills, from portrait and landscape drawing to architecture. In 1814, when British forces began threatening the Louisiana coast, Jackson made Latour his chief engineer and ordered him to draw plans for batteries on the lower Mississippi. Latour provided Jackson with valuable information throughout the New Orleans campaign.[17] His *Historical Memoir,* complete with accurate maps and dedicated to Andrew

MAJ.ᴿ Gᴬᴸ ANDREW JACKSON

Entered according to act of Congress

Figure 7.
Engraving attributed to Arsène Lacarrière Latour, after Jean François de Vallée, 1816. Historic New Orleans Collection; Museum/ Research Center, Acc. No. 73-12-L

Jackson, became a standard reference on the battle. Its likeness of Jackson, however, did not provide a satisfying look at the hero. In 1864 a much better engraving of Vallée's miniature appeared in Charles Havens Hunt's *The Life of Edward Livingston* [Fig. 8].

The Vallée miniature was passed down in the Livingston family from one generation to the next. Believed lost for a time, it resurfaced at Montgomery Place, the Hudson River estate Livingston inherited in 1828.

III

Until about 1819, the most prevalent and popular likenesses of Jackson were crude engravings, many of which were after an oil painting by Nathan W. Wheeler. Originally a native of Massachusetts, Wheeler was a veteran of the battle of 1815, and afterward he made his living as a distiller and artisan painter, principally in New Orleans. An article in the *Louisiana Courier* of January 1844 reported Wheeler as having been a pupil of Benjamin West.[18] He kept an art studio in the Third Municipality, where hung many of his works, including an unfinished painting of the Battle of New Orleans.

Notice of Wheeler's portrait of Jackson appeared in the *Louisiana Gazette* in early May of 1815. The artist advertised to "persons desirous of obtaining the likeness of Major General Andrew Jackson" that he planned to have five hundred copies engraved by the celebrated Philadelphia engraver David Edwin, after a likeness on view at Wheeler's Chartres Street studio.[19]

Based on comparisons with Edwin's engraving [Fig. 9], Wheeler's original oil painting has been discovered at the Historical Society of Pennsylvania [Fig. 10]. The two images are virtually identical, even to the six-pointed star on Jackson's right epaulet. For years this work lay in a storage vault, the artist unidentified. Recent conservation and cleaning have greatly enhanced the painting's warm colors.[20]

Figure 8.
Engraving by Alexander Hay Ritchie, after Jean François de Vallée, circa 1864.
National Portrait Gallery, Smithsonian Institution

What Wheeler lacked in artistic talent, Edwin made up for in engraving skill. Born in Bath, England, Edwin studied engraving in his native country and in the Netherlands. He sailed to the United States in 1797 and for a few years entered the employ of noted engraver Edward Savage. Not until Edwin began working independently did he establish his name, primarily through his portrait engravings after Gilbert Stuart. Edward Livingston noted the disparity between the original and the engraving in a letter to Jackson of November 7, 1816, in which he remarked, "There is an excellent engraving of the picture taken here [New Orleans] by Wheeler. . . . It is a pity the original was not a better likeness." With a touch of pride mixed with flattery, he added, "I find none that has Done you the least justice but Vallée in the miniature you gave me."[21]

Still another good print after Wheeler's portrait was engraved and published in New York City in 1816 by Thomas Gimbrede. In 1802 this French miniaturist came to America and eventually took up engraving. In 1819 he was appointed drawing master at the United States Military Academy at West Point, a position he held until his death in 1832. Gimbrede's print of Jackson is an oval image surrounded by clouds. The words "New Orleans" adorn the top, and depicted at the base are battle standards, cannon barrels, a sword, and an alligator. This engraving, titled *Major Genl. Andrew Jackson Of the United States Army,* is extremely rare [Fig. 11]. Unlike the Edwin likeness, Jackson faces the viewer's left and his coat is buttoned at the top. The middle buttons are open, however, suggesting a place to rest his hand in Napoleonic fashion. Such artistic license was no doubt the idea of this Frenchman.

The Edwin engraving reached a widespread audience. In 1817 it appeared as the frontispiece to a popular biography of Jackson that was published in Philadelphia. *The Life of Andrew Jackson* was begun by Jackson's military aide, John Reid. After Reid's sudden death in January 1816, the project fell into the hands of a young lawyer named John Henry Eaton, who later became Jackson's controversial secretary of war. Eaton showed great interest in the book's progress but had difficulty obtaining an image of his subject. Edwin's portrait was one option, however. "I have an engraved likeness," he told Jackson, "executed by Edwin which all who know you say is an excellent one, I think so too."[22]

GENERAL JACKSON.

Figure 9. Above.
Engraving by David Edwin, after Nathan W. Wheeler, circa 1816. Prints and Photographs Division, Library of Congress

Figure 10. Right.
Oil on canvas by Nathan W. Wheeler, 1815. The Historical Society of Pennsylvania

Figure 11. Below.
Engraving by Thomas Gimbrede, after Nathan W. Wheeler, 1816. The New-York Historical Society

David Edwin's engraving serves to document much of Andrew Jackson's early portraiture. It establishes the identity of the unsigned Wheeler portrait owned by the Historical Society of Pennsylvania. It also provides the key to interpreting perhaps the most confusing of Jackson's early portraits—a head-and-shoulders image now displayed in the White House, allegedly painted from life

Figure 12.
Oil on panel by John Wesley Jarvis, after
Nathan W. Wheeler, circa 1817. The
White House Collection; gift of Mr. and
Mrs. Gerard B. Lambert

by John Wesley Jarvis in 1815 [Fig. 12].[23] Of all of Jackson's early images, this appears to be the most lifelike. Consequently, it was never before suspected to be a copy of the Wheeler-Edwin likeness.

In about 1816 or 1817, John Wesley Jarvis was one of the foremost portraitists in New York and was working on a commission for City Hall to paint a series of portraits of heroes of the War of 1812.[24] Apparently, during this time he obtained a copy of the Edwin engraving. He may have even seen it reproduced in the Reid-Eaton biography. Jarvis took the Wheeler-Edwin likeness, which was basically a caricature, and gave it a measure of realism. In Jarvis's portrait, gone are the ill-proportioned shoulders, jib-like nose, and seemingly detached head. Jackson now looks real. Jarvis also saw fit to curl Jackson's bangs and simplify his military uniform. What he dared not change, however—and still have the portrait resemble what he supposed was a likeness of Jackson, albeit a crude one—were the lines of his face. These are identical to the ones in Edwin's print and in Wheeler's painting. On Jackson's right side, the artist's facial shading makes a dark funnel under the cheekbone, which tapers down to the jaw. To the left of this are two more shaded vertical lines. Even the mouth is the same. Of particular interest is the evolution of the small growth on the upper left side of Jackson's nose. In the Wheeler painting this is a shadow; in the Edwin engraving the shadow is inexplicably lightened and resembles a spot. In the Jarvis painting this has been misinterpreted to be a lump on Jackson's nose. The possibility exists that this portrait was the product of a painting lesson for the benefit of one of Jarvis's pupils, perhaps Henry Inman, who was apprenticed to Jarvis at the time.[25] The hurried brushstrokes in the background, especially around the head, appear to be the work of a novice. The portrait has an unfinished quality overall, indicating that it was never intended to be a serious artistic effort.

IV

On May 25, 1815, acting Secretary of War Alexander J. Dallas wrote to Joseph Hopkinson, president of the Pennsylvania Academy of the Fine Arts, about a special project. Dallas was seeking the academy's aid in making the gold medals that Congress had voted to several military heroes of the War of 1812, including, of course, Andrew Jackson. He made no specific requests, except to have the medals "executed in the best manner, to serve not only as a legislative testimonial of National gratitude, but as a lasting display of the skill and taste of the American artists, at the commencement of the nineteenth century."

Hopkinson replied five days later, conveying the academy's interest in the project. He recommended that each medal contain on one side the image of the officer for whom it was designed, and on the other an appropriate device. Such a plan would require less effort and expense than if different devices were designed for each side of each medal.[26] The War Department took Hopkinson's advice. Procurement of the officers' likenesses, however, proved tedious.

Sometime that spring, Dallas wrote to Jackson requesting his image. On July 11, Jackson replied by sending a miniature of himself, with the explanation, "though not very correct in the painting, [it] may be sufficiently so in the outlines to answer the purpose for which it is wanted." Because this was a government commission, he enclosed the artist's bill for thirty dollars, payable to J. B. West.[27] This was probably John B. West, who in 1814 was listed as a miniaturist living in Lexington, Kentucky.[28]

Just how Jackson and West had met remains a mystery; and no evidence exists of the miniature or an engraving of it. According to John Eaton, Jackson's biographer, the miniature was in the hands of the Pennsylvania Academy of the Fine Arts in 1817. Eaton considered using it for the frontispiece of his book but was unable to procure it. Nor was West's image of Jackson ever used for the congressional medal. In November of 1820, then-Secretary of War John C. Calhoun wrote Jackson and again requested a likeness.[29] Calhoun regretted the great delay in this commemorative endeavor, but explained that it was beyond his control.

The profile of Jackson that finally appeared on his medal, which was not finished until 1824, was the design of a better artist than John B. West. It was most likely the work of the die-sinker Moritz Fürst. The image resembles a unique Jackson portrait modeled in wax by Giuseppe Valaperta [Fig. 13]. This Italian sculptor had won acclaim for his carvings at Napoleon's palace, Malmaison, near Paris. After journeying to America in 1815, Valaperta advertised in a Baltimore newspaper his intent to execute likenesses on ivory, wax, or plaster of paris. Shortly thereafter he was in Washington working under the discerning eye of Benjamin Latrobe, architect of the Capitol. Latrobe needed skilled artisans and hired Valaperta to carve the great eagle on the frieze of the Hall of Representatives.[30]

Figure 13.
Red wax bas-relief on dark blue glass by Giuseppe Valaperta, circa 1815. The New-York Historical Society

His portrait of Jackson may have been taken from life. The image—a red wax bas-relief on dark blue glass—evinces fine craftsmanship and good detail. Valaperta had an opportunity to see Jackson in mid-November 1815, when the general and his lady visited Washington and remained for six weeks. During their stay, Jackson was entertained lavishly by President Madison, as well as informally in the homes of private citizens.[31] He was indeed a celebrity, and it would have been natural for Valaperta to have made every effort to take his likeness. The image of Jackson exudes realistic qualities similar to Valaperta's likenesses of James Monroe, James Madison, and Thomas Jefferson. Although the hair falling on Jackson's forehead is incongruous with more familiar depictions of him as President, other portraits executed before 1824 also reveal a man whose appearance was more often windswept than groomed.

V

Sometime in the fall of 1815, a little-known itinerant artist named Ralph Eleaser Whiteside Earl arrived in Savannah, Georgia. In his late twenties, he was the son of Ralph Earl, a successful portrait and landscape painter who had worked principally in Connecticut during the last quarter of the eighteenth century. The younger Earl inherited his father's interest in art but not his talent. Even so, beginning in 1809, the younger Earl visited England and France to further his education. In London he received instruction from John Trumbull and Benjamin West, and in Paris he viewed the fine collection of paintings that Napoleon Bonaparte had amassed from all over the Continent.[32]

At best, Ralph E. W. Earl's prospects as an artist were limited. His style was more primitive than refined, his portraits more wooden than lifelike. Earl probably would have had a difficult time sustaining himself in the cities along the eastern seaboard. His chances of success were not much better in the back country, where demand was less and, next to the axe and plow, portraits were deemed a luxury. Seemingly, the most he had in his favor were a few complimentary letters of introduction written on his behalf shortly after his arrival in Georgia.[33]

Yet Earl had a mission that, unbeknownst to him, would secure his future and immortalize his name as a portraitist. In the summer and fall of 1816, he passed through Augusta and Lexington, Georgia, working his way toward Nashville. His grand scheme was to obtain the likeness of Jackson, as well as two of his subordinate officers, John Coffee and William Carroll, with a view toward someday painting a picture of the Battle of New Orleans. As stated in a letter of introduction dated February 19, 1817, Earl planned to be at Jackson's home, the Hermitage, in "a few days, and remain there until he has finished his portrait."[34]

Earl apparently arrived on schedule but then never left, at least not emotionally. Nor did he ever finish painting likenesses of Andrew Jackson. It became his life's work. Little correspondence exists between artist and general to trace their extraordinary friendship, which lasted until Earl's death in 1838, a period of more than twenty years. The best documentation is the portrait record itself, which numbers more than three dozen paintings of Old Hickory.[35] Earl undoubtedly painted many others that either have not survived or have not been identified.

If Earl had plans of visiting other cities during that winter of 1817, he quickly abandoned them. Opportunities around Nashville were too plentiful to venture far from either there or the nearby Hermitage. Besides, Nashville was a good place for a young portraitist to make a start in his profession. It was refined enough to have a demand for portraiture but provincial enough to not expect masterpieces.

In the role of country gentleman, Andrew Jackson was truly the city's first citizen. Apparently he liked Earl from their first handshake. He had a soft spot in his nature for any honest young person struggling to make something of himself, and his house was always open to visiting relatives, friends, and weary travelers. Itinerant artists were no exception. Rachel Jackson, too, found a friend in Earl, based on their few surviving letters. In the spring of 1818, Earl married Jane Caffery, one of Rachel's favorite nieces. Yet before the couple could celebrate their first anniversary, Mrs. Earl died in childbirth.[36] Earl's family bond with the Jacksons survived this tragedy, and he remained thereafter in the lives of Rachel and Andrew.

Earl achieved considerable success as a portraitist during his first months in Nashville. He kept a memorandum book for 1817 and listed more than fifty-five commissions, totaling $4,721.[37] This sum was not inconsiderable; it approximated the government salary and expenses Jackson received as a major general.[38] Earl usually charged fifty dollars for a bust-size portrait and an additional twenty if it included a frame. That year he painted likenesses of many of Jackson's friends and nine portraits of the general himself. Typical of the person who wanted Jackson's portrait was the man in New Orleans who wrote to Earl in 1819, "I would wish at least to have his resemblance near me, that by daly [sic] viewing it I may endeavour to imitate his virtues, & follow in the foot steps of his political devotion."[39]

In 1818 Earl founded the Nashville Museum with the help of George Tunstall, the junior editor of the *Nashville Whig and Tennessee Advertiser.* The museum, a collection of portraits and "natural and artificial curiosities of the country," was similar in concept to the one Charles Willson Peale established in Philadelphia. Earl solicited donations from the public, which he received periodically. For instance, in 1821, he was presented with the jaw of a sawfish, fourteen feet long, caught off the coast of Florida.[40] But Earl primarily built the Nashville Museum around his own growing collection of portraits. That first year he exhibited likenesses of Brigadier Generals Coffee and Carroll, Jackson's principal lieutenants at New Orleans. He also had on display a portrait of Colonel Isaac Shelby, the aged former first governor of Kentucky. In October

1818 Shelby had assisted Jackson in securing a treaty with the Chickasaw Indians, effectually removing them from Tennessee and Kentucky. Of special interest was a portrait of President James Monroe, painted at the Hermitage in 1819. Monroe had stopped there during his southern tour. Yet unquestionably the museum's major attraction was a full-length painting of Andrew Jackson "reconnoitreing [*sic*] the position of the British Army before New-Orleans."[41] Earl depicted Old Hickory standing before a tent and holding a spyglass in his outstretched right hand [Fig. 14]. On May 9, 1818, the *Nashville Whig* observed: *In the contour of the head, and indeed of the whole figure, the fidelity of the representation cannot easily be excelled. . . . There is a characteristic in the forehead of the original, which is rarely to be met with—there is a stubbornness, or perhaps more properly speaking, a firmness almost amounting to obstinacy, which*

Above: Jackson was wearing this dark blue uniform coat in 1818 at the time that Ralph E. W. Earl was painting his life-size canvas of the general. Based on the similarity of the painted coat to the original, Earl's depiction of Jackson's features may indeed have been reasonably faithful. National Museum of American History, Smithsonian Institution

Figure 14. Right.
Oil on canvas by Ralph E. W. Earl, 1818.
Tennessee State Museum

the Painter has unequivocally struck. The expression of the eye, indicates a perfect confidence, as to the result of the contest which seems to be viewed with a fixed and determined resolution to overcome.[42]

The following September, Joseph Delaplaine of Philadelphia wrote to Earl about this full-length portrait of Jackson. Although unsuccessful in publishing a print of the Battle of New Orleans, Delaplaine did not lose interest in its hero. He now desired Jackson's image for his own museum, the National Gallery of Distinguished Americans, an undertaking in which he claimed to have invested nearly twenty thousand dollars. He wished to know how much Earl wanted for his full-length canvas.[43] As an alternative, the Philadelphian mentioned the possibility of acquiring, for no charge, another Earl portrait of Jackson; this head-and-shoulders image was owned by Jackson himself. Such a painting hangs in the Hermitage today, and may be the one to which Delaplaine was referring [Fig. 15]. Delaplaine also sought likenesses of John Coffee and William Carroll. In a postscript he noted his intention to have Earl's "portrait of Genl. Jackson engraved in the best style" for his national biographical work, the *Repository.*

Figure 15.
Oil on canvas by Ralph E. W. Earl, circa 1817–1818. The Hermitage: Home of President Andrew Jackson

Earl was in no hurry to respond. At the time he was enjoying his own success. He had portrait commissions to paint, a museum to manage, and a new and expectant wife to look after. Still Delaplaine pressed him. Finally, on December 13, Earl responded. Delaplaine would receive the portraits of Jackson and Coffee and possibly that of Carroll. He could not, however, have either copy portraits or engravings made without Earl's permission. Delaplaine agreed to the terms, asking when he might receive the portrait of Jackson.[44]

Delaplaine waited and grew impatient. That winter of 1819 he repeatedly wrote to Earl inquiring how the Jackson portrait would be shipped and when it would arrive. He coaxed Earl with an offer to send him several colors of paint, newly imported by a Frenchman and recommended by Thomas Sully. He flattered him with the news that fellow artists Charles Willson Peale, John Wesley Jarvis, and Thomas Sully had all painted Jackson's likeness, yet he still desired Earl's for his gallery.[45]

Meanwhile, in February, Earl's expectations for a family were shattered by his wife's death. The urgent requests coming from Philadelphia for his popular Jackson portrait must now have seemed trivial. Apparently, Earl ignored them. In the meantime, Delaplaine arranged for Charles Bird King to take Jackson's likeness when Jackson visited Washington in late January. On March 24, 1819, John Quincy Adams saw this painting in King's Washington studio. Four years later, the portrait, now unlocated, was exhibited at the Pennsylvania Academy of the Fine Arts.[46] In the event Delaplaine failed to acquire Earl's *Jackson,* he planned to have King's version engraved for a new volume of his biographical work. Unfortunately, this volume was never published. Delaplaine gave up on ever acquiring Earl's canvas of Jackson, which Earl himself kept before the public eye.

In January 1821, Earl made arrangements to exhibit the portrait, first in Natchez and then New Orleans, in hopes of enticing those cities into purchasing copies.[47] The painting generated interest in both places. The corporation of Natchez organized a subscription drive and agreed to raise one thousand dollars, payable to Earl, if he could furnish a copy portrait within four months. City officials planned to place the painting in "the large room of the new Court-house."[48] The story was much the same in New Orleans. Jackson wrote letters of introduction on the artist's behalf to his good friend Edward Livingston and to Mayor Joseph Roffignac, advising the mayor that Earl would "exhibit to view a more correct likeness of myself than perhaps you have ever seen."[49] After a committee appointed to examine the painting made its report, the city council resolved, on April 14, to allow the mayor to purchase a copy for one thousand dollars.[50] The next week, the noted naturalist painter John James Audubon visited Earl's quarters. In his journal he sarcastically labeled Earl "a New Phenomena in Painting." Of the portrait he exclaimed, "*Great God* forgive Me if My Jugment is Erroneous—I Never Saw A Worst painted Sign *in the Street of Paris.*"[51]

In the end, Earl's southern trip was only partly successful. The city of New Orleans did indeed commission a copy of Jackson's portrait, which has since disappeared. City officials in Natchez, however, were unable to raise the prescribed funds, since residents were reluctant to donate money "for ornamental purposes" during hard times.[52]

☙

In April 1825, Earl's original portrait was the focal point at a Nashville dinner honoring Jackson. He was returning from Washington, where as a senator he had just lost the presidency to John Quincy Adams in a contest decided by the House of Representatives. Appropriately, the portrait was decorated to reflect Jackson's popularity: over his head arched seven stars representing the states he had won in the recent election. Above this symbolic constellation were three wreaths of flowers circling the figure "99," and on either side, the words "electoral" and "votes." An inscription, "The People's Choice," decorated the top of the frame's molding.[53]

Earl's *Jackson* now hangs in the Tennessee State Museum in Nashville. It was owned by Judge John Catron of Nashville, one of President Jackson's last appointees to the United States Supreme Court. Catron bequeathed it, upon his death in 1865, to the state of Tennessee, and it hung for years in the Hall of Representatives.[54]

Notes

1. Parton, *Jackson,* vol. 1, pp. 110-11, 425, 547-48.

2. Andrew Barratt to Jackson, February 24, 1815, Papers of Andrew Jackson, Library of Congress; Andrew Jackson, *Correspondence of Andrew Jackson,* ed. John Spencer Bassett (Washington, D.C., 1926-1935), vol. 2, pp. 224-25 (hereafter cited as *Correspondence of Jackson*).

3. Joseph F. Loubat, *The Medallic History of the United States of America, 1776-1876* (New Milford, Conn., 1967), p. 239.

4. Joseph Delaplaine to Jackson, March 25, 1815, Jackson Papers, Library of Congress.

5. *Ibid.*

6. *Ibid.*

7. *An Album of American Battle Art, 1755-1918* (Washington, D.C., 1947), pp. 94-95.

8. Carl W. Drepperd, "Three Battles of New Orleans," *Antiques* 14 (August 1928): 129-31. Scacki also produced second strikes on new paper.

9. The inscription "West. Del" under the picture in the left corner implies that the original drawing was the work of an artist named West. It has been suggested that this was Kentucky portraitist William Edward West. But based on the quality of the composition, his less talented brother, John Brown West, was more likely to have been the artist. For further discussion, see John Carbonell's essay, "Prints of the Battle of New Orleans," in *Prints of the American West: Proceedings of the Ninth Annual North American Print Conference,* ed. Ron Tyler (Fort Worth, Tex., 1983), pp. 4-6.

Figure 16.
Oil on panel attributed to Nathan W. Wheeler, not dated. Hurja Collection, Tennessee State Museum

Figure 17.
Engraving by Charles Phillips, after John Wesley Jarvis, circa 1841. Private collection

10. Yeager also altered the hand gesture of Major General John Lambert (identified as "C"), who stands just to the right of Pakenham. In the first strike a handkerchief in Lambert's hand covered his face; now his index finger points in the direction of the bullet-riddled Union Jack nearby. See Carl W. Drepperd, "Selling Jackson's Great Victory," *Antiques* 38 (November 1940): 220-21; William C. Cook, "The Early Iconography of the Battle of New Orleans, 1815-1819," *Tennessee Historical Quarterly* 48 (Winter 1989): 221.

11. *Liberty Hall and Cincinnati Gazette,* March 2, 1827; *Correspondence of Jackson,* vol. 6, pp. 254-55.

12. Parton, *Jackson,* vol. 2, pp. 327-28.

13. Charles Henry Hart, "Life Portraits of Andrew Jackson," *McClure's Magazine* 9 (July 1897): 797; Susan Clover Symonds, "Portraits of Andrew Jackson, 1815-1845" (Master's thesis, University of Delaware, 1968), pp. 10-11. Vallée seems to have had a formula for painting hairstyles, regardless of the individual features of his sitters. For other examples of his work see Mrs. Thomas Nelson Carter Bruns, comp., *Louisiana Portraits* (New Orleans, La., 1975), pp. 58, 119, 222. Later portraits reveal that Jackson began wearing his hair longer and combing it straight back in a neater fashion in the early 1820s.

14. From Nashville on June 12, 1815, Jackson instructed Livingston, still in New Orleans, to ask Major Auguste Davézac, Livingston's brother-in-law, "whether the miniature was got" and delivered to Commodore Daniel T. Patterson, the American commandant of naval defenses in the New Orleans campaign. Jackson also inquired if Patterson had received his letter and the enclosed money for this purpose. The miniature Jackson was referring to cannot be determined. See *Correspondence of Jackson,* vol. 2, p. 209.

15. Remini, *Andrew Jackson,* vol. 2, pp. 249-50; Louise Livingston Hunt, *Memoir of Mrs. Edward Livingston with Letters Hitherto Unpublished* (New York, 1886), pp. 51-53.

16. *Correspondence of Jackson,* vol. 2, p. 263; vol. 6, p. 468.

17. Arsène Lacarrière Latour, *Historical Memoir of the War in West Florida and Louisiana in 1814-15, with an Atlas* (Gainesville, Fla., 1964), pp. xxxv-xliii. This is a facsimile reproduction of the 1816 edition, with an introduction by Jane Lucas de Grummond.

18. *Louisiana Courier* (New Orleans), January 25, 1844. Wheeler's obituary appeared in the *Daily Delta* (New Orleans), May 9, 1849. The *New Hampshire Gazette* (Portsmouth), April 10, 1810, reported that a Mr. Wheeler had taken a room in Portsmouth for the purpose of painting likenesses in miniature. See *Antiques* 46 (September 1944): 158. In August 1827, President John Quincy Adams, then at his home in Quincy, Massachusetts, noted having given a Mr. Wheeler of Cincinnati five sittings for a portrait, now lost. This artist was probably Nathan W. Wheeler. See Oliver, *Portraits of Adams,* pp. 137-38.

19. *Louisiana Gazette* (New Orleans), May 6, 1815.

20. The work was a gift to the Historical Society of Pennsylvania in 1917 from Mrs. Robert L. Aiken. Two copy portraits of the Wheeler likeness, different from both the original and each other, are known to have existed. The first is an oil on panel at the Tennessee State Museum [Fig. 16]. The other copy is now unlocated but appeared in a sale catalogue of Anderson Galleries in November 1926. See records of the Catalog of American Portraits, National Portrait Gallery, Smithsonian Institution, Washington, D.C.

21. *Correspondence of Jackson,* vol. 2, p. 263.

22. *Ibid.,* pp. 215, 283-84.

23. In 1842 an engraving by Charles Phillips appeared in the *United States Magazine, and Democratic Review* [Fig. 17]. It was labeled as being after an 1815 life portrait by Jarvis, then in the possession of Jonathan Hunt. The portrait was misdated, however, and it was not actually taken from life: in the years immediately after the Battle of New Orleans, Jackson and Jarvis's paths probably never crossed. Moreover, no contemporary account has been found of this painting, either in newspapers or letters, as was the case in 1819 when Jarvis painted his three-quarter-length portrait of Jackson now owned by the Metropolitan Museum of Art [see page 63].

24. Harold E. Dickson, *John Wesley Jarvis, American Painter, 1780-1840* (New York, 1949), pp. 171-79.

Figure 18.
Oil on panel attributed to Ralph E. W. Earl, circa 1817. Camden District Heritage Foundation

25. *Ibid.*, pp. 178-92.

26. Alexander J. Dallas to Joseph Hopkinson, May 25, 1815, and Hopkinson to Dallas, May 30, 1815, copies in Jackson Papers, Library of Congress.

27. George Graham to Hopkinson, November 25, 1815, copy in Jackson Papers, Library of Congress; Jackson to Dallas, July 11, 1815, Letters Received by the Accountant for the War Department, 1794-1817, Records of the General Accounting Office, RG 217, National Archives, Jackson Papers Project copy. For a published copy see *Correspondence of Jackson,* vol. 2, p. 213.

28. Anna Wells Rutledge, ed., *Cumulative Record of Exhibition Catalogues: The Pennsylvania Academy of the Fine Arts, 1807-1870* (Philadelphia, 1955), p. 251 (hereafter cited as Rutledge, *PAFA Exhibition Record*); Estill Curtis Pennington, *William Edward West, 1788-1857, Kentucky Painter* (Washington, D.C., 1985), p. 4.

29. *Correspondence of Jackson,* vol. 2, pp. 283-84; vol. 3, p. 34.

30. Valaperta disappeared suddenly in 1817. His will listed his place of birth as Milan and stated that he left a wife and three children. Among his possessions were several wax portraits of such prominent Americans as Albert Gallatin, Thomas Jefferson, James Madison, James Monroe, and Andrew Jackson. The Gallatin family later acquired these five and presented them in 1880 to the New-York Historical Society. See "Some American Wax Portraits," *Antiques* 12 (September 1927): 203; Wayne Craven, *Sculpture in America* (Newark, Del., 1968), pp. 60-62. These bas-reliefs are listed in *Catalogue of American Portraits in the New-York Historical Society* (New Haven, Conn., 1974).

31. Parton, *Jackson,* vol. 2, pp. 334-35.

32. Emma Look Scott, "Ralph Earl: Painter to Andrew Jackson," *Taylor-Trotwood Magazine* 7 (April 1908): 29-34; *Nashville Tennessean Magazine* (January 1, 1950): 9-11.

33. W. C. Daniell to C. W. Short, June 2, 1816, and W. Stephens to Thomas Flournoy, July 19, 1816, Ralph E. W. Earl Papers, American Antiquarian Society, Worcester, Massachusetts (hereafter cited as Earl Papers).

34. Charles Cassedy to John Coffee, February 19, 1817, Andrew Jackson Papers, Tennessee Historical Society, Nashville.

35. For a listing of Earl's portraits see Symonds, "Portraits of Jackson," pp. 98-105. More up-to-date records are in the Inventory of American Paintings, National Museum of American Art, Smithsonian Institution, Washington, D.C. See also Catalog of American Portraits.

36. Rachel Jackson to Earl, February 23, 1819, Jackson Papers, Library of Congress; *Nashville Tennessean Magazine* (January 1, 1950): 9.

37. Memorandum Book for 1817, Earl Papers.

38. Remini, *Andrew Jackson,* vol. 1, p. 321; Memorandum Book for 1817, Earl Papers.

39. James Sudder to Earl, April 12, 1819, Earl Papers.

A half-length portrait now in the collection of the Camden District Heritage Foundation, Camden, South Carolina, may possibly be one of Earl's earliest likenesses of Jackson [Fig. 18]. According to accession records, William F. Buckley, Sr., purchased the painting in Chicago in 1941. In his journal he referred to an inscription—"R.E.W. Earl 1815"—on the original liner, which has since been rebacked. In 1981 Buckley's son, Reid, presented the portrait on behalf of the family to Historic Camden. (For this information I am grateful to Shirley P. Ransom, acting director of Historic Camden.)

40. Jerome R. MacBeth, "Portraits by Ralph E. W. Earl," *Antiques* 100 (September 1971): 390; J. A. Duneto [?] to Earl, March 12, 1821, Earl Papers. Contemporary newspaper clippings about Earl's museum are also in this collection.

41. For Earl's list of portraits painted for his museum, see Earl Papers.

42. *Nashville Whig and Tennessee Advertiser,* May 9, 1818.

43. Joseph Delaplaine to Earl, September 20, 1818, Earl Papers.

44. Delaplaine to Earl, December 31, 1818, *ibid.*

45. Delaplaine to Earl, February 6 and 19, 1819, *ibid.*

46. Delaplaine to Earl, April 6, 1819, *ibid.*; Andrew F. Cosentino, *The Paintings of Charles Bird King (1785-1862)* (Washington, D.C., 1977), p. 136; *Twelfth Annual Exhibition of the Pennsylvania Academy of the Fine Arts, May, 1823* (Philadelphia, 1823), p. 13.

47. George Tunstall to T. W. Lorrain, January 17, 1821; Edward Turner to F. L. Turner, February 22, 1821; Isaac L. Baker to Richard Clague, February 23, 1821, Earl Papers.

48. *Correspondence of Jackson,* vol. 3, pp. 39-40; *National Intelligencer* (Washington, D.C.), August 6, 1821. A broadside of the Natchez subscription announcement is in the Tennessee State Library and Archives, Nashville.

49. Jackson to Edward Livingston, January 3, 1821, Edward Livingston Papers, Princeton University Library, New Jersey; Jackson to Joseph Roffignac, January 16, 1821, typescript in the Historic New Orleans Collection.

50. A typescript of the proceedings of the New Orleans City Council is in the Historic New Orleans Collection. See also *National Intelligencer,* August 6, 1821.

51. John James Audubon, *Journal of John James Audubon, Made During His Trip to New Orleans in 1820-1821,* ed. Howard Corning (Cambridge, Mass., 1929), p. 149 (hereafter cited as *Journal of Audubon*).

52. Edward Turner to Earl, July 12, 1821, Earl Papers.

53. *Sparta Review* (Sparta, Tennessee), April 27, 1825; Scott, "Ralph Earl," p. 30.

54. Records of the Catalog of American Portraits.

1819

January: Visits Washington to defend conduct in Seminole War; sits to portraitists Charles Willson Peale and Anna Claypoole Peale

February 8: Is exonerated by United States House of Representatives for seizure of Spanish West Florida

February 17: Visits Philadelphia and sits to Thomas Sully for portrait commissioned by the Association of American Artists

February 20: Arrives in New York City for visit of several days

February 23: Is requested by New York Common Council to sit for portrait by John Vanderlyn

Portraits painted by Samuel Lovett Waldo and John Wesley Jarvis in New York

February 27: Arrives in Baltimore; sits to Rembrandt Peale during three-day visit for portrait commissioned by the city council

June: Terra-cotta bust by William Rush exhibited in Philadelphia

Builds Hermitage mansion

1820

November: Stipple engraving published by James Barton Longacre after Sully's portrait

Chapter 2

The Real Man Emerges, 1819–1820

Until the winter of 1819, a faithful image of Andrew Jackson is not known to have been executed. The few artists who had depicted him had unintentionally captured caricature likenesses. But these efforts were in keeping with Jackson's own sense of modesty. He abhorred any activity that might suggest self-adoration.[1] For Jackson to grant a portrait sitting was in one sense like his marching off to war: both endeavors weighed heavily upon his sense of duty.

I

In January 1819 Jackson met his most critical test of character: his honor was at stake. The challenger this time was no petty duelist, but the United States government. The controversy centered on Jackson's conduct in the Seminole War of 1818. Jackson had marched an army into Spanish-held West Florida to quell Indian uprisings along the Georgia border. Before the campaign was over, Jackson had driven off the Spanish as well. Both houses of Congress were beginning to question the legality of this episode, and there was even talk of censuring Old Hickory. In addition, the House Committee on Military Affairs, assigned to investigate the matter, rebuked Jackson for ordering the executions of two British subjects, Robert Ambrister and Alexander Arbuthnot, who had been found guilty by a military court of aiding and abetting the Indians. The House committee also disapproved of Jackson's unauthorized seizures of St. Marks and Pensacola. Jackson had correctly guessed President James Monroe's secret desire to acquire Florida, but his reckless bayonet diplomacy embarrassed the administration and invited ugly confrontations with both Spain and England.

As Congress prepared for a major debate, Jackson grew restless in Nashville, wondering if he should venture to Washington in his own defense. Some of his friends advised him to do so, while others feared that he would lose his equanimity and only harm his cause.[2] Never one to sit idle and let others decide his fate, Jackson in the end hastened to the capital city.

No one expressed more excitement about his expected arrival than Charles Willson Peale, who had high hopes of painting Jackson's portrait. Born in 1741 in Queen Anne County, Maryland, Peale was enjoying the twilight of his splendid and varied career. At one time or another he had been a saddler, artist, soldier (in the Revolution), and naturalist. His reputation, however, rested on his portrait painting. In mid-November he journeyed to Washington with his wife, Hannah, and his niece, Anna Claypoole Peale, to take the likenesses of eminent personages.[3] He intended to place this new gallery of portraits in his Philadelphia museum, another great interest of his life.

As it happened, several of Peale's sitters were central figures in the Seminole

Figure 19.
Oil on canvas by Charles Willson Peale,
1819. The Masonic Library and Museum of
Pennsylvania

War imbroglio. First and foremost—besides Jackson—was President James Monroe, who was caught in the middle of the controversy. He could not praise Jackson, for fear of further enraging England or Spain, nor in good conscience could he openly criticize him for staking new boundaries into Florida.

Peale also had sittings with key members of the cabinet. The secretary of war, John C. Calhoun, resented Jackson for circumventing his authority, and argued for his being censured. Both the secretary of the treasury, William H. Crawford, and the attorney general, William Wirt, had aligned themselves with Calhoun. Yet the secretary of state, John Quincy Adams, sided with Jackson, arguing that the invasion was strictly defensive, since the Spanish had failed to control their Indian population.[4]

Peale timed his visit to coincide with the opening of the second session of Congress, and what a session it promised to be! Of all of Peale's sitters, no one took a more vocal stand against Jackson than Speaker of the House Henry Clay. Clay, too, was a westerner with presidential ambitions. What better way to clear his own path to the White House than to discredit any possible competition? A gifted orator, Clay could hush a packed gallery with his rhetoric or bring it to a crescendo of laughter with his sarcasm. His speech in the House was the highlight of the almost monthlong debate. He condensed the Seminole War controversy to a simple case of military infringement upon civil authority. In his judgment, Jackson's conduct was a threat to free government.

While Congress conducted its investigation, Peale grew restless waiting for Jackson to arrive. At one point, he heard that Jackson was not coming to Washington after all.[5] Peale decided to finish his portraits in hand and promptly return home.

Figure 20.
Watercolor on ivory by Anna Claypoole Peale, 1819. Mabel Brady Garvan Collection, Yale University Art Gallery

But on January 23, 1819, Peale was rewarded for his patience; Andrew Jackson had at last arrived in Washington. He paid his respects at the President's house but thereafter avoided most social gatherings during the investigation. He preferred instead to meet with his cohorts behind closed doors and plan his defense. Jackson, however, did consent to let Peale paint his portrait [Fig. 19]. On at least three occasions between January 24 and 29, he visited the artist's rented studio before breakfast. Peale was up even earlier on those cold winter mornings making a fire and preparing his colors. His niece, Anna, took advantage of the sittings with a brush of her own.[6] Born in Philadelphia in 1791, she was the daughter of miniaturist James Peale and the granddaughter of James Claypoole, who was reputed to have been the first native Pennsylvania artist. Charles Willson Peale had brought her along to Washington in hopes that she might receive a few commissions, which she succeeded in obtaining.

Apparently, Jackson's final sitting was primarily for Anna's benefit, so that she could finish her watercolor-on-ivory miniature [Fig. 20]. Her uncle left an account of this animated session in his diary. There sat Jackson, age fifty-one, conversing with a few friends who had come to keep him company and still smarting with indignation over the ongoing accusations against him. Anna, age twenty-seven, faced the great warrior, desperately sizing down his features to the confines of a 3 by 2½-inch oval piece of ivory. From nearby the seventy-seven-year-old Peale dabbed a seasoned brush in his own colors, retouching here and there while joining in the discussions. At an opportune time he felt disposed to give Jackson "a piece of advice" against fighting duels.[7] When Jackson asked how in some cases it could be avoided, Peale advised him to rise above ignominy. If Old Hickory winced at this—with a bullet embedded in his chest and another lodged in his shoulder, both the result of old personal feuds—Peale never noticed. Only afterward did he learn of Jackson's exploits on the field of honor.

⟡

During Jackson's trip east that winter of 1819, the public came to understand better the two conflicting sides of his character. Congress was vigorously investigating what it believed to be a darker side. Some members were charging that the hero of New Orleans was really just a headstrong military tyrant who had demonstrated little regard either for human life or civil law.[8]

Then there was Jackson the gentleman. A man in Washington noticed this side of his character one evening at a private social gathering. The next day he wrote to a friend: *I never was more disappointed, more interested, nor more delighted with any man I have ever yet met:* disappointed, *in meeting with an elegant, easy-mannered attractive gentleman, where I expected to find a savage;* interested, *in a conversation where modesty, good sense, and delicacy, formed so great a share in the relation of transactions where he himself appeared the least man, though deservedly the only hero in every sentence;* delighted, *because, with a free and graceful familiarity, he seemed to invite all around him to call for such information on those great achievements in which his country, his enemies and his friends, feel so much interest, as suited the temper, the talent, and the object of every individual present.*[9]

⟡

Then as now, the portraits by Charles Willson Peale and Anna Claypoole Peale helped the public see perhaps the truest likenesses of Old Hickory thus far executed.[10] In both images, Jackson has an almost sleepy look, and his hair is tousled as if he had just dragged himself out of bed—which of course he had. Charles's portrait hung in his Philadelphia museum until that collection was sold in the 1850s. Anna's miniature, signed and dated on the front "Anna C. Peale 1819," was exhibited that year at the Pennsylvania Academy of the Fine Arts.[11]

II

On February 8, 1819, the full House voted on the resolutions pertaining to Jackson's conduct in the Seminole War and vindicated him completely. Jackson's image had scarcely been blemished. With little more to accomplish in Washington, he journeyed north to New York with the intention of seeing his ward, Andrew Jackson Donelson, a cadet at West Point.

Jackson's three-week trip actually became a grand triumphal tour in every major city through which he passed. He arrived in Philadelphia about February 15. During his four days there, the city lavished praise and glory on him. A public dinner was held and toasts were made; and there were visits to the Olympic Theatre, to Delaplaine's National Gallery of Portraits, and to Peale's museum, where the latest chemical and philosophical experiments were on exhibit. A less ephemeral honor was the invitation from the Association of American Artists to sit for a portrait by Thomas Sully.[12]

At thirty-five, Sully had already established himself as one of America's premier painters. Born in England in 1783, he was brought to America at a young age. His elder brother Lawrence, a miniaturist, influenced his early development as an artist, as did Gilbert Stuart in Boston and Benjamin West in London. Sully, however, quickly mastered his own romantic style.

Figure 21.
Oil on canvas by Thomas Sully, 1819. New York State Office of Parks, Recreation, and Historic Preservation, Clermont State Historic Site

On February 17, with Jackson positioned in front of him, Sully began sketching a study portrait. At some point during the sitting, Jackson mentioned how difficult it was for his friend Ralph E. W. Earl to get decent picture frames in Tennessee. Later that day, Sully apparently passed this information along to his framemaker, James Earle, a local carver and gilder. Earle wrote to the Nashville artist, informing him that he would send him "six frames of different patterns" for Earl's inspection.[13] Meanwhile, Sully finished the study portrait a week later. According to his journal, he was paid one hundred dollars for the painting, which is apparently no longer extant.

Between March 26 and April 15, 1819, Sully painted his better-known three-quarter-length of Jackson for the association [Fig. 21]. Their intention was to have this work engraved by James B. Longacre and sold as a print. On April 19, the *Democratic Press* announced that Sully's finished portrait, for which he received two hundred dollars, could be seen for a few days at the association's room at 72 Chestnut Street—admission twenty-five cents.[14] Thereafter Mr. Longacre would commence an engraving.

❦

In 1819, the twenty-four-year-old Pennsylvanian James B. Longacre was just making the transition from apprentice to self-employed engraver. The opportunity to execute a portrait of Andrew Jackson was both a tribute to his newly learned skill and a harbinger of future success. He ultimately filled the shoes of David Edwin as the nation's leading stipple engraver, but he developed a different technique. For months he studied Sully's portrait, meticulously transferring the canvas image of Andrew Jackson to a steel plate and finally to paper. When his first proof impression was ready, he sent it to Sully for his suggestions [Fig. 22]. In what appears to be Sully's handwriting in the bottom margin, he instructed Longacre to "Lighten the Iris close to the pupil in both Eyes" in order to animate the face more.[15] He also suggested adding some fine wrinkles to the corners of the eyes and to the forehead. Moreover, the horse in the background needed darkening, especially around Jackson's head. Based on the finished print, copyrighted November 2, 1820, Longacre carried out Sully's instructions.

Figure 22.
Stipple engraving, proof, by James Barton Longacre, after Thomas Sully, 1819–1820. National Portrait Gallery, Smithsonian Institution

Shortly afterward, Longacre wrote to Jackson and enclosed a print for his inspection. Longacre admitted to the likelihood of some flaws, because this had been his first attempt at a work of such dimensions (the Jackson print ended up being his largest), and because there was a great distance separating the artist—in this case Sully—from the sitter, thus preventing corrections. Longacre explained that Sully considered the number of sittings insufficient for complete accuracy.

On February 20, 1821, Samuel Kennedy, a manager and trustee of the Association of American Artists, wrote to Jackson, officially thanking him for his politeness in granting the sitting. In appreciation, he enclosed "one framed and two unframed proof Impressions from the Plate."[16]

Longacre's print [Fig. 23] helped establish his name among his fellow artists. In 1821 he included the engraving in the annual exhibition of the Pennsylvania Academy of the Fine Arts. Except for the self-gratification and compliments he received for having completed an extraordinary job, Longacre was disappointed that he had earned no money from it. Considering his great expense in time, he wrote in 1821, the endeavor "so far, has been a losing concern for me."[17]

Sully, on the other hand, found that painting portraits of Andrew Jackson was worthwhile. In the course of his career he executed approximately a dozen likenesses, earning more than $1,400 in commissions.[18] Certain images, however, have been misleading, especially a study drawing on paper executed in the 1820s [Fig. 24]. It is labeled "Original sketch of Genl Jackson, taken immediately after the battle of New Orleans. T Sully."[19] Whether or not the inscription, which has been overdrawn, is Sully's is not known. What is certain, however, is that Sully was never in New Orleans "immediately after the battle." Also, Jackson's likeness is of a later period. In 1829 and 1858, Sully painted oil portraits based on this puzzling image.[20]

Only Sully's 1819 portrait is known to have been based on a life sitting. Exhibited that year at the Pennsylvania Academy of the Fine Arts, the painting is initialed and dated on the horse's bridle, just over Jackson's right shoulder. Today this painting is a part of the collection of the Clermont State Historic Park in Germantown, New York.[21]

III

During Jackson's four-day visit, another Philadelphia artist, William Rush, was apparently studying his features. Unfortunately, no contemporary record has been found to document that Jackson actually sat for Rush. Given the general's busy schedule, perhaps he did not. Yet Rush sculpted a bust of Jackson that some critics have considered to be his masterpiece.

Born in Philadelphia in 1756, Rush held a curious position within the artistic community of that city. In 1805 he was among a small group—which included Charles Willson Peale—that founded the Pennsylvania Academy of the Fine Arts; and in 1810 he was elected the first president of the Society of Artists, an independent organization. Although known as the Father of American Sculpture, Rush was principally an artisan whose genius lay in carving blocks of eastern white pine into ships' figureheads. Among his many creations were the symbolic figures of Nature and Genius that adorned the prows of two navy frigates, *Constellation* and *United States.*[22] During the first decade of the nineteenth century, American shipbuilding suffered severe setbacks, and this encouraged Rush to turn his artistic interests toward architectural sculpture and portraiture.

As a portraitist, Rush carved in wood before modeling in clay. His 1812–1813 busts of Philadelphia physicians Benjamin Rush, Philip Syng Physick, and Caspar Wistar were highly competent likenesses and were praised for their naturalistic style. With an eye toward the popular market, Rush made plaster replicas from the terra-cotta originals.[23]

Jackson's visit to Philadelphia in February 1819 offered Rush an excellent opportunity to execute yet another bust of an American hero. Rush could sculpt faithfully from memory, and his bust of Jackson may well have been the result of just such an exercise. He could have observed Jackson on any number of occasions—perhaps at Madame De Luce's concert, or at Peale's museum, or at the splendid public dinner given for Jackson at the Washington Hall Hotel. Regardless of where he had seen him, the image of Jackson was impressed in Rush's mind, and he spent the winter and spring transforming it into clay.

In June 1819, notice of Rush's finished bust appeared in various newspapers.[24] The *Nashville Gazette* reported that "the likeness is striking and true, as art can imitate nature, without flattery or deviation." Rush placed his newest work [Figs. 25 and 26] in a Philadelphia coffeehouse for inspection. He also proposed to make plaster replicas available to subscribers for a small fee.

By the fall of 1819, Rush had carried out his plan, and plaster casts were ready for sale in Philadelphia and Washington. In Washington, William Cooper, the proprietor of a music and book store on Pennsylvania Avenue, advertised: "The likeness is perfect, and the work another proof that the nation progresses not less in the arts than in arms. This probably will rank as Rush's masterpiece." The following spring, Rush exhibited his bust of Jackson at the Pennsylvania Academy of the Fine Arts.[25]

❧

No patron of the arts exhibited greater enthusiasm for Rush's *Jackson* than James Ronaldson. A native of Edinburgh, Scotland, Ronaldson immigrated to Philadelphia in 1794 and became an innovative and highly successful typefounder. One of the first to publicly support Jackson for President, Ronaldson did all in his means to perpetuate his candidate's image. Between October 1819 and January 1822, he presented four of Rush's plaster casts to prominent institutions: the American Academy of the Fine Arts in New York City, the Boston Athenaeum, the State Library of South Carolina in Columbia, and Peale's Philadelphia museum. In February 1820 Ronaldson also made presentations to former Presidents John Adams and Thomas Jefferson.[26]

Today, only one of Rush's plaster replicas is known to exist. Busts presented to the Boston Athenaeum and the American Academy disappeared years ago. The South Carolina State Library bust allegedly perished in the burning of Columbia at the close of the Civil War.[27] The replica given to Peale's museum

Figure 23.
Hand-colored stipple engraving by James Barton Longacre, after Thomas Sully, 1820. National Portrait Gallery, Smithsonian Institution

Figure 24.
Charcoal on paper by Thomas Sully, circa 1824. The Detroit Institute of Arts; gift of Mrs. Walter O. Briggs

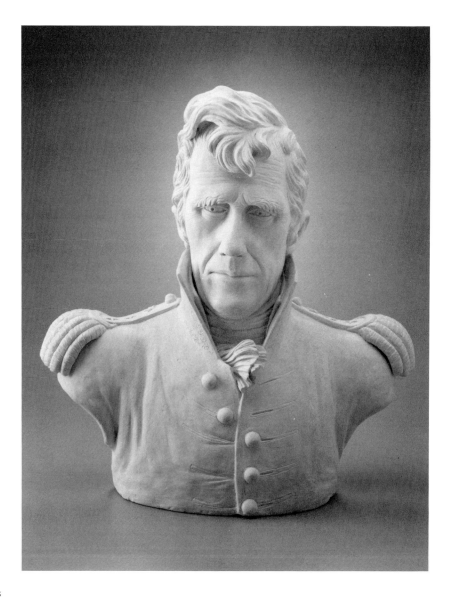

Figure 25. Right.
Terra-cotta by William Rush, 1819. The
Art Institute of Chicago; Bessie Bennett
Fund, W. G. Field Fund, Ada Turnbull
Hertle Fund, Laura T. Magnusson Fund,
Major Acquisition Fund, and restricted gifts
of Jamee J. and Marshall Field, and the
Brooks and Hope B. McCormick
Foundation, 1985.251

Figure 26. Above.
The scrollwork evident on the back of
Rush's *Jackson* reflects the artist's training as
an ornamental carver.

vanished when that institution went bankrupt in about 1850, and its collec-
tions were widely dispersed. A visual record of it has been preserved, however,
in the watercolor drawing *The Long Room* (1822), sketched by Charles Willson
Peale and finished by his youngest son, Titian Ramsey [Fig. 27]. In the 1820s
Peale housed his museum in the upper rooms of the Pennsylvania State
House. The drawing, a study for Peale's popular painting *The Artist in His
Museum,* depicts the main exhibition hall facing Chestnut Street. Rush's
Jackson is the fifth bust from the right, visible as the eye moves to the center of
the picture.[28]

What is believed to be Rush's only known extant plaster of Jackson was
discovered recently in the collection of Montgomery Place, the estate of
Edward Livingston. This replica may well have been yet another gift of James
Ronaldson to one of Jackson's staunch political defenders, or perhaps Livingston purchased it in 1819 at the advertised price of twelve dollars.

☙

Fortunately, Rush's original terra-cotta bust has resurfaced as well. Its provenance before 1940 remains a mystery. That year it was given to the Burlington County Historical Society in Burlington, New Jersey. There it re-

mained in storage for forty-two years, hidden under more than half a dozen coats of paint. The sitter's identity was not known, and the sculptor was presumed to be Jean-Antoine Houdon. In 1982 the bust was correctly identified, and conservation measures were undertaken. The discovery of Rush's original white lead paint prompted the society to repaint it. Usually Rush did not paint his terra-cotta works, except to disguise slight imperfections caused by firing the clay. Apparently this happened with his *Jackson,* which had a slight heat crack on the left side of the face and small singed areas on the hair and epaulets.[29] Further conservation has restored the original pinkish terra-cotta surface, revealing once again the naturalistic style of William Rush, as well as the vitality of Andrew Jackson.[30]

Figure 27.
The Long Room. Watercolor by Charles Willson Peale and Titian Ramsey Peale, 1822. The Detroit Institute of Arts; Founders Society Purchase, Director's Discretionary Fund

IV

At noon on February 20, 1819, Jackson and his entourage arrived in New York City to a chorus of artillery fire and huzzahs from thousands of well-wishers. Although the weather was dreary, it did not dampen the spirit of the occasion. Over the next few days the city hosted Old Hickory in high style, and Jackson handled himself with aplomb.[31] On the evening of February 22—Washington's birthday—a festive "Birth-Night Ball" was held at City Hall and attended by more than seven hundred people. The next day nearly four hundred citizens crowded Tammany Hall, bastion of the city's Jeffersonian Republicans, for a public dinner in Jackson's honor. Next, Jackson visited the theater, "the front of which was brilliantly illuminated on the occasion, and exhibited a full-length likeness of the Hero of New Orleans."[32] That day he had also toured the navy yard, the Academy of Arts, and the Institution for the Deaf and Dumb. In a ceremony that afternoon at City Hall, the mayor presented Jackson with the freedom of the city—a certificate and an inscribed gold box. In addition, the Common Council had resolved that Jackson "be respectfully requested to permit a full length portrait painting of him to be taken under the direction of the Corporation to be placed in the Gallery of Paintings in the City Hall."[33] John Vanderlyn was the artist elected for this honor. Vanderlyn, John Trumbull, and John Wesley Jarvis were among the finest portraitists in the city. Jarvis also painted a portrait of Jackson at this time, which some critics believed surpassed the work of Vanderlyn.

Figure 28. Above.
Oil on canvas by Samuel Lovett Waldo,
study, circa 1819. The Metropolitan
Museum of Art; Rogers Fund, 1906

Figure 29. Right.
Oil on canvas by Samuel Lovett Waldo,
circa 1819. Historic New Orleans
Collection; Museum/Research Center, Acc.
No. 1979.112

❧

Still another New York artist who took advantage of the opportunity to portray Jackson was Samuel Lovett Waldo. Born in Windham, Connecticut, in
1783, Waldo set up a studio in Hartford in 1803. Business was so bad that he
resorted to painting signs to sustain himself. By 1810 Waldo had settled in
New York City with every prospect of doing well. Within the next decade, he
established, with his pupil William Jewett, a partnership that lasted nearly forty
years.[34]

Facts surrounding Waldo's original study of Jackson are even sketchier than
the portrait itself, now in the collection of the Metropolitan Museum of Art
[Fig. 28]. Waldo apparently executed it in haste during Jackson's 1819 visit,
because the canvas is thinly painted. Jackson appears to have just turned his
head, as if distracted in a crowd. His eyes rivet the viewer, in effect making the
contact seem almost spontaneous. An inscription written later on the back of
the study dates it to 1817. This must be inaccurate, although Charles Henry
Hart, in his much-consulted article, "Life Portraits of Andrew Jackson," places
this study in that same year. He also states that Waldo used it as a model for a
full-length portrait that once hung in the Customs House in New Orleans.[35]
Allegedly, this painting was destroyed in the rebuilding of the Customs House
more than a century and a half ago.

Waldo made at least two, and possibly three, oil-on-canvas copy portraits from
his original sketch. Each is significantly different, however. The finest is now
owned by the Historic New Orleans Collection [Fig. 29].[36] Its obvious
distinguishing feature is the bright red sash around Jackson's waist. Further-
more, the eyes are more finished and focused than in the study canvas. The
mouth, however, has been left relatively undefined. At this stage in his life

Jackson was losing his teeth. Consequently, his lips were beginning to roll under slightly, making his mouth less full and pronounced. As he continued to age, his mouth became more linear, turning down at the corners. Waldo's portrait hints at this dental deterioration, as does Rembrandt Peale's oil portrait painted in Baltimore in March 1819.

The version owned by the state of Tennessee hangs in the governor's office in Nashville [Fig. 30]. The brushwork appears to be Waldo's, but the likeness is less satisfactory. Jackson's face is cadaverous, his eyes lack animation, and his chin is too full. The figure is draped in a dark blue cape with a red lining, and a gloved hand clutches the hilt of a sword. This added costuming unfortunately dwarfs Jackson's head and seemingly distorts his slender torso.[37]

Figure 30. Right.
Oil on canvas by Samuel Lovett Waldo, circa 1819. State of Tennessee, Governor's Residence

Figure 31. Far right.
Oil on canvas by Samuel Lovett Waldo, circa 1819. Addison Gallery of American Art, Phillips Academy, Andover, Massachusetts; gift of The Alfred and Margaret Caspary Foundation, Inc., in memory of Thomas Cochran

Figure 32. Below.
Engraving by Peter Maverick, after Samuel Lovett Waldo, circa 1819. National Portrait Gallery, Smithsonian Institution

The Jackson portrait in the collection of the Addison Gallery of American Art is the most curious of the three copy versions [Fig. 31]. Although a fairly accurate rendition of the original sketch, this painting has an entirely different feel to it. The brushwork comprising Jackson's features is more defined, particularly in the hair and the full lips. The painting of the belt buckle is precise and detailed, but the uniform lacks proportion around the neck and shoulder area. Jackson's left epaulet is attached to the lower collar instead of to the shoulder as in the other portraits. Also, Jackson's face is significantly rounder than in the other Waldo portraits. When compared with the Historic New Orleans Collection portrait, two different men seem to emerge. It may be that this version was not really the work of Waldo but was rather a copy by his longtime partner, William Jewett.[38]

In about 1819, Peter Maverick, one of New York's leading engravers and a founder of the National Academy of Design, made a line engraving after Waldo's likeness [Fig. 32]. Yet it is difficult to deduce just exactly what he copied—perhaps a portrait that is now lost—because his finished print differs in its details from all of the known Waldo images.[39]

V

The portraits of Andrew Jackson by John Wesley Jarvis and John Vanderlyn received appreciably more attention in their day than those of Samuel L. Waldo. Accounts of their work survive in published letters and in newspaper reports. John Pintard, a veteran merchant and one of New York City's most energetic civic leaders, recorded his thoughts about these two artists in relation to Jackson's visit. He attended the crowded ceremony at City Hall, where the mayor presented Jackson with the key to the city. Immediately afterward, Pintard wrote to his daughter: *I had a short but distinct view of his hard features sufft to qualify me to judge of the fidelity of the Portraits of two of our artists Vanderlyne [sic] & Jarvis, the first appointed to take the picture for the Corpn the second for himself. V. is not happy. His portraits are too stiff & minutely laboured. Jarvis executes with spirit & is very successful in giving character to his performances. He ought to have been the artist.*[40]

Precisely what portraits or study canvases Pintard was referring to, or where he might have seen them, cannot be ascertained. These likenesses apparently vanished years ago. The portrait by John Wesley Jarvis, now in the collection of the Metropolitan Museum of Art [Fig. 33], was probably done in the weeks after Jackson's New York visit. According to the *New York Evening Post,* Jackson did sit for Jarvis. Joseph Rodman Drake, a satirical rhymer, published several poetical accounts of Jackson's itinerary, and on March 11 he quipped:

> The board is met—the names are read;
> Elate of heart the glad committee
> Declare the mighty man has said
> He'll "take the freedom of the city."
> He thanks the council and the mayor,
> Presents 'em all his humble service;
> And thinks he's time enough to spare
> To sit an hour or so with Jarvis.

The following month, Samuel Swartwout, one of Jackson's political cronies in New York, penned the following to the general himself: *I have just been to see Jarvis' portrait of you. It is inimitable. He has already made 5 copies for different gentlemen. . . . My picture of you, is to be a three quarter full size. Jarvis has a full length for himself. I have not seen Vanderlyne's [sic] but understand it is uncommonly fine.*[41]

Swartwout disclosed more information about Jarvis's portraits of Jackson than all other contemporary sources combined. Unfortunately, the location of most of these paintings remains a mystery.[42] Only the three-quarter-length oil on canvas owned by the Metropolitan fits Swartwout's description. Its provenance, however, can be traced back only to 1964.[43]

The portrait is a skillfully executed work. This is especially evident in the belt buckle and in the stitching around the belt and between the fingers of Jackson's gloved hand. Jarvis could paint efficiently when he wanted to. No doubt such intricate painting slowed his progress considerably; it presents a sharp contrast to the breezier brushwork in the background.

Overall, the likeness of Jackson is convincing, although in comparison with images by Waldo, Sully, and Rush, Jarvis has painted Jackson's face to look squarer, stouter, and generally more robust than he must have actually appeared. The artist has aptly depicted his subject's characteristically shaggy eyebrows and slim stature, however.

Behind the figure the viewer moves from the real to the imaginary. Jackson appears unruffled amidst an almost turbulent landscape of foliage: his horse seems lost in the thicket. Such a setting is unique among portraits of Jackson. Jarvis painted similar but less dramatic backgrounds in likenesses of his first wife, Betsy Burtis (circa 1809), and of Mrs. John Williams, Jr. (1808).[44] Even more curious is the little figure of a man wearing a plumed hat, discernible in

Figure 33.
Oil on canvas by John Wesley Jarvis, 1819.
The Metropolitan Museum of Art; Harris
Brisbane Dick Fund, 1964

Figure 34.
Detail of Jarvis's *Jackson*

the lower left corner of the canvas [Fig. 34]. The explanation for this artistic aside is somewhat perplexing, as is the exact location of the setting. Is Jackson at New Orleans commanding the American troops, or is he in the woods of western Florida fighting the Seminole Indians? Or could he possibly be set in the forefront of the bewildering thicket that typified New York politics during the first quarter of the nineteenth century?

The figure in question clearly is wearing in his hat something resembling a bucktail. A faction of New York City Democrats, called Bucktails, wore such headpieces at patriotic gatherings.[45] The introduction of this curious little man may well have been suggested by Samuel Swartwout for the sake of associating Jackson with one of New York's viable political factions. Undoubtedly, he was not the inspiration of Jarvis himself. Although the artist had a well-deserved reputation as a prankster, Jarvis would not of his own volition have tinted his canvas with political overtones; to have done so would have been bad for future business. Yet the subtle juxtaposition of this political symbol beside Jackson's right hand is intriguing, and no doubt that was Jarvis's idea.[46]

As John Wesley Jarvis and Samuel Lovett Waldo produced multiple copy portraits of Andrew Jackson, John Vanderlyn became mired in ambivalence. Of the city's artists, Vanderlyn had landed the grand prize, the full-length portrait of Jackson commissioned by the Common Council. The finished painting was to be hung in City Hall, the premier portrait gallery in New York at that time. Artists who had already been honored with commissions included Waldo, John Trumbull, and Thomas Sully, in addition to Jarvis, who recently had painted a series of naval heroes of the War of 1812.[47] Vanderlyn should have been delighted at the prospect of this lucrative endeavor, especially in 1819, when a severe economic depression began drying the palettes of many of America's burgeoning artists. Yet Vanderlyn, as noted by John Pintard, was not satisfied.[48] His portrait of Jackson was the forced product of more than a year's frustration.

Much of Vanderlyn's problem was inertia, induced by more compelling artistic interests. Put simply, Vanderlyn disliked painting portraits. His ambition was to execute historical pictures. He had been trained in Paris for such a vocation and sought every opportunity to succeed in the United States. Yet in 1817 he lost a commission worth $32,000 to paint four murals for the Capitol rotunda in Washington, which Congress instead awarded to John Trumbull.[49]

By 1819 Vanderlyn was preoccupied with the opening of his Rotunda, a gallery for panoramas and pictures. Built on land leased from the city, it occupied the northeast corner of City Hall Park, at Cross and Chambers streets. Completed in 1818, the Rotunda was New York City's first museum devoted entirely to art. Construction costs, however, greatly exceeded Vanderlyn's expectations and taxed his resources to the point of insolvency. Understandably, he was anxious for his new endeavor to succeed. To offset his expenses, Vanderlyn concentrated on the grandest of his projects, a circular panoramic *View of the Palace and Gardens of Versailles,* which covered three thousand square feet of canvas.[50]

Meanwhile, the image of Andrew Jackson was fading in Vanderlyn's head. Dissatisfied with the first likeness he had hastily sketched while Jackson was in New York, Vanderlyn followed him to Washington in early March 1819. Again he painted a portrait of Jackson and again he was frustrated. Finally, on April 2 he reached out in desperation to a fellow artist—Ralph E. W. Earl. In a long letter Vanderlyn explained that he had learned about Earl from Jackson and his entourage in New York. In the hopes of getting a fresher, albeit peripheral, look at Jackson, Vanderlyn requested Earl to paint for him a small bust portrait. In the body of the letter, he enclosed a miniature sketch of the position and side view of the face he wanted. He instructed that the head should be "between 3 & 4 inches . . . from the chin to the top of the hair; such a size portrait painted on a piece of good elastic . . . canvas or on stout paper . . . might be sent on to me by mail."[51] Although strapped for funds, Vanderlyn underscored his willingness to remunerate Earl for his services.

Earl apparently responded fully, because among his papers lies a record of a one-hundred-dollar payment from Vanderlyn.[52] What Vanderlyn discovered when he opened his mail from Nashville can only be speculated upon. He apparently gleaned little inspiration from his appeal to Earl, however, and wrestled with the portrait of Andrew Jackson for more than another year.

Meanwhile, the corporation of New York City was already patiently waiting for Vanderlyn to deliver a full-length portrait of President James Monroe, commissioned in December 1817. To hasten the progress of this and the Jackson canvas, Vanderlyn returned to Washington in February 1820. Yet again he met with frustration. Vanderlyn was allowed to work in what he described as the "long room" in the President's house, but this space lacked a fireplace and was consequently cold and miserable.[53]

Back in New York during the summer months, Vanderlyn complained about his feeble health and his sagging spirits in general. The Rotunda, in which was displayed his panorama of Versailles, was not attracting the number of paying patrons he had anticipated. To meet daily expenses, Vanderlyn undertook several small portrait commissions, all of which interfered with progress on his larger canvases.[54]

Finally, in mid-September 1820, after nineteen months of disconcerted labor, Vanderlyn applied the last brushstrokes to his portrait of Andrew Jackson [Fig. 35]. While the canvas dried sufficiently, the corporation allowed Vanderlyn to retain it for several weeks at his Rotunda, where it was on view. Vanderlyn billed the city five hundred dollars for his efforts, two hundred of which had been an advance.[55] In December 1821, after he had completed the portrait of Monroe, the corporation awarded him an additional one hundred dollars for his "extraordinary trouble and expense in taking the two portraits."[56]

Figure 35.
Oil on canvas by John Vanderlyn, 1819–1820. The Art Commission of the City of New York

Figure 36.
Oil on canvas by John Vanderlyn, circa 1819. City Hall Collection, Charleston, South Carolina

೧೨

Reaction to the Jackson likeness was mixed. In April 1821 Vanderlyn, Jackson, and John James Audubon were by coincidence all in New Orleans at the same time. Vanderlyn was exhibiting a few of his best works; Jackson was on his way to Florida to assume his new duties as territorial governor; and Audubon was in residence, engrossed in his artistic study of the Mississippi bayou's native bird population. In his journal of April 27, Audubon mentioned having seen Jackson "thrice." He noted further that Vanderlyn's likeness was the only good one he had seen, and that Sully's plate (Longacre's engraving) was "miserable." It is not clear which image by Vanderlyn Audubon had admired. A notice of Vanderlyn's exhibition in the local paper on March 9 made no mention of a Jackson portrait on view.[57] In all likelihood, Audubon had not been to New York in the past six months, where he might have seen the newly finished portrait in City Hall. Nor is it probable that the corporation allowed Vanderlyn to borrow back the painting for the sake of his own traveling exhibition in the South, especially after waiting for so long to acquire it.

In February 1822 an agent in Savannah, Georgia, was managing another of Vanderlyn's exhibitions. By letter he informed Vanderlyn that he had received the Jackson portrait, but added that he did not think it worthy of his previous work, such as *Marius* or *Ariadne.*[58] In making such a comparison, he could

Figure 37.
French-made porcelain vase with a portrait of Andrew Jackson, after John Vanderlyn, circa 1825–1830. The White House Collection

Figure 38.
Engraving by Asher B. Durand, after John Vanderlyn, 1828. The New-York Historical Society

possibly—but not necessarily—have been referring to the full-length canvas.

Vanderlyn had executed other, smaller, portraits of Andrew Jackson. There was the first image—probably a study canvas—which he had done in New York during Jackson's visit. There was also the portrait he had journeyed to Washington in March 1819 to do. Of special interest, however, is a head-and-shoulders likeness, which is currently owned by the city of Charleston and hangs above the balcony of the council chambers in City Hall [Fig. 36]. This image is a variation of the full-length canvas, with slight differences in the jabot and positioning of the shoulders. In recent years this cabinet-sized portrait has received little notice, because it has literally hung in the shadow of Vanderlyn's superb 1824 full-length of Jackson. Then, too, the identity of the artist was questioned. This is ironic, since in its day this smaller likeness was the better known one. It was reproduced widely in engravings, particularly in Europe, and was even copied on a porcelain vase made in France about 1825, which is now a part of the White House collection [Fig. 37].

&

The New York City Hall canvas, which still hangs in this municipal landmark completed in 1811, was the first portrait of Jackson to be commissioned by a civic body. As early as 1815, Vanderlyn's name had been mentioned in connection with similar proposals for Jackson portraits in Washington, D.C., and Richmond, Virginia.[59] Either because of insufficient funds or lack of public interest, these portraits were never commissioned. In New York, Vanderlyn's portrait still evokes the grandeur once associated with the hero of New Orleans. Age and time have darkened the canvas in places, consequently hiding much detail from view; and the wrecked carriage of a cannon has all but vanished in the lower right corner. Fortunately, such incidentals remain crisply preserved in a line engraving published in June 1828 by Asher B. Durand of New York [Fig. 38].

Technically precocious and naturally talented, Durand by the age of thirty had established himself as one of the foremost engravers of his day. The publication of his large print, *The Declaration of Independence* (circa 1820–1823), after John Trumbull's recently completed mural in the rotunda of the United States Capitol, earned Durand considerable prestige and money. At the time Durand principally made his living from engraving bank notes and other commercial endeavors.[60] The field of portraiture aroused his artistic inclinations, however. In February 1828, notice appeared in the *National Intelligencer* announcing a subscription for a print of General Jackson after Vanderlyn's full-length painting. The print would measure 21 by 15 inches and would be published on "imperial French paper, of first quality." Durand further stipulated that instead of the usual printing of 2,000 to 3,000 copies, only 850 prints would be produced, thus ensuring that they would "be considered proofs, or perfect impressions."[61] Each print would sell for nine dollars. Published four months before the presidential election of 1828, Durand's engraved portrait was a timely icon for Jacksonians.

VII

Andrew Jackson retraced his route during his Northeast tour of 1819 back to the city of Baltimore. Upon his arrival by steamboat in the early morning of February 27, celebrations ensued, much as they had in Philadelphia and New York. There were military reviews and presentations, a visit to "Mr. Guy's splendid exhibition of landscape paintings," as well as a tour of Fort McHenry, Baltimore's own shrine to the War of 1812. On the evening of March 1, a

Figure 39.
Oil on canvas by Rembrandt Peale, 1819.
Baltimore City Life Museums

sumptuous public dinner was held at Williamson's Hotel, attended by more than two hundred citizens. Behind Jackson was lofted a "transparency inscribed with the names of places at which he had chiefly distinguished himself." Among the many toasts drunk was one for "Old Hickory, who took up a big cudgel and knocked down the folks who made unlawful love to your sister Louisiana—a yankee of the breed of former times."[62]

A special tribute was the city council's unanimous resolution inviting Jackson to have his likeness painted by Rembrandt Peale, the city's foremost portraitist. Peale's artistic interests were nurtured in his youth by his remarkable father, Charles Willson Peale. In 1814 Rembrandt had opened his own museum in a newly erected three-story brick building on North Holliday Street. Although he had fashioned his collection of paintings and natural history curiosities after his father's successful example in Philadelphia, the structure itself—built specifically as a museum—was the first of its kind in the country. As the collection grew, its strength leaned toward the sciences, in spite of Peale's preoccupation with portrait painting.[63]

In 1816 the city council had commissioned Peale to paint the likenesses of four local heroes, all of whom had displayed patriotic valor in defending the city against the British.[64] In 1818 the councilmen returned to Peale for a portrait of the late Commodore Joshua Barney, a naval hero of the Revolutionary War. So when Jackson visited the following year, it was only natural that Peale was requested once more to begin mixing his colors.

Jackson sat for Peale three times during his three-day visit. The morning after his departure for Washington, a notice appeared in the local newspaper announcing that Peale's portrait of the general would be placed on display in the museum for that evening only. Simply a study, this canvas may not yet have been completed. Several days later, Peale's daughter Rosalba wrote to a Philadelphia relative with news that her father had just painted an excellent likeness of Jackson and was making a copy for the City Hall.[65]

What became of Peale's study portrait is not known, but the Baltimore City Hall painting is now in the collection of the Peale Museum in Baltimore [Fig. 39]. Of all the three 1819 Jackson images by the Peale family, Rembrandt's gave the truest glimpse of the subject's declining state of health, especially in the area of the mouth.

ဆ

Baltimore was the last stop on Jackson's tour. He made a hasty departure when he learned that the Senate committee, which, like the House, had been investigating his conduct for the seizure of Spanish West Florida, had just released its report. It was highly critical, and Jackson was furious. Fortunately for all concerned, the congressional session was ending, allowing no time for constructive debate on this emotional topic. In addition, Spain, in signing the Adams-Onís Treaty in Washington on February 22, 1819, ceded East and West Florida to the United States, thereby abandoning their grievances over Old Hickory's unauthorized invasion of 1818. Since the hostile report had virtually become a dead issue, Jackson could finally return home to Nashville.[66]

Jackson left behind a generally favorable public impression, which corroborated his own oft-repeated message that he had performed his duty for the good of the country. America believed him and retained confidence in him. Jackson was still the hero of New Orleans.

The visual record said as much. In portraits varying in size and composition from Anna Claypoole Peale's miniature to John Vanderlyn's full-length state portrait, Jackson was depicted in military garb—in some instances bedecked with sashes, in others bedecked with swords. Yet behind the regulation dark blue uniform with the gold braid trimmings of a major general, a composite likeness of Jackson emerged. Those who knew him were already familiar with his features: the long face, the deep-set eyes, the overhanging brows, the linear mouth, and the shock of graying hair that fell on his lined forehead. Others had only to admire the most recent works by some of America's best portraitists to gain for themselves some notion of the appearance of their distinguished countryman.

Notes

1. In 1826, Major Henry Lee, son of the famed Revolutionary War general "Lighthorse Harry" Lee, proposed writing a biography of Jackson. Jackson agreed to assist him but warned: "I cannot speak of myself, or relate anecdotes of myself which have not been worded by others—should I attempt this, the most secret recess, could not conceal my shame." See *Correspondence of Jackson*, vol. 3, p. 327.

2. *Ibid.*, vol. 2, p. 403.

3. Charles Coleman Sellers, *Charles Willson Peale*, Volume 2: *Later Life, 1790–1827* (Philadelphia, 1947), pp. 318-19.

4. Remini, *Andrew Jackson*, vol. 1, pp. 366-73. For a list of Peale's sitters, see Charles Willson Peale to Angelica Peale Robinson, January 8, 1819, Peale-Sellers Papers, American Philosophical Society, Philadelphia.

5. Charles Willson Peale to Rubens Peale, January 19, 1819, Peale-Sellers Papers.

6. Charles Willson Peale to Rembrandt Peale, January 23, 1819; Charles Willson Peale to Rubens Peale, January 24, 1819, Charles Willson Peale Diary, January 29, 1819, *ibid.*

7. Charles Willson Peale Diary, January 29-30, 1819, *ibid.*

8. This unfavorable view was substantiated by reports of Jackson's behavior while in Washington that winter of 1819. Rumors circulated throughout the capital that he had threatened to cut the ears off of every member of the Senate committee (which was conducting its own investigation) who spoke against his actions in the Seminole War. Reputedly at special risk was Senator John W. Eppes of Virginia, the son-in-law of Thomas Jefferson. Based on a diary entry by John Quincy Adams on March 12, several friends kept Jackson up one night until two or three o'clock in the morning, trying to dissuade him from challenging Eppes to a duel. In January, Eppes had sat for Peale and informed the artist that he had learned Jackson was not coming to Washington. Unfortunately for the misinformed senator, Jackson arrived in town looking for a fight. Nothing, however, came of his anger. See Charles Willson Peale to Rubens Peale, January 19, 1819, *ibid.*; Parton, *Jackson*, vol. 2, pp. 551, 570-71; Remini, *Andrew Jackson*, vol. 1, pp. 376-77; John Quincy Adams, *Memoirs of John Quincy Adams, Comprising Portions of His Diary from 1795 to 1848*, ed. Charles Francis Adams (Philadelphia, 1847-1877), vol. 4, pp. 291-95 (hereafter cited as Adams, *Memoirs*).

9. Extract of a letter published in the *New York Columbian*, February 20, 1819.

10. An oil-on-canvas portrait of Jackson owned by Lafayette College in Easton, Pennsylvania, appears to be the work of one of the Peales. It has been attributed to Rembrandt, but stylistically it more resembles the brush of Charles Willson. For instance, the acorn design in the belt is identical to that shown in Peale's portrait executed in Washington. The artist must have been determined to include Jackson's belt and buckle at the bottom of the canvas, because as depicted they are unnaturally high on Jackson's abdomen. Rembrandt avoided these intricate details altogether, preferring instead to hide them under Jackson's coat. The image itself differs significantly from Charles Willson Peale's Washington, D.C., portrait, particularly as it is a more frontal view. Yet the depiction of the mouth in both paintings is almost identical. If Charles Willson Peale did not actually paint the portrait owned by Lafayette College, his 1819 portrait influenced it.

11. Subsequently, Charles's portrait passed through the hands of several private owners before John Wanamaker, the successful Philadelphia retailer, presented it in 1922 to the Grand Lodge F. & A.M. of Pennsylvania Masonic Temple in Philadelphia. Anna's portrait is now part of the Mabel Brady Garvan Collection at Yale University.

12. Parton, *Jackson*, vol. 2, pp. 557-58; *Democratic Press* (Philadelphia), February 16-22, 1819.

13. James Earle to Ralph E. W. Earl, February 17, 1819, Earl Papers.

14. Sully's interest in this business venture amounted to four shares of stock. Monroe H. Fabian, *Mr. Sully, Portrait Painter: The Works of Thomas Sully (1723-1872)* (Washington, D.C., 1983), p. 72; *Democratic Press*, April 19, 1819; Edward Biddle and Mantle Fielding, *The Life and Works of Thomas Sully (1783-1872)* (Philadelphia, 1921), p. 186.

15. This proof is in the collection of the National Portrait Gallery, Smithsonian Institution.

16. James Barton Longacre to Andrew Jackson, n.d. (handwritten transcript not in Longacre's hand), Longacre file, Print Department, National Portrait Gallery, Smithsonian Institution; *Correspondence of Jackson*, vol. 3, p. 40.

17. Longacre to G. Fairman, October 30, 1821, James Barton Longacre Papers, Archives of American Art, Smithsonian Institution, Washington, D.C. Another Philadelphia artist who claimed to have lost money on engraving a portrait of Jackson was Joshua Shaw. On September 7, 1823, Shaw mentioned in a letter to Secretary of War John C. Calhoun that he had paid seven hundred dollars "for engraving that of General Andrew Jackson, by which I lost 125 Dollars cash besides all my labor." Neither the image nor the engraving has been

identified. See John C. Calhoun, *The Papers of John C. Calhoun,* ed. W. Edwin Hemphill *et al.* (Columbia, S.C., 1959–1983), vol. 8, p. 259.

18. The Historical Society of Pennsylvania owns Sully's original "Account of Pictures," commonly referred to as the register. The New York Public Library has a version, not in Sully's handwriting, which is also on microfilm in the Archives of American Art. For a published and annotated listing, see Biddle and Fielding, *Sully,* pp. 186–87.

19. This study sketch is owned by the Detroit Institute of Arts.

20. The 1829 portrait measures 8¾₆ by 6⅛ inches and is owned by the Historical Society of Pennsylvania. In July of 1858, Sully painted a similar, even larger portrait (33⅞ by 27¾ inches) for the noted American actor Edwin Forrest. In 1988 this painting was put up for auction at Christie's of New York. See Biddle and Fielding, *Sully,* List of Paintings, nos. 880 and 886.

21. In 1962, Mrs. John Henry Livingston donated this painting to the state of New York. A card attached to the back of the canvas by John H. Livingston traces the provenance to the Swartwout family of New York. Samuel Swartwout was an early Jacksonian supporter in that state.

22. *William Rush, American Sculptor* (exhibition catalogue, Pennsylvania Academy of the Fine Arts, Philadelphia, 1982), pp. 10–20, 57, 61–64, 85–91.

23. *Ibid.,* pp. 54–55; *Third Annual Exhibition of the Columbian Society of Artists and the Pennsylvania Academy, 1813* (Philadelphia, 1813), p. 12. At the end of his career, Rush regretted not having had the time to sculpt in marble, the medium most desired by artists and patrons alike.

24. *Nashville Gazette,* June 19, 1819. See also the *Farmers' Repository* (Charles Town, [West] Virginia), June 2, 1819; Naeve, "William Rush's Terracotta and Plaster Busts," p. 28.

25. *National Intelligencer,* December 14, 1819; *Ninth Annual Exhibition of the Pennsylvania Academy of the Fine Arts, June, 1820* (Philadelphia, 1820), p. 12. Regrettably, this catalogue did not specify the medium. Subsequent exhibition records, however, listed a "cast" bust.

26. *William Rush, American Sculptor,* pp. 157–58.

Both elder statesmen gratefully acknowledged this gesture. The occasion prompted Adams to call Jackson one of the greatest military figures that North America had ever produced. At Monticello, Jefferson promised to venerate Jackson in his tea room along with busts of Washington, Franklin, and Lafayette. See James Ronaldson to Jefferson, February 1, 1820, Thomas Jefferson Papers, Library of Congress; Naeve, "William Rush's Terracotta and Plaster Busts," p. 31.

27. *Nashville Whig,* March 7, 1821. See also Cyrus Townsend Brady, *The True Andrew Jackson* (Philadelphia, 1906), pp. 414–15.

28. Jessie J. Poesch, "A Precise View of Peale's Museum," *Antiques* 78 (October 1960): 345; *William Rush, American Sculptor,* p. 158.

A photograph of President Abraham Lincoln's body lying in state inside New York's City Hall on April 29, 1865, reveals a bust of Jackson by Rush resting on a pedestal in the background. This was probably a plaster cast. This photograph by an unidentified photographer is in the Illinois State Historical Library, Old State Capitol, Springfield.

29. Naeve, "William Rush's Terracotta and Plaster Busts," p. 32.

30. In 1985 the society auctioned the bust of Jackson through Christie's of New York City. The estimated price was set between $250,000 and $300,000. It was purchased by Hirschl & Adler Galleries, Inc., and subsequently acquired by the Art Institute of Chicago.

A marble copy of Rush's Jackson by an unidentified artist was presented to the Ladies' Hermitage Association in 1907 by the Honorable Lawrence Cooper of Huntsville, Alabama [Fig. 40]. Nothing further has been discovered about this piece. For mention of other extant copies by artists other than Rush, see *ibid.,* p. 36.

31. *National Advocate* (New York), February 23–24, 1819; *American and Commercial Daily Advertiser* (Baltimore), February 26–27, 1819; *Democratic Press,* February 23, 1819.

Figure 40.
Marble by unidentified artist after William Rush, not dated. The Hermitage: Home of President Andrew Jackson

32. *National Advocate,* February 24, 1819; *American and Commercial Daily Advertiser,* February 27, 1819; Parton, *Jackson,* vol. 2, pp. 561-63; William Allen Butler, *A Retrospect of Forty Years, 1825-1865* (New York, 1911), pp. 128-29.

33. *Minutes of the Common Council of the City of New York, 1784-1831* (New York, 1917), vol. 10, p. 255; *American and Commercial Daily Advertiser,* February 25, 1819.

34. Frederic Fairchild Sherman, "Samuel L. Waldo and William Jewett, Portrait Painters," *Art in America and Elsewhere* 18 (February 1930): 81-82.

35. Purchased by the Metropolitan Museum of Art in 1906, Waldo's study had previously been owned by George H. Story and earlier by John M. Hoe of New York. Hart, "Life Portraits," p. 795; Russell Walton Thorpe, "The Waldo Portraits: Of Our Seventh President," *Antiques* 53 (May 1948): 364-65.

36. The Historic New Orleans Collection purchased the piece from Hirschl & Adler Galleries, Inc., of New York City in 1978. Fifty years earlier, this portrait was auctioned as part of the late Lyman G. Bloomingdale collection of oil paintings. It sold for $29,000, then a record for an American portrait. In the 1940s Mr. and Mrs. William A. Fisher of Detroit owned the painting.

37. In 1971 the state of Tennessee purchased the portrait for $52,000 from the auction house of Adam A. Weschler and Sons in Washington. Three years before, Hirschl & Adler had offered it for sale at $95,000 but found no takers. Before this, the painting was the property of the Chaille family of New Orleans. See *Washington Post,* March 2, 1971. At the time of the sale, a portrait of Jackson similar in size and composition was loaned to the Louisiana State Museum in New Orleans by the Chalmette Chapter of the United States Daughters of 1812. At one time, a local art authority questioned its being the work of Waldo. See New Orleans *Times-Picayune,* March 21, 1971.

38. The early provenance of the work in the Addison Gallery remains a mystery. In 1940 Mrs. Louise Vanderbilt of New York sold it to a dealer, Miss Inglis Griswold, for $3,800. She in turn disposed of it through the Milch Galleries of New York. See *New York Herald-Tribune,* July 28, 1940. In 1955 Mr. Alfred H. Caspary presented it to the Addison Gallery.

39. A portrait of Jackson owned by Philipse Manor Hall State Historic Site, Yonkers, New York, has been attributed to Samuel L. Waldo. In style and composition, this painting differs radically from Waldo's more familiar Jackson portraits. The image resembles a portrait attributed to Rembrandt Peale (but stylistically more like Charles Willson Peale), which is now in the possession of Lafayette College, Pennsylvania (see n. 10).

40. John Pintard, *Letters from John Pintard to His Daughter, Eliza Noel Pintard Davidson, 1816-1833* (New York, 1940-1941), vol. 1, pp. 166-69.

41. *New York Evening Post,* March 11, 1819; Dickson, *Jarvis,* pp. 213-15; Parton, *Jackson,* vol. 2, pp. 559-64; *Correspondence of Jackson,* vol. 6, p. 471.

42. At least two other Jackson portraits attributed to Jarvis are extant. One is owned by the Union Club in New York City, and the other is at the Charlotte Court House Library in Virginia. The former depicts Jackson in uniform, the latter in civilian dress. Neither portrait, however, exudes lifelike qualities.

43. The Manhattan Club sold the painting to the Metropolitan in that year.

In April 1841, a notice appeared in a New York City newspaper announcing a sale of paintings at Frazer's, 122 Broadway. The notice stated that among the lot was "a portrait of General Jackson, from the spirited pencil of Jarvis. It was painted many years ago when General Jackson was on a visit to this city, and exhibits that remarkable man in all the vigor of middle life." What portrait this may have been cannot now be ascertained. See *New York Evening Post,* April 8, 1841.

44. These portraits are illustrated in Dickson, *Jarvis,* nos. 16 and 37. For an analysis of Jarvis's changing style as a painter see pp. 322-36.

45. David M. Ellis *et al., A History of New York State* (Ithaca, N.Y., 1957), pp 144-49.

46. In relation to the horse and the landscape in general, the small figure is out of perspective, which suggests that Jarvis depicted him for subtle symbolism rather than composition.

Two copy miniatures of the figure of Jackson have been recorded by the Catalog of American portraits as being in private collections. One is signed on the front "R.E.W.E. 1823," and the other has a paper label on the back that is partly illegible, stating the artist as Aaron H. Corwine. Corwine was a noted Cincinnati portraitist and became friends with Jarvis, who used to pass periodically through that city during his travels. On one occasion Jarvis was seen on a street, "contemplating a swinging sign, upon which was daubed a wretched likeness of Gen. Jackson." A friend approached him and asked what he thought of the painting. "Painting!—Gen. Jackson!" chuckled Jarvis. "I'll rub my dog's tail on the pallet, and he'll *wag a better likeness than that!*" See *Daily Picayune* (New Orleans), June 15, 1841.

47. These portraits, all painted between 1814 and 1816, were of Commodore Isaac Hull, Commodore William Bainbridge, Captain Thomas Macdonough, General Jacob Jennings Brown, and Commodore Oliver Hazard Perry.

48. Pintard, *Letters,* vol. 1, pp. 168–69.

49. Louise Hunt Averill, "John Vanderlyn, American Painter (1775–1852)" (Ph.D. diss., Yale University, 1949), pp. 99–100, 109–10, 128–29; Salvatore Mondello, "John Vanderlyn," *New-York Historical Society Quarterly* 52 (April 1968): 174–76.

In 1820, Vanderlyn was deprived again when the city of New Orleans rebuffed his proposal to paint a scene of Jackson's famous battle.

50. Mondello, "John Vanderlyn," p. 176.

51. The text of this letter has been reproduced in full in Averill, "John Vanderlyn," pp. 254–55, and in part in *Americana, Mainly the Collection of a New Jersey Historian and California Pioneer . . .* (auction catalogue, Anderson Galleries, New York, 1923), p. 47.

52. Earl Papers.

53. This was the unfinished East Room, which Jackson as President decorated for the first time in 1829. See John Vanderlyn to John H. Purviance, June 8, 1820, John H. Purviance Papers, William R. Perkins Library, Duke University, Durham, North Carolina.

54. Vanderlyn to Purviance, July 16, 1820, *ibid.*

55. *Minutes of the Common Council,* vol. 11, p. 315.

56. *Ibid.,* vol. 12, p. 163.

57. *Journal of Audubon,* p. 151; *Le Courrier de la Louisiane,* March 9, 1821.

58. Averill, "John Vanderlyn," p. 265.

59. *Ibid.,* p. 246.

60. Wayne Craven, "Asher B. Durand's Career as an Engraver," *American Art Journal* 3 (Spring 1971): 39–50.

61. *National Intelligencer,* February 13, 1828. See also *National Banner and Nashville Whig,* December 15, 1829.

62. *American and Commercial Daily Advertiser,* March 4, 1819; *Niles' Weekly Register* (Baltimore), March 6, 1819.

63. Wilbur Harvey Hunter, *The Story of America's Oldest Museum Building* (Baltimore, Md., 1964), p. 2.

64. The heroes were Major Edward Johnson; Major General Samuel Smith, commander in chief of the land and sea forces; Brigadier General John Stricker, commander at North Point; and Lieutenant Colonel George Armistead, commander of Fort McHenry. See *ibid.,* p. 12; David Meschutt, "The Peale Portraits of Andrew Jackson," *Tennessee Historical Quarterly* 46 (Spring 1987): 6.

65. *American and Commercial Daily Advertiser,* March 2, 1819; Rosalba Carriera Peale Underwood to Titian Peale, March 14, 1819, Peale-Sellers Papers.

66. Remini, *Andrew Jackson,* vol. 1, pp. 375–77.

1821

Is appointed governor of Florida Territory

November 13: Resigns governorship and returns to Tennessee

1822

July 20: Is nominated for President by Tennessee legislature

1823

December 3: Arrives in Washington to take seat in United States Senate

1824

January: Is requested by Charleston City Council to sit for portrait by John Vanderlyn

March 16: Receives gold medal voted by Congress

April: Jackson portrait exhibited in Washington by Robert Street

Portrait painted by Joseph Wood and engraved by James B. Longacre

November: Receives plurality of electoral votes in presidential election

1825

February 9: Loses presidential contest to John Quincy Adams in House election

March: Returns home via Cincinnati; portrait painted by Aaron Houghton Corwine and bust sculpted by Frederick Eckstein

October: Resigns Senate seat; is nominated for President by Tennessee legislature

1826

June 1: Engraving published by Charles Cutler Torrey after portrait by Earl

1828

Engraving published by James B. Longacre after 1826 portrait by Earl

May 12: Likeness taken by O. H. Throop

August 25: Engraving published by Throop in Baltimore

November: Is elected President of the United States

December 22: Rachel Jackson dies

Chapter 3

Presidential Timber, 1821–1828

Beginning in the early 1820s, the perception of Andrew Jackson progressively changed from military hero to presidential candidate. George Washington was the first American to have undergone this transformation, and Jackson would be the next. Much like his Virginia predecessor, Jackson was driven by a sense of duty to his country, and in the expanding realm of national affairs the opportunities to serve seemed endless. Already Jackson had answered his nation's call in the Creek War of 1813–1814, in New Orleans in 1814–1815, and in the Seminole campaign of 1818. Three years later, Jackson returned to Florida, newly acquired from Spain, as territorial governor. This appointment did not work out for him, however, and he held it for only a few months. In the fall of 1821 Jackson arrived home, exhausted and nearly broken in health, but satisfied in having once again served his government.[1]

For all of his patriotism, Jackson recognized his limitations. There were times when it behooved men of power and prominence to be mere spectators upon the national stage. This was especially so in the fledgling arena of republican politics, where it was not yet the accepted practice for presidential contenders to enthusiastically advance their own candidacy. It was not surprising, then, that Jackson would not promote himself for the presidency or even let it appear to the electorate that he approved of the tactical politicking of his ambitious friends. In his letters and business dealings, Jackson assumed the image of a gentleman farmer, content in retirement.[2]

I

Notwithstanding some gaps in the portrait record of the 1820s, the extant likenesses of Jackson reveal how his physical appearance and political image changed as he marched off the battlefield and toward the presidential mansion. The most obvious difference was dress. With one or two exceptions, artists preferred depicting Jackson in traditional civilian attire—black coat and white jabot—rather than in a general's uniform. This squirely image was consistent with his new station in life. Moreover, it refuted the slur of Jackson as a "Military Chieftain," cast by such political enemies as Henry Clay. Jackson never really understood the negative connotations of this charge. "He who fights, and fights successfully," he wrote to a friend in 1825, "must according to his standard be held up as a 'Military Chieftain': even Washington could he again appear among us might be so considered."[3]

Another significant change in Jackson's appearance was his hair, which he began brushing back from his high forehead in a neater fashion. While he probably adopted this style because of personal preference, it did enhance his Washington image, both as a senator in 1823–1825 and later as President. Moreover, his hair became his most distinctive feature.

In the 1820s Jackson's aging and gauntness became more evident. The hollows in his cheeks were more pronounced, and the lines running down his face and across his forehead were deeper. The gunfights, the battlefield campaigns, and the years of malnutrition had taken their toll. From about 1814 until his death in 1845, he suffered constantly with one ailment or another—intestinal disorders or rheumatism. More alarming was the periodic congestion in his chest, which probably was caused by the bullet that had lodged near his heart since May 30, 1806, when he had fought a duel with Charles Dickinson over a horse race.[4] Jackson killed Dickinson, but not before the latter had hit his mark.

Some of the remedies that Jackson and his doctor tried were almost as lethal as the maladies. Still this veteran warrior possessed a will of iron. On occasion, determination alone kept him on his feet. Describing the person most people encountered, an acquaintance remembered his appearance in the summer of 1828: *Picture to yourself a military-looking man, above the ordinary height, dressed plainly, but with great neatness; dignified and grave—I had almost said stern—but always courteous and affable, with keen, searching eyes, iron-gray hair, standing stiffly up from an expansive forehead, a face somewhat furrowed by care and time, and expressive of deep thought and active intellect, and you have before you the General Jackson.*[5]

II

Jackson's portrait record of the 1820s commenced with unfinished business dating back five years. The War Department still had to proceed with making the gold medals voted on by Congress in February 1815, which would honor heroes of the War of 1812—including, of course, Jackson. Reasons for the delay were many, but one obstacle was the lack of qualified artists to perform the necessary work. In August 1819, Joseph Hopkinson, president of the Pennsylvania Academy of the Fine Arts, who was charged with supervising production of the medals, informed Secretary of War John C. Calhoun of his difficulty in finding skilled engravers. A few days later Calhoun responded with a letter he had received from one Moritz Fürst, who indicated an interest in doing the engraving.[6]

Fürst was born in Hungary in 1782. He studied die-sinking in Vienna before immigrating to the United States in 1807, where he went into business for himself. Perhaps because of more pressing departmental matters, it took more than a year for Calhoun to offer the job to Fürst, and then only on the condition that Hopkinson had not already engaged another artist. Meanwhile, Fürst was asked to supply the names of those officers who had not yet furnished a likeness, and "for whom a device has not been already adopted."[7]

Jackson's name was on Fürst's list, as were most of the other officers. After digging in back files, Calhoun discovered that in 1817 the War Department had failed to instruct the generals to return the designs for the reverse of the medals once they had inspected them. He wrote to Jackson on November 30, 1820, and requested him to return his design immediately if it was still in his possession. Calhoun added, "Your likeness has been received and is now in the possession of the artist [Fürst]." This likeness was undoubtedly the crude one executed by John B. West, which Jackson had mailed to the War Department in the summer of 1815. At the time Jackson had not been impressed with it. Apparently, neither were Fürst or Hopkinson—Calhoun enclosed an extract from Hopkinson asking Jackson to send a "profile likeness" instead. A month later Jackson replied from his home outside of Nashville, explaining that filling the request might take time on account of "there being no miniature painter in this country at present."[8] As far as Jackson was concerned, that was the end of it. The profile that ultimately appeared on the obverse of Jackson's medal was no doubt the contrived work of Moritz Fürst.

Jackson apparently never returned the device for the medal's reverse to Calhoun either. Designs for the reverses of these army medals were executed by Thomas Sully, who left a record of having drawn one for Jackson's medal in September 1817.[9] He produced a replacement design on September 27, 1822, and the following day Fürst wrote to the War Department and explained the symbolism behind Sully's drawing. It depicted the allegorical figures Victory and Peace, with the former engraving "Orleans" on a tablet and the latter extending a restraining hand. Calhoun approved of the design.[10]

Meanwhile, Fürst progressed steadily in his work. By 1823 he had exhibited several of the medals, including Jackson's, at the Pennsylvania Academy of the Fine Arts. These were probably struck in bronze.

Finally, on February 7, 1824, Hopkinson informed Calhoun that Jackson's gold medal had been struck [Fig. 41]. Each medal, he noted, contained approximately $140 worth of gold. He added in closing, "I am sure the President [James Monroe] will be pleased when he sees the Army medals."[11]

On March 16, 1824, President Monroe presented the medal to Jackson in the presidential mansion. Jackson was accompanied by his Senate colleague from Tennessee, John H. Eaton, and his old friend and former aide-de-camp, Edward Livingston, now a member of the House, representing the district of New Orleans. The ceremony, although brief, received ample notice in the next day's *National Intelligencer.*[12]

Figure 41.
Gold medal engraved by Moritz Fürst, 1824. The American Numismatic Society

Today Jackson's gold medal is in the collection of the American Numismatic Society in New York City. Allegedly it was discovered in a pawnshop. A number of bronze replicas were stamped, two of which are in collections at the Hermitage and the Smithsonian Institution.[13]

III

Andrew Jackson's arrival in Washington in the winter of 1823–1824 was the outcome of a chain of events initiated two years earlier, with his nomination for President by the Tennessee legislature. Although Jackson was then enormously popular throughout the state, he did have personal and political adversaries in influential positions, one of whom was Colonel John Williams of Tennessee, a candidate for reelection to the United States Senate in 1823. Williams vehemently opposed Jackson's nomination, preferring the highly regarded William H. Crawford, secretary of the treasury under Monroe. Because those were still the days when congressional caucuses hand-picked presidential candidates, Jackson's political backers saw the danger in returning Williams to Washington. If Tennessee did not support Jackson, who else could be expected to do so? For Jacksonians in the state there was only one thing to do: run their man against Williams for the Senate seat.[14] This they did with surprising success.

Senator-elect Andrew Jackson arrived in Washington the morning of December 3, 1823. The care with which he had packed his bags, however, belied his true feelings. He had serious reservations about whether to go at all. At the age of fifty-six, he would have been perfectly happy to remain at the Hermitage, where he could oversee his plantation, comfort his wife Rachel, and dote on the nieces and nephews that frequently filled his house. Besides, the Senate held no real attraction for him. He understood what his new duties would entail; in 1798 he had been a senator for one session before resigning his seat. His almost blank record clearly indicated that he was out of his element. Temperamentally, Jackson was ill-suited for settling differences of opinion through tedious debate, which often continued for weeks, only to end in compromise.

Why, then, did Jackson place himself once again in the swirl of political intrigue? Part of the reason had to do with his sense of duty. Another part was his need for involvement. Throughout his adult life, Jackson exhibited a keen interest in national affairs. He was a regular student of the newspapers and enjoyed expounding his views in correspondence. Although the Senate was scarcely an ideal forum for him, it presented him with an opportunity to be directly involved in monitoring the country's destiny during a time of peace. Jackson agreed to at least give it another try. And if nothing else, the senatorial election of 1823 had been a contest. It was another chance to confront a personal rival and beat him. Such an endeavor was a sensible challenge for a retired duelist who in earlier days had actively honed his competitive edge at cockfights and horse races.

After Andrew Jackson's arrival in Washington at the end of 1823, his new personality began to emerge. His colleagues noted changes, especially in his improved attitude and controlled temperament. This time the capital city apparently agreed with him. Jackson enjoyed much better health than he had for some time. His spirits rallied as well. Although he disliked being away from Rachel, the city's social life enveloped him. As a hero and a presidential contender, he was the center of attention. Shortly after he reached town, Jackson's friend John Eaton wrote to Rachel that her husband was "constantly in motion to some Dinner party or other."[15]

Jackson added a remarkable postscript to Eaton's letter, telling Rachel that he was "now at peace with all the world." This suggests another facet to his perplexing character. He could control his temper when it benefited him to do so and in the next moment could stage a tantrum when circumstances required a show of conviction. As a presidential candidate, Jackson was well aware that politicians throughout the country were scrutinizing his every move. One false step or diplomatic stumble could jeopardize his future in Washington. Fate, too, played a hand in shaping his new attitude. Jackson discovered that his seat in the Senate chamber was next to an old friend turned adversary, Thomas Hart Benton of Missouri. A trivial misunderstanding back in 1813 had pitted Benton and his brother Jesse against Jackson in a gunfight in Nashville. Jackson suffered a near-fatal bullet wound in his left shoulder. Fellow members now offered to exchange seats, but Jackson refused. The two men resolved to face each other and dismiss the past.[16] An unexpected and strong friendship was renewed. Jackson also mended his relations with others, most notably General Winfield Scott and Henry Clay, each of whom had criticized Jackson's military performance. Clay especially had voiced his concerns during the Seminole War hearings of 1819. A significant change, however, had come over Jackson since that time. The new Jackson, as noted by Congressman Sam Houston, was "calm, dignified, and makes as polished a *bow* as any man I have seen at court." No one was more pleased with the change than Jackson himself, who confided in a letter to a Nashville friend, "I am told the opinion of these whose minds were prepared to see me with a Tomahawk in one hand, and a scalping knife in the other has greatly changed and I am getting on very smoothly."[17]

In late January 1824, as Jackson settled into his senatorial duties, he received a communiqué from John Geddes, intendant of the city of Charleston, South Carolina. Three years earlier it had been Geddes's pleasure as governor to accept James Ronaldson's gift of a Jackson plaster bust by William Rush for display in the Legislative Library in Columbia. Now he was writing on behalf of the Charleston City Council to request Jackson to sit for an oil portrait by John Vanderlyn. Since 1790 the council had been commissioning portraits of notable figures who were in some way connected with the region.[18] The honor for Jackson was twofold: he was a native son of the state, and he had participated in the Revolutionary War Battle of Hanging Rock as a boy of just thirteen.

Vanderlyn was an obvious choice to undertake this commission. He was well known in the South, in part because of his exhibitions in New Orleans, Savannah, and Charleston in 1821 and 1822. On May 22, 1821, he was made an honorary member of the South Carolina Academy of Fine Arts. Moreover, his full-length portrait of Jackson for the corporation of New York City was an endorsement in itself.

Jackson responded favorably to the city's request and seemed genuinely honored by it. For Vanderlyn the project meant being in Washington while Congress was in session. He made the most of his visit in February, exhibiting his large circular panorama, *View of the Palace and Gardens of Versailles.*[19] Predictably, Vanderlyn was distracted from portraiture by grander artistic interests. Consequently, he drew only Jackson's head.

Back in New York the following August, Vanderlyn was working on the torso of his portrait when John James Audubon stopped by his studio. Vanderlyn eyed the young naturalist-painter and determined that he was just about Jackson's size. He asked Audubon to pose, and Audubon complied, filling his time by sketching Vanderlyn's landlady and her child. Vanderlyn's *Jackson* [Fig. 42], for which he received six hundred dollars, was completed in time to be included in the fourth annual exhibition of the South Carolina Academy of Fine Arts, held in Charleston in March 1825. As a work of art, it was not the equal of Jacques-Louis David's spectacular *Bonaparte Crossing the Alps,* also on display. Yet as an icon, the popular *Jackson* more than held its ground.[20]

Vanderlyn may have been inspired to pose his Charleston portrait after a full-length painting of Daniel D. Tompkins, executed by John Wesley Jarvis in about 1820.[21] At the time, Tompkins, a former governor of New York, was the Vice President of the United States. In both paintings the figure is turned slightly to the viewer's right; the right arm is extended downward and rests on the hilt of a sword, and the left hand clutches a glove at the waist. Even the background scenery, a curving coastline, is similar in both.

Although less animated than Vanderlyn's earlier work, this new *Jackson* is a better painting technically, for the artist had an easier time executing the face and head. Jackson is depicted in transition: his countenance bespeaks the rejuvenated senator from Tennessee, whose hair is now combed neatly over his head. His blue eyes are firm yet relaxed. Overall, he appears rested, as if he is indeed enjoying a spell of good health and is at peace with all the world. The figure, on the other hand, garbed in the smart dress blues of a major general, places Jackson in the more familiar context of hero of New Orleans. Both depictions were accurate. Although he was now a serious candidate for the presidency, his credentials had United States Army stamped all over them.

In spite of Vanderlyn's most recent accomplishment, portraiture in the grand manner left him unsatisfied. In a letter to his nephew in 1825, he offered the following advice: "Were I to begin life again, I should not hesitate to follow this plan, that is, to paint portraits cheap & slight, for the mass of folks can't judge of the merits of a well finished picture."[22]

V

In the early spring of 1824, Robert Street, a young portraitist from Philadelphia, was in Washington painting works for exhibition. Little is known of Street, who inspired four of his six children to become artists themselves.

Figure 43.
Oil on canvas by Robert Street, 1824.
Sedalia Public Library

Family portraits and religious, historical, and landscape paintings occupied the bulk of his career. In 1840 he exhibited more than two hundred of his paintings at the Artist's Fund Hall in Philadelphia. Portraits of notable persons did not figure in his oeuvre. This was especially evident during his visit to Washington. The city bustled with personalities who were making headlines and history—men like Monroe, Clay, Calhoun, Webster, Adams, and Jackson. Yet, based on what is known of Street's work, only an image of Jackson survives.

Why just Old Hickory? Was he the only public servant in whom Street was interested; or perhaps was he the only sitter available? These questions make his oil portrait of the Tennessee senator even more intriguing. For the first time on a documented canvas—signed "R Street. 1824"—Jackson appears in civilian attire [Fig. 43]. He wears a black suit and white jabot. The background and props enhance his statesmanlike image. He is seated in a red upholstered chair typical of the Federal period. A classical column borders the edge of the canvas. Jackson's left arm rests upon a table surrounded by tokens of his illustrious past. His forefinger points to a paper entitled "Fortification of New Orleans." The golden hilt of a sword, in the shape of an eagle's head and draped with two tassels, protrudes into the picture. These mementos are subtle, yet they are placed in the foreground. Jackson calls attention to them with his hands, especially his right hand, which conveys a feeling of motion. The play of light and shadow upon the fingers and cuff of Jackson's shirt represents some of Street's best brushwork. The countenance is not handsome, but it is dignified. In the tired eyes and in the lines of his face, Jackson shows his age more than in any previous portrait. Although the presidency was still four years away, he bears more the look of a successful candidate than a seasoned general, in spite of the allusions to New Orleans.

That April, Street exhibited his new portrait in Washington. At least two of Jackson's cronies, John H. Eaton and William C. Neal, examined it and signed a statement attesting to its accuracy as a likeness. The catalogue of Street's 1840 exhibition in Philadelphia mentioned that the portrait was sent to the White House, where it remained for some time.[23] From there, it somehow made its way to the Sedalia Public Library in Missouri. Apparently no one there knew anything about it or realized who the artist was. In 1901, while the library's effects were being transferred into a new building, the portrait was examined. On the back was discovered the name of J. G. Wilson of Nashville, and the date of June 15, 1822. This was assumed to have been the artist, but it has since become evident that Wilson was the framemaker. Subsequent restoration has removed decades of grime and revealed Street's name on the canvas.[24] Until this discovery, his portrait of Andrew Jackson had seemingly disappeared.

VI

Debate and passage of the tariff bill of 1824 kept Jackson in Washington until the middle of May. He voted for this legislation, which was designed to protect domestic manufacturers, and promptly headed home to Nashville. In the six months that he had spent in the federal city, at least three artists had made likenesses of him: Vanderlyn, Street, and Joseph Wood.

Although Wood was also listed in the Baltimore directory, he undoubtedly executed his *Jackson* in his Washington studio. The painting, a cabinet-size miniature (the genre in which Wood principally worked) is no longer extant. Nevertheless, the likeness has been well preserved. In the mid-1820s, it was the most widely published image of Andrew Jackson.

Born near Clarkstown, New York, in about 1778, Wood had a restless streak in him from the day when, as an adolescent, he ran away from his father's farm. In New York City he worked at odd jobs, fiddled on the violin, and learned to paint portrait miniatures. In about 1802, after realizing his ambition to be an artist, he formed an eight-year partnership with John Wesley Jarvis. Together the two excelled at painting quick portraits, for which they charged handsomely. When the partnership ended in about 1810, Wood traveled south, setting up his easel in Philadelphia, Baltimore, and finally Washington, where he lived the last years of his life.[25]

By 1824 Wood was struggling, not so much with his artistic talents as with his tavern cronies, who encouraged his frivolity. When sober, Wood could still paint a deft likeness. His charming watercolor of Daniel Webster, executed in 1824, displays skillful control of color, as well as an insightful delineation of the sitter's commanding personality. One may suppose that Wood's portrait of Jackson, perhaps painted in oils, was done in a similar fashion.

Many of Wood's works were produced for the sole purpose of being engraved.[26] Of Jackson alone, David McNeely Stauffer listed seven different engravings after Wood in his *American Engravers upon Copper and Steel.*

Figure 44.
Engraving by James Barton Longacre, after
Joseph Wood, 1824. National Portrait
Gallery, Smithsonian Institution

ANDREW JACKSON

Engraved by J.B. Longacre from an Original miniature by J. Wood.

Published by B.O. Tyler Washington City

MAJ. GEN. ANDREW JACKSON.

Figure 45.
Stipple engraving by Peter Maverick, after
Joseph Wood, 1825. National Portrait
Gallery, Smithsonian Institution

Perhaps the earliest and best was James B. Longacre's stipple engraving, first
published by B. O. Tyler of Washington in 1824 [Fig. 44]. Set in an ornamental frame, the engraving has Jackson facing right and wearing a cloak. In
1829 Longacre displayed this print in the annual exhibition of the Pennsylvania Academy of the Fine Arts. From 1821 to 1828, with the exception of
1823, Longacre had exhibited his engraving of Jackson after Sully.

Wood's image appeared as the frontispiece for several popular Jackson biogra-
phies. In 1824 John H. Eaton used an engraving by Gideon Fairman and
Cephas G. Childs in his embellished *The Life of Andrew Jackson*. This revised
edition was designed to enhance Jackson's political image and consequently
proved to be even more laudatory than the 1817 first edition. In 1825 a stipple
engraving by Peter Maverick appeared in Samuel Putnam Waldo's *Civil and
Military History of Andrew Jackson* [Fig. 45]. Then in 1831 a cruder print by
an unidentified engraver illustrated *A Brief and Impartial History of the Life and
Actions of Andrew Jackson, President of the United States* by William Joseph
Snelling.

Of the frontispiece engravings, that by James W. Steel in *The Jackson Wreath, or National Souvenir* is the most appealing [Fig. 46]. The book itself, published in the winter of 1829, commemorated Jackson's recent election to the presidency. Like Longacre's 1824 stipple engraving, this image is surrounded by a decorative border, which gives the portrait a finished appearance, as if it were framed. These two prints present an interesting comparison of different engraving techniques.

ை

By happenstance, Joseph Wood's image of Andrew Jackson took on political connotations. There is no reason to believe that Wood painted the portrait to promote Jackson's candidacy; yet Eaton used the likeness in his political biography. A few years later, the image also appeared in a rare campaign engraving presumably by William Harrison, Jr. On a single sheet of paper, Harrison juxtaposed small medallion portraits of John Quincy Adams and Andrew Jackson, clearly evoking the presidential rivalry of these two ideologically different men [Fig. 47].

A portrait lying in storage at the Hermitage further connects the Wood image to Jackson's political fortunes. Allegedly it was painted by an obscure New York artist, Franklin Witcher, for the 1828 presidential campaign [Fig. 48]. This small oil-on-panel likeness was copied from an engraving after Wood. The crude execution of this work helps explain Witcher's anonymity. Although the colors have faded, a hint of blue is still visible in Jackson's eyes, his hair is gray, and he wears a rust-colored cape with a red collar and brass clasp. The portrait is representative of the type of icon that would have been hastily executed for display at a political rally or dinner.[27]

ை

Portraits of national heroes and political figures executed in traditional mediums, whether paintings or sculpted busts, failed to satisfy the curiosity of the overwhelming majority of Americans, who never saw these images firsthand. Engravings greatly helped to fulfill public demand, as did ribbons, medals, snuff boxes, and chinaware bearing portrait images. These items were principally intended as souvenirs. Yet, as presidential campaigns grew more sophisticated, many such objects became political memorabilia. The Wood portrait of Jackson was one such image; it found its way onto Staffordshire dishes [Fig. 49] and copper lusterware pitchers [Fig. 50].[28] These glazed images carried Jackson's name at the top and identified him as "The Hero of New Orleans."

Figure 46.
Engraving by James W. Steel, after Joseph Wood, 1829. Private collection

Figure 47.
John Quincy Adams and Andrew Jackson. Hand-colored engraving by W. Harrison, after Thomas Sully and Joseph Wood, circa 1828. Private collection

Figure 48.
Oil on panel attributed to Franklin
Witcher, after Joseph Wood, circa 1828.
The Hermitage: Home of President Andrew
Jackson

Figure 49.
Lusterware plate with image of General
Jackson, after Joseph Wood, circa 1828.
National Museum of American History,
Smithsonian Institution

Figure 50.
Copper lusterware pitcher with image of
General Jackson, after Joseph Wood, circa
1828. National Museum of American
History, Smithsonian Institution

In 1825 the glass-making establishment of Bakewell, Page, and Bakewell of
Pittsburgh commenced making cut-glass tumblers, in the bottoms of which,
"by a very ingenious process," were embedded likenesses of either Jackson or
Lafayette. "The likeness," reported the *Pittsburgh Mercury,* "is formed of a
composition having the appearance of silver, and although presented in bold
relief, every part of it is inclosed in solid glass, and is consequently indelible."
The medallions were executed "from miniature profiles drawn by Mr. Wood,
in Washington" and were "intended to perpetuate in an imperishable material" their likenesses.[29] Unfortunately, no such tumbler bearing Jackson's image
has since been identified.

VII

In late March of 1825, Senator Andrew Jackson ended his second session in
Congress and left Washington, making the long journey home to the Hermitage. Only days before, he had personally extended his congratulations to the
nation's sixth President, John Quincy Adams. For Jackson the election of 1824
had been a bitter disappointment. Although he had won a plurality of popular
votes, it had not been enough to assure him a victory. The House of Representatives decided the matter by the narrowest of margins, largely because Speaker
Henry Clay, himself an unsuccessful candidate, threw his considerable support
to Adams. His action was thoroughly constitutional and no doubt philosophi-
cally honest. Yet the Jackson camp smelled intrigue and corruption when Clay
was offered, and then accepted, the cabinet post of secretary of state. At that
time, this was the surest path to the White House.

Jackson felt cheated. Of the three leading contenders—himself, Adams, and
Crawford—he had been the single favorite. Jackson was outraged at what he
considered to be a collapse in the democratic process. In his letters, he vented
his anger by calling Clay the "*Judas* of the West," who could be bought for
thirty pieces of silver: "Was there ever witnessed such a bare faced corruption
in any country before?"[30] Many westerners shared his disillusionment and told
him so in the cities and towns through which he passed. "Barter and Bargain,"
they cried; their echoes reverberated until the next election.

Tired, angry, and bitter: such was Jackson's state of mind on his homeward
trek. His route via the National Road took him over the Allegheny Mountains
near Cumberland, Maryland, and westward to the banks of the Ohio River at
Wheeling. On Sunday, March 27, the steamboat *General Neville* landed
Jackson and his suite, including Rachel, onto the dock at Cincinnati. In this
city—the largest in the West—they remained four days.

Jackson's schedule was full. On the day of his arrival, he twice visited the First
Presbyterian Church, undoubtedly on the arm of his devout wife. Most of
Monday was occupied with receiving visitors. In the afternoon he attended a
review of five companies of uniformed volunteers. In the evening he was off to
the theater, where the Thespian Society performed a specially arranged play to
a packed gallery. The activities of Tuesday and Wednesday were just as busy
and included visits to the new hospital and to the Western Museum. On the
evening of his departure, Jackson sat down to a public dinner before boarding
the steamboat *General Pike* for Louisville.[31]

Jackson journeyed from city to city, mustering his energy for the next deluge
of public affection. His stop in Cincinnati had been routine, just another
hospitable respite on his way home. Nothing about it was especially memo-
rable, except for what he left behind. Sometime during his four-day visit, he sat
for a portrait by a young artist named Aaron Corwine.

Figure 51.
Oil on canvas by Aaron H. Corwine, 1825.
Mr. and Mrs. Jackson P. Ravenscroft

Aaron Houghton Corwine was born in 1802 near Maysville, Kentucky. Like his New York contemporary, Joseph Wood, Corwine grew up on a farm, which he left at about the age of fifteen to further his education. Unlike Wood, however, Corwine departed with the blessings of his father to become an artist. He arrived in Cincinnati in 1818, a self-taught and promising portraitist. Through the generous patronage of friends, Corwine took advantage of the opportunity to study in Philadelphia under Thomas Sully, where he had a studio in the house of framemaker James Earle. No better place could have been found for the visual study of art, because here the best paintings and engravings in the city were brought to be framed. It was said that Corwine would stretch himself on the floor in front of a picture and dissect it, line by line, stroke by stroke.[32]

Corwine was working again in Cincinnati at the time of Jackson's visit. During April 1825 he was adding the finishing touches to his newest work. On May 4 the *Cincinnati Advertiser* announced: *We have had a great pleasure in the inspection of a painting of General Jackson, by our ingenious young citizen, Mr. Corwine. It is assuredly not only an excellent likeness of the hero, but a finely finished picture; it does great credit to the artist, and will give satisfaction to every one who has seen the original, and who admires the character of the man.*[33]

Such accounts generally tended to be flattering, almost as if surreptitiously written by the artists themselves. This one, however, was no exaggeration. Corwine's portrait does conjure up "the original" better than any previous likeness. Jackson appears much the way he must have looked—tired, yet in earnest and a little peeved. This is the man who had just been denied the presidency by a single vote. One would not want to confront this veteran gunfighter in a blind alley with a score to settle.

Corwine painted a western-style portrait of a great westerner [Fig. 51]. The fur collar lends a ruggedness to the image, which belied Jackson's physical health at the time. Only two months before, he had stumbled in the dark on some stairs, nearly falling to the floor. The jolt to his system reinjured an old shoulder wound, laying him up for a week.[34]

Corwine's portrait marked a high point in a short career. Seven weeks later he painted a portrait of General Lafayette during the Frenchman's visit to Cincinnati. The local paper praised this likeness, which was executed aboard a steamboat. (Jackson may have sat under similar, less-than-ideal circumstances.) That summer, both paintings went on display in the Western Museum.[35]

In the mid-1820s Corwine was Cincinnati's leading portraitist. In 1829 he traveled to England on the advice of Thomas Sully to improve his artistic skills and regain his health. In London he executed a self-portrait revealing the influence of Sir Thomas Lawrence, court painter to King George IV. Curiously enough, he depicted himself wearing a fur collar similar to the one in his Jackson portrait.[36] Ultimately Corwine's health deteriorated further, necessitating his return to the United States. On Independence Day in 1830, he died of tuberculosis in Philadelphia.[37]

❧

In a postscript to Jackson's 1825 visit, the *Cincinnati Advertiser* reported in May that Frederick Eckstein, a local sculptor, had modeled a portrait bust of the general. The paper called it "an excellent likeness, and when finished, it being yet to be bronzed, will be considered a piece of statuary that would do honor to the sculpture of an European capital."[38]

Prussian-born Frederick Eckstein had arrived in Cincinnati in December 1823. He was in his late forties and was the son of Johann Eckstein, a sculptor

Figure 52.
Engraving by Charles Cutler Torrey, after
Ralph E. W. Earl, 1826. National Portrait
Gallery, Smithsonian Institution

ANDREW   JACKSON.

Figure 53.
Oil on canvas by Ralph E. W. Earl, circa
1817 or after. Alabama Department of
Archives and History

and modeler in wax formerly employed by Frederick the Great. Following in
his father's footsteps, Eckstein developed skills in drawing and sculpting. Little
appreciated today, he is remembered as the teacher of two prominent American sculptors, Hiram Powers and Shobal Clevenger. The fate of his bust of
Jackson remains a mystery.[39]

VIII

At a point in their careers when a few of the best portraitists in the East—such
as John Vanderlyn, John Wesley Jarvis, and Joseph Wood—were facing either
despair or insolvency, Ralph E. W. Earl of Nashville was getting on quite
comfortably. He was doing exactly what Vanderlyn had advised his own
nephew—painting many inexpensive portraits quickly. Earl, however, enjoyed
the advantage of being a close friend of Jackson. Whoever wanted a portrait of
Old Hickory—and there were many—invariably consulted Earl. Men like John
Overton made repeated and even special requests. "I wish you to paint me a
portrait of our Friend Genl. Jackson," he wrote in September 1824, "with
more of a front view than your last." This last may have been a portrait that

Figure 54.
Oil on canvas by Ralph E. W. Earl, circa 1817 or after. The Hermitage: Home of President Andrew Jackson

Figure 55.
Oil on canvas by Ralph E. W. Earl, circa 1817 or after. National Portrait Gallery, Smithsonian Institution; transfer from the National Gallery of Art, gift of Andrew W. Mellon, 1942

Earl painted in 1817. Even as late as 1829, Overton was requesting still another Jackson likeness.[40]

Earl stayed busy. He received all types of portrait commissions. In 1825 a certain gentleman for whom Earl had painted two likenesses, probably of family members, sent the artist a horse as payment. Earl returned the animal with the explanation that he had no use "for a riding horse at this time, and much less talent in the art of trading horses." Earl asked the gentleman if instead he would send "*one hundred dollars*," his usual fee for two portraits. The gentleman replied that he would never have commissioned the paintings if he had understood that Earl would accept only hard cash.[41] The man stated that he did not have the money and sent back the by now exhausted horse.

In December 1823 Earl received another kind of request. This one must have flattered him. It came from Charles Cutler Torrey, by way of a letter of introduction. Torrey, age twenty-four, was a native of Massachusetts, where in Salem he had been working as an engraver. He had recently moved to Nashville. Jackson was, of course, the big attraction, and Earl was the man to see about Jackson portraiture. Torrey suggested engraving a portrait of the general, provided he could get permission to copy Earl's most recent work.

It took two-and-a-half years, but Torrey did succeed in his endeavor, publishing a print in Nashville on June 1, 1826 [Fig. 52]. That fall, the *National Banner and Nashville Whig* alerted subscribers that the print was ready for delivery and that samples could be inspected at a local bookstore.[42] This proved to be one of Torrey's last works. He died in 1827.

Torrey's engraving, framed with a decorative border, depicts General Jackson in uniform. In the bottom margin it is stated that the original picture was in the possession of Major Henry M. Rutledge, an aide of Jackson's in Florida in 1821. That original is now owned by the state of Alabama and for years has hung in the capitol in Montgomery [Fig. 53].[43]

Two replicas are in the collections of the Ladies' Hermitage Association and in the National Portrait Gallery. Roughly sketched in the background of the first replica are what appear to be four soldiers mounted on horses [Fig. 54]. The second replica also depicts four figures, but only one is mounted [Fig. 55]. Unfortunately, the provenance of the Hermitage canvas, which was purchased in 1897, is incomplete. The history of the one at the National Portrait Gallery is considerably better. Records indicate that it had been painted for John Decker of Nashville. Decker operated a confectionery store on Court House Square; one floor above was Ralph E. W. Earl's Nashville Museum.[44]

Still another oil-on-canvas copy is owned by Historic Deerfield, Inc. This likeness varies the most from the original and was probably the work of another artist. For instance, the Nashville *Politician* on June 13, 1845, reported that George P. A. Healy, having just recently taken the last life portrait of Jackson only days before his death, was about to copy an earlier likeness by Earl in the possession of the family of the late Major Rutledge. The Historic Deerfield portrait may well have been the result of this or some other similar endeavor.[45]

⁊

In the mid-1820s, demand for Jackson portraiture increased with the circulation of relatively inexpensive engraved prints. How much profit Earl may have realized from the sale of Charles Torrey's engraving is not known. The endeavor, however, was successful enough to encourage Earl in another similar venture.

Figure 56.
Oil on canvas by Ralph E. W. Earl, circa
1826. The Hermitage: Home of President
Andrew Jackson

In September 1826 Earl received a letter from Archibald Woodruff, an acquaintance in Cincinnati. Woodruff was writing on behalf of his son, William, an engraver who had worked in Philadelphia and Cincinnati and had known Earl in Paris years earlier. The younger Woodruff desired to make an engraving of Jackson and had already collected about a hundred subscribers. It was his understanding that Earl was preparing to publish an engraving himself; therefore he inquired if the Nashville artist would be interested in their collaborating.

From Earl came silence. The following February, Archibald Woodruff again wrote and asked if the artist could furnish his son with a correct likeness of Jackson. By now William H. Woodward, a fervent Jacksonian and a Cincinnati bookseller, had also become interested in the project. He promised to be instrumental in distributing the proposed print and emphasized the general's growing support in Cincinnati.[46] In light of this, Woodruff presumed that Earl would reply favorably.

Earl evidently had his own agenda, one that excluded Woodruff and his son. During the spring of 1827 he was supervising the engraving of a portrait painted the previous year. This is the first likeness by Earl to portray Jackson in

ANDREW JACKSON.

Figure 57.
Engraving by James Barton Longacre, after
Ralph E. W. Earl, 1828. Prints Collection,
Miriam and Ira D. Wallach Division of Art,
Prints and Photographs, The New York
Public Library; Astor, Lenox and Tilden
Foundations

Subscription list for an engraving by James
Barton Longacre, after Ralph E. W. Earl,
1828. The Hermitage: Home of President
Andrew Jackson

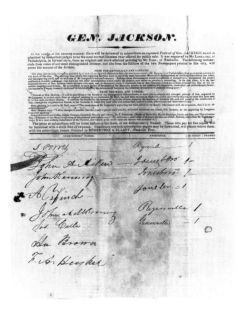

civilian attire. Based on one contemporary account, his effort was well liked. From New Orleans, a friend of Jackson's wrote to Earl in April 1827, stating that he had seen the painting the previous summer during a visit to the Hermitage, and "there accorded with general opinion that it was evidently the most correct likeness that had fallen within my observation." He was delighted to know that an engraving was to be made from it, which he sincerely hoped would "extensively spread among the people of the United States who alone appreciate properly the important services rendered by the General to our Common Country, and who will award him by an elevation to the first office within their control."[47] The original canvas has not been located, but the image is known by a published engraving, in addition to a copy portrait owned by the Hermitage [Fig. 56].[48]

Earl selected James B. Longacre of Philadelphia to execute the engraving [Fig. 57]. Longacre had already engraved images of Jackson after portraits by Sully in 1819 and by Wood in 1824. By Earl's account, Longacre was doing another superb job. After receiving an unfinished proof sheet, Earl wrote to the Philadelphia artist on May 7, 1828, and expressed his complete satisfaction: "The engraving I consider to be an exact copy from my original likeness, and am perfectly satisfyed with its correctness as well as the elegance of the execution thus far."[49] In fact, Earl considered the likeness so perfect that he feared Longacre would never be able to duplicate it, should it ever be reengraved.

Earl instructed Longacre to run an initial printing of five hundred impressions on the best-quality paper. He wanted one hundred of them framed and all five hundred forwarded to the bookselling firm of Robertson & Elliot in Nashville. They were acting as his agent and were in charge of the subscription lists and the circulation of prints in that section of the country. Already, Earl was claiming that he had garnered enough subscribers to cover Longacre's costs for engraving and printing.[50]

The printed subscription list, circulated by Earl's agent in Nashville, contained glowing testimonials of the engraving.[51] Praise came from Jackson himself and from several of his friends, including Tennessee governor Sam Houston. Quotations from two Nashville newspapers are interesting for what they said about the general. The Nashville *Republican and Gazette* reported that Jackson was portrayed as he was "known to thousands of the American people, in the costume of a hospitable, benevolent and philanthropic *farmer,* surrounded by a happy domestic circle, not to be disturbed by the calumnies of faction or the infamous detractions of political demagogues." The *Whig and Banner* struck a similar note, saying that the engraving "exhibits the General in the costume of a private citizen, enjoying the comforts of domestic life, and will preserve the recollection of him, amongst his neighbors and friends, in the character in which they most value and esteem him—that of a kind, affectionate and benevolent citizen."[52]

Kind and benevolent: that was the image of Jackson painted by the partisan Nashville press. No longer was he the conqueror of redcoats and Indians (at least not for the time being); he was now the "philanthropic *farmer,*" happy in the midst of peaceful domesticity. Since Jackson was again a presidential candidate in the contest of 1828, his political backers liked to think in such terms, because it tempered his gladiator image and aligned him with the nation's nobleman—the farmer. In reality, Jackson was a large landowner whose various cotton plantations were worked by dozens of slaves. There was never really much field dirt under his fingernails.

In addition, Jackson's domestic tranquillity became a political issue, particularly his besmirched union with Rachel Donelson Robards. Unknown to them at the time, their wedding ceremony, which took place in about 1791, proved to be an irregular affair, which Jackson's political adversaries later touted as a national scandal. The trouble stemmed from Rachel's unfortunate marriage in 1785 to Lewis Robards, a jealous spouse who had suspected her affections. While he was resolving his suspicions, he banished Rachel back to her family's home on the Cumberland, ten miles from Nashville. There Jackson found lodging upon his arrival in the city in 1788, and there he first gazed into the "lustrous dark eyes" of Rachel. Apparently she was guilty of nothing more than polite sociability with Jackson or anyone else. But no one could convince Robards of this, and in 1790 he sued for divorce, the final proceedings of which he inexplicably delayed for two years. Later, when Andrew and Rachel discovered that their own marriage had been premature, they shamefully endured a second ceremony in 1794.[53] During the presidential campaign of 1828, many Americans were hearing this slanderous tale for the first time from the wagging tongues of Jackson's enemies. Was such a salacious man fit to be President of the United States, they asked?

With the circulation of Longacre's flattering print, Ralph E. W. Earl was helping to answer that question affirmatively. He was also making a profit. Portraiture was his livelihood, and he approached his profession with a certain business acumen. Naturally he felt a strong devotion, both personally and politically, to Jackson, but he also had every monetary reason to capitalize on Jackson's popularity, as long as someone was willing to buy an oil portrait or an engraved icon. Consequently, he did all in his power to ensure that his newest print would be "spread among the people." Via one friend or another, he notified newspapers in cities throughout the South of its pending availability.

Earl set a price of three dollars per print. Those who paid for five would receive a sixth free of charge. For one mounted in a gilt frame, the price was six dollars. In a record book labeled "Memorandum of my Jackson Prints 1828," Earl kept a detailed account of their distribution.[54] Wherever faithful Jacksonians could be found, he sent engravings, whether to New Orleans, St. Louis, Cincinnati, Memphis, or Pittsburgh. Favored recipients included merchants, army veterans, steamboat captains, a newspaperman, an owner of a museum, Jackson's wife, and finally an old school chum of the general's. Some received framed engravings as gifts; some paid for the privilege; and still others were asked to disperse and sell as many as two dozen single sheets.[55]

༚

In contrast to the success of Earl's published engraving, replica portraits after his original 1826 likeness became a source of vexation both for Earl and for those who commissioned them—two of whom were Captain Richard Keith Call and his wife Mary. As a youth of eighteen, Call had won Jackson's admiration in 1814 during the Creek War in the Mississippi Territory, where Call remained on duty when his company of Tennessee volunteers abandoned the field at the expiration of their three-month enlistment. Then in 1821 Call wished to wed Mary Kirkman. When her mother objected to the match, Jackson advised the young couple either to elope or forget each other, and he even offered to assist in making wedding arrangements.[56] The two were finally married at the church Jackson had built on his estate, and naturally the Calls felt a strong attachment to Old Hickory. So it was that early in 1826 Captain Call requested his former commander and Mrs. Jackson to sit to Earl for their portraits. Jackson replied that they would be pleased to do so, and that he would see Earl about it presently.[57]

There the matter seemingly stood until April 1828, when Mrs. Call notified Jackson that she would not accept Earl's portrait of him. She and Captain Call

Figure 58.
Snuff box with portrait of Andrew Jackson.
Oil on lacquered wood by unidentified
artist, possibly Ralph E. W. Earl, circa
1829. The White House Collection; gift of
Hays Rittenhouse Browning

considered it an entire failure. She requested Earl to tell her what to do with it and expected him to send a good likeness.[58]

Whatever portrait the Calls considered unacceptable cannot be determined. In a letter of reply, Jackson tried to make amends. He informed the Calls that Earl had been apprised of the difficulty and offered them the original portrait that Mrs. Call had first admired. Meanwhile, Earl had shipped that painting to Philadelphia to be engraved by Longacre. Jackson assured the young couple that as soon as the original canvas arrived back in Nashville, where it was expected any day, it would be sent to them with instructions for the disposition of the one they had.[59]

From bits and pieces gleaned from Earl's correspondence, it seems that portrait requests routinely kept the artist busy almost to the point of distraction. Unfortunately, Earl was lax about fulfilling his many obligations. For instance, if a casual admirer happened to fancy a particular painting, Earl was apt to surrender the prize, thus leaving potential patrons waiting, as was true in the case of the Calls.

That spring of 1828, Earl had another dissatisfied customer. Again, a replica of the 1826 likeness was at the heart of the matter. Unfortunately, the exact nature of the complaint remains unclear, because the only record of it is a vague letter of reply that Earl wrote to a certain Dr. E. S. Davis of Abbeville, South Carolina.[60] Davis seems to have been miffed at having paid Earl fifty dollars for a portrait that the artist called a present from Jackson himself.

ↄ৶

At least two miniature variations of the 1826 image still exist. Unfortunately, it cannot be determined if Earl painted these, though he rarely painted miniatures. In the collection of the White House is a handsomely crafted wooden snuff box [Fig. 58].[61] A small circular portrait of Jackson decorates the top of the box. A similar likeness painted on a piece of card is now owned by the R. W. Norton Art Gallery in Shreveport, Louisiana. Both images resemble the engraving by Longacre, especially in the area of the ruffles of the jabot, more than the copy portrait at the Hermitage.

Figure 59.
Silhouette on paper attributed to William James Hubard, 1828. Tennessee State Museum

Figure 60.
Rachel Donelson Jackson(?). Silhouette on paper attributed to William James Hubard, 1828. Tennessee State Museum

Ralph E. W. Earl's 1826 likeness of Andrew Jackson depicted a lean man with a long, sharp face and a pitched forehead, capped with a shock of bristling gray hair. This image has been perpetuated in part by a puzzling silhouette, which, according to a printed label on the back, was "Cut with Scissors by Master Hubard without Drawing or Machine" [Fig. 59]. Based upon certain irregularities of the features, it was probably also cut without Jackson. Another inscription supplies additional information, or perhaps misinformation: "To my friend Edward Livingston Charleston S.C. 1828." The obvious implication is that Jackson was in that city at that time and had his profile cut by the teenage sensation William James Hubard.

Several problems surround this intriguing paper miniature. The penned inscription is not in Jackson's hand and was undoubtedly written after the fact. Also, Jackson was never in Charleston in 1828, or at any time thereabout. Moreover, the whereabouts of Hubard are difficult to trace. His early life is sketchy, but he was born in England in 1809.[62] As a silhouette artist he was a child prodigy. In about 1822 Hubard joined a troupe of adolescent artists organized by an enterprising man named William C. Smith. From country town to bustling city, Hubard perfected his skill until he could cut an exact bust of anyone in only a few seconds. He soon became the main attraction of the "Hubard Gallery." His nimble scissors attracted the attention of the Duchess of Kent, who arranged for other members of the royal family to sit to him, including Victoria, the future queen of England.[63] All the while manager Smith traveled the troupe, and by September of 1824 they had crossed the Atlantic, landing in New York City.

Between 1824 and 1826, Hubard was the drawing card of the "Papyrotomia or . . . Gallery of Cuttings," which toured the Northeast. But in Boston during the winter of 1826, hints of friction between Hubard and Smith began to emerge, and Hubard broke with the troupe.[64]

The most perplexing aspect about Jackson's silhouette is the image itself. Based on the composite portrait record, Jackson's nose was straighter than it was cut, and his chin was not as prominent. Also, the lump on his forehead is inexplicable. It almost seems as if the artist had been working from a sketchy memory and misplaced Jackson's thick, bushy eyebrows. Hubard was known to have relied upon his recollection, but just when and where he could have seen Jackson, or even a profile image of him from which to cut a likeness, cannot be determined.[65]

The silhouette of the woman reputed to be Mrs. Jackson lends even more weight to the theory that Hubard occasionally worked from something besides life models, in this case perhaps even his own imagination [Fig. 60]. By all contemporary accounts, Rachel Jackson was a corpulent woman, whose charm lay not in her features or figure, but rather in the sweet disposition with which she indulged the general and his circle of friends.[66] The black paper image is that of a young woman fashionably attired in a Vandyke ruff. Her hair is neatly pulled behind her, and she has the svelte chin of a sixteen-year-old. It is hard to envision this woman smoking a corncob pipe in a rocking chair on the porch of the Hermitage.

Like the silhouette of Andrew, the one of "Rachel" bears a written inscription stating that it was cut at Charleston in January 1828 by Master Hubard. Based on a letter dated January 4, 1828, Hubard was about to leave New York for Charleston. Coincidentally, an advertisement in the *Charleston Courier* of January 10 announced the opening of the Papyrotomia in that city. Master

ANDREW JACKSON.

John Hankes, however, was billed as the featured artist.[67] It is probable that both artists were there at the same time.

Seemingly, the circumstances behind the paper cuttings of Andrew Jackson and, allegedly, Rachel will remain a mystery. Both likenesses are identical in size, with matching background papers, indicating that they were to form a pair. Their execution has been attributed to Hubard, but even this is open to conjecture. What seems a certainty, based on the gross inaccuracies of the profile images, is that the Jacksons never sat for these silhouettes. As likenesses, they are inferior to the faithful ones of President John Quincy Adams and his wife Louisa, cut from life by Hubard in 1828 and by Hankes several months later.[68] They are, nonetheless, charming bits of Americana, which were passed down through the hands of the Livingston family of New York.[69]

X

Unlike the puzzling silhouettes traditionally attributed to Hubard, a rare print of Andrew Jackson, engraved by O. H. Throop in 1828, is amply recorded in contemporary letters and newspapers [Fig. 61]. Born in 1798, in Oxford, New

York, Orramel Hinckley Throop in his early adulthood was trying to establish himself as an engraver. In late April 1828 he arrived in Nashville, brimming with the prospect of sketching a life portrait of Andrew Jackson. He was aided by R. Dasha and John Henry Eaton, both of whom wrote letters of introduction to Ralph E. W. Earl and Andrew Jackson respectively.[70] If successful, Throop planned to return home to Baltimore, where he would engrave and publish a print.

Almost three weeks passed before Throop was rewarded for his patience. In the meantime, Jackson had suffered another severe physical attack. While recovering, he kept up his political correspondence, defending his wife's good character and his own honor, and castigating his rivals in general.[71] Finally, on May 12, he obliged the young artist by granting a sitting.

The following week, notice appeared in the *United States Telegraph* about Throop's plans to publish an engraved portrait. This paper was the principal Jacksonian voice in Washington until the *Globe* replaced it. Two years earlier, Jackson had lent its new editor, Duff Green, three thousand dollars with which to get the presses rolling. Of Throop's engraving of Jackson, the *Telegraph* reported: "Most, if not all of the portraits heretofore published, have represented him as a military character. This engraving presents him as a civilian, both in employment and costume, a character which he has deservedly acquired as that of the citizen soldier."[72]

Underscoring this theme, Throop placed Jackson in an intellectual setting, one in which John Quincy Adams would have felt most comfortable. The hero is seated in an ornately carved chair amidst shelves full of books, an inkwell with two pens, a tasseled curtain, and a Doric column. The only battlefield reminder is a rolled document in Jackson's left hand, inscribed "Plan—8th of January 1815."

Before leaving the Hermitage, Throop requested written proof of the sitting from Jackson. Consequently, the engraving, first published in Baltimore on August 25, 1828, bore the following inscription in the bottom margin: "This is to Certify that I [Jackson] did sit to Mr. O. H. Throop on the 12th inst. for My Likeness." A facsimile of Jackson's signature appeared with it.

By the end of February 1829, Throop had left Baltimore for Washington, where he opened a printing shop on Pennsylvania Avenue between Ninth and Tenth streets, Northwest. In a local paper he introduced himself as a pupil of the late Gideon Fairman, the celebrated bank-note engraver. He proposed engraving a wide variety of items, "all of which will be executed in the very best style."[73] High on his agenda was making a restrike of Jackson, soon to be President, which he deliberately postponed until the inauguration. The advertised price was three dollars a sheet.[74]

☙

Throop's charmingly awkward likeness of Andrew Jackson proved to be a timely icon. As President, General Jackson was assuming a new role in an unfamiliar setting. Many foes believed that he was ill-suited for the demanding job at hand. Jackson, however, not only filled the shoes of his six illustrious predecessors, but expanded the powers of the presidency for all time.

Notes

1. Remini, *Andrew Jackson*, vol. 1, pp. 422-24.

2. In December 1824 Jackson wrote: "I would rather remain a plain cultivator of the soil as I am, than to occupy that which is truly the first office in the world." See *Correspondence of Jackson*, vol. 3, pp. 268-69.

3. *Ibid.*, p. 279.

4. Remini, *Andrew Jackson*, vol. 2, pp. 1-3; *Correspondence of Jackson*, vol. 3, p. 161.

5. Quoted in Parton, *Jackson*, vol. 3, p. 160.

6. Calhoun, *Papers*, vol. 4, pp. 270-71.

7. *Ibid.*, vol. 5, pp. 445-46.

8. *Correspondence of Jackson*, vol. 3, p. 34. Concerning the 1815 likeness, see vol. 2, p. 213. The image by West has since disappeared.

9. Calhoun, *Papers*, vol. 5, pp. 458-59; vol. 7, pp. 170-71, 290, 299; Biddle and Fielding, *Sully*, p. 186. Sully charged fifty dollars for each image. The first measured 6 by 6 inches, and the second measured 10 by 12 inches.

10. R. W. Julian, *Medals of the United States Mint: The First Century, 1792-1892*, ed. N. Neil Harris (El Cajon, Calif., circa 1977), p. 127. For Sully's explanation of his design, see Sully to Joseph Hopkinson, January 31, 1818, Letters Received by the Secretary of War, M41, RG 107, National Archives.

11. Calhoun, *Papers*, vol. 8, pp. 525-26, 568, 580.

12. Parton, *Jackson*, vol. 3, p. 38; Adams, *Memoirs*, vol. 6, pp. 258-59; *National Intelligencer*, March 17, 1824.

13. Julian, *Medals of the United States Mint*, p. 127.

14. Remini, *Andrew Jackson*, vol. 2, pp. 48-53.

15. *Ibid.*, p. 59; *Correspondence of Jackson*, vol. 3, p. 217.

16. Parton, *Jackson*, vol. 3, p. 47.

17. *Correspondence of Jackson*, vol. 6, p. 480; vol. 3, p. 222.

18. *City Gazette and Commercial Daily Advertiser* (Charleston), February 12, 1824; Anna Wells Rutledge, "Paintings in the Council Chamber of Charleston's City Hall," *Antiques* 98 (November 1970): 794-96.

19. John Vanderlyn to John Vanderlyn, Jr., March 8, 1824, John Vanderlyn Papers, Roswell Randall Hoes Collection, Senate House Museum, Kingston, New York.

20. *The Life of John James Audubon, the Naturalist* (New York, 1901), p. 107; *Charleston Courier*, March 14, 1825.

In 1846 the Georgia state legislature commissioned William Wilson to paint a copy of the Vanderlyn *Jackson*. Wilson was a native of England and immigrated to the United States before 1836. He resided principally in Charleston until his death in 1850. His *Jackson* is an adequate full-size replica, although it lacks the detail of the original. The painting now hangs in the capitol in Atlanta. See *Daily Delta*, August 12, 1847; Anna Wells Rutledge, "Early Painter Rediscovered: William Wilson," *American Collector* 15 (April 1946): 8-9; *Charleston Mercury*, January 13, 1851.

21. An illustration of this painting, now in the New-York Historical Society, appears in Dickson, *Jarvis*, pl. 81.

22. Vanderlyn to John Vanderlyn, Jr., September 9, 1825, Vanderlyn Papers, Senate House Museum; Averill, "John Vanderlyn," pp. 134-35.

23. *Catalogue of Robert Street's Exhibition, of Upwards of 200 Oil Paintings . . .* (Philadelphia, 1840), p. 15. When Jackson occupied the presidential mansion, his good friend Major

William B. Lewis lived in the house and assisted with the refurnishing. Over the mantel on the west wall of the entrance hall, he hung a portrait of Jackson to appease the multitudes of visitors who were denied personal access to the President. The unidentified portrait was probably painted by Ralph E. W. Earl. See Remini, *Andrew Jackson,* vol. 3, pp. 391-92; William Seale, *The President's House, A History* (Washington, D.C., 1986), vol. 1, p. 188.

24. *Sedalia Evening Democrat* (Missouri), October 18, 1901; conservation report of Henry Tully Moss to Donald G. Morton, February 11, 1976, Sedalia Public Library.

25. George C. Groce, Jr., and J. T. Chase Willet, "Joseph Wood: A Brief Account of His Life and the First Catalogue of His Work," *Art Quarterly* 3 (Spring 1940): 149-51.

26. George C. Groce, Jr., "The First Catalogue of the Work of Joseph Wood," *Art Quarterly* 3 (supplement) (1940): 393-400.

27. The provenance of the painting is all but lost. Records of the Ladies' Hermitage Association state that it was purchased from a relative of the artist. Eleanor Fleming Morrissey, comp., *Portraits in Tennessee Painted Before 1866* (n.p., 1964), p. 61.

Figure 62.
Oil on canvas by unidentified artist, after Aaron Corwine, not dated. Tennessee Botanical Gardens and Fine Arts Center, Inc., at Cheekwood

28. Donald Ackerman, "Dating Jackson Historical China," *APIC Keynoter* 87 (Spring 1987): 27-29.

29. Reported in *Cincinnati Advertiser,* June 15, 1825.

30. *Correspondence of Jackson,* vol. 3, p. 276.

31. *Cincinnati Advertiser,* April 2, 1825.

32. Edward H. Dwight, "Aaron Houghton Corwine: Cincinnati Artist," *Antiques* 67 (June 1955): 502-3; William Dunlap, *A History of the Rise and Progress of the Arts of Design in the United States* (New York, 1834), vol. 3, pp. 107-8.

33. *Cincinnati Advertiser,* May 4, 1825. A copy portrait by an unidentified artist is owned by the Tennessee Botanical Gardens and Fine Arts Center, Inc., at Cheekwood in Nashville [Fig. 62]. Also, a miniature copy, signed "AHC 1825," is in a private collection. See Catalog of American Portraits.

34. Remini, *Andrew Jackson,* vol. 2, pp. 91-92.

35. *Cincinnati Advertiser,* June 11, 1825.

36. This self-portrait, owned by the Maysville and Mason County Public Library, Maysville, Kentucky, is illustrated in Dwight, "Aaron Corwine," p. 502.

37. Corwine's portrait of Andrew Jackson suffered the fate of misattribution throughout the first half of the twentieth century. In the mid-1950s, Edward H. Dwight, former director of the Munson-Williams-Proctor Institute in Utica, New York, engaged upon a thorough study of Corwine and his paintings. An article published in *Antiques* magazine in June 1955, entitled "Aaron Houghton Corwine: Cincinnati Artist," broke new ground. In November 1963, *Antiques* again reported on Dwight's research, this time correcting the errant attribution of the Jackson portrait. Somehow it previously had been believed to be the work of Boston artist Chester Harding. In Dwight's opinion, however, the style of the portrait was clearly Corwine's. Since it was documented that Corwine had painted a portrait of Jackson in 1825, the subject's age in the likeness corroborated this date. The picture's dimensions, 27 by 22 inches—a favorite size of Corwine's—also offered a clue. Moreover, not a shred of evidence has ever been found to suggest that Harding ever painted a portrait of Andrew Jackson. At the time in question, Harding was in Europe.

The origin for the misattribution is not clear, though in February 1951 *Art Digest* illustrated the Jackson portrait in an article about a new exhibition at the Corcoran Gallery of Art. The show, "Privately Owned," included international works produced from the time of ancient Greece to the twentieth century, which were then owned by prominent Washingtonians. The Jackson portrait was lent by Mrs. Albert H. Ely, who had inherited it from her father, Walter Jennings of New York. He had purchased it in 1921 at auction through the American Art Association in New York. See "Corcoran Investigates What Washington Collects," *Art Digest* 26 (February 1952): 9. The provenance cannot be traced back further than this; but in 1841 William Neville, a large property holder in Cincinnati, owned a portrait of Jackson by

Corwine, which he lent for exhibition in that city. In more recent years, Corwine's original *Jackson* has been in the possession of Mr. and Mrs. Jackson P. Ravenscroft.

38. *Cincinnati Advertiser,* May 4, 1825.

39. *Liberty Hall and Cincinnati Gazette,* March 17, 1826, January 12, March 27, 1827; Craven, *Sculpture in America,* p. 111.

40. John Overton to Ralph E. W. Earl, September 23, 1824; Overton to Earl, March 26, 1829, Earl Papers.

41. Earl to H. Petway, August 12, 1825; Petway to Earl, August 13, 1825, *ibid.*

42. [Illegible] to Earl, December 22, 1823, *ibid.; National Banner and Nashville Whig,* October 25 and November 8, 1826.

43. The portrait passed through Rutledge's descendants into the possession of Confederate General John Horace Forney, whose daughter, Annie Rowan, married Clarence W. Daugette in 1897. It was through Daugette, president of the state normal school in Jacksonville, that that institution acquired the portrait. It was subsequently transferred to the Alabama Department of Archives and History. See records of the Ladies' Hermitage Association and the Catalog of American Portraits.

44. Information on the National Portrait Gallery portrait is in the Catalog of American Portraits. With regard to John Decker, see Marquis James, *The Life of Andrew Jackson, Complete in One Volume* (Indianapolis, Ind., 1938), pp. 340, 342.

Decker bequeathed the portrait to his daughter, Mrs. Harriet D. McKean. In January 1885 Captain E. R. McKean lent the painting to the National Gallery in Washington. Subsequently it was owned by Thomas B. Clarke of New York, and then by Andrew W. Mellon, who donated it to the new National Gallery of Art in 1942. In 1965 the portrait was transferred to the National Portrait Gallery, where it has hung in the Hall of Presidents.

45. Nashville *Politician,* June 13, 1845; records of the Catalog of American Portraits. The Historic Deerfield portrait was a bequest of C. Alice Baker in 1909 to the Pocumtuck Valley Memorial Association of Deerfield.

46. Archibald Woodruff to Earl, September 20, 1826; Woodruff to Earl, February 21, 1827, Earl Papers; *Cincinnati Advertiser,* March 30, 1825.

47. William L. Robeson to Earl, April 23, 1827, Earl Papers. For the possible political connotations of this engraving, see Georgia Brady Bumgardner, "Political Portraiture: Two Prints of Andrew Jackson," *American Art Journal* 18 (1986): 84-89.

48. In the spring of 1962, Mr. and Mrs. William Randolph Hearst, Jr., presented Earl's copy of his 1826 likeness to the Ladies' Hermitage Association. The painting had been acquired by Hearst's grandparents, Senator and Mrs. George Hearst of California. See Mrs. William Randolph Hearst, Jr., to Mrs. A. MacDowell Smith, April 18, 1962, and Smith to Hearst, April 20, 1962, Ladies' Hermitage Association; *Nashville Banner,* May 16, 1962.

The painting's frame bears an inscription that provides additional information. Around the top of the oval window is inscribed the following: "Presented to Gen'l. Waddy Thompson. By Gen'l. Andrew Jackson." Waddy Thompson served as a congressman from South Carolina from 1835 to 1841. The following year he was appointed minister to Mexico, where he was influential in gaining the release of some three hundred prisoners captured during the war between Mexico and Texas. In July 1843 Jackson corresponded with Thompson on behalf of a prisoner named John Bradley. See *Correspondence of Jackson,* vol. 6, p. 224. The relationship between Thompson and Jackson before this is not clear. Thompson, a South Carolinian by birth, was an ardent nullifier during the crisis of 1832-1833 and was made a brigadier general in defense of the state. As President, Jackson was fully prepared to crush the Carolina recalcitrants with federal forces, if necessary.

49. Earl to James B. Longacre, May 9, 1828, Earl Letters, Tennessee State Library and Archives.

50. *Ibid.*

51. Subscription lists are in the Earl Papers and the Ladies' Hermitage Association.

52. *Ibid.*

53. John William Ward, *Andrew Jackson, Symbol for an Age* (New York, 1962), pp. 41-45; Bumgardner, "Political Portraiture," p. 86.

54. This memorandum is in the Earl Papers. Earl's framemaker in Philadelphia was Charles N. Robinson. See Robinson to Earl, September 9, 1828, Earl Papers.

55. Allan D. Campbell to Earl, August 28, 1828, *ibid.*

56. James, *Life of Jackson*, pp. 398-99.

57. *Correspondence of Jackson*, vol. 6, p. 483.

58. Robert Butler to Jackson, April 23, 1828, Jackson Papers, Library of Congress.

59. Jackson to Richard K. Call, May 12, 1828, *ibid.*

60. The letter is instructive about how Earl conducted business: *But Sir to my great surprise and astonishment is an extract in your letter to me of the 28th . . . respecting Genl. Jackson's Portrait having been presented to you by the Genl. himself. If your paying me fifty dollars for his picture can be called a presentation from him (the Genl.) to you, of course my full length Portrait of him painted for the Corporation of the City of New-Orleans in 1821 and for which I received $1,000 must also be a present from the same source; or I might add a dozen more donations presented in the same way from the Genl.—and besides has not Genl. Jackson the same privileges of any other citizen to present his Portrait to a friend if he thinks proper? And you I presume if applyed to by a friend for a copy, or the original copy are entitled to the same privilege, particularly after having paid me [for] the portrait, are you not?*

The Portrait you have is a copy of my original painting taken from the Genl. at the Hermitage in 1826, which has for 12 months past been in the hands of Mr. Longacre (the engraver) of Philadelphia.

I perfectly well recollect when you first arrived in Nashville, that you applyed to me for a portrait of Genl. Jackson, and said you must have one before you left Tennessee at any price I thought proper to charge for it. I observed to you that I had a copy of the one then in Philadelphia, which I had left at the Hermitage subject to my order—this picture I informed you was at your service provided the likeness when you saw it met with your approbation. Earl to E. S. Davis, May 2, 1828, Earl Papers.

61. An inscription inside states that it was made in Braunschweig, Germany, by Strobwassers Fabrik. A second inscription on the underside of the rectangular lid indicates that it was an inaugural gift (1829) from Andrew Jackson to Jacob Hayes, an unidentified Jacksonian.

62. Hubard's tombstone in Hollywood Cemetery, Richmond, Virginia, lists his date and place of birth as August 20, 1807, in Warwick, England. The Boston *News Letter and City Record* for April 8, 1826, however, states that Hubard was born in 1809 at Whitechurch. This later date is corroborated by a passenger list for the ship *Hanibal*, which arrived in New York City on September 6, 1824, from Liverpool. Hubard's age was listed as fifteen. See Passenger Arrival for "Ship *Hanibal*," Port of New-York, September 6, 1824, Records of the United States Customs Service, RG 36, National Archives; *William James Hubard, 1807-1862: A Concurrent Survey and Exhibition, January, 1948* (exhibition catalogue, Valentine Museum, Richmond, Va., 1948), p. 3; Mabel M. Swan, "Master Hubard, Profilist and Painter," *Antiques* 15 (June 1929): 497; Helen G. McCormack, "The Hubard Gallery Duplicate Book," *Antiques* 45 (February 1944): 68.

63. *William James Hubard*, pp. 3-4; Swan, "Master Hubard," pp. 496-97.

64. Swan, "Master Hubard," pp. 498-99.

65. For mention of a silhouette of Lafayette that Hubard cut from recollection, see *Fourteenth Annual Exhibition of the Pennsylvania Academy of the Fine Arts* (Philadelphia, 1825), p. 12.

66. Parton, *Jackson*, vol. 3, pp. 160-61.

67. Mabel M. Swan, "A Neglected Aspect of Hubard," *Antiques* 20 (October 1931): 222; McCormack, "Hubard Gallery Duplicate Book," p. 68.

68. For illustrations of these, see Oliver, *Portraits of Adams,* pp. 144-46.

69. Previous to their accession into the collection of the Tennessee State Museum in 1982, they were owned by Stanley F. Horn, an avid collector of Jackson memorabilia.

70. R. Dasha to Earl, April 22, 1828, Earl Letters, Tennessee State Library and Archives; John Henry Eaton to Andrew Jackson, April 22, 1828, Jackson Papers, Library of Congress.

71. *Correspondence of Jackson,* vol. 3, pp. 402-3.

72. *United States Telegraph* (Washington, D.C.), May 17, 1828; Remini, *Andrew Jackson,* vol. 2, pp. 125-26.

73. *United States Telegraph,* May 25, 1829.

74. *Ibid.; Old Print Shop Portfolio* 25 (1966): 135. An example of this 1829 version has not surfaced. Yet one was offered in February 1966 for $125 by the Old Print Shop in New York City, and was illustrated in their *Portfolio.* It was captioned "Andrew Jackson, President of The United States—engraved and published by O. H. Throop, City of Washington, D.C. March 4, 1829."

1829

March 4: Is inaugurated seventh President of the United States

September 23: Portrait painted and subsequently engraved by James B. Longacre

1830

Full-length portrait painted by Auguste Hervieu

Portrait painted by Francis Alexander

Portrait painted by William James Hubard

May 28: Signs Indian Removal Bill

October 19: Hubard portrait lithographed by Albert Newsam and published by Cephas G. Childs

1831–1832

Jackson's Indian peace medals, engraved by Moritz Fürst, struck in three different sizes

1832

November: Is reelected President

1833

January 1–2: Receives miniature portrait of himself, mounted as breastpin, executed by Henry Hoppner Meyer; sends it to daughter-in-law Sarah Yorke

June: Embarks upon grand tour of New England

Portrait painted by Philip Hewins of Hartford, Connecticut

1834

May 31–June 5: Clay bust modeled by John Frazee inside presidential mansion

June: Sits for wax sculpture by Theodatus Garlick

1834–1835

December–January: Clay bust modeled by Hiram Powers inside presidential mansion

1835

January 8: Presented with marble bust executed from life sittings in 1829 by Luigi Persico

March: Sits for portrait by Asher B. Durand

Portrait painted by David Rent Etter

Miniature painted by S. M. Charles

1836

April: Bust modeled by Ferdinand Pettrich

Cabinet-size full-length portrait painted by John P. Merrill

1837

March: Leaves office and retires at the Hermitage

Chapter 4

President Jackson, 1829–1837

Unlike the previous presidential election, the contest of 1828 went decidedly to Andrew Jackson. He won 647,276 popular votes and 178 electoral votes, as opposed to 508,064 popular votes and 83 electoral votes garnered by the incumbent, John Quincy Adams.

On March 4, 1829, Jackson became the seventh President of the United States. During his eight years in office, more than a dozen artists executed portraits of him. Inevitably, the record would have been richer had he displayed as much interest in portraiture as his predecessor. Although Jackson's images vary in medium, taken together they depict a uniformly revealing likeness of him as President.

Figure 63.
Andrew Jackson peace medal with beadwork necklace and eagle claw ornament. Silver, engraved by Moritz Fürst, 76 mm. (3 in.) diameter, circa 1832. National Museum of the American Indian, Smithsonian Institution

I

Since George Washington's administration, it had been the government's practice to mint and issue Indian peace medals. These tokens of friendship were bestowed upon chiefs and other important tribesmen on such special occasions as the signing of treaties, visits to Washington by tribal delegations, and official government tours through Indian territories. The Indians themselves wore the medals around their necks and valued them as badges of power and prestige [Fig. 63]. Former administrations had given high priority to keeping the presidential images up to date, but not Jackson.[1]

He had not been in office for two weeks before Thomas L. McKenney, head of the Bureau of Indian Affairs, wrote to John Henry Eaton, the new secretary of war, requesting authority to hire an engraver to execute the peace medals, as was customary. Moritz Fürst had engraved the medals for the last two Presidents—Monroe and Adams—so McKenney sought to rehire him. Once again McKenney wanted the medals engraved in three different sizes, and he requested that a total of three hundred be struck in silver at the United States Mint in Philadelphia.

Eaton apparently ignored this initial request, and McKenney applied to him again at the end of the year.[2] Eaton's continued unresponsiveness reflected the administration's disinterest in the practical application of the fine arts, and was in keeping with Jackson's reluctance to appease America's natives in any way. In early December 1829, in his first annual message to Congress, Jackson jolted the legislature with a proposal to move virtually all of the Indians to unoccupied lands west of the Mississippi. After heated debate, the Indian Removal Bill was signed into law in May 1830. Bold and rash, the measure was typically Jacksonian in nature.

The execution of Jackson's medal was a long, tedious, and neglected affair.

Figure 64.
Silver Indian peace medal, engraved by
Moritz Fürst, 51 mm. (2 in.) diameter, circa
1832. The Hermitage: Home of President
Andrew Jackson

Figure 65.
Reverse of small Jackson Indian peace medal

The first striking was not until the end of 1831, and then only in the smallest size [Fig. 64]. Medals in the two larger sizes were struck later. Reasons for the delay varied; they included the administration's lack of appreciation for the Indian peace medal as a token of peace and friendship, as well as the general disruption in the War Department, especially in the administration of the Indian Bureau itself. Lesser setbacks were caused by breakdowns in the heavy presses used to strike the medals and by the poor health of the chief coiner, Adam Eckfeldt.[3]

Finally, in the winter of 1832, three years after Jackson had taken office, a requisite number of his medals were struck in all three sizes and were ready for shipment. Records show that they consisted of eighty-seven large, fifty-eight medium, and seventy-one small medals, in addition to a box of twenty-six medals of unspecified sizes. Although this total was less than the original order of three hundred medals, they were long overdue and much welcomed by such frontier agents as William Clark at St. Louis, who was sent seventy-three of them that April.

Jackson was pleased with his medal.[4] Typically, he did not record ever having sat to Fürst for his likeness—the artist probably worked from secondary sources. For each size medal—76 millimeter, 62 millimeter, and 51 millimeter—Fürst engraved similar impressions. Thus, the finished medals all reveal slight differences in the portraits. The most notable and deliberate variation was evident in the largest medal, in which Fürst added a cape around Jackson's torso. The reverse of the medals bears the inscription "Peace and Friendship" and depicts a crossed tomahawk and peace pipe over the clasped hands of a white man (wearing a cuff) and an Indian [Fig. 65]. This design had been used since the administration of James Madison.

II

That spring of 1830, Frances Trollope and her artist friend Auguste Hervieu arrived in the federal city. This enterprising Englishwoman had journeyed to America with her family in 1827, with the notion of establishing an emporium in Cincinnati. Hervieu assisted in this grand scheme and took advantage of what appeared to be the city's promising artistic opportunities as well. Born near Paris in 1794, Hervieu had taken an early interest in drawing, as well as in the revolutionary underground that plotted the overthrow of King Louis XVIII. Exiled from France in 1823, Hervieu sought refuge in England and shortly thereafter became the drawing master for the Trollope children. From then on, Hervieu was connected in one endeavor or another with the Trollopes.[5]

After Mrs. Trollope left Cincinnati in 1830, she began compiling material for her widely read travelogue, *Domestic Manners of the Americans.* Published in England in 1832, it chronicled her sojourn in the mid-Atlantic and northeastern sections of the country and candidly denounced what the author considered to be the social and cultural vulgarities of American life. In one sense, it was an early portrait of the Jacksonian era. The book proved to be an instant success in England, bringing fame to Mrs. Trollope. Naturally, the work was less well received in the United States.[6]

Meanwhile, Mrs. Trollope, accompanied by Hervieu, had just commenced her tour of the East when she visited Washington. Congress was then debating the Indian Removal Bill, which she considered "a base, cruel, and most oppressive act of their *great father.*"[7]

While Mrs. Trollope wrote about Washington, Hervieu had the opportunity to

Figure 66.
Oil on canvas by Auguste Hervieu, 1830.
Redwood Library and Athenaeum

paint. His full-length, life-size canvas of the hero of New Orleans is pure historical genre, from Jackson's black knee-high boots up to his uniform collar [Fig. 66]. The head, however, is an intriguing likeness of the nation's seventh President. Perhaps because of the incongruity of face and figure, Hervieu's *Jackson* has been largely overlooked as a reputable image. Jackson's gangly legs, for instance, are almost stiltlike. Yet a careful study of certain facial characteristics, especially the creases on the left side of his mouth, suggests that Hervieu got a precise look at his subject. It may have been at one of the President's levees, held on alternate Wednesday evenings. Mrs. Trollope wrote of these, describing the White House reception rooms as handsome and splendidly

105   A Portrait Study

Figure 67.
Lithograph after Auguste Hervieu, 1832.
The New-York Historical Society

furnished. If only, she mused, the company in attendance were as elegant.[8]

Hervieu kept a sketchbook in hand during his stay in Washington, as he had throughout his entire American sojourn. Twenty-four of his original drawings appeared as Hogarthian lithographic illustrations in *Domestic Manners*. One depicts Jackson sitting on a horse in front of a columned building and clutching the reins of a second horse standing beside him [Fig. 67].[9]

Unlike this sketch, Hervieu's oil on canvas was a serious artistic effort. His decision to depict Jackson as a general instead of a statesman no doubt reflected the artist's higher opinion of the man, and perhaps also his business acumen of what was marketable as pictorial history.[10]

III

Shortly after Jackson assumed his duties as President, a young Italian sculptor, Luigi Persico, introduced himself. His object was to model a clay likeness of Jackson, from which he would later sculpt a marble bust.

Persico was born in Naples in 1791. In December 1817 he was in Baltimore with his brother, drawing miniatures and full portraits. By the mid-1820s, after working in Lancaster and Philadelphia, Persico went to Washington, where he won a commission to sculpt three figures representing the "Genius of America" for the east portico of the United States Capitol. This occurred during the administration of John Quincy Adams, who sat to the artist as well.[11]

In April 1829 Persico returned to his studio in Naples, where he spent the next five years carving a marble bust of Jackson, among other objects. Meanwhile, he shipped a plaster cast of his bust of Adams back to the ex-President, with the renewed intention of someday chiseling one in stone.

Persico embarked for Washington again in the fall of 1834. He brought a trove of art, including a collection of pictures by other Italian masters, which he hoped to sell on speculation. On December 26, Adams noted in his diary that Persico had invited him up to his rooms on Capitol Hill, where he viewed these works, including the marble bust of Andrew Jackson [Fig. 68].[12] Persico stated his intention of presenting it to the President on January 8. Adams encouraged him to do so.

On the twentieth anniversary of the Battle of New Orleans, Persico kept his promise. Jackson, of course, left no account of having received this splendid gift, but the Washington newspapers described it as the "best bust of the President ever executed."[13] Jackson seemingly favored Persico's likeness himself, because it was one of the few that he owned. After the Civil War, a visitor impressed by the likeness reported that "the shape of the head and the outline of the face had a power and decision which seemed to penetrate into you."[14]

IV

By the fall of 1829 the lean, angular features of Andrew Jackson were already familiar to James Barton Longacre of Philadelphia. Longacre had executed engravings of Jackson after portraits by Thomas Sully (1819), Joseph Wood (1824), and Ralph E. W. Earl (1826). These were just a few of the highlights of his early career, yet he could scarcely make a living. Most of the work he undertook was piecemeal, sometimes involving ten-hour days, for which he

Figure 68.
Marble by E. Luigi Persico, 1829–1834.
The Hermitage: Home of President Andrew
Jackson

was undercompensated. An exception to this involved the series of more than
two dozen portrait engravings that he made for John Sanderson's *Biography of
the Signers to the Declaration of Independence.* A number of these engravings
were from original drawings that Longacre had executed himself. He prized his
creative talents and saw the advantages of engraving his own work. With this
in mind, Longacre paid a visit to the White House to view firsthand the
celebrated countenance of Andrew Jackson.[15]

If the information printed on Longacre's published stipple engraving was
accurate [Fig. 69], he painted a likeness of Jackson on September 23, 1829.[16]
This image, done in watercolor on artist board, is in the collection of the
National Portrait Gallery [Fig. 70]. The print would seem to indicate that this

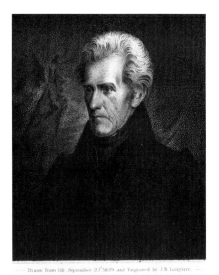

Drawn from life, September 23 1829, and Engraved by J.B Longacre.

ANDREW JACKSON
OF TENNESSEE
PRESIDENT OF THE UNITED STATES.

Figure 69. Above.
Stipple engraving by James Barton
Longacre, 1829. Print Collection, Miriam
and Ira D. Wallach Division of Art, Prints
and Photographs, The New York Public
Library; Astor, Lenox and Tilden
Foundations

Figure 70. Right.
Sepia watercolor on artist board by James
Barton Longacre, 1829. National Portrait
Gallery, Smithsonian Institution

portrait endeavor was an isolated one. Yet Longacre's mission may have been twofold. About this same time, he conceived the idea of putting together his own illustrated biography of famous Americans.[17]

Longacre ultimately carried through with his plan, but in conjunction with James Herring, a New York artist who had a similar ambition. *The National Portrait Gallery of Distinguished Americans* appeared in its final form as a four-volume work, published between 1834 and 1839. It was sold through subscription, and Jackson himself was among the subscribers.[18] For Longacre the undertaking was enormous, and it is the one for which he is best remembered. Of the 144 engraved likenesses, Longacre drew the originals for 12 and engraved 24 altogether.

Jackson's portrait appeared in the first volume of the *Portrait Gallery,* and the image was the same one that Longacre had drawn and engraved in 1829. Although there is nothing particularly egregious about it, the image lacks life and is stilted. A second watercolor drawing is similar in its ripple-like execution, as if Jackson's image was reflected upon water [Fig. 71]. This effect proved to be characteristic of Longacre's style. This second watercolor was no better as a likeness, although Jackson appears less posed. Longacre changed the

Figure 71. Right.
Sepia watercolor on artist board by James
Barton Longacre, 1829. National Portrait
Gallery, Smithsonian Institution; gift of the
Swedish Colonial Society through Mrs.
William Hacker

Figure 72. Below.
Watercolor on ivory by James Barton
Longacre, circa 1829. Mr. and Mrs. Mack
A. Lewis, Jr.

composition slightly by adding a white standing collar and including a column
and tasseled curtain in the background. Apparently, he executed both drawings
at about the same time and selected only the one for engraving.

Longacre occasionally tried miniature painting, with varying degrees of success.
Examples of his work in this medium, however, are extremely rare. In 1831
Longacre sent to the President a miniature of Mrs. Jackson copied after a
portrait by Ralph E. W. Earl, with instructions to return it if it was not
accurate. Jackson, disappointed in this new image of his beloved, did just
that.[19] A more successful effort was Longacre's watercolor-on-ivory miniature
of Jackson [Fig. 72], copied after his first watercolor drawing. The background, embellished with a column and tasseled curtain, is reminiscent of his
second drawing.[20]

V

During the winter of 1830, excitement stirred in the city of Washington, from
one end of Pennsylvania Avenue to the other. In the Senate chamber Daniel
Webster lectured Robert Hayne, his Carolina colleague and defender of states'
rights, and the nation at large on the superior tenets of the Union. Soon after,
Jackson himself would have something to say about this when he offered his
famous toast, "Our Union: It must be preserved."[21]

Meanwhile, the administration was caught in its own turmoil over the Peggy Eaton scandal. This stemmed from John Henry Eaton's recent marriage to a twenty-nine-year-old Washington belle whose background was considered sordid by city socialites. In January, Jackson directed his cabinet to stop ostracizing the secretary of war and his beguiling wife.[22] The controversy would fester for another year, however.

Amid this flurry of national news and Washington gossip, a young artist from Connecticut arrived in the capital, intent upon taking the likeness of Andrew Jackson. Born in Windham County in 1800, Francis Alexander did not fully discover his talent for painting until early in his twenties. Initially he aspired only to be a sign painter. Yet, after making two trips to New York City, where he received instruction from Alexander Robertson, secretary of the American Academy of Fine Arts, Alexander discovered portraiture. He returned home, plied his newfound skills on the local populace, and became a neighborhood sensation with his charmingly accurate likenesses. Although aspects of his painting needed improvement, his natural ability impressed Gilbert Stuart, the grand master of American portraiture.[23]

In Washington during the winter of 1830, Alexander was just entering upon the most productive phase of his career. He had still to paint portraits of such notables as Henry Wadsworth Longfellow and Charles Dickens. In 1835 he executed a dramatic likeness of Daniel Webster. The "Black Dan" portrait revealed a new romanticism in his style, invariably gleaned from a recent two-year tour through the art capitals of Europe.[24]

His simple, straightforward portrait of Andrew Jackson was quite different [Fig. 73]. A description of Jackson written by James Stuart, a Scotsman touring the United States at that time, corroborated Alexander's likeness. Jackson, wrote Stuart, *has very little the appearance or gait of a soldier. . . . He is extremely spare in his habit of body—at first sight not altogether unlike Shakespeare's starved apothecary—but he is not an ungenteel man in manner and appearance; and there are marks of good humour, as well as of decision of character, in his countenance.*[25]

Alexander also painted a splendid likeness of Secretary of State Martin Van Buren at about this time. But for reasons unknown, the artist was partial to the Jackson portrait. He retained it in his possession, carrying it to Florence, Italy, in 1853.[26] There, with his wife and only child, he established his home until his death in 1880.

VI

Given Jackson's busy schedule, it was somewhat surprising that he should have granted consecutive sittings to William James Hubard during the first week of March 1830. It had been almost four years since Hubard broke with the English troupe of silhouette cutters, of which he had been the star attraction. The young artist had discovered the more challenging medium of oil painting, falling under the spell of Gilbert Stuart in Boston and later Thomas Sully in Philadelphia. Not only did this new endeavor expand his oeuvre, but Hubard obviously realized the increased remuneration it promised. No longer would he have to travel the countryside cutting paper likenesses in a carnival-like atmosphere; nor would he have to submit to the regimentation of a shrewd, profiteering manager.[27]

Only about twenty years of age, Hubard allowed neither his youth nor his inexperience to discourage him from taking the likenesses of the nation's most celebrated figures. In an 1830 letter to Cephas G. Childs, a pioneering lithographer in Philadelphia, Hubard reported having had three sittings with Jackson and expecting to have one more. Brimming with confidence, he anticipated taking the likenesses of Webster and Van Buren as well.[28]

Hubard painted his likeness of Jackson as a full-length, with Jackson seated in a chair. In June 1830 the *United States Telegraph* gave a glowing account of it. "The President," the paper reported, *is seated in his cabinet closet, with a countenance lighted up with a conversational expression. The eyes and mouth are managed with consummate judgement and accuracy. The hair is inimitable, and on the whole, the corporeal resemblance of expression and air, are so exactly* familiar *to the living subject, that this likeness is recognized at the first glance.*[29]

Unfortunately, Hubard's *Jackson* no longer exists, but the image became popular through contemporary lithographs. It was also used to illustrate campaign broadsides in 1832, funeral ribbons in 1845, and state banknotes in the 1850s. Hubard may have executed it with publication in mind; his correspondence keeping Cephas Childs apprised of his progress lends credence to this view. On October 18, 1830, Childs published a lithograph after Hubard's work [Fig. 74]. In early November the *National Gazette* praised this

Figure 74.
Lithograph by Albert Newsam, after
William James Hubard, published by
Cephas G. Childs lithography company,
1830. National Portrait Gallery,
Smithsonian Institution

ANDREW JACKSON,

new print, calling the likeness by Hubard "excellent." Of the lithograph itself,
the newspaper speculated that it "may be styled the most remarkable drawing
on stone hitherto achieved in this country."[30]

Albert Newsam deserved credit for the "drawing on stone." Born in 1809,
Newsam was deaf, mute, and orphaned as a young child. A talent for drawing,
however, offered hope for his future. In 1820 he won admittance into Philadelphia's new Asylum for the Deaf and Dumb. In 1824 he and several
schoolmates visited Harrisburg to demonstrate their learning before the
legislature. Asked by some of Andrew Jackson's friends if he could draw a
picture of the hero, the fourteen-year-old artist swiftly complied, to everyone's
complete satisfaction.[31] Back in Philadelphia, his talent won the attention of
Thomas Sully, Rembrandt Peale, and James R. Lambdin. Lambdin actually

Figure 75. Right.
Lithograph by Albert Newsam, after
William James Hubard, published by
Childs and Lehman lithography company,
1834. National Portrait Gallery,
Smithsonian Institution

Far right: Cloth broadside of Jackson
electors, with an image of Andrew Jackson
after William James Hubard, 1832. Hurja
Collection, Tennessee State Library and
Archives

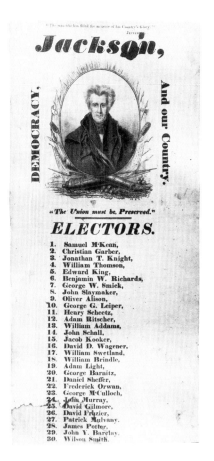

tried to teach him to paint portraits but doubted his future success, on account
of his inability to animate his sitters with conversation.

In 1827, and for the next four years, Newsam was apprenticed to Cephas
Childs. For a brief period in 1830, Newsam and Hubard, both the same age,
were living under Childs's roof. Because the art of lithography was just gaining
favor as a commercial enterprise in the United States, Newsam was trained in
that field. His 1830 lithograph of Hubard's portrait represented one of his
earliest works; in a rare instance he is identified on the lithograph as "Pupil to
C. G. Childs."[32] In 1834 Newsam made another drawing, which was published by Childs and his new associate, George Lehman [Fig. 75]. However,
his earlier lithograph was the better of the two. In it, Jackson's image is
considerably more animated and the lines of his face more detailed. Even the
contrast of light and dark in Jackson's attire and in the surrounding furnishings is more refined. In 1832 John Sartain, the noted English engraver who
had arrived in Philadelphia in 1830, produced it as a mezzotint.

VII

On January 2, 1833, Andrew Jackson wrote to his daughter-in-law, Sarah
Yorke. She was accomplished and comely, and from the family of a successful
Philadelphia merchant. In 1831 her charm and talents captivated the restless
heart of Jackson's adopted son, Andrew Jackson, Jr. [Fig. 76]. Although
Jackson never fathered a child of his own, he was the legal guardian of several
children of relatives and friends. Of these, Andrew J. Donelson is best remembered, for he became the President's private secretary. But only Andrew

Figure 76. Above.
Andrew Jackson, Jr. Oil on canvas by Ralph
E. W. Earl, circa 1833. The Hermitage:
Home of President Andrew Jackson

Figure 77. Right.
Sarah Yorke Jackson. Oil on canvas by
Ralph E. W. Earl, circa 1833. The
Hermitage: Home of President Andrew
Jackson

Jackson, Jr., was doted upon as a son. He was really the nephew of Andrew
and Rachel, but they had taken legal custody of him as an infant. Jackson had
learned from experience to question many of the decisions of his impulsive,
debt-ridden charge, and the young man's marriage seemed no exception. Yet
Jackson quickly came around to this union after meeting the amiable Sarah
[Fig. 77].[33] The newlyweds lived in the President's house for a brief time, but
when Sarah became pregnant, the couple moved to the Hermitage, which
Jackson was having remodeled. On November 1, 1832, Jackson had become a
grandfather, with the birth of little Rachel.

With the closest members of his family far away from him on the cold second
day of the new year, Jackson filled his letter with sentiments of love and
affection. Because he could not be with Sarah in person, he enclosed a small
keepsake—a new breastpin, presumably given to him the day before, during
the traditional New Year's Day levee. The occasion had been a fatiguing one.
Jackson wrote that he had never seen the "House more crowded than it was
and I was kept three hours on my feet labouring all the while under one of my
severe headaches."[34]

Jackson's presidential levees were events that received considerable notice in
memoirs and travelogues of the day. Proper Washingtonians, accustomed to
the genteel social gatherings of former administrations, now literally brushed
shoulders with the common man. On one occasion a visiting Scotsman
recalled that there were in attendance "men begrimed with all the sweat and
filth accumulated in their day's—perhaps their week's—labour. There were
sooty artificers, evidently fresh from the forge or the workshop; and one
individual . . . —either a miller or a baker—who, wherever he passed, left marks
of contact on the garments of the company."[35]

The New Year's Day levee of 1833 was no exception to this custom. It was

probably during this crowded affair that Henry Hoppner Meyer presented
Jackson with a miniature portrait, mounted as a breastpin. Although delicately
executed, this stock likeness was suggestive of the work of Ralph E. W. Earl
and may well have been a copy by Meyer. The Jackson family always treasured
it, and Sarah Yorke bequeathed it to her daughter. This brooch portrait, now
lost (identified in an old photograph in the records of the Ladies' Hermitage
Association), was oval in shape and set under glass in a gold case about the size
of one of the lenses in Jackson's spectacles, that is, 1½ inches in length.[36]

Fortunately, Meyer's likeness has been preserved in a stipple engraving by
Thomas Illman [Fig. 78]. Illman was working in New York as a stipple and
mezzotint engraver in 1833, before moving his business to Philadelphia in
about 1845. Meyer began his career as an engraver, but then turned to
drawing and painting portraits. After painting for a number of years in the
United States, Meyer eventually returned to England, where he died in 1847.[37]

Figure 78.
Stipple engraving by Thomas Illman, after
Henry Hoppner Meyer, circa 1833.
National Portrait Gallery, Smithsonian
Institution

VIII

Jackson's portrait record for 1833 is almost nonexistent. What survives are
mostly vivid descriptions of him recorded by his contemporaries. A common
observation centered on the President's declining health. New York diarist
Philip Hone attended Jackson's second inaugural in March and noted that he
looked "exceedingly feeble." Hone admitted that if he were a gambling man,
he "would bet large odds that he [Jackson] does not outlive the present term of
his office."[38]

At times, Jackson must have entertained similar doubts. He endured almost
constant pain and discomfort from headaches and hemorrhages in his chest,
and he was often incapacitated for days. Yet in spite of his physical debilitation,
Jackson kept the wheels of government turning. His signing of the Force Bill
and the Compromise Tariff on March 2 effectively squelched the nullification
crisis in South Carolina. In addition, having vetoed the bill to recharter the
Bank of the United States the previous July, Jackson now made preparations
to remove the Bank's deposits.

In the midst of this brewing controversy and in spite of his failing health, the
sixty-six-year-old Jackson embarked upon his celebrated "Grand Triumphal
Tour" of New England. The trip lasted through most of June and went into
the first week of July. From start to finish, Jackson's endurance was tested with
welcoming celebrations, military reviews, crowded receptions, banquets, and
assorted sightseeing adventures, and it all took a toll on his delicate constitution. Well before he reached New England, friends in Philadelphia encouraged
him to submit to a physical examination by the renowned surgeon Dr. Philip
Syng Physick. Reluctantly Jackson consented. After explaining his symptoms
to the doctor, he declared, "There are only two things I can't give up: one is
coffee, and the other is tobacco."[39] Physick, believing his patient's ailments to
be largely beyond medical remedies, simply urged Jackson to keep up the fight,
to which the old man took heart.

After a prolonged stop in New York City, Jackson's entourage journeyed into
Connecticut, first to Bridgeport, then to New Haven, and finally to Hartford.
On the morning of June 17, a grand procession of city magistrates and militia
escorted Jackson into town. The local newspaper reported that "the President
was on horseback, and most of the time with his hat off, bowing to the
multitudes who thronged the streets and filled the windows of the houses."[40] It
may well have been that somewhere in the crowd artist Philip Hewins was
watching intently.

Born in Blue Hill, Maine, in 1806, Hewins entered the dry-goods business as a youth. In Albany he developed a passionate interest in art after sitting for his own portrait by Reuben Rowlery. Hewins studied under Rowlery for a year, but mostly he taught himself. About the time of Jackson's visit, he moved to Hartford, where he became one of the city's first portrait painters, noted especially for his ability to execute portraits rapidly.[41]

Hewins's portrait of Old Hickory is scarcely accurate, indicating that he undoubtedly painted it hurriedly from memory [Fig. 79]. Still, it is revealing; the image embodies many of Jackson's most characteristic features, notably his bristling gray hair, his gold-rimmed spectacles, and his wrinkled mouth. Jackson holds another familiar trademark—his beaverskin hat, still draped with a black band or "weeper" in memory of his wife's death on December 22, 1828. On the inside of the brim Hewins painted his initials.[42] Two weeks after his portrait was painted, Jackson abruptly canceled the remainder of his tour. His delicate health, weakened by fatigue and overexertion, necessitated his immediate return to the White House.

In the spring of 1834, John Frazee was passing through Washington on his way home to New York. Frazee was one of the nation's pioneering sculptors and was returning from Richmond, where he had taken the likeness of Chief Justice John Marshall. Upon reaching the nation's capital, Frazee did not anticipate lingering more than a day, until an opportunity detained him. Frazee explained the delay to his new wife, Lydia. "Some of my friends, and the friends of Genl. Jackson," he wrote, "have urged me so much to take the Bust of the Old Hero, that I have consented to do so." Frazee was writing from inside the presidential mansion before fixing his clay in preparation for a first sitting with Jackson the next morning. "I shall make quick work of him," he promised, "so as to be home next week."[43] In a second letter, Frazee reported, "I am getting on with the head of Genl. Jackson very well. . . . The Old Veteran is beginning to get acquainted with me; and if I can only gain his *affection,* why then I shall feel doubly sure of his *Friendship* and *favor.*" Frazee was happy enjoying small hospitalities such as sitting next to Jackson at the dining table.[44]

Five days after he had had his first sitting, on the afternoon of June 5, Frazee finished Jackson's clay bust. Next he needed to make a mold to be used later in the casting of plaster replicas. One such cast is in the Art Museum at Princeton University [Fig. 80].[45]

When he returned to his New York studio, Frazee was under no obligation to do anything further with this likeness, since it had not been commissioned. He had more lucrative projects to pursue, such as carving in stone a bust of John Marshall.[46] Some fifteen years elapsed before Frazee seriously turned his attention once more to Andrew Jackson. He was working upon a large marble bust of Jackson when he collapsed in 1851. Never again strong enough to continue sculpting, Frazee died the following year. It is believed that a pupil of his named Nelson Swezey finished the bust, which was presented to the city of Memphis in 1859. The bust was placed in the middle of Court Square, upon a pedestal bearing a version of Jackson's famous Jefferson's birthday toast of 1830—"Our Federal Union, It Must and Shall Be Preserved." During the Civil War, a southern sympathizer armed with a chisel took issue with these words. Decades of exposure to natural elements also took their toll on the monument, which was relocated in about 1920 inside the Shelby County Courthouse [Fig. 81].[47]

Surprisingly, Frazee's likeness failed to capture the most readily visible feature of Andrew Jackson—his long, narrow face. Frazee's depiction is square and compact. The principal flaw is the stubby chin, which is flattened on the underside as if Jackson had been resting it on something. Just how egregious this is can only be appreciated when compared with the lifelike busts sculpted by Hiram Powers and Ferdinand Pettrich in 1835 and 1836. The strength of Frazee's likeness lies just above this distorted area, in Jackson's downturned mouth; it lends a feeble, almost melancholy aspect to his expression, which was noted on different occasions by his contemporaries.[48]

In an undated engraving, Waterman Lilly Ormsby, a New York bank-note engraver, gave Frazee's image new credibility [Fig. 82]. Ormsby wisely selected a profile view, which greatly enhanced Jackson's countenance. Adept at inventing devices that would facilitate his work, Ormsby employed what he called a pentographic machine to create the appearance of a shallow relief. The three-dimensional aspect makes this one of the most appealing engraved portraits of Andrew Jackson. An inscription under the image states that Ormsby engraved it after a model by Robert E. Launitz, Frazee's friend and

Figure 80.
Plaster by John Frazee, 1834. The Art Museum, Princeton University; Museum purchase, John Maclean Magie and Gertrude Magie Fund

business partner. This suggests that at least two plaster casts were once in existence, and there may well have been several more. Only the one at Princeton has come to light.[49]

❧

John Frazee had no sooner departed the capital when Theodatus Garlick arrived in mid-June 1834, hoping to model a portrait of the President. Garlick was born in Middlebury, Vermont, in 1805, and as a youth he traveled with an older brother to Pennsylvania and Ohio, where he learned blacksmithing and stonecutting. Like Frazee, Garlick tested his skills by carving tombstones. His real interest, however, was the study of medicine, which he pursued in the evenings until he had saved enough money to attend the University of Maryland in the fall of 1833. Garlick earned his medical degree the following spring and shortly thereafter returned to Ohio, where he began a distinguished eighteen-year practice as a surgeon.[50]

Garlick's fascination with portrait sculpture began in Baltimore during the winter of 1834. In the office of Barnum's Hotel, his place of lodging, Garlick admired a bas-relief medallion by Alfred S. Waugh, an Irish sculptor and

Figure 81.
Marble begun by John Frazee and thought
to have been completed by Nelson Swezey,
begun circa 1850. Shelby County
Courthouse, Memphis

Figure 82.
Engraving by Waterman Lilly Ormsby, after
a model of John Frazee's bust made by his
partner Robert E. Launitz, not dated. The
New-York Historical Society

miniature painter. Charmed by its beauty, Garlick was determined to learn the
art. His subsequent miniature wax likenesses of some of his professors and of
David Barnum, the hotel proprietor, won him attention in Baltimore.[51] At the
urging and request of John Stuart Skinner, postmaster of the city, Garlick
journeyed to the White House.

In his autobiography written years later, Garlick recalled that the President
welcomed him in a kindly fashion and introduced him to the cabinet members
who were present at the time. Jackson, however, was disinclined to sit for his
portrait, citing his busy agenda, especially with Congress about to close its long
session for the summer. He was eager to clear his desk before escaping to the
Hermitage for a rest. Still Garlick gently persisted, armed with letters of
introduction and the likeness of Barnum, with whom Jackson was acquainted.
The President mentioned that he had just recently sat for Frazee. He wanted
to know the number and length of sittings Garlick would require. Upon
learning that it would be four half-hour sessions, Jackson nodded his consent,
instructing Garlick to report back the next morning at ten o'clock.[52]

At the appointed hour Garlick arrived with his modeling wax and tools. After
Jackson was seated, he asked the artist if he might converse; Garlick encouraged it. Next he asked if he could smoke his pipe, a long-stemmed clay model.
Again Garlick expressed no objection. He finished that day's session in less
than thirty minutes. After the fourth and final sitting, Garlick spent nearly a
week perfecting the model, from which he made a cast out of beeswax and
white flake. The completed work had the appearance of the finest Parian
marble. The likeness, a full-length miniature, depicted Jackson seated in a
chair. Garlick placed it in a handsome frame and presented it to the President
who, in company with Mrs. Andrew Jackson Donelson, the wife of Jackson's
private secretary, pronounced it a perfect likeness.[53]

Regrettably, Garlick's miniature sculpture does not survive. By his own
account, the portrait was a small but unique highlight of his varied and
distinguished career. Later as a surgeon, Dr. Garlick employed his artistic skills
in the making of complex and lifelike anatomical models. He accomplished
perhaps his greatest work in the new field of reconstructive surgery.[54]

IX

When Hiram Powers of Cincinnati journeyed to Washington in the autumn
of 1834, he just missed crossing the path of Theodatus Garlick, who was
returning to Ohio. Both men were twenty-nine years old, born within a half
year and fifty miles of each other on farms in Vermont. Both were beginning
careers that would take them to the top of their respective professions, Garlick
as a surgeon and Powers as a sculptor. At that time, as in subsequent times,
America held more promise for a man of Garlick's interest than it did for one
such as Powers. For artists, economic risks seemed to be stitched into the
national fabric. Powers must have shouldered his own doubts when he left his
wife, children, and log cabin in search of the nation's most prominent figures,
especially Andrew Jackson. The young sculptor's credentials amounted to little
more than a local reputation and one or two letters of introduction.[55]

Cincinnati had been home to Powers since 1819, when his family left New
England. He went to work early in life for a clockmaker and organ-builder,
demonstrating a knack for mechanical tinkering. It was also about this time
that he became fascinated with portrait sculpture after admiring a plaster cast
of Houdon's *Washington*. Under the watchful eye of Frederick Eckstein,
Powers learned the rudiments of modeling and casting.

By 1834 the budding artist Powers had outgrown Cincinnati. Through a generous benefactor, Nicholas Longworth, he was able to travel briefly, free from the worry of having to provide for his wife and young children.[56] Powers chose Washington as his destination, and he reached the capital on about December 1, 1834, where he remained for four months. In that time he modeled clay busts of Andrew Jackson, John Marshall, John C. Calhoun, and Colonel Richard M. Johnson. "The likenesses are perfect," reported the *National Intelligencer,* "and we think that we could trace in each of them the true character and indicia of talent peculiar to their prototypes."[57]

Jackson was the first to sit to Powers. Although the exact dates were not recorded, it must have been in early December.[58] Powers used a vacant room in the White House as a studio. In approximately three one-hour sessions, Jackson passed the time by smoking his pipe and reading newspapers from his part of Tennessee. Once Powers was invited to dinner, where he observed that Jackson touched neither meat nor wine, but ate only bread and milk from a large bowl. During the meal, Jackson's secretary, Major Donelson, made mention of a number of recent astronomical discoveries. "It's nonsense," retorted Jackson, raising his thin voice, "to talk about a little spark, twinkling away up in the sky, as if we knew just how far off it was, and just how big it was." Donelson suggested that without scientific knowledge it would be impossible, for instance, to chart the positions of the stars and planets, or predict eclipses years in advance. "That's all very easy, sir; very easy," replied Jackson. "It's done by *tradition,* sir. The stars move in regular orbits. Their places are observed, at certain times, and noted; and when they come again to the same places, it's observed and handed down. . . . It's all very simple."[59]

Jackson had spoken, and wisely the topic was allowed to drop. The President had a knack for simplifying things, whether it be the complexity of the solar system or the tenets of American democracy.

As Powers was finishing the bust, Major Donelson stopped in as he had on previous occasions to inspect the work. He highly approved, except for the mouth, which he felt had been copied too faithfully, "alleging that the General had lost his teeth, or rather, laid them aside, and that his mouth had fallen in, which left him, in that respect, unlike his former self." Powers was not persuaded, but he thought best to consult Jackson about it. "Make me as I am," Jackson ordered. "I have no desire to *look* young as long as I *feel* old."[60]

Jackson never inspected the bust until the end of the last session. He declined giving his opinion, exclaiming that he was no judge, especially of his own portraits. Critical praise came from elsewhere. The Baltimore *Patriot* reported: *Mr. Powers has succeeded to a charm. He presents the old man precisely as he looks when receiving company in the East Room on a levee night. There is a peculiar position of the head, when listening to the compliments of flatterers, the chin thrown a little forward, the wrinkles all over the face in full play, and the mouth just ready to speak. It is General Jackson to the life.*[61]

The Philadelphia *National Gazette* was just as laudatory. Powers, it claimed, "has executed a bust of Gen. Jackson, that excels any thing of the kind ever seen here [Washington] in clay or marble. The curve of the lips and the very indentation produced by the constant smoking of the pipe are true to nature."[62] The indentation on the left side of Jackson's bottom lip was actually an old scar from his adolescence.

❧

During the next two years, Powers made other trips to Washington, more or less coming and going with Congress. In October 1835 he presented Jackson with a plaster bust of the late John Marshall (the Chief Justice had died three

Figure 83.
Marble by Hiram Powers, 1838–1839. The Metropolitan Museum of Art; gift of Mrs. Francis V. Nash, 1894

months earlier), which was accepted with "much pleasure." The following January, Powers was "at work upon the little Magician," Vice President Martin Van Buren, with every prospect of achieving a "wonderful likeness."

In early October 1837 the Powers family sailed for Florence, Italy. In this new and foreign setting, surrounded by many of the icons of American democracy, Powers began carving marble versions of Jackson, Marshall, and Webster. In January 1839, as the bust of Jackson was becoming recognizable, Powers engaged a native workman to assist with the drapery, "not wanting to trust him upon the flesh parts" until Powers was confident in his abilities. A few weeks later he was proclaiming the piece nearly finished [Fig. 83].

As yet, Powers had no takers for this masterpiece. He began the marble with the understanding that the bust would go to the Library of Congress, by means of a congressional subscription for five hundred dollars. Because only one hundred twenty dollars had actually been collected, Powers felt absolved of this commitment. Thus began a long and frustrating endeavor to sell what many critics believed was his finest portrait bust. In a letter to Longworth,

Powers offered it to "the good Jackson boys of Cincinnati" if only they would meet his price. At five hundred dollars—twice what Italian sculptors were demanding—the bust was scarcely a bargain. Nevertheless, Horatio Greenough, who was in Italy working on a colossal statue of George Washington for the Capitol, was convincing his compatriot that it ought really to bring one thousand dollars.[63]

Months turned into years, and still Powers had not been able to dispose of his *Jackson.* For one, his attention had turned to ideal sculpture, including such works as *Eve Tempted, Greek Slave,* and *Fisher Boy.*[64] Then, too, Powers refused to return to America to look after his own interests, in spite of the coaxing of friends.

In the case of the Jackson bust, Charles J. M. Eaton of Baltimore offered his assistance, as others had previously done unsuccessfully. In May 1846 Powers shipped the bust to New York City, where Eaton had it stored until a buyer was found. The political climate of the country, however, made this difficult. Jackson, Eaton learned, was "a dead lion." When efforts to muster interest in Washington—a city preoccupied with the Mexican War—failed, Eaton turned to the Tammany men of New York. The asking price in May 1846 was eleven hundred dollars; six months later Eaton was offering it for fifteen hundred dollars.[65] Remarkably, the price kept rising, despite the general antipathy for the bust. Powers, it seemed, could only give it away, which was basically what happened.

In September 1847 Eaton turned the bust over to Miner Kilbourne Kellogg, Powers's old artist friend from Cincinnati. Kellogg, in a generous effort to advance Powers's interests in America, organized a two-year tour of three of his statues, as well as the bust of Jackson. Then, in 1850 Kellogg broke with Powers and kept the bust of Jackson to cover exhibition expenses. Eventually, the bust was presented to the Metropolitan Museum of Art. Although Powers made numerous copies of some of his popular ideal works, it is believed that his marble head of Jackson, a little larger than life and signed on the back "Hiram Powers Sculp.," was the only one he cut in stone.[66]

Powers's plaster model is in the National Museum of American Art, Smithsonian Institution [Fig. 84]. Apparently, the artist left several other casts in the care of his uncle, Boyd Reilly, in Washington. On September 4, 1849, he asked Reilly what model Clark Mills was using for his grand equestrian statue of Jackson. He instructed Reilly not to allow any of his casts to go out, since Powers anticipated carving his own statue of Jackson someday. Ten years later, however, Powers reversed himself and sent a plaster cast (of just the head) to George Peter Alexander Healy.[67] Healy was painting a full-length portrait of Jackson ordered by the Congress and wanted Powers's likeness to corroborate his own, taken from life in 1845.

Throughout his career Powers always maintained a healthy sense of his own worth. The sculptor once stated that he had never had a more striking subject than Andrew Jackson, and he doubted whether he would get another like it. Powers held that his bust of Jackson "was the original cause of all my success since. It brought me into notice & from that time I have never been in want of an order."[68]

Figure 84.
Plaster by Hiram Powers, 1835. National Museum of American Art, Smithsonian Institution; Museum purchase in memory of Ralph Cross Johnson

X

Andrew Jackson was fortunate. Perhaps, too, as he himself believed, Providence had played a benevolent hand. In any event, nothing like the attempted assassination of the President as he was leaving the Capitol on January 30, 1835, had ever occurred in the nation's history. This event sobered the republic, leaving it somehow older and less innocent. Fortunately for Jackson, the two pistols that a lunatic aimed at his heart from only a few yards away failed to fire in the thick mist of an exceedingly damp winter day. His life had been miraculously spared. As it was, Jackson's health was precarious. His body endured constant pain from one ailment or another, and on some days he simply did not get out of bed.[69]

During that winter of 1835 the President's peace of mind also left something to be desired. Debt was his primary worry. Although he had just successfully retired the national debt, he was having trouble meeting his own financial obligations. These were compounded by his incorrigible adopted son, Andrew Jackson, Jr., who was left to manage the family's farms in his father's absence. Then, too, the French owed twenty-five million francs to the United States in reparations for losses suffered by American shipping interests during the Napoleonic wars. The French were dragging their feet on this matter, and Jackson was losing his temper, almost to the point at which war loomed on the horizon.[70]

Amid these burdens of personal and national concern involving the President, Asher B. Durand arrived in Washington with his paints and brushes. Durand was from New York and had established himself as one of the nation's leading engravers. Just that February, the *National Intelligencer* announced the sale of three of his most recent prints, including *The Signing of the Declaration of Independence*.[71] In 1828 he had published a popular line engraving of Andrew Jackson after John Vanderlyn's full-length portrait executed for the City Hall of New York. Durand's trip to Washington reflected a decided change in his career, one toward painting portraits, and then painting landscapes in the mode of the Hudson River School.

In late February Durand embarked upon his journey with two goals: foremost to paint a likeness of Henry Clay for Charles Augustus Davis of New York, and secondly to execute one of Andrew Jackson for Luman Reed, also of New York. Durand's reception in Washington was frosty. Snow covered the ground, and the prospects of his obtaining the desired sittings seemed bleak. Clay refused to cooperate, citing his full agenda with the impending close of Congress. In the case of Jackson, Durand complained of "having to dance attendance on 'great men' two or three days before one can get an answer to a simple question."[72] Ultimately, Jackson agreed to sit, but only after the end of the congressional session.

Durand waited ten days, growing restless and thinking of returning home. Luman Reed, however, persuaded him otherwise. In a cluster of letters sent to the discouraged and homesick artist, Reed asked to have John Quincy Adams's portrait as well; in fact, he instructed Durand to paint likenesses of all the former Presidents. Of those not living, Durand was supposed to make faithful copies of Gilbert Stuart's portraits.

Reed, a prosperous New York merchant and a leading benefactor of the arts, intended to present the presidential series to some public institution of science and natural history. He suggested that Durand inform Jackson and Adams of this and implored him to spare no pains, either of time or expense, in getting perfect likenesses. "I am anxious that these two portraits be the standard portraits of the nation," he noted.[73]

When Durand finally got his chance at Jackson, he made the most of it [Fig. 85]. The general, he wrote, "has been part of the time in a pretty good humor, but some times he gets his 'dander up' & smokes his pipe prodigiously." Durand was only able to obtain about four or five sittings. He would have liked to have had more. He was also at work upon the portrait of Adams, who

Figure 85.
Oil on canvas by Asher B. Durand, 1835.
United States Naval Academy Museum

sat for a total of eleven hours. Not surprisingly, Durand was better satisfied with this effort. After he had returned to New York with his paintings, the *New York Mirror* considered the *Jackson* to be Durand's best likeness. The *Knickerbocker* went even further, labeling it "not merely a likeness, but a facsimile."[74]

This was indeed high praise, but was not necessarily an exaggeration. Not since Aaron Corwine's portrait ten years earlier had there emerged such a convincing painting of Jackson.[75] It conjures up the description left by an unidentified American who had interviewed Jackson in August 1831. *His face is unlike any other: its prevailing expression is energy. . . . His eye is of a dangerous fixedness, deep set, and overhung by bushy gray eyebrows, his features long, with strong, ridgy lines running through his cheeks; his forehead a good deal seamed; and his white hair, stiff and wiry, brushed obstinately back, and worn quite with an expression of a* chevaux de frise *of bayonets. In his mouth there is a redeeming suavity as he speaks; but the instant his lips close, a vizor of steel would scarcely look more impenetrable.*[76]

Figure 86.
Oil on canvas by Asher B. Durand, 1835.
The New-York Historical Society

Figure 87.
Oil on canvas by David Rent Etter, 1835.
Independence National Historical Park

❧

In December 1835, Luman Reed gave his presidential canvases painted by Durand to the Brooklyn Naval Lyceum. When the Lyceum closed in 1892, the paintings were transferred to the United States Naval Academy Museum at Annapolis, Maryland, where they now hang. Durand painted copy portraits for Reed's private collection, which are now in the New-York Historical Society [Fig. 86].[77]

❧

In contrast to Durand's close likeness, David Rent Etter of Philadelphia painted in 1835 a portrait of Jackson that, although contrived, is interesting for its symbolism [Fig. 87]. Etter, born in 1807, was at one time a member of the Pennsylvania legislature. As a painter, he was only an amateur and is remembered for a few portraits and fire-engine panels. His nearly full-length canvas of Jackson recalls the President's commitment to preserving the federal union during the nullification crisis. Jackson's left hand points to his Proclamation addressed to the people of South Carolina, issued on December 10, 1832. On top of this rests the Constitution, behind which lies a sword, symbolic of Jackson's determination to use military force, if necessary, to uphold the laws of the land. Two of the books standing on the table are the *Life of Jefferson* and *Life of William Penn.*

The inspiration for Etter's portrait was principally Joseph Wood's 1824 likeness, which was reproduced in numerous engravings of the period. For instance, the three folds of the cape running down the left side of Jackson's chest are almost identical to those reproduced in the frontispiece of the popular *Jackson Wreath,* a souvenir volume of the 1828 election [see page 84]. Etter's portrait is signed and dated in the lower left corner and is believed to have been presented as a gift to the city of Philadelphia by the commissioners of neighboring Southwark in about 1854. The painting now hangs in the portrait gallery of the Second Bank of the United States, Independence National Historical Park.[78]

❧

A miniature portrait of Jackson by an unidentified artist, now in the Hermitage collection, dates to 1835, and in some respects it resembles Etter's canvas [Fig. 88]. Jackson's hairline is almost identical in both images, as are also the right eyebrow, the nose, the mouth, and the chin. This watercolor on ivory, set in a gold brooch, was presented to John Donelson Coffee by Andrew Jackson in 1835, as inscribed on the back, probably on the occasion of young Coffee's marriage. Coffee was the son of General John Coffee, Jackson's former commander of cavalry in the Creek War and at New Orleans, and afterward, an intimate friend and adviser.[79]

XI

An especially faithful likeness of President Jackson was executed during the final year of his administration, in 1836. This image, an unsigned marble bust, evokes the lifelike intensity of works by both Hiram Powers and Asher Durand. Whereas their portraits received widespread praise in their day, this one went virtually unnoticed, even though four marble copies were sculpted. Fortunately, after nearly a century of anonymity, the artist was identified by a chance discovery.

The *Official Catalogue* of the Tennessee Centennial and International Exposition, held in Nashville in 1897, listed a "large bust of Jackson himself (and

Figure 88.
Watercolor on ivory by unidentified artist,
1835. The Hermitage: Home of President
Andrew Jackson

Figure 89.
Marble by Ferdinand Pettrich, 1836.
Ursuline Convent Archives and Museum

pedestal) made by Fettuick, April 16, 1836, at Washington, D.C."[80] This was just one of many pieces of Jackson memorabilia on exhibition. The contents of this particular citation proved puzzling because of the mention of an unknown artist. Only when a fortuitous letter surfaced among the papers of Ralph E. W. Earl was the sculptor's real identity revealed.

On March 20, 1836, Thomas Sully wrote to Earl at the President's house. He apologized for troubling Earl with a letter of introduction on behalf of a certain "Mr. Petterich," who was about to leave Philadelphia for Washington on business. Sully described his acquaintance as an artist and a stranger, new to the country, and struggling with a foreign language. Sully added that he was a pupil of Thorwaldsen and that he excels in "works of magnitude."[81]

Having thus established that Pettrich was in Washington in the spring of 1836, it became clear that his name had been misinterpreted in the 1897 exposition catalogue. When a comparison was made of the bust of Jackson with other portrait busts of him, the mysterious sculptor was readily recognized to be none other than Ferdinand Pettrich.[82]

Born in Dresden, Germany, in 1798, Pettrich learned the rudiments of carving from his father, the court sculptor to the king of Saxony. As a young man he journeyed to Rome, where he perfected his skills under Bertel Thorwaldsen, the famed Danish-born sculptor. In 1835 he and his wife sailed for the United States, settling in Philadelphia. Precisely what took him to Washington the following year can only be surmised, since Sully did not elaborate in his letter of introduction. Pettrich probably hoped to be included among the select group of artists winning government commissions, but he was largely unsuccessful. For one thing, there was a movement among certain legislators to employ only American-born artists like Horatio Greenough. Also, Pettrich was apparently not well liked, perhaps because of his aggressiveness in competing for scarce work. In May 1842 he barely survived a murder attempt, when two men entered his studio one night and inflicted three serious knife wounds. The provocation for this attack was never determined.[83]

For various reasons, Pettrich's few years in Washington were not as productive as he would have liked; the artist struggled to put food on the table for his wife and children. The modeling of portrait busts became both a necessity for existence and an activity to fill his idle hours. His likenesses of Henry Clay, John Forsyth, Amos Kendall, Joel Poinsett, and Martin Van Buren all received favorable notice in the newspapers of the day. Oddly, no such record has been discovered for the bust of Andrew Jackson.[84] What little evidence survives suggests that Pettrich met the President in early April 1836. If his primary goal was to seek Jackson's special favor in winning government commissions, Pettrich also took advantage of the opportunity to study the eminent face before him. Judging from the fidelity of the finished likeness, Jackson may even have granted Pettrich several sittings.

The bust most likely to be the original is now in storage at the Ursuline Convent Archives and Museum in New Orleans [Fig. 89]. Unfortunately, it has suffered severe damage, the head having broken off at the neck.[85] At least four copies exist: all are marble and all are within an inch of being the same size as the original. The major variation from the original lies in the modeling of Jackson's coiffure. In the copies, it is more freely executed and stands out further from Jackson's head.

These copies have surfaced in a variety of places. In 1968 the United Daughters of the Confederacy in Alexandria, Virginia, discovered one in storage at their Confederate home during its restoration. This bust, now unfortunately missing its nose, is on loan to the George Washington National Masonic

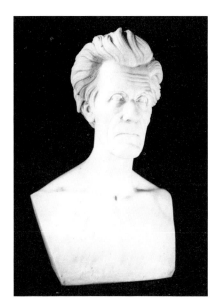

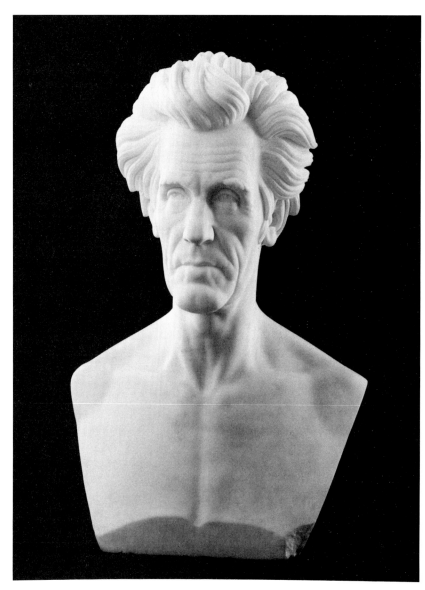

Temple. Other copies are owned by the Chrysler Museum in Norfolk, Virginia [Fig. 90], the Historical Society of Pennsylvania [Fig. 91], and the Maine Historical Society.[86]

Two of Pettrich's best-known works are a plaster model of General Washington in the act of resigning his commission as commander of the army and a marble version of *The Dying Tecumseh.* His bust of Jackson, although much less ambitious in scale, evinces the same high quality of workmanship. Pettrich once mentioned this portrait in a letter to Thorwaldsen, but apart from this the bust has remained something of a mystery.[87]

Why so many superbly executed copies of it were carved is another puzzlement. At this same time, Hiram Powers was desperately seeking a buyer for his own highly touted masterpiece. It is doubtful that Pettrich had commissions for his replicas. One can only suspect that he, being a foreigner, badly miscalculated the shifting political winds in Washington and beyond. Fortunately, over the years Pettrich's likeness has risen above the anonymity of its creator to speak eloquently of the seventh President near the end of his reign.

Figure 92.
Oil on canvas by John P. Merrill, 1836. Mr.
and Mrs. John R. Neal

ↄ

Sometime during the last months of Jackson's administration, a little-known
portrait and genre painter from Philadelphia named John P. Merrill executed a
unique and charming likeness of the President standing on the front grounds
of the Hermitage [Fig. 92]. Although Jackson visited his home late in the
summer of 1836, Merrill painted the portrait in Washington, based on an
inscription at the bottom of the canvas. Several incongruities in the setting
corroborate this contention. For one, the mansion is depicted as it looked in
1831, after the wings were added. In 1834 the house burned to the ground.
Redesigned and rebuilt during the next two years, the new dwelling is what
survives today.[88] The inclusion of the brick wall in the foreground was undoubtedly the artist's invention, because no such structure has ever been
documented.

It is uncertain whether Jackson ever sat for this small full-length portrait, given
his relatively robust and idealized appearance in it. The fall foliage is perhaps

symbolic of the autumn of his life. With a cloak draped over his arm, Jackson holds his familiar beaverskin hat and favorite cane and appears as if he had just returned from a morning walk. Although Jackson still occupied the presidential mansion, Merrill's romanticized rendering of him at home was in one sense an accurate portrayal of what lay deepest in the old man's heart.[89]

Notes

1. Francis Paul Prucha, *Indian Peace Medals in American History* (Lincoln, Nebr., 1971), pp. xiii–xiv; Thomas L. McKenney to John Henry Eaton, March 13, 1829, M21, roll 5, Records of the Bureau of Indian Affairs, RG 75, National Archives.

2. Prucha, *Indian Peace Medals,* pp. 103–4; McKenney to Eaton, December 21, 1829, M21, roll 6, RG 75, National Archives.

3. Samuel S. Hamilton to Samuel Moore, October 10 and December 8, 1831, M21, roll 7, RG 75, National Archives; Prucha, *Indian Peace Medals,* pp. 104–5.

4. Prucha, *Indian Peace Medals,* pp. 104–5.

5. Frances Trollope, *Domestic Manners of the Americans,* ed. Donald Smalley (New York, 1949), pp. vii–viii, xxii–xxv. Hervieu was not only accompanying Frances Trollope on her travels, but was actually financing her tour, in large part, through his art (*ibid.,* p. liii).

6. *Ibid.,* pp. viii–xiii, li–liii.

7. *Ibid.,* p. 221.

8. Hart, "Life Portraits," p. 796. Hervieu's painting corroborates Luigi Persico's bust, which was modeled about this time. Trollope, *Domestic Manners,* pp. 229–30.

9. Trollope, *Domestic Manners,* pp. 328, 431.

10. For more than a century, Hervieu's *Jackson* has hung in the Redwood Library of Newport, Rhode Island. Newport was the birthplace of portraitist Charles Bird King, who presented the portrait as a gift in 1861, the year before he died. Hervieu may have left the painting with King in his Washington studio before returning to England with Mrs. Trollope in 1831.

11. *American and Commercial Daily Advertiser,* December 30, 1817; Adams, *Memoirs,* vol. 8, p. 123; *Compilation of Works of Art and Other Objects in the United States Capitol* (Washington, D.C., 1965), pp. 367, 378.

12. Adams, *Memoirs,* vol. 9, pp. 193–94.

13. *National Intelligencer,* January 17, 1835.

14. Quoted from an unidentified newspaper clipping in the Andrew Jackson Donelson Papers, Library of Congress. The bust was inherited by Jackson's adopted son, Andrew Jackson, Jr., and in turn by his son, whose wife, Amy Rich, left it to the Ladies' Hermitage Association. See records of the Ladies' Hermitage Association.

15. Wendy Wick Reaves, ed., *American Portrait Prints* (Charlottesville, Va., 1984), pp. 46–47; Longacre Papers, roll P-2, frame 20.

16. This engraving is listed as no. 2017 in David McNeely Stauffer and Mantle Fielding, *American Engravers upon Copper and Steel* (New York, 1907), vol. 2, p. 332.

17. Reaves, *American Portrait Prints,* p. 58.

18. Receipts for orders (vols. three and four) dated January 26, 1837, and February 28, 1839, are in Jackson Papers, Library of Congress.

19. Ralph E. W. Earl to James B. Longacre, May 15, 1836, Longacre Papers, roll P-1, frames 1007–9.

20. Records of the Catalog of American Portraits.

21. The occasion was a subscription dinner in Washington on April 13, 1830, to celebrate the birthday of Thomas Jefferson. Anticipating that the nullifiers in attendance might use the

event as a political pitch for states' rights, Jackson drafted an appropriate rebuttal. But in delivering his toast, he unintentionally deleted the word "federal." Before the newspaper was given the text of his message, he was persuaded to insert the missing word. Thereafter, his full toast—"Our Federal Union: It must be preserved"—was quoted frequently and appeared on several of his portraits. See Remini, *Andrew Jackson,* vol. 2, pp. 235-36.

22. *Ibid.,* pp. 212-13.

23. Dunlap, *Arts of Design,* vol. 3, pp. 233-40; Catharine W. Pierce, "Francis Alexander," *Old-Time New England* 44 (October-December 1953): 30-34.

24. Pierce, "Francis Alexander," p. 34; Constance Grosvenor Alexander, comp., *Francesca Alexander: Memories* (Cambridge, Mass., 1927), pp. 12-13; Lucia Gray Swett, comp., *John Ruskin's Letters to Francesca and Memoirs of the Alexanders* (Boston, 1931), p. 213; James Barber and Frederick Voss, *The Godlike Black Dan: A Selection of Portraits from Life in Commemoration of the Two Hundredth Anniversary of the Birth of Daniel Webster* (Washington, D.C., 1982), p. 36.

25. James Stuart, *Three Years in North America* (Edinburgh, 1833), vol. 2, pp. 43-45.

26. The portrait was eventually brought back to the United States and remained in the possession of Alexander's heirs until 1925, when it was sold to a private collector. See records of the Catalog of American Portraits; Pierce, "Francis Alexander," pp. 41-43; Catharine W. Pierce, "Further Notes on Francis Alexander," *Old-Time New England* 56 (October-December 1965): 38.

27. Swan, "A Neglected Aspect of Hubard," p. 222; McCormack, "Hubard Gallery Duplicate Book," p. 68.

28. A portion of this letter, dated March 3, 1830, appeared as item 111 in *Autographs,* list 51, n.d., a dealer catalogue published by Joseph Rubinfine of Pleasantville, New Jersey. As evidence of his productivity, portraits of Chief Justice John Marshall, Henry Clay, and John C. Calhoun do survive. These are owned by the National Portrait Gallery, the University of Virginia, and the Corcoran Gallery of Art, respectively. See records of the Catalog of American Portraits.

29. *United States Telegraph,* June 7, 1830.

30. *National Gazette and Literary Register* (Philadelphia), November 8, 1830.

31. Joseph O. Pyatt, *Memoir of Albert Newsam* (Philadelphia, 1868), pp. 35-36.

32. Reaves, *American Portrait Prints,* pp. 89-93.

33. Remini, *Andrew Jackson,* vol. 2, pp. 333-34.

34. *Correspondence of Jackson,* vol. 5, p. 1.

35. Thomas Hamilton, *Men and Manners in America* (Edinburgh, 1843), pp. 301-2.

36. The Meyer miniature was still in Mrs. Rachel Jackson Lawrence's possession in 1897 when Charles Henry Hart recorded it in his article in *McClure's Magazine.* In 1927 it was listed in the inventory of the Ladies' Hermitage Association, but by 1961 the piece had disappeared. This photograph is filed in a folder pertaining to a pearl necklace inherited by Sarah Yorke Jackson. See records of the Ladies' Hermitage Association; Hart, "Life Portraits," p. 796. What appears to be a copy miniature is illustrated in Cyrus Brady's *True Andrew Jackson.* See also William T. Hord to Samuel Smith, January 6, 1977, records of the Ladies' Hermitage Association.

37. Theodore Bolton, *Early American Portrait Painters in Miniature* (New York, 1921), p. 113.

38. Hone, *Diary,* vol. 1, p. 89.

39. Quoted in Parton, *Jackson,* vol. 3, p. 489; Remini, *Andrew Jackson,* vol. 3, pp. 63, 66.

40. *Connecticut Courant* (Hartford), June 24, 1833.

41. Henry W. French, *Art and Artists in Connecticut* (Boston, 1879), pp. 71-72.

42. The portrait was presented to the Connecticut Historical Society in 1903 by Francis H. Parker. See portrait records of the Connecticut Historical Society, Hartford; Remini, *Andrew Jackson,* vol. 3, pp. 82–83.

43. John Frazee to Lydia Frazee, May 30, 1834, John Frazee Papers, Archives of American Art; Frederick S. Voss, *John Frazee, 1790–1852, Sculptor* (Washington, D.C., 1986), p. 39.

44. Frazee to Lydia Frazee, June 2, 1834, Frazee Papers.

45. The Art Museum acquired the plaster cast of Frazee's bust in 1948 from the estate of Frank M. Widner, Jr., of Brooklyn. He obtained it from one of Frazee's nieces at an unknown date.

46. John Frazee to Lydia Frazee, June 5, 1834, *ibid.* In 1835, Frazee was trying to interest Congress in a statue of Thomas Jefferson for the Library of Congress. He was also thinking about executing a marble bust of Jackson. See Frazee to Aaron Ward, February 2, 1835, Aaron Ward Papers, Boston Public Library.

47. Voss, *John Frazee,* pp. 93, 95; *Boston Post,* December 13, 1858.

48. For such a description see Henry Tudor, *Narrative of a Tour of North America . . .* (London, 1834), vol. 2, p. 469.

49. Stauffer and Fielding, *American Engravers,* vol. 1, pp. 194–95.

50. Autobiography of Dr. Theodatus Garlick, 1805–1884 (typescript), pp. 1–13, 18–19, The Western Reserve Historical Society, Cleveland.

51. *Ibid.,* pp. 7–8.

52. *Ibid.*

53. *Ibid.,* pp. 8–9, 20. Among his other portrait sculptures, Garlick mentioned having executed one of Henry Clay, but like the one of Jackson, this seems no longer to exist.

54. *Ibid.,* pp. 12–13.

55. Hiram Powers to Elizabeth Powers, December 1, 1834, Hiram Powers Papers, Archives of American Art.

56. Craven, *Sculpture in America,* pp. 111–12; Henry W. Bellows, "Seven Sittings with Powers, the Sculptor," *Appleton's Journal of Literature, Science, and Art* 1 and 2 (1869): 403–4.

57. *National Intelligencer,* March 25, 1835.

58. Before the President granted his consent, he wanted to know if it was the artist's practice to daub anything over his face by which to obtain the likeness. Jackson had heard of the frightful experience of Thomas Jefferson in 1825, when sculptor John Henri Isaac Browere had coated Jefferson's head with thin layers of grout, which prematurely hardened. Browere had to chisel the grout off of Jefferson's face. Jackson was not interested in having his ears pulled off in a similar process. See C. Edwards Lester, *The Artist, the Merchant, and the Statesman, of the Age of the Medici, and of Our Own Times* (New York, 1845), vol. 1, p. 62; Alfred L. Bush, *The Life Portraits of Thomas Jefferson* (Charlottesville, Va., 1962), p. 95.

59. Bellows, "Seven Sittings with Powers," vol. 1, p. 342; vol. 2, p. 106.

60. Lester, *Artist, Merchant, and Statesman,* vol. 1, pp. 65–66.

61. Reported in the *Cincinnati Daily Gazette,* March 25, 1835.

62. Reported in *ibid.,* February 5, 1835.

63. Donald Martin Reynolds, "Hiram Powers and His Ideal Sculpture" (Ph.D. diss., Columbia University, 1975), pp. 70–71; Memorandum Book for 1839, entries of January 2, February 24, March 13, Powers Papers; Powers to Nicholas Longworth, April 22, 1839, Powers Papers.

64. William Kloss, *Treasures from the National Museum of American Art* (Washington, D.C., 1985), p. 189.

65. Charles J. M. Eaton to Powers, May 29, July 12, December 10, 1846, and January 28,

1847, Powers Papers. For other failed attempts to dispose of the bust see John Slidell to Powers, August 22, 1841, and Isaiah Townsend to Powers, September 15, 1842, *ibid.*

66. Eaton to Powers, September 28, 1847, and January 18, 1850, *ibid.;* Richard P. Wunder, "Hiram Powers, Vermont Sculptor, 1805–1873," unpublished manuscript, curatorial files, National Museum of American Art, p. 186. For many years the bust by Luigi Persico at the Hermitage was misattributed to Powers, in spite of the inscription on the back. Colonel Andrew Jackson III inherited the Persico bust and apparently perpetuated the misattribution when he lent it to an art exhibition in Cincinnati in 1896. Then in 1897 Charles Henry Hart confused it in his article on Jackson portraiture. See Hart, "Life Portraits," p. 796; records of the Catalog of American Portraits.

67. Powers to Boyd Reilly, September 4, 1849; Powers to Theodore Dehon, June 22, 1859; George P. A. Healy to Powers, September 12, 1859, Powers Papers.

68. Powers to Reilly, January 31, 1839, *ibid.;* Lester, *Artist, Merchant, and Statesman,* p. 66.

69. Remini, *Andrew Jackson,* vol. 3, pp. 228–30, 237–38.

70. *Ibid.;* Parton, *Jackson,* vol. 3, pp. 580–82.

71. *National Intelligencer,* February 7, 1835.

72. Asher B. Durand to Mary Durand, February 28, 1835, Asher B. Durand Papers, Archives of American Art; John Durand, *The Life and Times of A. B. Durand* (New York, 1894), pp. 107–8. Henry Clay also refused to sit for Hiram Powers. See Powers to William C. Preston, March 29, 1839, Powers Papers.

73. Durand to Mary Durand, March 5, 1835; Luman Reed to Durand, March 10, 11, 12, and 17, 1835, Durand Papers.

74. Durand to John Durand, March 15, 1835; Durand to Mary Durand, March 17, 1835, *ibid.;* Oliver, *Portraits of Adams,* p. 169; *New York Mirror,* May 23, 1835; New York *Knickerbocker* 5 (1835): 552.

75. That spring of 1835, Durand exhibited his *Jackson* in the annual exhibition of the National Academy of Design. A local paper commented on the previous lack of good likenesses of Jackson. "There is one now," the paper added, "in the Exhibition, by Durand, lately painted, and a most excellent one indeed, but it represents the hero in his old age, and is much less interesting than if taken at an earlier period of life, when the features were unbroken and stamped with visible character." See the *Nashville Union,* June 10, 1835; *National Academy of Design Exhibition Record, 1826–1860* (New York, 1943), vol. 1, p. 135.

76. Quoted in Parton, *Jackson,* vol. 3, p. 598.

77. Reed died in June 1836. The paintings remained in family hands and were displayed in a gallery in Reed's house. John Quincy Adams visited in 1840 and commented on seeing the seven presidential likenesses hanging in their proper order. Reed's heirs relinquished the collection, which through private subscription became the New York Gallery of Fine Arts. In 1858 this collection, including the copy of Jackson, was transferred to the New-York Historical Society. See Oliver, *Portraits of Adams,* pp. 175, 179.

78. Harry B. Etter to Wilfred Jordan, January 1916, records of Independence National Historical Park, Philadelphia.

79. The miniature remained in the hands of Coffee's descendants until 1969, when the Ladies' Hermitage Association purchased it from Harry F. Long II. See records of the Ladies' Hermitage Association.

Another work that can be dated to 1835 is a rare lithograph of Jackson by John T. Bowen, an Englishman who was working in New York City in the 1830s. Bowen's image, purportedly drawn from life, is a head-and-shoulders depiction. A wooden quality about it is reminiscent of the work of Ralph E. W. Earl. Also in 1835 at the National Academy of Design exhibition, a case of "conchylia portraits" of General Andrew Jackson was on view. This represented some of the first work of George W. Jamison, a part-time sculptor turned actor who became a familiar figure on the New York stage. See *Old Print Shop Portfolio* 47 (1987): 25; *National Academy of Design Exhibition Record, 1826–1860,* vol. 1, p. 264.

80. *The Official Catalogue of the Tennessee Centennial and International Exposition, Nashville, Tennessee, U.S.A., May 1st to October 31st, 1897* (Nashville, Tenn., 1897), p. 106.

81. Thomas Sully to Earl, March 20, 1836, Earl Papers.

82. See Pettrich files in Catalog of American Portraits.

83. R. L. Stehle, "Ferdinand Pettrich in America," *Pennsylvania History* 33 (October 1966): 389-98, 403-4; Craven, *Sculpture in America,* p. 68; *National Intelligencer,* April 25, 1836, May 31 and June 4, 1842; *Daily Evening Transcript* (Boston), June 1, 1842.

84. *Daily Evening Transcript,* April 20, 1838; *New York Evening Post,* July 10, 1840.

85. An illustration made before its ill fate appeared in the second volume of Marquis James's Pulitzer Prize-winning biography, *The Life of Andrew Jackson* (1938). The image was then owned by Dr. Isaac M. Cline of New Orleans and was on loan to the Louisiana State Museum. In 1939 the Chalmette Chapter of the United States Daughters of 1812 purchased it, and they too loaned it to the museum, in which they shared organizational facilities. When this arrangement was terminated, they disposed of their possessions. The bust of Jackson went to the Ursulines. See Sr. Joan Marie Aycock to James G. Barber, November 30, 1988, records of the Catalog of American Portraits.

86. The Chrysler Museum's *Jackson* appeared on the cover of *Antiques* magazine in September 1964 and was credited then as being in the collection of James H. Ricau. He purchased it at a junk shop near Providence, Rhode Island, in about 1955.

In 1906 the Historical Society of Pennsylvania accepted as a gift a marble bust of Jackson from Mrs. F. F. Stilson and Mrs. S. H. Fay.

The Maine Historical Society's *Jackson* lacks any records about its acquisition, which suggests that it has been in the collection since the nineteenth century, when accession records were not systematically kept. See records of the Catalog of American Portraits.

87. Stehle, "Ferdinand Pettrich," pp. 406-7.

88. Stanley F. Horn, *The Hermitage, Home of Old Hickory* (Richmond, Va., 1938), pp. 22-26.

89. The canvas, inscribed on the front "J. P. Merrill Wash 1836," was purchased in the mid-1980s from the Vose Gallery in Boston by Mr. and Mrs. John R. Neal. It now hangs in their restored property, Clifton Place, the former home of General Gideon J. Pillow. In 1941 the portrait was displayed in the New York art gallery of C. W. Lyon, Inc., and in 1842 it was included in the annual exhibition of the Pennsylvania Academy of the Fine Arts. See New York *Sun,* February 1, 1941; Rutledge, *PAFA Exhibition Record,* p. 140.

1829
Jackson invites Earl to live in presidential mansion

1830
Cabinet-size full-length portrait painted by Earl, showing Jackson on grounds of Hermitage

1831-1832
Earl's 1830 portrait lithographed by John Henry Bufford and published by William S. Pendleton

1833-1836
Portrait series of Jackson in military uniform painted by Earl, including canvas depicting the general astride Sam Patch

1836-1837
December-January: Large full-length "National Picture" painted by Earl for the city of Washington

Chapter 5

Ralph E. W. Earl, the "King's Painter"

Ralph Eleaser Whiteside Earl was truly a phenomenon, wryly observed John James Audubon in New Orleans in 1821 after viewing a portrait of Jackson. Audubon, himself a meticulous naturalist painter, based his judgment solely on what he considered to be the inferior quality of Earl's work. More astounding, however, was the sheer quantity of it. During Jackson's eight years in the White House, Earl painted more than two dozen portraits of the President. The variety of sizes, settings, and poses in Earl's canvases was seemingly endless and the demand seemingly insatiable. Jackson, however, always looked the same, as if the artist had reproduced his facial features with a large rubber stamp!

I

It all began in 1817, when Earl arrived at the Hermitage to paint a portrait of a man he did not yet know but had heard much about. Before the year was over, he had completed at least nine likenesses of the hero of New Orleans. As a frequent guest at the Hermitage, Earl enjoyed a sense of family under Jackson's roof. The general—who always spelled Earl's name with a persistent final "e"—conferred on his good friend the affectionate title of colonel. Yet Earl did not become a permanent member of the household until after the general moved into the presidential mansion. Until that time, the artist mostly enjoyed a life of his own; he had his museum in town to look after, and some winters he painted his way down the Mississippi River valley to New Orleans.[1]

Because of Earl's affection for the Jacksons, he routinely did favors for them. For instance, when in Nashville, Earl checked the post office for Rachel in her husband's absence. During the presidential contest of 1828, Earl smoothed Jackson's feathers, ruffled by the malicious opposition press, with letters of sympathetic outrage.[2]

The best indicator of how intimately Earl was connected with the Jacksons surfaced in the family's financial ledgers. As early as 1818, and for the rest of his life, Earl was beholden to the general for periodic financial assistance. When his commissions were either scant or delayed, it was not uncommon for Jackson to write him a check for any amount between twenty and one hundred twenty dollars.[3]

Because of Rachel's death on December 22, 1828, the two widowers now shared a mutual empathy in addition to their common residence, the White House. Jackson found it to be a terribly lonely abode. Not even the press of new business—the seating of the new cabinet or the winnowing of hundreds of applicants—could dismiss thoughts of Rachel. Only days after Jackson took office he was inquiring of Earl, who was still in Nashville, about the progress on her tomb and lamenting that the artist could not join him in Washington.[4]

Earl arrived soon enough with his canvases, paints, and brushes. He unpacked his belongings in a second-story room on the northeast side of the mansion. Other occupants at this time included Major William B. Lewis and Jackson's secretary, Andrew Jackson Donelson, his wife Emily, and their children. Earl was privy to the day-to-day business of Jackson's administration. For instance, it was in his studio that members of the Kitchen Cabinet drafted the famous veto on the bill to recharter the Bank of the United States.[5] While the great issues of the day were hammered out, Earl kept at his easel, seemingly oblivious to it all.

Earl was a quiet, gentle person, the perfect companion for the headstrong old warrior on walks about Washington and on rides into the neighboring countryside. Earl usually accompanied the President on long-distance trips as well. Jackson no doubt saw in the younger man a link to his own past. In part, it was through Earl's portraits that Jackson clung to those most dear to him. Earl painted several likenesses of Rachel, which never failed to stir Andrew's heart. In July of 1830, during a visit back to the Hermitage, Earl recalled that scarcely had Jackson reached the house before he visited Rachel's grave.[6] He then entered the mansion teary-eyed, excused himself for his emotion, and went immediately into the front parlor where hung a portrait of his wife. The sight of her only compounded his grief.

In James Parton's nineteenth-century biography of Jackson the author wrote, "it was well understood by the seekers of presidential favor that it did no harm to order a portrait of General Jackson from Ralph E. W. Earl."[7] This may or may not have been true, but regardless of the motive, it seemed that the majority of Jackson's good friends had paintings by Earl.

A typical request arrived in the form of a letter addressed to Earl at the President's house. The artist received at least three such letters between March and October of 1834. One was from Captain William H. Chase, who requested Earl to inscribe near the lower corners of his picture the dates of Jackson's Bank veto message and of the paper read to the cabinet on the removal of the deposits. Another letter came from C. Biddle of Philadelphia, who was writing on behalf of Samuel Rhoads Fisher. He was inquiring about a full-length portrait for which Fisher had contracted with Earl several years earlier. Earl received another letter from Philadelphia, this one from a married couple desiring a locket-size miniature of Rachel Jackson, as well as a cameo image of the President.[8] Besides the intrinsic value of such a portrait as a true and original likeness, the couple would treasure it as an heirloom. Another portrait that passed through family hands was painted by Earl in 1834, depicting Jackson wearing a cape lined in red [Fig. 93].[9]

Figure 93.
Oil on panel by Ralph E. W. Earl, 1834.
Mr. R. Gwin Follis

II

Not every portrait Earl painted was commissioned; sometimes he produced works that he retained temporarily. Such was the case in the spring of 1831. The previous year Earl had executed a small, full-length likeness of Jackson standing jauntily on the grounds of the Hermitage. He is depicted wearing an open cape, and his right hand grasps his white beaverskin hat and walking stick, while his other hand clutches a glove. Earl once referred to this likeness as "Farmer Jackson" [Fig. 94].[10] In reality, Jackson was a large landowner, a country squire in the mold of the prosperous southern planters. But, regardless of how Earl interpreted Jackson, he succeeded admirably in portraying the President at the height of his grandeur.

Figure 94.
Oil on canvas by Ralph E. W. Earl, 1830.
Private collection

The portrait was Earl's best of Jackson up to that time. Naturally, it won admirers, one of whom was George Bates of Boston. In April 1831 Bates and his son visited Washington and met Jackson and Earl at the White House. Bates, a physician and art connoisseur, discussed with Earl the possibility of having the portrait engraved. On April 29 Bates, home again in Boston, wrote to Earl recommending that William S. Pendleton, the proprietor of Boston's first successful lithography firm, execute the proposed work. Bates enclosed three of Pendleton's prints for Earl's inspection.[11] A lengthy correspondence ensued between Bates, Earl, and Pendleton.

In late June Earl escorted the President to the Rip Raps, a government-owned islet off of Hampton Roads, Virginia. This proved to be a favorite retreat for Jackson when the capital city turned muggy, and that summer Jackson desperately needed a recess after a tumultuous winter and spring. In February, he had read his Vice President, John C. Calhoun, out of the Democratic party. Calhoun's offense was his public disclosure that he had supported Jackson's censure in 1818 for his conduct in the Seminole War campaign in Florida. The Carolinian's ambitions for the presidency further alienated Jackson, who was himself considering running for a second term. Then in April, the President accepted the resignations of his cabinet, which had grown irreconcilably divided. Van Buren's rivalry with Calhoun had created underlying friction, and the Peggy Eaton scandal had shot sparks throughout the administration. From the start, Jackson stubbornly defended the reputation of this maligned wife of Secretary of War John H. Eaton.

Meanwhile, the "Farmer Jackson" was shipped to Boston in July. Work on the lithograph proceeded in the hands of John Henry Bufford, an apprentice in Pendleton's firm. In August, Bates wrote to William B. Lewis, informing him of the progress: *I am in hopes this picture will be worthy* [of] *the painter and of the original, it has been remarked by many that almost all the prints and paintings of Gen. Jackson were mere caricatures. They have had the strong lines of his features magnified rather than softened, whereas Mr. Earl's portrait gives that expression of frankness and mild benevolence which every one who has seen him always spoke of and which have been remarkably characteristic of his whole life.*[12]

Bates requested Earl's permission to allow the painting to go on public exhibition for a short while, promising that it would not delay the printing process. In another letter he informed the artist of an eager buyer; if Earl was interested in selling the portrait, he wrote, he should state his price.[13]

By October 26, Earl received from Bates a proof impression. He was distressed at what he saw, as were the President and his friends. It "is altogether too black and woolly," Earl complained to Bates, "and wants that clearness of touch and brilliancy I expected from a lithograph of Mr. Pendleton." Earl instructed how best to correct the damage. *The entire person of the President from head to foot, would have to be altered, to make the print acceptable; and this would not be attempted without running the risk of making a botch of the whole. The shortest plan, and the safest, will, therefore, be to* obliterate the drawing *from the stone.*[14]

Pendleton understood perfectly the reasons for the failure, blaming the poor impression on a long spell of rainy weather before it was cold enough to warrant the building of a fire. Consequently, the copy was continuously exposed to the damp atmosphere and "the alkali of the Crayons absorbed so much moisture as to diffuse its qualities with those of the other components of the Crayons below the upper, down to the lower surface of the Stone."[15] He explained further that the problem was not perceptible before printing, and he hoped that Earl would give him a second chance.

Pendleton received his wish. On March 14, 1832, he sent Earl, via Bates, a

Figure 95.
Lithograph by John Henry Bufford, after Ralph E. W. Earl, published by Pendleton lithography company, 1832. National Portrait Gallery, Smithsonian Institution; gift of Mrs. Katie Louchheim

Figure 96.
Oil on canvas by Ralph E. W. Earl, circa 1833. Private collection

proof sheet of the newest lithograph. Earl responded enthusiastically the next week. Pendleton advised Earl that subsequent impressions would be "firmer, fuller, & generally better." Earl, hoping that this would be true, was concerned about the lines of Jackson's face, which were "scarcely visible" in the proof. Particularly he thought the line around the brim of the hat should be defined more to distinguish it from the sky. Finally, he wanted the inscription "At the Hermitage, 1830," placed under Jackson's signature so that it would be perfectly clear where he was standing.[16]

Bates, who was active in seeing that the lithograph received adequate newspaper publicity and a wide distribution, consulted Earl about the sale price. Most subscribers, he stated, would not be wealthy patrons of the fine arts. Rather, the majority would be "men devoted in heart to our excellent President and who are therefore desirous of possessing the best likeness of him at a cheap rate." In Boston, where Jackson had few supporters, Bates predicted a low number of sales and recommended that the first impressions be sold for five dollars each and later impressions be sold for three dollars.[17]

By the end of July, 950 impressions had been sent to New York, Albany, Philadelphia, Washington, Norfolk, Charleston, New Orleans, Cincinnati, Nashville, and Louisville. Just in time for the forthcoming presidential election, Bates singled out Baltimore, which would be hosting the Democratic-Republican Convention in late May. "The excitement of the election will help the sale and the presence of the picture will help the election," Bates predicted.[18] It is questionable just how successful the lithograph was as a commercial endeavor, much less as a political icon [Fig. 95].[19] As late as December 1833, a dealer in Philadelphia reported selling only seven impressions, and this was with a 25 percent discount.

❧

Meanwhile, on March 20, 1832, Bates informed Earl that the "Farmer Jackson" painting was being shipped to him that week. Earl apparently had no interest in selling it at that time, in spite of having at least one eager buyer available. Shortly thereafter it came into the possession of Francis Preston Blair, and is still in the hands of his descendants.[20] In contrast to the lithograph, the painting exhibits a subtle but interesting detail. The columned, domed tomb of Rachel Jackson is clearly visible in the background beside the mansion house, which is depicted before the front portico and wings were added in 1831. Although contemporary newspaper accounts mentioned the inclusion of Rachel's tomb in the lithograph, it was described as a gable-roofed structure with a window. The domed memorial was not built until December 1831, many months after Earl had painted his original likeness. Naturally, an accurate portrayal of it would not have appeared in the original painting, from which Bufford executed the lithograph. Yet upon careful inspection of the canvas, it is evident that Earl later painted the columned tomb over the old structure. Surprisingly, he did not first blot out this area with new paint, because the original lines of the roof and window are faintly visible. These would not be perceptible without the lithographic image as a guide.

A copy of this portrait is in a private collection and differs significantly [Fig. 96]. Jackson has been depicted without spectacles, and his entire countenance has been slightly altered. Three horses have been added in the foreground to his right, and the grapevine no longer spirals gracefully up the tree beside him.

This portrait may well be the one mentioned in a letter of May 21, 1833, from John H. Eaton in Washington to Joseph Hemphill of Philadelphia. Hemphill, a counselor-at-law, was seeking a copy of Earl's "Farmer Jackson," and he made his application to the artist through Eaton. In his reply, Eaton men-

Figure 97. Above.
Oil on canvas by Ralph E. W. Earl, circa
1830. The Daughters of the American
Revolution Museum; Friends of the
Museum purchase

Figure 98. Right.
Oil on canvas by Ralph E. W. Earl, not
dated. The Hermitage: Home of President
Andrew Jackson

tioned that James Barton Longacre, also of Philadelphia, had a reduced-size
sketch of this likeness. Eaton wrote that Longacre was expected in Washington, presumably to make portrait sketches for his soon-to-be-published
National Portrait Gallery. He suggested that, by means of a drawing machine,
Longacre could reduce—to any size—a brand new painting of Earl's, which just
happened to be before Eaton as he wrote.[21] Based on Eaton's description, this
latest portrait included the same subject matter as Earl's original canvas, in
addition to three horses grazing in the foreground.

Earl painted at least two head-and-shoulders versions based on his original full-
length canvas. One is now owned by the Daughters of the American Revolution Museum in Washington, D.C. [Fig. 97]. The other portrait was illustrated in *Antiques* magazine in November 1955, in an advertisement for Vose
Galleries of Boston. It is now unlocated.[22]

In another full-length portrait contemporary with Earl's "Farmer Jackson," the
artist used a similar approach to create an altogether different likeness. This
painting, dubbed the "Tennessee Gentleman," depicts Jackson, wearing his hat
and a long-tailed coat, standing directly in front of his distant mansion [Fig.

Figure 99. Right.
Engraving by Henry B. Hall, after Ralph E. W. Earl, circa 1860. National Portrait Gallery, Smithsonian Institution

Far right: This white beaver hat was "Made expressly for His *Excellency Gen'l Andrew Jackson*" by Orlando Fish of New York and Washington in about 1829. It became one of Jackson's trademarks and is depicted in many of his portraits. The black "mourning" band was in remembrance of his deceased wife, Rachel. Tennessee Historical Society Collection, Tennessee State Museum

Jackson's cherry cane with gold head, engraved on top: "General Andrew Jackson." The Hermitage: Home of President Andrew Jackson

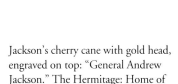

98]. Once again the house appears as it did before the December 1831 renovation. The portrait is now in the collection of the Ladies' Hermitage Association, and no copies are known to exist. Allegedly this portrait was painted for William C. H. Waddell, a successful politician from New York.[23]

In 1861 an engraving of the "Tennessee Gentleman" by Henry B. Hall appeared as the frontispiece to the third volume of James Parton's *Life of Andrew Jackson* [Fig. 99]. Then in 1897, Charles Henry Hart illustrated the portrait in an article for *McClure's Magazine*.[24]

III

Only in rare instances did Earl sign and date his portraits, now making it impossible to chronicle his extensive work with absolute accuracy. In the early 1830s he began portraying Jackson again in military uniform. One such likeness, a half-length owned by the Memphis Brooks Museum of Art in Tennessee, is signed and dated in the lower right corner, "R. E. W. Earl Pinxt 1833" [Fig. 100]. This portrait is greatly idealized when compared with Earl's painting of "Farmer Jackson," itself a flattering image. In the newer likeness, the President appears younger and more robust, despite being three years older and in declining health. In the fall of 1834 Jackson sent this portrait to Sir Edward Thomason, an English inventor and merchant, in acknowledgment of a series of medals that the latter had bestowed upon him. Thomason was pleased with the portrait and remarked that its imposing style did honor to Earl.[25]

The Washington *Globe* had inspected the painting before it was sent to England. It considered the likeness the best representation of the President that it had seen, and added that "the attitude, the coloring, and the accessories,

Figure 100.
Oil on canvas by Ralph E. W. Earl, 1833.
Memphis Brooks Museum of Art; Memphis
Park Commission purchase, 46.2

combine to present an almost speaking portrait of the Chief Magistrate."[26] The
Globe's high praise was typical of editor Francis P. Blair's unflinching loyalty
to Jackson's administration.

Copies of the Thomason portrait are in the collections of the National
Museum of American Art [Fig. 101] and Montgomery Place, the former
home of the Livingston-Delafield family of New York.[27] Both portraits are
half-length and depict Jackson in a general's uniform. His left arm is folded
across his waist, and his hand grasps a sword. On the scabbard is inscribed
Jackson's famous Jefferson's birthday dinner toast of April 13, 1830, urging
the preservation of the federal union.

Earl thoroughly disregarded historical perspective in these paintings. He not
only portrayed the President in military uniform, but the uniform itself is not
even regulation for a veteran of the War of 1812. Rather, it reflects a newer
style introduced in the 1830s, which replaced the single-breasted officer's
jacket with a double-breasted swallow-tailed coat. The collar, cuffs, and lining
were all buff-colored, reminiscent of the design worn by American officers of
the Revolution.[28]

❧

Figure 101. Above.
Oil on canvas by Ralph E. W. Earl, 1835.
National Museum of American Art,
Smithsonian Institution; transfer from the
National Institute

Figure 102. Right.
Oil on canvas by Ralph E. W. Earl, circa
1835. The Hermitage: Home of President
Andrew Jackson

Still another Earl portrait of Jackson in uniform that dates from the mid-1830s is in the collection of the Ladies' Hermitage Association [Fig. 102].[29] This image depicts Jackson with his coat buttoned to the collar. His head is turned toward his right shoulder, over which is draped a red-lined cape. On December 22, 1835, the *Nashville Republican* reported favorably on Earl as an artist and cited his close familiarity with the President as giving him an unusual advantage in executing spirited likenesses. The paper singled out for praise "a half length portrait of the President, in a general's uniform, of the simple and dignified revolutionary pattern." This portrait was probably the one now at the Hermitage. "The style of this picture," the paper added, "is singularly simple and effective: the features express with remarkable force and dignity the character of the man, and cannot fail to impress the spectator most powerfully with those attributes of energy and decision, which have most distinguished General Jackson."[30]

❧

Perhaps the most widely illustrated and popular of all Jackson images by any artist is the portrait of the general mounted on Sam Patch, the beautiful white horse presented to him in 1833 by the citizens of Philadelphia [Fig. 103]. This painting now hangs in the Hermitage. (A copy portrait depicting only Jackson from the waist up is owned by the Columbia Museum of Art in South Carolina [Fig. 104].) Jackson's granddaughter Rachel always admired the equestrian work, because it brought back fond memories.[31] As a young girl she enjoyed after-breakfast rides with the retired President around the farm, visiting the stables and talking with the servants, either at their cabins or in the cotton fields. When Sam Patch died, she recalled that he was buried on the estate with military honors.

The *Nashville Republican* lavishly praised this "splendid picture," adding, *The charger has been copied from that celebrated model to succeeding artists, in Vandyke's Charles I, and has all the grace and spirit of the original, but the noble looking animal has rarely been excelled as an effect of the pencil; the dignified bearing of the General, and his habit of command, tell with fine effect in the upright figure and firm countenance, every line of which the painter has made alive with expression. We consider this portrait, as a painting, one of the best efforts of American art which we have seen.*[32]

IV

Ralph E. W. Earl saved his best for last. In December 1836, just a few months before the end of Jackson's administration, Earl was at work upon a full-length, life-size portrait of the President. The last time he had painted such a grand canvas was back in 1821, when he executed a copy portrait for the city of New Orleans. Earl began by painting a small study [Fig. 105]. For whatever reason, he asked John Pemberton, a friend of Jackson's living in Philadelphia, to consult with Thomas Sully about this newest likeness. Sully discouraged the inclusion of spectacles, arguing that they would hide Jackson's fine, deep-set eyes. "By the by," Pemberton told Earl, "the eyes, in all the portraits I have ever seen of the General, are too prominent."[33]

Pemberton took the opportunity to press Earl about his own portrait of Jackson, which he believed to be still in the artist's possession after some two

Figure 105. Above.
Oil on canvas by Ralph E. W. Earl, study,
1836. The Hermitage: Home of President
Andrew Jackson

Figure 106. Right.
Oil on canvas by Ralph E. W. Earl, 1836–
1837. National Museum of American Art,
Smithsonian Institution; transfer from
United States District Court for the District
of Columbia

years. (Based on past practices, Earl may well have inadvertently given this portrait to someone else by this time.) Pemberton especially valued this particular likeness because the President had sat for it in his presence. He hoped that Earl would send it after he had finished his full-length in 1837.

Meanwhile, Earl painted his grand canvas for the city of Washington, calling it the "National Picture" [Fig. 106]. He depicted the President standing on the south portico of the presidential mansion in civilian dress, with his scarlet-lined military cloak draped over his shoulders. His right hand rests on his cane, and his white hat with the black band lies on a side chair. These personal props recall Earl's "Farmer Jackson" painted almost seven years before. Yet the national setting, with the Capitol in the background, lends a stately air to this portrait. A reporter, after viewing the painting at the White House prior to its removal to City Hall, saw symbolism in the fact that Jackson's back was "*turned upon Congress*," with which he had quarreled unceasingly for eight years. Another source considered the "autumnal sunset emblematic of his bright and glorious official retirement."[34]

Earl had painted more faithful portraits of Jackson, but none were as dramatic as this full-size "National Picture." The "perspective is beautiful," wrote the *Spirit of the Times,* and "the conception is admirable." Perhaps the *Boston Statesman* best summed up this image: "It combines the qualities of a portrait, a landscape, and a historical painting." Earl considered it his masterpiece.[35]

Earl's canvas, which measures 126 by 93 inches, has hung for years in the United States Court of Military Appeals, on loan from the National Museum of American Art. The small study portrait remained in the Jackson family until 1926, when it was sold to the Ladies' Hermitage Association.

In January 1838 Earl was contemplating having an engraving made from the study. This was the understanding of S. D. Langtree, one of the founders of a new literary magazine, the *Democratic Review.* The second issue of the *Review* announced, somewhat prematurely, a forthcoming engraving from Earl's latest picture. In a letter to the artist, Langtree hoped that Earl would have found time "amid the shades and quiet of the Hermitage to retouch, with the last finish of an artist's care, the original sketch of the large painting."[36] With that done, Langtree urged Earl to send the portrait to Washington so that the engraving process could commence.

But in September 1838, Earl died unexpectedly at the Hermitage. Jackson, himself weak and debilitated, related the details in a letter: *Our faithful friend Col. Earle is no more, he departed this life on the morning of 16th instant in the short illness of eight days and without the least intimation from the physicians until the morning before he departed that his case was dangerous; he daily assured me he was better, without pain, his medicine operating well, with a good pulse. The first simptoms [sic] of alarm his hand became cold, but every other part warm with a good pulse, but heat could not again be restored to his hands, and in 24 hours after this simptom of alarm, he expired without a groan.*[37]

Jackson was stunned. As explained many years later by Rachel Jackson Lawrence, a young girl of five at the time, Earl had been engaged in laying out the front lawn and driveway into a guitar shape. The idea for this unusual design was inspired by Rachel's mother, Sarah Yorke. Earl drew the plans and supervised the work. He enjoyed landscape gardening, having earlier drawn the plan for flower beds in the center of the garden and around Mrs. Jackson's tomb. On this particular day, Earl stayed out too long in the sun and suffered heat stroke, which became fatal.[38]

Jackson had Earl buried in the corner of the garden, not far from where he himself would soon rest. In letter after letter, the old warrior vented his grief. "He was an invaluable friend," wrote Jackson, "a most upright and honest man." Jackson especially valued Earl as a traveling companion. Their last major journey together had been in March 1837, when Jackson retired from the presidency and returned once and for all to the Hermitage.[39]

Earl's death was a premonition for Jackson. He knew that his own path ahead was short, and suddenly it had become lonely. Friends sympathized with him, for they too mourned Earl's loss. Francis P. Blair "felt a sincere friendship" for the artist, "indeed a sort of fraternal affection." For seven years, he, like Earl, was in the habit of looking upon Jackson as a patron. "Poor Earl," Blair lamented, "in his facetious way, frequently spoke of our relationships, saying that he, was the *King's Painter* and I the *King's Printer.*"[40]

છ

Portraits of Andrew Jackson by Ralph E. W. Earl hang today in museums, in state capitols, in governors' mansions, in the White House, and in private collections across the country. These portraits all depict a common image of a remarkable man. Although largely deficient in the finer points of physical accuracy, Earl's likenesses, in the universality of their appeal, mirror the great national legacy of Andrew Jackson. In this sense, they are Jackson's best portraits.

Notes

1. Earl's closest relatives, his mother and sister, lived in Troy, New York. For unknown reasons, he had not communicated with either of them since his trip to England in 1809.

2. Rachel Jackson to Ralph E. W. Earl, July 3, 1819, and Earl to Andrew Jackson, July 17, 1828, Jackson Papers, Library of Congress.

3. For a record of checks that Jackson wrote to Earl, see such dates in the Library of Congress collection as July 28, 1831, April 16 and August 2, 1832, September 24, 1833, and June 2 and July 4, 1836.

4. Jackson to Earl, March 16, 1829, roll 928, Charles Henry Hart Papers, Archives of American Art.

5. Remini, *Andrew Jackson,* vol. 3, p. 384; John C. Fitzpatrick, ed., *Annual Report of the American Historical Association for the Year 1918 . . . the Autobiography of Martin Van Buren* (Washington, D.C., 1920), vol. 2, p. 377 (hereafter cited as Van Buren, *Autobiography*); Arthur M. Schlesinger, Jr., *The Age of Jackson* (Boston, 1945), pp. 89–90.

6. Scott, "Ralph Earl," pp. 33–34; Horn, *Hermitage,* p. 126.

7. Parton, *Jackson,* vol. 3, p. 165.

8. William H. Chase to Earl, March 16, 1834; C. Biddle to Earl, September 17, 1834; J. N. Barker to Earl, October 24, 1834, Earl Papers.

9. See J. N. Barker to Earl, November 29, 1834, *ibid.*; records of the Catalog of American Portraits.

The 1834 Earl portrait, owned by R. Gwin Follis, probably came to his family through his great-great-grandfather, James Gwin, who allegedly had been Jackson's chaplain during the New Orleans campaign.

10. Earl to George Bates, June 28, 1831, Earl Papers. In 1832 this likeness was lithographed by John Henry Bufford and published by William S. Pendleton of Boston. In extolling this print, the *National Banner and Daily Advertiser* of April 23, 1832, reported that it represented Jackson at the Hermitage during his last visit. This would have spanned the months of July through September 1830. Earl may have painted the original likeness at this time.

11. Bates to Earl, April 29, 1831, Earl Papers.

12. Bates to William B. Lewis, August 22, 1831, *ibid.*

13. Bates to Earl, August 8, 1831; Bates to Earl, October 4, 1831, *ibid.*

14. Bates to Earl, October 20, 1831; Earl to Bates, October 26, 1831 (and copy letter of same date), *ibid.*

15. William S. Pendleton to Earl, October 31, 1831, *ibid.*

16. Pendleton to Earl, November 12, 1831; Bates to Earl, March 14, 1832; Pendleton to Earl, March 14, 1832; Earl to Pendleton, March 22, 1832, *ibid.*

17. Bates to Earl, March 28, 1832, *ibid.* For critical acclaim of the lithograph, see Washington *Globe,* April 12, 1832.

18. Bates to Earl, April 21, May 16, 18, June 2, 16, July 24, August 31, 1832, Earl Papers.

19. For a political interpretation of this lithograph, see Bumgardner, "Political Portraiture," pp. 89–95. See also A. M. Howell to Earl, December 17, 1833, Earl Papers.

20. The *Nashville Republican* of December 22, 1835, mentioned that a full-length portrait of General Jackson at the Hermitage was then in the possession of Blair. Undoubtedly, this was the "Farmer Jackson." In addition, the article reported that a small number of unsatisfactory lithographs of the portrait had been published by Endicott before the stone was crushed and destroyed in the printing process.

In about 1860, William Rumney, a Boston figurehead carver, made a wooden version, 78 ¼ inches high, of Earl's 1830 likeness [Fig. 107]. This carving is in the Metropolitan Museum of Art, New York City. See records of the Catalog of American Portraits.

21. John H. Eaton to Joseph Hemphill, May 21, 1833, Longacre Papers.

22. The DAR portrait traces back to the descendants of George Bryan Porter. In 1831 Jackson appointed Porter territorial governor of Michigan, a post he held until his death in 1834. See records of the Catalog of American Portraits; *Antiques* 68 (November 1955): 420.

23. Subsequently, the portrait passed through the hands of Seymour Van Santvoord, his brother George B. Santvoord, and William H. Frear, all of Troy, New York. In 1944 Mrs. Charles W. Frear presented it to the Ladies' Hermitage Association. See records of the Ladies' Hermitage Association.

24. *Ibid.*; Parton, *Jackson,* vol. 3, p. 599; Hart, "Life Portraits," p. 800.

25. *Nashville Republican,* March 10, 1835; *Nashville Union,* June 10, 1835.

The portrait remained in family hands, eventually passing down to P. R. Thomason, the great-grandson of Sir Edward Thomason. Knoedler Galleries of New York City owned the painting in the 1950s, prior to its acquisition by the Memphis Brooks Museum of Art. See records of the Memphis Brooks Museum of Art.

26. Washington *Globe,* February 23, 1835.

27. The portrait now at the National Museum of American Art had originally been the property of Major William H. Chase. Chase presented the portrait in 1844 to the National Institute (now the Smithsonian Institution). It is signed and dated in the lower right corner, "R. E. W. Earl Pinxt. 1835."

The portrait at Montgomery Place was initially owned by Edward Livingston. Subsequently it passed through the hands of the Delafield family, relatives by marriage. This canvas is neither signed nor dated, and the background is different. Instead of the United States Capitol in the distance, a nautical scene with a sailing vessel is clearly visible just beside Jackson's left elbow. In the spring of 1831 Jackson had appointed Livingston secretary of state. Two years later he resigned to become minister to France. The distant vessel might represent Livingston's mostly successful efforts to win twenty-five million francs from the French government, as indemnity for spoliation suffered principally by American merchants under the Berlin and Milan decrees.

28. H. A. Ogden and Henry Loomis Nelson, *Uniforms of the United States Army* (New York, 1959), p. 27.

29. The Ladies' Hermitage Association acquired this portrait in about 1908 from the estate of Jackson's grandson, Colonel Andrew Jackson III.

30. *Nashville Republican,* December 22, 1835.

31. This painting was once owned by Colonel Andrew Jackson III, Jackson's grandson. Rachel Jackson Lawrence, "Andrew Jackson at Home," *McClure's Magazine* 9 (September 1897): 793.

32. *Nashville Republican,* December 22, 1835.

33. John Pemberton to Earl, December 19, 1836, Earl Papers.

34. *Spirit of the Times* (New York), March 25, 1837; *Boston Statesman,* February 25, 1837.

Figure 107.
Painted poplar carving by William Rumney, circa 1860. The Metropolitan Museum of Art; purchase, Rogers Fund, The J. M. Kaplan Fund, Inc., and Mrs. Frederick A. Stoughton Gifts, Harris Brisbane Dick and Louis V. Bell Funds, 1978

35. *Spirit of the Times,* March 25, 1837; *Boston Statesman,* February 25, 1837.

36. S. D. Langtree to Earl, January 5, 1838, Earl Papers.

37. Earl died before Jackson could learn of his wishes concerning his worldly goods. He was survived by a sister, and until word came from her, nothing could be done with his belongings, including his painting apparatus. A set of Earl's brushes is now in the collection of the Tennessee State Museum. See *Correspondence of Jackson,* vol. 5, pp. 565–66, 570.

38. Lawrence, "Jackson at Home," p. 793; Horn, *Hermitage,* p. 127. Earl's obituary appeared in the *Nashville Union,* September 19, 1838.

39. *Correspondence of Jackson,* vol. 5, p. 566; Remini, *Andrew Jackson,* vol. 3, pp. 448–49; Horn, *Hermitage,* p. 127; Lawrence, "Jackson at Home," pp. 792–93.

40. *Correspondence of Jackson,* vol. 5, p. 567.

1829-1830
Administration is buffeted by Peggy Eaton scandal

1831
April: Accepts cabinet resignations; Edward Williams Clay publishes noted cartoon *The Rats leaving a Falling House*

1832
July 10: Vetoes bill to recharter second Bank of the United States

December 10: Issues Proclamation against nullification to people of South Carolina

1833
March 4: Attends second inaugural

April 6: Meets Black Hawk, captured Sauk and Fox warrior, at White House

1834
March 28: Is censured by Senate

1835
January 30: Survives assassination attempt

1836
February: Resolves French spoliations claims controversy

July 11: Issues Specie Circular

1837
March 4: Issues Farewell Address

Chapter 6

"King Andrew": Cartoons, Caricatures, and Carvings

Figure 108.
Hand-colored engraving published by J. Sidebetham, 1819. Tennessee State Museum

James Parton, in his *Life of Andrew Jackson,* observed that "some of the most characteristic and life-like portraits of the General are to be found in the caricatures of the time."[1] Writing some fifteen years after Jackson's death, and on the eve of the Civil War, Parton was able to collect twenty works in which Jackson was the principal figure. Of these, he noted that an extraordinary number were produced during the last five years of Jackson's presidency.

Today, after decades of thorough collecting by such research depositories as the Library of Congress and the American Antiquarian Society, Parton's figure can easily be doubled, if not tripled. Most of these caricatures are cartoon lithographs pertaining to Jackson's tumultuous eight years as President. Issues that received ample lampooning included Jackson's war on the Bank of the United States, his Kitchen Cabinet, and the influence of his political protégé Martin Van Buren. Over and above their value as portraiture, these political cartoons form a veritable record—biased to be sure—of Jacksonian democracy.

I

Jackson debuted in caricature long before he became President. An early reference to him appeared in a cartoon etched in 1815 by William Charles. *John Bull Before New Orleans* depicts a brutish fellow, the burly personification of England, being pulled out of the Louisiana mud by his ears. His Yankee antagonist orders, "Come along you old Rascal you did not know the brave Americans and their old Hickory."

As a medium of portraiture, caricature was still in its infancy in America. The Revolutionary War and the War of 1812 eras each produced only a handful of cartoons when compared with the mid-nineteenth century. For the most part, the new nation lacked the artists, the engravers, and the technical apparatus to do justice to even the most important issues and events of the period.[2]

The English were far more prolific and sophisticated. Consequently, one of Jackson's earliest caricatures was a cartoon published in London in April 1819. *American Justice!! or The Ferocious Yankee Genl. Jack's Reward for Butchering Two British Subjects!!!* savagely ridiculed Jackson for ordering the execution of British officers Robert Ambrister and Alexander Arbuthnot [Fig. 108].

In *American Justice,* the marauder Jackson accepts the "Government of the Floridas" from the United States as a reward for his alleged exploitations against the Indians and British. By the process of hand-coloring, the red blood dripping from Jackson's daggers forms the focal point of this busy sketch. In the upper left corner, emerging from the clouds of eternity, the figures of Ambrister and Arbuthnot cry out to Britannia, "Revenge! Revenge!" By any standard, this cartoon published by J. Sidebetham is a ghoulish commentary on Jackson in particular and American democracy in general.

℮৲১

In 1819 James Akin was intent upon enhancing Jackson's heroic image by means of a caricature. Born about 1773 in Charleston, South Carolina, Akin spent most of his adult years in Philadelphia, working in a variety of print mediums, including etchings, wood engravings, and lithographs.

To help counter the violent abuse leveled at Jackson by certain members of Congress, Akin proposed "to place their preposterous proceeding in as ridiculous [a] point of view as can be." The cartoonist, however, needed the assistance of Ralph E. W. Earl. While visiting Washington in February, Akin divulged his scheme in a letter to the artist. Specifically, he was inquiring whether Earl would furnish him with a portrait sketch of the general. "I merely want the strong outlines of feature and figure, required in caricature," wrote Akin.[3] As an inducement, he promised not to intrude upon any plans Earl might have for publishing Jackson's portrait.

Figure 109.
Aquatint by James Akin, 1824. Prints and Photographs Division, Library of Congress

Figure 110.
Lithograph by James Akin, not dated. American Antiquarian Society

Whatever reply, if any, that Akin may have received is not recorded. Apparently his cartoon endeavor was postponed for several years. In any event, by November 1824 he had finally completed a favorable caricature of Jackson, a copy of which he enclosed in a letter of gratitude to Earl.[4] Printed just before the national election, *Caucus Curs in full Yell, or a War-Whoop to saddle on the People, a Pappoose President* [Fig. 109] depicts Jackson as the hero of New Orleans, standing resolute against the congressional caucus that had endorsed William H. Crawford of Georgia for President. Akin criticizes Crawford, then the secretary of the treasury, for alleged corruption in his department and labels him the "Pappoose President." This characterization refers to a paralyzing stroke that he had suffered in August 1823. His political career was virtually at an end. Still, Crawford had his supporters, as depicted by the "Caucus Curs," representing the partisan newspapers who were growling at Jackson.

In costume and posture, Akin's portrayal of Jackson resembles Earl's full-length canvas painted in 1818 [see page 44]. For instance, in the painting Jackson holds a telescope in his outstretched right hand; in the cartoon he rests it upon a sword bearing Caesar's famous quote, "I came, I saw, I conquered."

It is uncertain when the artist changed his opinion about the hero of New Orleans, but by the end of Jackson's first term as President, Akin was caricaturing him savagely. In 1832 he published a satirical pamphlet, *The House That Jonathan Built, or Political Primer for 1832*. Among the sixteen pages of parody (drawn from an old English nursery rhyme) were twelve woodblock cartoons cut by Akin ridiculing the administration.

Akin proved to be a clever and versatile caricaturist. He once reprinted one of his satires (not of Jackson) on chamber pots for increased effect.[5] He even drew a respectable likeness of Jackson that, when inverted, transformed into a jackass [Fig. 110]. The accompanying verse read:

> What have we here? A human head!
> "The tree known by its fruit"!
> A brainless, sappy, lump of lead;
> The card turn'd—shows the Brute!!!
>
> A stupid Jack he now appears!
> An awkward dolt—a Beast!
> "By the Eternal," Uncle Sam fears,
> On Liberty he'll feast!!!

Figure 111.
Central to President Jackson's reform program was the need to rid government of inefficiency and corruption. Believing that many officeholders were incompetent or dishonest, Jackson advocated their replacement. "Rotation in office," he postulated, "will perpetuate our liberty." Critics, however, considered this a "spoils system," whereby the politically faithful were rewarded with jobs and patronage. This popular cartoon, *Office Hunters for the Year 1834*, depicts Jackson as the devil, tantalizing the people with the fruits of victory. Lithograph attributed to James Akin, 1834. Peters Collection, National Museum of American History, Smithsonian Institution

OFFICE HUNTERS FOR THE YEAR 1854.

Cartoonists portrayed Jackson both favorably and unfavorably, in such guises as a king, a devil [Fig. 111], a lion, a turtle, a cat, an eagle, and even a decrepit old lady. But the favorite personification was that of a jackass.[6] Perhaps the President's surname suggested it. In any event, Jackson's adversaries found the comparison appropriate. Eventually, the jackass, or donkey, emerged as the symbol of the Democratic party.

II

Few presidential elections have provoked more character assassination than the contest of 1828 between incumbent John Quincy Adams and Andrew Jackson. In August Jackson complained: *The whole object of the* [opposing] *coalition is to calumniate me, cart loads of coffin hand-bills, forgeries, & pamphlets of the most base calumnies are circulated by the franking privelege* [sic] *of Members of Congress, & Mr. Clay. Even Mrs. J. is not spared, & my pious Mother, nearly fifty years in the tomb . . . has been dragged forth . . . & held to public scorn as a prostitute who intermarried with a Negro.*[7]

If not outright lies, these allegations were hyperbole at best. Jackson did his best to counter such slanders in his correspondence, but he was still vulnerable. Particularly vexing was the "coffin" handbill published by John Binns, editor of the Philadelphia *Democratic Press*. It purported to contain factual details about the six militiamen who, at the close of the Creek War in September 1814, disputed the length of their enlistments. They were later found guilty of desertion and mutiny and were ordered by General Jackson to be executed. Binns circulated several thousand of these disparaging supplements in his daily, triweekly, and weekly editions. The original version, labeled *Monumental Inscriptions!*, depicted six large black coffins, each bearing the name and a brief account of one of the condemned militiamen.

Versions of the original handbill appeared in anti-Jackson newspapers throughout the country and chronicled other offenses as well. The most widely circulated one was entitled *Some Account of some of the Bloody Deeds of General Jackson*. Several versions exist, most of which depict a figure representing Jackson thrusting a sword through the back of a man bending over to pick up

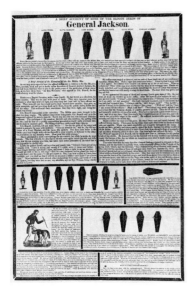

Figure 112.
Handbill, 1828. Private collection

Figure 113.
Lithograph by Edward Williams Clay,
1829. National Portrait Gallery,
Smithsonian Institution

a stone [Fig. 112]. The accompanying text explained that Andrew Jackson made this brutal assault upon one Samuel Jackson in the streets of Nashville. Old Hickory was indicted for this violent act but argued self-defense and was acquitted. "Gentle reader," posed the handbill, "it is for you to say, whether this man, who carries a sword cane, and is willing to run it through the body of any one who may presume to stand in his way, is a fit person to be our President."

Ultimately, the coffin handbill turned against its zealous creator. On repeated occasions, angry mobs threatened to rout the editor from his premises and bandy him about town in an empty coffin.[8] Then Binns began to lose much of his patronage, until financial difficulties necessitated the discontinuance of his paper. His fate was caricatured in part in an anonymous cartoon, *The Pedlar and His Pack or the Desperate Effort, an Over Balance,* depicting Binns being overburdened with coffins. Henry Clay and John Quincy Adams are balanced precariously on top. Clay acknowledges that in his bid for the presidency he is sinking like Binns, but he urges Adams to hold on to the presidential chair. Adams replies that he will hang on in spite of the coffin handbills and the "wishes of the people."[9]

III

Jackson's election to the presidency in 1828 roughly coincided with the beginning of commercial lithography in America. The process, invented in about 1795 by a Bavarian, Alois Senefelder, and first introduced in the United States by Bass Otis in 1819, was much simpler for the artist than engraving or woodcutting, although a special press and knowledgeable printer were required. Lithographs were also cheaper to produce and sell and, at approximately fifteen cents a sheet, were no longer an extravagance for the common man. Appropriately, lithographs became the most popular art medium in the age of Jackson.

Andrew Jackson also contributed to the sudden emergence of political caricature in the United States.[9] No previous President had been more colorful or controversial. Naturally, his administration invited commentary.

❧

What is believed to be the first caricature of Jackson in office was titled *A Grand Functionary. "The Lord High Keeper"* [Fig. 113]. Drawn by Edward Williams Clay, this cartoon depicted Jackson locking up Tobias Watkins, the fourth auditor in the Treasury Department, for government fraud. When it was discovered that his accounts were short by some seven thousand dollars, Watkins fled the city, only to be caught and convicted. The case, occurring just weeks after the inauguration, was a national sensation. Jackson had promised to cleanse the government of corruption. This initial and surprising success clearly demonstrated the timeliness of his reform movement.

Edward Williams Clay chose not to interpret it that way, however, and portrayed Jackson as a sinister jailor. Clay's Jackson is today reminiscent of the character Montresor in Poe's classic tale "The Cask of Amontillado," who shackles the stupefied Fortunato in an underground crypt for his "thousand injuries." In the cartoon, Watkins's hands reach out for justice through the barred window of the prison door. As Jackson double-locks it he warns, "I'm acting in my Magisterial Capacity!!!! D—n the fellow he opposed my election and if he is released he'll set up a Newspaper against me. Here let him rot!!!"[10]

Clay was never among Jackson's ardent supporters. Unfortunately for the

President, this graphic jester proved to be the most prolific cartoonist of the 1830s and 1840s. Born in Philadelphia in 1799, Clay trained in the law. He had a deft mind and obviously appreciated the many nuances of political satire. Unlike some caricaturists who chose to remain anonymous, preferring not to risk letting politics jeopardize their business prospects, Clay often signed his work, using a variety of signatures, at times "C," "EC," "EWC," "Clay," and in at least one instance, a rebus.[11]

Certain unsigned works can be attributed to Clay based on his characteristic portrayals of Jackson. An original pencil sketch of Jackson's left profile has survived [Fig. 114]. His features—pursed mouth, straight nose, bushy eyebrows, lined forehead, bristling locks—have been faithfully replicated, even to the folding adjustable spectacles that rest on his brow. Clay used this view in many of his cartoons, suggesting that it was his principal model.

His sketch may well have been taken from life in Washington in 1831. It may also have been a model for his most popular cartoon of Jackson, *The Rats leaving a Falling House* [Fig. 115]. First published in the capital in April of that year, this was Clay's only satire since 1829, when he produced *A Grand Functionary.* Unlike his earlier image of Jackson, which was truly a caricature, this one, also a frontal view, was nearly lifelike.

Clay composed this cartoon hastily after Jackson had accepted the resignations of his cabinet in mid-April of 1831. Most of the nation knew little about the discord among Jackson's chief advisers. The festering rivalry between Secretary of State Van Buren and Vice President Calhoun, both presidential aspirants, divided the Democratic party. Ultimately, Calhoun's public airing of sensitive correspondence between himself and Jackson concerning the Seminole War only brought ridicule on the administration and led to the President's reading Calhoun out of the party.[12] To distance himself from this imbroglio, Van Buren cagily resigned. Secretary of War John Henry Eaton followed suit.

Eaton was another story altogether. He and his wife, Peggy, the former Mrs. Margaret O'Neale Timberlake, had been themselves the cause of much rancor. They first became acquainted in about 1818 when Eaton, a new senator from Tennessee, began living in the Washington boarding house run by Peggy's father. At the time she was the wife of John B. Timberlake, a navy purser who died in 1828, amid rumors of malfeasance and suicide. Eaton's subsequent courtship of Peggy seemed only to confirm the slander of his intimacy with her before she had become a widow. Jackson, himself a former boarder at the O'Neales' during his own brief Senate career, was an old friend of Eaton and an admirer of Peggy. To end the local gossip alleging that the Eatons had had a premarital relationship, he encouraged their marriage, which occurred on January 1, 1829. Still, persistent rumors followed Jackson and Eaton into office and kept smug Washingtonians buzzing for the next two years. Affairs degenerated to the point that the wives and daughters of several cabinet members refused to attend social gatherings and state dinners to which Mrs. Eaton had been invited. Even Mrs. Andrew Jackson Donelson, wife of the President's private secretary and resident of the presidential mansion, did the same. Jackson, having weathered stormy allegations of living in adultery himself, took all of this personally. Incensed by the acrimonious rumors and slights, he defended Peggy's honor as if it were that of his own deceased and beloved Rachel.[13]

The nation at large was never aware of all this turmoil in the administration. Consequently, there was great surprise when the resignations dropped on Jackson's desk for seemingly no reason and without clear explanation. Nothing like this had ever occurred before in the nation's history.[14] Was the government

Figure 114.
Pencil on paper by Edward Williams Clay, 1831. National Portrait Gallery, Smithsonian Institution; gift of J. William Middendorf II

Figure 115.
Lithograph by Edward Williams
Clay, 1831. The Library Company
of Philadelphia

Figure 116.
Lithograph by Edward Williams Clay,
1831. The Library Company of
Philadelphia

collapsing, as suggested by Clay in his cartoon? He depicted the President looking perplexed and forlorn and sitting in a broken chair against a backdrop of resignations. Beside him, a column labeled "Public confidence in the stability and harmony of this administration" is toppling. Also falling is a cracked podium inscribed "Altar of Reform," upon which stands a winged jackass holding a worn-out broom. Upon entering office, Jackson had invariably likened the federal bureaucracy to an "Augean Stable," which he proposed to sweep clean. In the cartoon, on the floor at his feet, four rats with human heads scamper out of harm's way. From left to right, they represent Eaton, Secretary of the Navy John Branch, Van Buren, and Secretary of the Treasury Samuel D. Ingham. (Attorney General John McPherson Berrien had not yet resigned and consequently was not included in Clay's cartoon.) Jackson steps on the tail of the Van Buren rat, preventing his escape—an allusion to retaining him until his replacement could be named.

The Rats, although it shed little light on the inner workings of the administration, was both effective and widely published. For instance, when Van Buren's son was asked when his father would be returning to New York, he replied, "When the President takes off his foot." On April 25, John Quincy Adams, who never let much of consequence escape his diary, recorded that two thousand copies of the cartoon had been sold that day in Philadelphia and that ten thousand more would be disposed of within a fortnight. He viewed this as "an indication of the estimation in which Jackson and his administration are held."[15]

Adams could be astute as well as cynical. It was his understanding that the President looked upon his cabinet as a unit "which had come together in great harmony." Adams's hypothesis proved to be correct. Since two individuals of the unit had voluntarily resigned, Jackson thought it necessary to reorganize the entire body. That was the explanation he rendered to Branch and Ingham in requesting their resignations. It was also the explanation circulated in the newspapers that published Jackson's correspondence.

In a more sophisticated reworking of his earlier cartoon, Clay cleverly satirized Jackson's concept of a unit. The result, published by the artist in Philadelphia in 1831, was titled *,00001—The value of a unit with four cyphers going before it* [Fig. 116]. The gist of this revised cartoon was basically the same—the unraveling of the administration.[16] Yet this time, Clay added to the cast of characters. Calhoun appears in the guise of a terrier, intent upon stopping Van Buren from ascending the "Ladder of Political Preferment." In the background, two other presidential contenders, Daniel Webster and Henry Clay, look on with contempt. To their right, John Randolph of Virginia blames Clay for all of the trouble. These two statesmen had been bitter enemies for a long time. In 1826 they faced off in a harmless duel over a spate of political name-calling. Lastly, the human rat under Jackson's arm labeled "snug" appears to be William B. Lewis, the President's personal adviser and his only companion in the White House at that time.

Jackson survived the "Eaton Malaria," replaced his official cabinet, and went about the business of reforming the government as if nothing extraordinary had occurred. What emerged, however, was something unique in itself, a small circle of intimate advisers known as the "Kitchen Cabinet." Remarkable for their unflinching loyalty to the President, men like Francis P. Blair and Amos Kendall, both experienced newspaper editors, exerted an influence in Washington "unknown to the Constitution and to the country."[17] Unlike the official "parlor" cabinet, these men allegedly slipped in and out of Jackson's second-floor study via the kitchen.

Figure 117.
Hand-colored lithograph published by
George Endicott and Moses Swett
lithography company, 1834. Prints and
Photographs Division, Library of Congress

Figure 118.
Lithograph by Edward Williams Clay, circa
1834. Tennessee Historical Society
Collection, Tennessee State Museum

Inevitably, the Kitchen Cabinet provoked ridicule, as illustrated in the cartoon *"The Government." "*[I] *Take the Responsibility"* [Fig. 117].[18] In 1834 Endicott and Swett of New York City published this anonymous work, which was signed facetiously "Hassan Straightshanks." Jackson appears as a jackass being led by the ear by Van Buren, who is carrying a crown in his pocket. Burdening the President is a cart labeled "KC." Implements of the hearth and stove are stacked to represent a driver. To the rear, a servant dumps refuse into the cart. The whole contraption is labeled "The Government." Although Jackson is depicted as being subservient to both Van Buren and the Kitchen Cabinet, in reality no previous President had wielded more authority over his administration.

Edward Williams Clay dramatized Jackson's apparent sovereignty in a popular broadside, *King Andrew the First, "Born to Command,"* published in about 1834 [Fig. 118]. The President is shown bedecked in regal splendor; a jeweled crown adorns his head and an ermine-lined cape cascades from around his shoulders. "A King," states the artist, "who, possessing as much power as his Gracious Brother William IV., makes a worse use of it." Jackson tramples on the Constitution, internal improvements, and the Bank of the United States. In his left hand is a scroll marked "veto." Jackson exercised this executive power more than all of his predecessors combined and was the first President to use the pocket veto. Such power amply wielded troubled many of his critics, such as Supreme Court Justice Joseph Story, who observed during the fever of the Bank war, "Though we live under the form of a republic we are in fact under the absolute rule of a single man."[19]

❧

In the 1832 election the people again cast their ballots overwhelmingly for Old Hickory, in spite of poignant cartoons especially distressing to the incumbent, as shown in yet another work by Clay, *A Political Game of Bragg. Or the best hand out of four* [Fig. 119].[20] Seated around a card table are the presidential contestants. To the left sits Henry Clay, candidate of the National Republicans, later called Whigs. He lays down a hand of "internal improvements," "domestic manufactures," and the "U. S. Bank." Opposite him, Jackson hunches over cards marked "Intrigue," "Corruption," and "Imbecillity." To

Figure 119.
Hand-colored lithograph by Edward
Williams Clay, 1832. The Library
Company of Philadelphia

A POLITICAL GAME OF BRAG.
Or the best hand out of four.

his left, Calhoun plays the "Nullification" and "Anti Tariff" cards, while across
from him sits William Wirt, candidate of the Anti-Masonic party, which was
organized in protest of secret societies. In Edward Williams Clay's game of
bragg, an early version of poker, Jackson clearly is the loser. How different was
the reality!

IV

No single issue better exemplified Jackson's iron will than renewal of the
charter of the second Bank of the United States. In his first annual message to
Congress, in December 1829, Jackson expressed concern about the Bank's
constitutionality, about the expediency of the law that had created it, and
about the general soundness of paper money in lieu of gold and silver specie.
Amid these rumblings, Nicholas Biddle, the Bank's president, grew uneasy
about the future of his financial institution. Intent upon provoking the issue in
an election year, and with Henry Clay's urging, Biddle applied to Congress in
January 1832 for a new charter, four years before the expiration of the existing
one. Jackson sensed political maneuvering, and suddenly defeat of the Bank of
the United States became his obsession. He considered it to be a monopoly,
inherently established to benefit the privileged classes. Its powers, independent
of federal and state regulations, were immense and growing. The Bank was a
veritable government in itself, exclaimed the President, *"but I will kill it!"*[21]

On July 10, 1832, Jackson vetoed the bill to recharter the Bank. Then he
made arrangements for removing the government's funds and depositing them
in state banks. Biddle struck back by calling in loans, thus causing a mild
economic contraction through the end of 1833 and into 1834. Public opinion
about the Bank was sharply divided, depending upon whose income or
business was most affected by this fluctuating economy. Ultimately Jackson,
because of his enduring hold on the American psyche, survived his own
tenuous monetary policy. His successor, Martin Van Buren, inheriting the
panic and depression of 1837, did not.

Figure 120.
Lithograph by unidentified artist, circa
1834. The Library Company of
Philadelphia

The Bank war spawned numerous political cartoons. Although two-thirds of
the press supported the Bank, caricaturists tended either to side with Jackson
or remain ambivalent. *I Take It on My Responsibility* was a notable exception
[Fig. 120]. In this anti-Jackson cartoon, Nicholas Biddle is shown leading his
cohorts in an attack against the President and his Kitchen Cabinet, who all
scurry off for protection among the Greek Revival columns of the United
States Bank in Philadelphia.

Edward Williams Clay, in an about-face from earlier works, actually portrayed
the President favorably in *The Downfall of Mother Bank* [Fig. 121]. In the
forefront stands Jackson, holding up an "order for the Removal of the Public
Money." As if struck by lightning, Biddle's financial temple topples around the
demonic Biddle himself, along with Webster and Clay, two chief congressional
proponents of the Bank. Strewn on the floor are partisan newspapers, depen-
dent on the Bank for loans and patronage. On the far right, the foppish figure
of Major Jack Downing takes his hat off to Jackson while patting him on the
back. Downing was a facetious literary figure created in about 1830 by Seba
Smith, editor of the *Portland Courier*. In 1833 Smith effectively cast Downing
as Jackson's confidant during the President's well-publicized tour of the
Northeast. Instantly Downing became a popular character of political folklore
and was pirated by other more hostile satirists, as well as cartoonists such as
Clay.[22]

Pugilistic contests were favorite themes for cartoonists, as illustrated in an
anonymous 1834 work, *Set to Between Old Hickory and Bully Nick* [Fig. 122].
Here Jackson, seconded by Van Buren and Major Downing, squares off with
Biddle, seconded by Webster and Clay. Class distinctions are clearly underscored in the characters of the bottle holders: a frontiersman in buckskins tends
a jug of Old Monongohala Whiskey, while a corpulent Old Mother Bank
stands ready with a carafe of port.

General Jackson Slaying the Many Headed Monster drew its inspiration from
Jackson himself, who once referred to the Bank as a "hydra-headed monster"
[Fig. 123].[23] In this cartoon by Alfred M. Hoffy, Jackson attacks the beast with

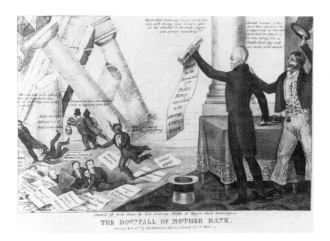

THE DOWNFALL OF MOTHER BANK.

SET TO BETWEEN OLD HICKORY AND BULLY NICK.

GENERAL JACKSON SLAYING THE MANY HEADED MONSTER.

ON THE WAY TO ARABY!

Published March 1836 by the proprietor H.R. Robinson 48 Courtland St New York.

Figure 121. Top left.
Lithograph by Edward Williams Clay,
1833. American Antiquarian Society

Figure 122. Top right.
Lithograph attributed to Edward Williams
Clay, 1834. Prints and Photographs
Division, Library of Congress

Figure 123. Bottom left.
Lithograph by Alfred M. Hoffy, circa 1836.
Prints and Photographs Division, Library of
Congress

Figure 124. Center right.
Lithograph by Edward Williams Clay,
1836. Prints and Photographs Division,
Library of Congress

Figure 125. Bottom right.
Hand-colored lithograph attributed to
Edward Williams Clay, 1834. The Library
Company of Philadelphia

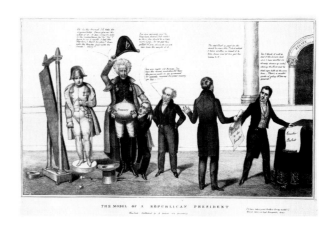

THE MODEL OF A REPUBLICAN PRESIDENT

his walking stick labeled "veto," while imploring his new Vice President, Martin Van Buren, to take a clear stand on the issue. To the right, Major Jack Downing offers the President his assistance. The many heads of the monster represent state branches of the Bank. The large central figure wearing the hat labeled "Penn" is Nicholas Biddle, who managed the Bank's thirty-five-million-dollar assets from the home office in Philadelphia.

Jackson, in defense of his war on the Bank, once informed a delegation from Philadelphia that, instead of living in a country where such a powerful institution prevailed, he would seek asylum in the wilds of Arabia.[24] In 1836, the year the Bank's charter expired, Edward Williams Clay satirized Jackson's threat in *On the Way to Araby!* [Fig. 124]. The portly Biddle stands on the step of the old Bank of the United States and holds up a multifaced demon's mask. (Biddle was able to keep his branch office functioning, since the Pennsylvania legislature had incorporated it as a state bank.) Jackson, clutching a broken "veto" stick, exclaims as he flees, "The Monster! the many headed Monster's come to life! Old Nick! Old Nick! I'll cut stick and fly to Araby! by the Eternal!" Left behind on the ground is Van Buren, clinging to the President's self-styled mantle and musing, "I hope it will fit!"

☙

Jackson paid heavily for killing the Bank of the United States. Spurred by Henry Clay, the Senate censured the President, on March 28, 1834, for assuming power and authority not conferred by the Constitution. This legislative act was unprecedented, and Jackson's pride suffered a severe blow. Predictably, he struck back with a written protest, which was composed largely by his attorney general, Benjamin F. Butler. When the Senate rebutted this, Jackson fired a codicil. He wanted his protest entered into the Senate journal, but the Senate, again led by Clay, refused on grounds that it was an infringement upon its privileges.[25]

Jackson's removal of the deposits, and his subsequent censure and protests, have been cleverly illustrated in an anonymous cartoon titled *The Model of a Republican President* [Fig. 125]. This work, which closely resembles that of Edward Williams Clay, was meant to be viewed from left to right. Jackson, aspiring to resemble France's dictatorial Napoleon, stands before a mirror dressed in his military uniform; his familiar beaverskin hat, walking stick, and long-stemmed clay pipe lie at his feet. To his left stoops Secretary of the Treasury Roger B. Taney, who holds a pillow labeled "Treasury" in front of Jackson's stomach. "You are certainly very like Napoleon," quips Taney, "but rather too thin. You should be a little more *pursy,* let me put this *pillow* on you, if you think you can bear the weight of it." As Van Buren placidly looks on, Benjamin F. Butler hands the "Protest to the Senate" to Amos Kendall for the President's signature. As an intimate member of the Kitchen Cabinet, Kendall helped draft both the protest and the paper on the deposit removal. In the cartoon, he stands ready with the "Counter Protest."

In marked contrast to the relative complexity of the above work, *Symptoms of a Locked Jaw* is almost modern in its straightforward simplicity [Fig. 126]. Jackson and Clay alone compose this sketch. Clay restrains the President in a chair and stitches his mouth shut, long believed to be a false allusion to the Kentuckian's support for censure and his fight to keep Jackson's protest from being recorded in the Senate journal. In reality, this cartoon had appeared in 1827, the same year that Henry Clay published a pamphlet refuting Jackson's charges that a corrupt bargain had been struck in the presidential election of 1824–1825.

Symptoms of a Locked Jaw, signed "DCJ," was the work of David Claypoole

PLAIN SEWING DONE HERE

SYMPTOMS OF A LOCKED JAW

RICHARD III.

Figure 126. Above.
Lithograph by David Claypoole Johnston, 1827. American Antiquarian Society

Figure 127. Right.
Engraving and stipple by David Claypoole Johnston, circa 1828. The New-York Historical Society

Johnston. Like his contemporary, Edward Williams Clay, Johnston was born in Philadelphia in the spring of 1799. Unlike Clay, he only occasionally dabbled in political caricature, as he lacked Clay's financial independence. At an early age Johnston considered a career as a painter, but instead directed his graphic ambitions toward the more lucrative field of engraving. After an apprenticeship under Francis Kearney, he discovered that this field, too, had entered a period of contraction, especially for novices. Johnston became an actor for several years, only to return again to the burin in about 1826. By then he was living in Boston and beginning a successful career designing prints for booksellers and publishers.[26]

Johnston had a special flair for caricature. His talent was such that print and book dealers, fearing libel suits, shunned his satiric sketches. A composite portrait of Jackson, titled *Richard III,* illustrated just how venomous his work could be [Fig. 127]. In this sketch Johnston derided Jackson's entire military career. Although undated, it was probably published in 1828 as a kind of pictorial coffin handbill. Naked corpses compose the general's face and the braids of his epaulets. These are no doubt allusions to the executions of the six militiamen and to Ambrister and Arbuthnot. From behind the prison grates across Jackson's chest, two figures hold out a white sheet labeled "Habeas corpus." This cleverly contrived jabot alludes to Jackson's arrest of Louis Louailler in New Orleans in 1815 for a petty violation of martial law. When Judge Dominick A. Hall issued a writ of habeas corpus, Jackson jailed him, too. Johnston plumbed the depths of his imagination in this work: cannons become coat collars and a tent becomes a hat, the plume of which is a gun barrel billowing smoke. He probably based his design on an 1813 German caricature of Napoleon, whose visage was also composed of carcasses.[27] Johnston, a veteran of the stage, tapped Shakespeare for the title, *Richard III,* and

Figure 128.
Lithograph published by George Endicott and Moses Swett lithography company, 1833. Prints and Photographs Division, Library of Congress

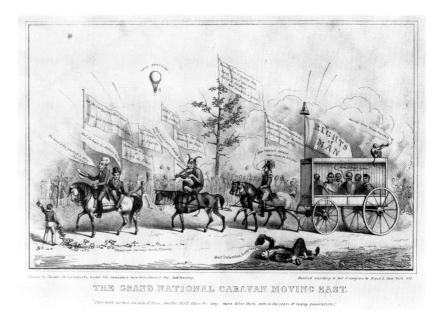

THE GRAND NATIONAL CARAVAN MOVING EAST.

"There hath not been the like of them, neither shall there be any more after them, even to the years of many generations."

borrowed a line from act 5, scene 3: "Methought the souls of all that I had murder'd, came to my tent."

V

In February 1833 a citizens' committee in Hartford, Connecticut, invited the President to visit New England to personally inspect her "institutions of Republican Freedom." Jackson accepted, and in early June embarked upon a nearly monthlong tour. Politically, such an excursion made good sense. Although New Englanders enthusiastically approved of his uncompromising stand against southern nullifiers, the financiers, businessmen, and industrialists among them deplored his war on the Bank as an unwarranted economic menace. The trip would provide Jackson with an opportunity to mingle with the people, explain his agenda, and possibly win adherents to the Democratic party.

Unlike the press, which seemingly reported Jackson's every move, the sole cartoon to mark the event was *The Grand National Caravan Moving East* [Fig. 128]. The inscription reads, "Drawn by Hassan Straightshanks, under the immediate superintendence of Maj. Jack Downing," but the real artist of this work, which was published by Endicott and Swett in 1833, is unknown. At the head of the caravan rides Jackson on a horse. "I've kissed & I've prattled to fifty fair maids," he boasts. Much was made of the Yankee girls who lined the President's route.[28]

Characteristically, Van Buren, who joined the party in New York, rides behind Jackson on the President's horse. Besides hoping to establish a measure of political clout in New England, Van Buren was along to offer counsel about the removal of deposits from the Bank of the United States. Although he understood better than Jackson the economic upheaval that such a bold measure could trigger throughout the country, he was careful not to discourage the President, whose mind was made up. "Had I a heart for falsehood fram'd," sighs the Little Magician.

Of particular note, Black Hawk and his five warrior companions bring up the rear, caged like wild beasts in a barred, horse-drawn wagon. The year before, Black Hawk had led his people, the Sauk and Fox tribes, in a desperate but futile war against federal and state troops in northern Illinois. In defeat, the tribes were forced once and for all across the Mississippi River. Black Hawk and five of his warriors were captured and held as prisoners before a military escort returned them home again. The liberty pole and cap, from which trails a flag labeled "Rights of Man," satirizes their predicament, as does Black Hawk, who states, "Home! Sweet home!" The balloon, captioned "rising generation," alludes to the ascent made by aeronaut Charles Ferson Durant at Castle Garden, New York City, on June 14, the same day upon which both Jackson and Black Hawk arrived.[29]

Indian affairs were routinely ignored by cartoonists during Jackson's presidency. *The Grand National Caravan Moving East* touched on them, but merely as an aside to the President's tour. At least one contemporary cartoon is known to have dealt squarely with Indians. Unfortunately this lithograph, in the collection of the William L. Clements Library at the University of Michigan, has been cropped, removing any possible record of the artist, publisher, or date [Fig. 129]. The sketch is simple and straightforward. Jackson, depicted as the Great Father, sits in the presidential chair, holding two of his Indian "children" on his lap; six more mingle at his feet and look up to him. The cartoon satirizes Jackson's compassion for the Indians, which was anything but embracing. His policy of removal was intended to clear Native Americans off their ancestral lands, thereby removing them west of the Mississippi River. The President's attitude was paternalistic and racist. It was also mainstream American, which is one explanation why so few caricatures of this nature were published.

VI

On June 24, 1833, Andrew Jackson was to have participated in ceremonies at the Charlestown navy yard on the occasion of dry-docking the forty-four-gun frigate *Constitution,* popularly called *Old Ironsides* for its steadfast service in the War of 1812. But the President was ailing that day in neighboring Boston. Meanwhile, Vice President Van Buren filled in at the navy yard, where he was entrusted with a special gift for the President, a cane carved from the ship's rotting timber.[30]

In its refurbished state, the *Constitution* was to carry a carved pine figurehead of Andrew Jackson to replace the weathered fiddle scroll billethead that it had carried since the War of 1812. The idea originated with Commodore Jesse D. Elliott, the new commandant of the navy yard. Elliott was a great admirer of Jackson. During the nullification crisis, he had commanded the navy's squadron at Charleston, South Carolina, and supported the President's uncompromising stance, as did all of New England. Gauging that the political climate was now right in Boston, Elliott reasoned that by placing "the image of the most popular man of the West upon the favorite ship of the East," westerners might develop a new and favorable opinion of the United States Navy.[31]

Then Jackson ordered the removal of the government's deposits from the Bank of the United States. Whatever graces the President had garnered in the North vanished. Outraged Bostonians rallied against desecrating the venerable vessel with the image of a tyrant. Buffeted by angry Whig newspapers, threatening handbills, and volatile cartoons, Elliott ordered the carving suspended, while he consulted with his superiors about the wisdom of fitting it onto another ship. The work later resumed, but the carver, Laban S. Beecher, was allegedly bribed one thousand dollars to allow his work to be pilfered. Elliott then had it

Figure 130.
Wooden figurehead by Laban S. Beecher,
carved for frigate *Constitution*, 1834.
Replacement head carved in 1835 by
Dodge and Son. Museum of the City of
New York; gift of the Seawanhaka
Corinthian Yacht Club

surreptitiously moved to the navy yard, where it was completed.[32] At last the
Constitution had a new ornament on its bow, a nearly ten-foot-tall, full-length
sculpture of Jackson, standing in his familiar cloak and holding his hat in his
left hand and the Constitution in his right [Fig. 130]. Beecher's folksy carving
looked like a reincarnation of a portrait by Earl.

∾

Daring has always had its own rewards. Therefore, the one hundred dollars
offered to an eighteen-year-old merchant marine to decapitate the figurehead
of Andrew Jackson was merely a bonus. The real prize would be the notoriety,
albeit anonymous, that inevitably would follow. In the late hours of July 3,
during a twilight storm, the deed was done. The next morning, Independence
Day, all of Boston was astir with the astonishing news. Jackson's many enemies
lauded the feat. The *National Intelligencer* learned that the derring-do was
accomplished by a lone young man, who with muffled oars rowed out to the
Constitution.[33] An hour later, Jackson's wooden head splashed into the harbor

without a sentinel's notice.

Commodore Elliott offered one thousand dollars for discovery of the culprit, but to no avail. Then he learned that the severed trophy had been proudly exhibited at a large party and that bits of it had been cut off and distributed as souvenirs. A chip was even sent to Elliott himself. Equally adept at political sniping, Elliott later wrapped the body of the mutilated figurehead with a five-striped flag, the emblem of New England's defiance of the War of 1812, when the ship finally left port.[34]

In a diary entry made on April 1, 1835, Secretary of the Navy Mahlon Dickerson identified the mysterious assailant.[35] That day he was visited by a young man, who, after introducing himself as Samuel W. Dewey, confessed his guilt. The motive, he claimed, was to protect the ship from any possible damage inflicted on it by others who were vehemently opposed to the figurehead. Dewey's addled revelation proved to be no April Fool's joke, when later that day he presented Dickerson with the evidence, neatly sawed off just below the nose and ears. Because there were no laws forbidding such destruction, Dewey walked away freely. Although its present whereabouts are unknown, a sawed-off wooden head of Jackson thought to be the original was illustrated in a 1936 *Antiques* magazine article.[36]

In the mid-1850s the *Constitution* was again overhauled, and a new figurehead of Jackson was mounted.[37] It served the ship until the mid-1870s, when it was replaced with a traditional fiddlehead.

The original body, which Elliott had wrapped in the flag, is in the collection of the Museum of the City of New York. A replacement head was attached in March of 1835 by Jeremiah Dodge & Son of New York City.[38]

∽

The cartoon *The Decapitation of a great Blockhead by the Mysterious agency of the Claret coloured Coat* presents an allegorical explanation of what had transpired [Fig. 131]. Two demons hold a saw and axe, and an ominous cloud at the bow of the ship, from which emerges a coat and the head of Jackson, heightens the sense of mystery. This sketch corroborated the *Boston Commercial Gazette,* which reported, "The night was dark, the rain fell in torrents, the thunder rolled, the lightning flashed, and the sentinels slept upon their posts!"[39]

According to the Boston *Daily Evening Transcript,* "the 'Glory' of yesterday was this morning wrapped up in mail cloth, 'to hide its diminished *head*' from the impertinent gaze of admiring multitudes."[40] An anonymous cartoon, *Fixing a block-head to the Constitution or putting a wart on the nose of old Ironsides,* depicts the head of Jackson wrapped in such a cloth [Fig. 132]. Anthony Imbert of New York, however, may have published this undated work before the mutilation took place, because the cartoon concerns the original controversy of the figurehead's installation. The uniformed character with his back turned represents Commodore Elliott, urging the dockhands on with a "double allowance of grog" for mounting the figurehead. The scroll that Jackson holds reads, "my interpretation of the Constitution." To the right, the drummer admonishes the fifer for playing the "rogue's march" instead of *Hail Columbia.*

VII

The attempted assassination of President Jackson on January 30, 1835, prompted a lithograph that was as unique for its news commentary as the actual event was in the national experience. Never before in the forty-year history of the presidency had such a deadly assault been attempted. A com-

Figure 131. Above.
Lithograph by unidentified artist, 1834.
Prints and Photographs Division, Library of
Congress

Figure 132. Right.
Lithograph published by Anthony Imbert,
1834. The Library Company of
Philadelphia

Figure 133.
Lithograph published by George Endicott,
1835. Prints and Photographs Division,
Library of Congress

paratively minor incident had occurred in May 1833, when a disgruntled young man pushed his hand into Jackson's face aboard a steamboat at Alexandria, Virginia. Although this provocation, for which one Robert B. Randolph was later arrested, caused much excitement, it was not life-threatening.[41] That Jackson survived this latest attempted assault was miraculous.

The incident occurred immediately after funeral services had been held in the House chamber for Representative Warren R. Davis of South Carolina. As Jackson, leaning on the arm of Treasury Secretary Levi Woodbury, was leaving the Capitol rotunda, a young man sprang from the crowd and leveled a pistol at the President. Since the day was damp, the powder inside the barrel did not ignite. A second pistol proved equally harmless. As a presidential escort knocked the assailant to the ground, Old Hickory had to be restrained from thrashing him with his cane. Jackson was then whisked back to the safety of the White House, where Vice President Van Buren observed him, moments later, "sitting with one of Major Donelson's children on his lap and conversing with General [Winfield] Scott, himself apparently the least disturbed person in the room." The assailant, Richard Lawrence, an unemployed house painter, was arrested, tried, and found innocent by reason of insanity.[42]

The Attempted Assassination, of the President of the United States, Jan. 30. 1835, published by George Endicott of New York, was neither caricature nor satire, but straightforward news coverage packaged as a lithograph [Fig. 133]. Said to be "Drawn from a Sketch by an eye witness," this work was the type of graphic reporting that the Harper brothers and Frank Leslie would make popular twenty years later in their illustrated magazines. Although the lithograph is scarcely accurate as a likeness, the principal figures have been drawn in greater detail and identified against a background of amorphous faces: depicted from left to right are Lieutenant Gedner, the naval officer who wrestled Lawrence to the ground; the President; Levi Woodbury; and Lawrence himself, shown attempting a second shot.

≈

Meanwhile, Jackson's diplomacy in settling the French spoliation claims was no less controversial than most of his executive actions, with one notable exception—for once his hard-line rhetoric and uncompromising posture united the entire nation. The antagonist this time was the French government. The trouble stemmed from its delinquency in paying the first of six installments of a twenty-five-million-franc indemnity for depredations against United States shipping interests during the Napoleonic wars. The initial payment was to have been made a year after the treaty's ratification on February 2, 1832. By September of 1833 the United States had not yet received anything. The American minister, Edward Livingston, had no difficulty in persuading the king and the ministry to meet the obligation. The chambers, however, which had to vote its approval, remained obdurate in view of French public opinion, which considered the claim exorbitant.

Convinced that a show of force might be required, Jackson ordered the navy to be ready in June 1834. Skittish Americans sensed war. In his annual message to Congress that year, Jackson strongly suggested that if France continued to shirk her duty, the United States should seize enough French property to satisfy the claim. The President's belligerent tone offended the French minis-

Figure 134.
Hand-colored lithograph by unidentified artist, 1835. Tennessee State Library and Archives

THE OLD LION, AND THE COCK WHAT WON'T FIGHT.

try, which abruptly recalled its representative from Washington. Soon after, the chambers voted in favor of honoring the treaty, but with the proviso that Jackson first make a satisfactory explanation of his offensive message.[43] The Americans held that since the President's address was intended solely for the consideration of Congress, the French, in effect, had no right reading over Uncle Sam's shoulder.

An anonymous hand-colored lithograph, *The Old Lion, and the Cock What Won't Fight,* illustrated the impasse as it stood the spring of 1835 when the *Globe,* the administration's organ, blared, "France will get no apology" [Fig. 134]. Jackson, depicted as a lion standing upon his government's claim, roars at King Louis-Philippe, "What! You want me to apologize? You think yourself Cock of the walk, but, By the Eternal! I'm a Roarer!" Philippe replies as he turns tail, "Ah! my dear friend. I ras only crack de leetle joke. Sacristi!"

In reality, Philippe agreed with the American claim. In confidential discussions with Livingston, he advised that Jackson be forthright about the issue as a diplomatic way of nudging the chambers to vote the money. The President's bristling message of 1834, however, surprised even the king. Privately, he

Figure 136.
Andrew Jackson and Louis-Philippe. Wood
carving by Pierre Joseph Landry, 1836. The
Hermitage: Home of President Andrew
Jackson

thought that Jackson's contrived belligerency was most amusing. The French
government, however, did not view it as such and demanded an explanation.

In his annual message of 1835, Jackson tempered his language toward France
without necessarily changing his attitude. Finally, with the aid of British
mediation, the French accepted Jackson's assurances that he had never
intended any menace or insult. The controversy was quickly resolved, the
indemnity was forthrightly paid, and the relationship between the two
countries was greatly improved.[44]

American cartoonists gloated in victory. Edward Williams Clay's *Grand
Virginia Reel and Scamperdown at the White House . . .* caricatured the nation's
jubilation [Fig. 135]. Jackson clutches a full bag of francs and reels in glee as
Louis-Philippe stumbles to the floor. To the left, Vice President Van Buren
leads the cabinet band, while in the background, heads of state from around
the world watch and comment. "Wy! Lo! What a set of flunkies!" quips the
emperor of China. Regardless of the cartoonist's satiric look at the affair, its
successful settlement bolstered America's image as a world power.[45]

In contrast to the biased caricatures, a primitive wood carving by Pierre Joseph
Landry commemorated the event with simple dignity. Born in France in
1770, Landry immigrated with his family to Louisiana at the age of fifteen,
where he became a successful planter. Landry began wood carving in late
middle age after a chronically bad knee relegated him to a life of sitting.

The conclusion of the French spoliation claims controversy in 1836 proved to
be inspirational for Landry. His wood carving of Andrew Jackson and Louis-
Philippe clasping arms around a tree is emblematic of peace, yet takes no sides
[Fig. 136]. Its simple message is friendship. The carved base, portraying two
ships, each sailing toward the other against a distant sun, holds forth the
promise for new ties between the two nations. Landry, a veteran of the New
Orleans campaign of 1815, allegedly presented his sculpture to Jackson.[46]

VIII

In June 1836 President Jackson addressed an unprecedented national problem—what to do with approximately twenty million dollars of excess federal
revenue. This situation had been created in the previous year by the eradica-

tion of the national debt. For the first time in its history, the country did not owe anyone a single dollar. This, coupled with the successful resolution of the French spoliations claims, meant that the nation was not only fiscally flush but also at peace.

Yet Jackson was deeply perplexed. It was not the government's function to be accumulating largess at the taxpayer's expense, nor would it be deemed responsible to hand money back, either to the states or to the people, with instructions on how it should be spent. This would result in the one practice that Jackson detested most—government interference in the lives of the citizens.[47]

Caucus on the Surplus Bill by Edward Williams Clay captures a rare moment of indecision on the part of the President [Fig. 137]. With the Distribution Bill lying on the table before him, Jackson contemplates his options: "What the devil shall I do Matty, with this Bill?—If I veto it the cursed Whigs are strong enough to pass it!!" Van Buren, sitting opposite, replies that he is "dead against giving away a dollar, but as you say, needs must when the devil drives!!" The figure seated in the middle represents Roger B. Taney, the former treasury secretary and the newly appointed Chief Justice of the Supreme Court. Taking advantage of Taney's fiscal experience and deft legal mind, Jackson had asked him to prepare a paper on the question, which Taney wrote as a veto message. In the cartoon he laments, "It's hard to part with our Surplus, but the people are too strong for us!!"

Ultimately Jackson signed the Distribution Bill, partly because it was attached to legislation designed to regulate the deposit banks. The President was anxious to bring order to the national banking system before it became unwieldy and self-serving. He also acted for political reasons.[48] Since the administration was determined to divide the surplus among the states, the endorsement of the bill would invariably boost Vice President Van Buren's popularity in the upcoming presidential election.

ℰ⃞

The contest of 1836 was something of a political free-for-all. Van Buren was of course the choice of Jacksonian Democrats, with Hugh Lawson White of Tennessee winning support in the South. Daniel Webster was the favorite in the North, especially in Massachusetts. General William Henry Harrison of Ohio defeated Henry Clay to become the choice of the West and the Whig party's leading contender.

Edward Williams Clay's *Grand Match Between the Kinderhook Poney and the*

Figure 137. Below.
Lithograph by Edward Williams Clay, 1836. Prints and Photographs Division, Library of Congress

Figure 138. Right.
Lithograph by Edward Williams Clay, 1836. Prints and Photographs Division, Library of Congress

THE MODERN BALAAM AND HIS ASS.

Ohio Ploughman caricatured the contest as it stood in April 1836 [Fig. 138]. In
a game of high-stakes billiards, Harrison attempts to outshoot Van Buren. His
real opponent, however, is Jackson, who is shown holding a spotter at the
opposite end of the table. Richard M. Johnson, the Democratic vice-presiden-
tial candidate, stands beside Van Buren, while Webster and Clay, arm in arm,
encourage Harrison. The artist interjected his own bias in the portraits on the
wall: behind Jackson hangs the emperor Napoleon, and behind Harrison
hangs the hero Washington.[49]

Van Buren's decisive victory in the election reflected Old Hickory's popular
hold on the common man and the working classes. Unfortunately for his
successor, the President could not transfer his hero's mantle, but rather only a
worsening national economy bordering on collapse. Jackson's myopic fiscal
policies were not entirely to blame for the Panic of 1837 as the Whigs claimed,
but they did have unforeseen detrimental consequences, beginning with the
demise of the Bank of the United States. In its place, the newly designated
state banks, flush with federal assets and largely unregulated, increased the
money supply by issuing large quantities of bills backed with insufficient
specie. This monetary expansion stimulated a frenzy of internal improvements
and western land speculations. To curb the latter, Jackson issued his Specie
Circular on July 11, 1836, against the advice of his cabinet and during the
congressional recess.[50] This executive order stipulated that future sales of public
lands could be negotiated only with gold or silver. Consequently, when the
demand for specie rose, it far outstripped the supply. Hundreds of banks
unable to redeem their notes were forced to close.

An anonymously produced colored lithograph, *The Modern Balaam and His
Ass,* ingeniously satirized the Specie Circular and its catastrophic effects on the
banking system [Fig. 139]. The genius of this cartoon lay in the adaptation of
an Old Testament passage. Balaam was a Syrian diviner who was hired to
curse the Israelites. Three times during his journey, the ass upon which he rode
was stopped by the angel of God standing before it. Because the angel's
presence was invisible to Balaam, he beat the ass to proceed. After the third

Figure 140. Above.
Lithograph attributed to Edward Williams
Clay, 1837. Prints and Photographs
Division, Library of Congress

Figure 141. Right.
Hand-colored lithograph by Napoleon
Sarony, 1837. American Antiquarian
Society

time, the ass spoke to Balaam, inquiring why he was being beaten. Only then
was Balaam able to see the angel, who permitted him to continue, on condition that he speak strictly in God's name. Upon reaching Moab, Balaam
blessed the Israelites instead of cursing them and delivered four oracles promising prosperity and good fortune for Israel.

Given its Biblical framework, *The Modern Balaam* provokes contemplation
that transcends an initial reading. At first glance Jackson appears to be beating
the hesitant beast, carrying "Specie Currency," onward. Apparently Jackson
has not yet noticed the apparition before him representing the bankruptcies of
1837. Nor in reality was Jackson prepared for the banking crises. His original
motive in issuing the Specie Circular was to curtail the wild and often corrupt
land speculations that were putting homesteads out of the financial reach of
many honest settlers.[51] He was also concerned about protecting the government's deposits, which were being used to finance this dangerously infla-
tionary spending spree.

The cartoon's captions, however, tell a different story. The ass, representing the
Specie Circular, asks of its rider, "Am not I thine Ass, upon which thou hast
ridden ever since I was thine unto this day?" Jackson, now aware of the
financial hardship he has wrought, professes that he would strike down the
Specie Circular with a veto. Like his Biblical namesake, Jackson, the modern
Balaam, has reversed himself completely. Behind him trails the new President,
Martin Van Buren, who appears foolish by his announcement, "I shall tread in
the footsteps of my illustrious predecessor." In the background are several
Manhattan banks advertising "No specie."

In the absence of specie, certain cities, businesses, and even individuals
throughout the country began issuing paper money in small denominations to
be used like change. As currency these "shinplasters" were virtually worthless.
They did, however, inspire several caricatures, two of which H. R. Robinson
published in 1837.[52] Based on artistic style, *Fifty Cents Shin Plaster* was
probably the work of Edward Williams Clay [Fig. 140]. Jackson, chasing the
"Gold Humbug," rides a pig recklessly toward a precipice. Thomas Hart
Benton follows, astride a jackass (Benton vigorously supported the Specie
Circular and advised Jackson in drafting it). The quill pen he carries, labeled
"Expunger," alludes to his successful fight in the Senate to have Jackson's
censure eradicated from the record. In the rear, President Van Buren, ever the
wily politician, rides a fox down a safer path. "Although I follow in the
footsteps of Jackson," he professes, "it is expedient, at this time to deviate a
little!!" Van Buren now advocated an independent "Sub-Treasury" as a means
of reorganizing the national banking system. John C. Calhoun, in a sudden
swing back to the Democratic fold, strongly endorsed similar legislation.[53] In

Figure 142.
Lithograph by Edward Williams Clay,
1837. Peters Collection, National Museum
of American History, Smithsonian
Institution

Figure 143.
Hand-colored lithograph by Henry Dacre,
circa 1840. Prints and Photographs
Division, Library of Congress

Treasury Note 75 cents, Napoleon Sarony satirized this surprising alliance in
support of an independent treasury, through which public funds would be
managed by government officials without the aid of banks [Fig. 141]. Decorat-
ing the side margins of this mock shinplaster are caricature vignettes of
Jackson, who is no longer the center of national attention.

For the remainder of his life and after, Jackson would be caricatured in such
cartoons as Clay's *The Times,* which depicts the dire effects of the Panic of
1837 [Fig. 142]. In some instances he would appear as a person; in others,
such as *Weighed & Found Wanting* by Henry Dacre, he would appear as an
apparition lurking in the background, tipping the scales in favor of the
common man [Fig. 143].

Notes

1. Parton, *Jackson,* vol. 3, p. 599.

2. Allan Nevins and Frank Weitenkampf, *A Century of Political Cartoons: Caricature in the
United States from 1800 to 1900* (New York, 1975), pp. 11–12, 16; Nancy Reynolds Davison,
"E. W. Clay: American Political Caricaturist of the Jacksonian Era" (Ph.D. diss., University of
Michigan, 1980), pp. 107–10.

3. James Akin to Ralph E. W. Earl, February 17, 1819, Earl Papers.

4. Akin's letter is published in William Murrell, *A History of American Graphic Humor* (New
York, 1933–1938), vol. 1, p. 135.

5. Davison, "E. W. Clay," p. 133.

6. Nancy R. Davison, "Andrew Jackson in Cartoon and Caricature," in *American Printmaking
Before 1876: Fact, Fiction, and Fantasy* (Washington, D.C., 1975), p. 23.

7. Jackson's letter is published in *Virginia Magazine of History and Biography* 29 (April 1921):
191–92.

8. *Correspondence of Jackson,* vol. 3, pp. 455, 463; John Binns, *Recollections of the Life of John
Binns: Twenty-nine Years in Europe and Fifty-three in the United States* (Philadelphia, 1854),
pp. 243, 245–46, 255–56. Binns had once been an admirer of Jackson. In 1815, during a
celebratory illumination in Philadelphia for Jackson's New Orleans victory, Binns had a large
transparency painted, nearly covering the front of his house, representing the hero on
horseback at the head of his staff, in pursuit of the enemy.

9. Murrell, *American Graphic Humor,* vol. 1, pp. 115-16; Davison, "E. W. Clay," pp. 110-11; Stephen Hess and Milton Kaplan, *The Ungentlemanly Art: A History of American Political Cartoons* (New York, 1975), p. 67.

10. Remini, *Andrew Jackson,* vol. 2, pp. 186-87; Davison, "E. W. Clay," pp. 114-15.

11. Davison, "E. W. Clay," pp. 131-32.

12. Remini, *Andrew Jackson,* vol. 2, pp. 306-8.

13. Parton, *Jackson,* vol. 3, pp. 195-96.

14. Remini, *Andrew Jackson,* vol. 2, pp. 316-17.

15. Frances Trollope, herself mystified by the resignations, considered Clay's work to be "the only tolerable caricature" she had seen in the country. See *Domestic Manners,* pp. 331-32. John Quincy Adams, *The Diary of John Quincy Adams, 1794-1845,* ed. Allan Nevins (New York, 1951), pp. 418-19.

16. Davison, "E. W. Clay," pp. 127-29.

17. William J. Duane, quoted in Schlesinger, *Age of Jackson,* p. 67; Remini, *Andrew Jackson,* vol. 2, p. 326.

18. Cartoonists delighted in the sayings of the President. "By the Eternal" and "I take the responsibility" were two that were especially suited for satire. Jackson uttered the former repeatedly; the latter he used in reference to an administration paper calling for the suspension of government deposits in the Bank of the United States. See Van Buren, *Autobiography,* vol. 2, p. 608; Schlesinger, *Age of Jackson,* p. 101.

19. Schlesinger, *Age of Jackson,* pp. 110, 276; Remini, *Andrew Jackson,* vol. 2, p. 255.

20. Davison, "E. W. Clay," pp. 130-31. This cartoon marked Clay's first association with Henry R. Robinson of New York, who was one of the primary publishers of political caricature in the United States between 1836 and 1849.

21. Remini, *Andrew Jackson,* vol. 2, pp. 342-43, 366-67; Van Buren, *Autobiography,* vol. 2, p. 625.

22. Davison, "Jackson in Cartoon and Caricature," pp. 21-22; Ward, *Symbol for an Age,* pp. 81-86.

23. Remini, *Andrew Jackson,* vol. 2, p. 366.

24. Schlesinger, *Age of Jackson,* p. 109.

25. Remini, *Andrew Jackson,* vol. 3, pp. 150-60.

26. Notice of the publication of *Symptoms of a Locked Jaw* appeared in the Washington *National Journal,* August 16, 1827. I am grateful to Harold Moser, editor of the Jackson Papers Project, for making this discovery and for bringing it to my attention. Dunlap, *Arts of Design,* vol. 3, pp. 111-17; Murrell, *American Graphic Humor,* vol. 1, pp. 103, 119-20.

27. Davison, "Jackson in Cartoon and Caricature," p. 23. An illustration of this unusual caricature of Napoleon appears in John Ashton, *English Caricature and Satire on Napoleon I* (New York, 1968), p. 358.

28. Fletcher M. Green, "On Tour with President Andrew Jackson," *New England Quarterly* 36 (June 1963): 226-27.

29. Black Hawk mentions this astonishing ascent in *Black Hawk, An Autobiography,* ed. Donald Jackson (Urbana, Ill., 1964), p. 147.

30. *Niles' Weekly Register,* June 29, 1833; Remini, *Andrew Jackson,* vol. 3, p. 77.

31. Ward, *Symbol for an Age,* pp. 115-16; Charles E. Harris, "Figureheads of the 'Constitution,'" *Antiques* 30 (July 1936): 10-12.

32. Ward, *Symbol for an Age,* pp. 117-18; Washington *Globe,* August 1, 1834.

33. *National Intelligencer,* July 14, 16, 1834; Washington *Globe,* July 8, 1834.

34. *Niles' Weekly Register,* July 12, 1834; Ward, *Symbol for an Age,* pp. 119–20.

35. This entry is published in Frederick A. Canfield, "The Figure Head of Jackson," *Proceedings of the New Jersey Historical Society* 7 (July 1922): 222–23.

36. Harris, "Figureheads," p. 12.

Dickerson retained possession of the wooden head in his New Jersey home until his death in 1853. With the sale of his effects the following year, the head, which had been set on top of some bookcases, was claimed by the purchaser of Dickerson's library.

37. This figurehead, now at the United States Naval Academy at Annapolis, is shorter and more idealized than the original. Still holding the Constitution in his right hand, Jackson places his left in a double-breasted jacket, à la Napoleon. Oddly, the sculpture, with its generously carved shoulders and ample girth, resembles more the figure of Daniel Webster. *New York Times,* January 13, 1932, and January 12, 1936.

38. In about 1861 Jonathan Bowers of Tyngsboro, Massachusetts, purchased the figurehead in a Boston junk shop. In about 1925, industrialist Henry Ford, who was then scouring the countryside for early Americana with which to build his own museum, offered Bowers's sons ten thousand dollars for it. This price was topped by an elderly New England collector who had a lifelong interest in *Old Ironsides.* Although at the time he wished to remain anonymous, his identity seems to have been that of Max Williams. In 1928, after his death, Anderson Galleries of New York sold his effects. William B. Leeds purchased the figurehead and subsequently donated it to the Seawanhaka Corinthian Yacht Club at Oyster Bay, from which it was acquired by the Museum of the City of New York. See *New York Times,* May 3 and November 9, 1925; January 12, 15, 1936; *Niles' Weekly Register,* March 21, 1835.

39. As reported in the Washington *Globe,* July 8, 1834.

40. *Ibid.*

41. Remini, *Andrew Jackson,* vol. 3, pp. 60–61, 227–29.

42. Van Buren, *Autobiography,* vol. 2, p. 353; Carlton Jackson, "Another Time, Another Place—The Attempted Assassination of President Andrew Jackson," *Tennessee Historical Quarterly* 26 (Summer 1967): 189–90.

43. John Spencer Bassett, *The Life of Andrew Jackson* (Hamden, Conn., 1967), pp. 663–69; Remini, *Andrew Jackson,* vol. 3, pp. 230–31.

44. Parton, *Jackson,* vol. 3, pp. 568–78; Bassett, *Life of Jackson,* pp. 671–72.

45. Remini, *Andrew Jackson,* vol. 3, p. 289.

46. Lester Burbank Bridaham, "Pierre Joseph Landry, Louisiana Woodcarver," *Antiques* 72 (August 1957): 157–59; records of the Ladies' Hermitage Association.

In 1923 Marshall Lawrence, a great-grandson of Jackson, donated Landry's work to the Ladies' Hermitage Association.

47. Remini, *Andrew Jackson,* vol. 3, pp. 318–20.

48. *Ibid.,* pp. 323–25.

49. Davison, "E. W. Clay," pp. 161–62.

50. Remini, *Andrew Jackson,* vol. 3, pp. 327–28.

51. *Ibid.,* pp. 326–27.

52. Thomas C. Blaisdell, Jr., *et al., The American Presidency in Political Cartoons, 1776–1976* (Berkeley, Calif., 1976), pp. 66–69; Davison, "Jackson in Cartoon and Caricature," p. 23.

53. Remini, *Andrew Jackson,* vol. 3, p. 438.

1838

June: Portraits painted by Thomas J. Jackson and B. W. Jenks at Hermitage

July 15: Joins Presbyterian Church, fulfilling promise to Rachel made in 1826

September 16: Earl dies at Hermitage

December: Bust commissioned by Jacksonian Democrats in Kentucky modeled at Hermitage by Joel Tanner Hart

1840

January: Attends Silver Jubilee of victory in New Orleans

Portraits executed by R. Brand, Jacques Amans, and Edward D. Marchant in New Orleans

Portrait painted by Trevor Thomas Fowler aboard steamer *Vicksburg*

Miniature executed by James Tooley, Jr., after Marchant's likeness

March–April: Portrait commissioned by Cincinnati Democrats painted at Hermitage by Miner Kilbourne Kellogg

1842

March: Miniature painted by John Wood Dodge at Hermitage

1843

Engraving of Dodge's miniature published by Moseley Isaac Danforth

1844

June: One-thousand-dollar prize awarded by city of New Orleans to Jacques Amans and Theodore Sidney Moise for large equestrian painting

1845

April: Is photographed by Edward Anthony at Hermitage

May 29: Last life portrait painted by George P. A. Healy

June 8: Dies at Hermitage

June 10: Buried in Hermitage garden beside Rachel

Chapter 7

Sage of the Hermitage, 1838 –1845

Figure 144.
Oil on canvas by Thomas J. Jackson, 1838.
The Hermitage: Home of President Andrew
Jackson

Home again at the Hermitage, Andrew Jackson lived out the remainder of his life. The worries of executive leadership now rested on the shoulders of his successor, Martin Van Buren. The unsolicited counsel that filled Jackson's letters suggests that a part of him yearned to be in Washington, in spite of such domestic concerns as the severe drought that devastated his harvest during the summer and fall of 1838. Still, this setback did not dissuade Jackson's thirty-year-old son from purchasing another extensive plantation, miring the household estate deeper in debt. Jackson's health also remained precarious.

A brighter note was the fulfillment of Jackson's eighteen-year-old promise to his now-deceased wife, Rachel, that he would become a Christian. On Sunday, July 15, 1838, in a special service at the Hermitage church that Jackson had built for Rachel in 1823, he joined the Presbyterian faith. Tragically, Ralph E. W. Earl died two months later.

As if this news were not bad enough, by the end of the year Jackson learned of the scandal unfolding around Samuel Swartwout, a Jackson appointee to the post of collector of the customs house in New York City. Following the expiration of his appointment in March 1838, Swartwout was discovered to have misappropriated more than a million dollars. He escaped prosecution by fleeing to England. His defalcation tainted Jackson's administration with corruption unprecedented in the nation's history. Jackson, who had sworn to curb such government fraud, was mortified when apprised of this latest development.[1]

I

It was also in 1838 that two new portraits of Jackson were painted. Such occasions were notable because relatively few artists passed through the Nashville area, and those who did invariably made arrangements to visit the Hermitage. This was the case with Thomas J. Jackson and B. W. Jenks, both of whom arrived in June on separate visits.

Little has been recorded about the life of Thomas J. Jackson. He was born in Woodbridge, New Jersey, in 1815. His name was listed in the New York City directories in the mid-1830s, and he painted in New Orleans in the early 1840s. A New Orleans newspaper summed up his modest talent: "His likenesses are always good, but his peculiar forte is in draperies."[2]

It was probably during the artist's southern travels that he met the retired President and painted a small portrait of him [Fig. 144]. The likeness is crude and smacks of being a true representation only in the depiction of Jackson's most obvious features: his bristling white hair, his spectacles, and his long, deeply creased face.[3]

Figure 145.
Marble by Joel Tanner Hart, circa 1850.
Kentucky Historical Society

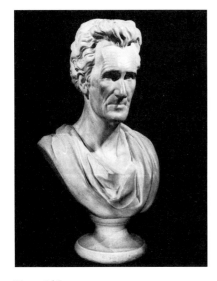

Figure 146.
Plaster by Joel Tanner Hart, 1838 or after.
The Stradlings

Information relating to B. W. Jenks is sparser still. In the early 1840s he worked the Mississippi and Ohio River valleys, from New Orleans to Cincinnati and into western Virginia. His portrait of Jackson has not been identified and is known only through a contemporary newspaper account. On June 9, 1838, the *Nashville Union* reported: *We had the pleasure last Saturday of examining an unfinished portrait of Gen. Jackson, painted by Mr. B. W. Jenks, for some gentlemen of Louisville. The drapery, background, &c. require the last touches of the artist, but the face and head is complete. The General is represented sitting in a chair, dressed in a plain black coat, the figure slightly stooping, the features rather pale, and the fire of his eye somewhat subdued by recent illness—the outline of the features is perfect, and the expression true to life.*[4]

It was the newspaper's understanding that Jackson would not sit for another portrait, thus seemingly distinguishing Jenks's likeness as the last one taken from life. Fortunately, this proved not to be the case.

❧

Before the close of 1838, the last life bust of Jackson was executed. The request for the sitting arrived in the form of a letter. Jackson received dozens of letters every month from admirers throughout the country. Some wanted his autograph, others requested locks of his hair, and still others wrote just to praise him for his many years of dedicated public service.

In early November a committee representing a group of friends in the vicinity of Lexington, Kentucky, invited Jackson to sit for a portrait bust to be modeled by Joel Tanner Hart. Their letter introduced Hart as a young sculptor who "has already exhibited extraordinary genius, taste and proficiency in his art."[5] Jackson pondered the proposition in light of his feeble health. Never wanting to disappoint, he mustered his energy and complied with the committee's request.

Born in Clark County, Kentucky, in 1810, Hart grew up in a family hard-pressed to make a living. By self-study, Hart compensated for his lack of formal schooling. He went to work in his early teens as a stonecutter, and in Lexington his boyhood interest in sculpture burgeoned into his life's passion. Hart's subsequent success, particularly with a bust of Kentucky politician and abolitionist Cassius M. Clay, propelled his fledgling career to professional heights.[6]

Exactly when in December, or for how long, Hart visited at the Hermitage is not known. Predictably, he was encouraged to stay for as long as he needed, or for as long as Jackson's health held out. Hart had completed his work by Christmas Eve. That day Jackson wrote to the committee from Lexington, apprising them that the likeness "is esteemed by all who have seen it a good" one. "I think it equal to any that has been taken of me," he confessed.[7]

Hart's white marble bust, copied from a plaster model, was indeed a realistic representation of Old Hickory in his golden years [Fig. 145]. The wrinkles and furrows are all there; only the spontaneity of expression discernible in the works by Powers and Pettrich is missing. Hart's *Jackson* completed a distinguished series of portrait sculpture dating back to 1819, when William Rush executed his terra-cotta bust.

Today Hart's *Jackson* is owned by the Kentucky Historical Society and is on display in the Old State House in Frankfort.[8] A plaster version has been recently discovered by a New York City antiques dealer [Fig. 146]. Although the provenance is all but lost, the work closely resembles a plaster bust of Jackson by Hart illustrated in the *Lexington Herald-Leader* of March 20, 1938.[9]

As a likeness, the plaster version is almost identical to the marble, with the notable exception of Jackson's hair. In the marble bust, it is straight and swept behind him; in the plaster, Jackson sports a wavy pompadour reminiscent of the work of Luigi Persico. Coincidentally, Persico's marble bust, taken from an 1829 sitting, was in the Hermitage at the time of Hart's visit. Perhaps it influenced Hart in making his original clay model. Yet, when it came time to carve the marble, he obviously reconsidered and fashioned Old Hickory's hair in a manner truer to life.

II

The Silver Jubilee of Jackson's victory at New Orleans was scheduled to take place in that city on January 8, 1840. Jackson was disinclined to attend: a trip of more than five hundred miles in frigid weather and with his fragile health scarcely made sense. But that was before creditors began knocking more loudly on the doors of the Hermitage. Little did the old man know that he had been hearing the abridged version only from Andrew Jackson, Jr. To his surprise and mortification, he learned of still other significant debts.

With these unforeseen circumstances thrust suddenly upon Jackson, a trip to New Orleans began to seem like a good idea, provided he could stop along the way to make favorable arrangements with certain of his son's creditors. The advance that Jackson secured for his cotton crop would ease the situation slightly, and his word of honor, he hoped, would cover the balance for the time. The trip would also allow Jackson the chance to personally lend his prestige to the Democratic ticket in its bid for the reelection of President Martin Van Buren. Nearly three years had passed since Jackson last made a public appearance. The time was right to demonstrate again the principles of democracy that he had been espousing for more than a decade.[10]

Figure 147.
Crayon on paper by R. Brand, 1840.
Louisiana State Museum

On Christmas Eve, Jackson left for New Orleans with Major Donelson, arriving on January 8. The victory spirit of twenty-five years before soothed his wearied body and burdened mind like an elixir. A convoy of four steamboats, "laden with passengers and soldiers, with cannon firing and colors streaming," escorted the general to the city wharf.[11] There, a crowd of several thousand waved hats and handkerchiefs as he stepped off the boat. Thus began the first of several festive days filled with parades, military pageantry, speeches, and dinners. It was a chance for Jackson and the citizens of the Crescent City to relive a proud moment. Not surprisingly, it also provided an opportunity for the execution of several new portraits of the hero of 1815.

Among the artists of New Orleans, R. Brand remains anonymous, except for a signed profile sketch of Jackson made during this visit. With crayon and paper Brand depicted Jackson sitting in an open carriage passing in front of a building lined with spectators [Fig. 147]. The scene is reminiscent of the newspaper reports of the grand welcoming procession of soldiers and citizens that escorted Jackson to the State House, the Place d'Armes (Jackson Square), and St. Louis Cathedral. Along the levee and over Canal and Chartres streets Jackson rode in a barouche drawn by four white horses. "*Amid a sea* of human heads," all eyes jockeyed to see him. Balconies were literally white with handkerchiefs waved by ladies, "as though at every step of the *cortege,* a thousand snowy and glittering birds were *started, and took wing.*"[12] Jackson bowed in humble acknowledgment. "His head was white," reported the *New-Orleans Commercial Bulletin,* "as if the snow of a hundred winters had fallen upon it; and the palid [*sic*] and wan aspect of his features indicated the near approach of the aged Hero to 'that bourne whence no traveller returns.'"[13]

Somewhere in the throng of humanity stood Brand, mentally taking note of the aged hero. The artist was obviously struck with Jackson's weathered appearance: both his stately mien and his feebleness are captured in this amateur sketch, perhaps the only one of its kind that Brand drew. The drawing is owned by the Louisiana State Museum in New Orleans.

❧

No portrait of Jackson was officially commissioned in commemoration of the Silver Jubilee, but the likeness executed by Jacques Guillaume Lucien Amans might now claim that distinction. In the 1840s and early 1850s Amans was the finest portraitist in New Orleans. Born in Belgium in 1801, he studied art in Paris, exhibiting in the salons there before sailing to Louisiana in 1836. Virtually unknown outside of his adopted state, Amans won local recognition for his oil portraits of Andrew Jackson and Zachary Taylor.

At the urging of his fellow townsmen, Amans on January 10 addressed a letter to the general requesting a portrait sitting. "If this favor should be granted by you," wrote the artist, "my intention is to present the portrait to the city of New-Orleans." Four sessions of an hour each would be sufficient, and Jackson would not even need to interrupt his conversations with friends and visitors.[14]

The sittings no doubt took place at the French Exchange Hotel on St. Louis Street, where a suite of rooms had been readied for Jackson's comfort. There is no way of knowing just how much time he actually granted Amans; however, it was enough for the artist to have painted a careful likeness. Jackson appears tired, almost exhausted. Two weeks of travel were wearisome for him, not to mention the activities scheduled since his arrival. The first day Jackson had found it necessary to postpone visiting the plain of Chalmette—the scene of his historic battle—because of fatigue.[15]

Amans's likeness compares favorably with the best. Considering Jackson's health and exhaustion, his expression naturally lacks vitality. He appears attentive, however, much as he does in the portrait by Asher Durand painted five years earlier.

Four portraits of Jackson by Amans are extant. Unfortunately, their provenances are not sufficient to determine the order in which they were painted. The smallest version measures 21⅝ by 17⅛ inches. Based on its size, it is tempting to view this painting as the original study canvas. Yet there is a hand-me-down quality to the likeness, which suggests that it was probably a replica. This small canvas, which was illustrated in 1968 in *Antiques* magazine, has now slipped from view.[16]

Two larger versions, both measuring approximately 60 by 49 inches, are owned by the Chicago Historical Society and the Historic New Orleans Collection. In the latter likeness, which may indeed be the original, lifelike qualities are evident in the concentrated focus of Jackson's eyes and in his overall pensive expression [Fig. 148]. Something resembling a pillow has been lightly sketched in behind Jackson's back. The only trace of pentimento occurs here, as if the artist was uncertain about including this cushioning device, which he left out in the other three canvases. Generally the brushwork in this canvas is finer, particularly in the background detail.[17] On a folded piece of paper lying on the circular table, Amans signed his surname and dated the portrait "8 Janvier 1840." Since it was not until January 10 that he first approached Jackson about sitting, this date refers only to the anniversary of the Battle of New Orleans. The painting at the Chicago Historical Society is also signed but is dated less precisely, "Janvier 1840" [Fig. 149].[18]

Figure 148.
Oil on canvas by Jacques Guillaume Lucien
Amans, 1840. Historic New Orleans
Collection; Museum/Research Center, Acc.
No. 1982.11

Figure 149.
Oil on canvas by Jacques Guillaume Lucien
Amans, 1840. The Chicago Historical
Society, 1920.54

Figure 150.
Oil on canvas by Jacques Guillaume Lucien
Amans, not dated. Tennessee State Museum

An unsigned and undated version of this likeness, measuring 72 by 48 inches, hangs in the Tennessee State Museum in Nashville [Fig. 150]. The image itself is clearly a diluted copy when compared with the New Orleans portrait: for example, Jackson's hands and black suit appear as if they had been hastily painted. The portrait has been simplified overall, especially in the lack of detail in Jackson's jabot and in the background composition. A curtain acts as a backdrop instead of a columned interior, as in the other paintings. Paradoxically, because of its simpler composition, this is the portrait that one would have expected Amans to have roughed out in the precious time in which Jackson sat for him. Old Hickory's trademark—his beaverskin hat—even lies on the table. Yet it lacks the intensity of the other canvases.[19]

୧୨

Edward Dalton Marchant apparently never made multiple replicas of his portrait of Andrew Jackson painted during the Silver Jubilee, as did Jacques Amans. In fact, no such likeness was known to exist until just recently [Fig. 151]. According to one source, Jackson granted Marchant three sittings. The completed canvas went on view in the artist's studio at 12 Exchange Place, with portraits of other notable figures, including Henry Clay and General

Figure 151.
Oil on canvas by Edward Dalton Marchant,
1840. The Union League of Philadelphia

Figure 152.
Watercolor on ivory by James Tooley, Jr.,
after Edward Dalton Marchant, 1840.
National Portrait Gallery, Smithsonian
Institution; gift of Mr. William H. Lively,
Mrs. Mary Lively Hoffman, and Dr.
Charles J. Lively

William Henry Harrison, the Whig presidential candidate. Most of what is
known about Marchant's *Jackson* has been gleaned from contemporary
newspaper accounts. Although Marchant's was only a head-and-shoulders
image, it was considered "as highly wrought and imposing" as Earl's full-length
painted for the city in 1821. "Age seems to have a benignant effect on the
features of Andrew Jackson," observed the *Mississippi Free Trader,* "adding a
new and softened dignity to a contour of head and countenance that ever
expressed the lineaments of his high destiny." Even the *New-Orleans Commercial Bulletin,* a local Whig sheet, after touting the portrait of General Harrison,
praised the *Jackson* as "a very natural likeness."[20]

A surprise discovery in the *Natchez Weekly Gazette* of January 22, 1840, has
resulted in the identification of Marchant's heretofore lost likeness of Jackson.
The *Gazette* stated that Marchant had given James Tooley, Jr., permission to
copy the portrait of Jackson, as well as that of Harrison. Tooley, a miniaturist
and landscape painter, was active in the Mississippi Valley in the early 1840s,
especially in Natchez and New Orleans. His miniature of Jackson is a rectangular watercolor on ivory [Fig. 152].[21]

The Tooley miniature was assumed to have been painted from life. The
likeness is animated and is consistent with that by Amans, although less
detailed. However, its newfound status as a copy has in no measure diminished

its artistic or historical luster; it has raised its own value by aiding in the identification of the Marchant likeness, now in the collection of the Union League of Philadelphia. For many years this oil on canvas portrait, measuring 30 by 25 inches, had been attributed to Henry Inman.[22] Yet no record has surfaced to suggest that Inman ever painted a portrait of Andrew Jackson. The probability that the Union League portrait is really by Marchant is almost certain, based on the uncanny similarity to James Tooley's miniature. The two likenesses are nearly identical in the execution of Jackson's facial lines and shadings. This is particularly evident in the shadow cast by the bifocals, the inner lenses of which folded back neatly against the frames along Jackson's temples. The Silver Jubilee paintings are the only ones to depict Jackson wearing this unique style of eyeglass. After viewing the Marchant portrait, a contemporary source observed that Jackson's "ancient spectacles, of Jack Downing memory, stand off in firm perspective, casting a mellow shade back upon the dimmed eye and faded cheek."[23]

The Union League portrait fits the above description. This likeness, however, lacks a certain quality of melancholy about the eyes that is characteristic of Jackson's later portraiture. The mouth also poses a problem in that it has been too youthfully depicted; there are no pursed lips indicating the sitter's severe dental deterioration. Surprisingly, James Tooley, in his miniature, better conveyed Jackson's aura of fatigue and his fragile constitution.[24]

❧

When the Jubilee festivities ended, Jackson bade farewell to the city of New Orleans. The timbre of this mutual adieu communicated a sense of finality. Every person knew that Jackson would never again be returning to the place where he had achieved enduring fame. Naturally, there was an urge to cling to the fleeting memories. This was demonstrated the following week when the "plain, but rich and massive" bedstead used by Old Hickory during his stay was auctioned for the exorbitant price of $130.[25]

Jackson may have been leaving town forever, but he was not going without a motley escort. The *Vicksburg*, upon which he made the return voyage, was crowded beyond capacity. No less than 120 people had taken berths on the floor. Rather than "snore in concert with so many bedfellows," a reporter bound for Natchez elected to wait for another boat.[26] At some point during this tedious journey, Trevor Thomas Fowler painted a portrait of Jackson, now in the collection of the Chicago Historical Society [Fig. 153]. Fowler was an Irishman, born in Dublin in 1800. He exhibited in the royal academies of his native city and also in London before immigrating to the United States. In 1837 and 1838, he was listed in New York City, and by 1840 he had ventured as far as New Orleans. "His paintings are life-like," noted the *Daily Picayune* in 1842, "and there is a classical finish about them, which none could give but he whom nature endowed with the spirit of an artist."[27]

In composition, Fowler's head-and-shoulders likeness is similar to those by Marchant and Tooley. Jackson faces left, he wears bifocals, his hair is brushed back in characteristic fashion, and he is dressed in a dark suit of clothes. Although Fowler's image is breezier and less studied than the Marchant-Tooley likenesses, it is no less accurate in conveying an impression of physical decline. Jackson's age and precarious health—accentuated by the walking stick he clutches—emanate from this canvas as they do in no previous one. A replica portrait, slightly more finished, especially in its facial brushwork, is in the collection of the National Portrait Gallery [Fig. 154].

Figure 153. Above.
Oil on canvas by Trevor Thomas Fowler,
1840. The Chicago Historical Society,
1947.8

Figure 154. Right.
Oil on canvas by Trevor Thomas Fowler,
1840. National Portrait Gallery,
Smithsonian Institution

III

With the exception of the year 1819, more portraits were executed of Andrew Jackson in 1840 than in any other twelve-month period. Jackson made victory trips in both of those years, which placed him in the midst of such talented artists as the Peales, Sully, Jarvis, Vanderlyn, Amans, Marchant, and Fowler. A likeness painted in April 1840 by Miner Kilbourne Kellogg was noteworthy because, as friends of the general exclaimed, it represented "the sage of the Hermitage at Home."[28]

Born in 1814 in Manlius Square, New York, Kellogg moved with his parents to Cincinnati when he was almost four. The boy showed an early interest in music and drawing. In about 1828, along with Hiram Powers, Kellogg received introductory art lessons from sculptor Frederick Eckstein. In 1831 he furthered his instruction, now in oil painting, under portraitist Abraham G. D. Tuthill. Then in 1840, a group of Cincinnati Democrats selected Kellogg to call upon Jackson. For the young artist, the assignment proved to be a golden opportunity.[29]

Sometime in late March, Kellogg arrived at the Hermitage. His reception was warm and heartfelt. As was customary for any guest there, he was made to feel at home. Kellogg imbibed on this spirit of goodwill and remained six weeks. Jackson appreciated having company; the only other occupant in the house at this time, besides servants, was Andrew Jackson Donelson.

Kellogg occupied a room on the second floor and set up his studio in an adjacent chamber. Given the extended duration of his visit, he naturally was not painting Jackson's portrait full time. There were days when the old man's health would not allow him to write a letter, much less to climb stairs. On occasions when Jackson was incapacitated, the artist enjoyed plinking at squirrels in the company of Andrew Jackson, Jr.[30]

Kellogg painted an insightful likeness. He had the tremendous advantages of time and proximity to observe Jackson in his daily routine. For instance, there was Jackson at the breakfast table, dissuaded from reading the bundles of newspapers critical of his administration. Later there was Jackson at the dinner table, nibbling on the blandest of food. Then there was Jackson distressed about the stray house kittens who wandered from their mother, and about the chimney swallows whose nest had fallen into his bedroom fireplace and had been disturbed by a chambermaid. On other occasions there was Jackson reminiscing about war and politics. Inevitably, there was Jackson at the side of Rachel's tomb. "They murdered her," he once mused, in reference to his political enemies in the election of 1828.

As Kellogg progressed with his work, he heard the same story told in earnest to his predecessors, that Jackson was sitting for the last time. "There is still fire left in the old man's eye," observed Kellogg, "but it is blended with the benevolence of his character, and the inward consciousness of having done his duty to his country." Kellogg wrote of having difficulty translating Jackson's expressions onto canvas, because his mood changed with the topic of discussion. The task for Kellogg was in directing the conversation to his best advantage. When speaking of the Bank or the British, Jackson's eyes would "light up with indignant fire," Kellogg noted.[31]

After the portrait's completion, a few of Jackson's friends, including Governor James K. Polk of Tennessee, were invited to the house. They assembled in a room in the middle of which the likeness was placed. As all eyes moved from canvas to subject and back again, a discussion followed as to the painting's merits. Jackson, of course, enjoyed the repartee swirling around him, and, as if on cue, he knew when to interject. Prompted by Major Donelson's criticism of the scar depicted on the left side of Jackson's lower lip, he sprang to the artist's defense. The scar, a souvenir from Jackson's youth, was inflicted by a former adversary with whom he had tangled triumphantly. He was inwardly proud of this badge of bravado and outwardly adamant that Kellogg be true to nature in his art.[32] Perhaps recalling a similar incident at the White House five years earlier, involving Hiram Powers and his lifelike bust, Major Donelson passed Kellogg a sly wink. Afterward he explained to the artist that he made the brazen remark to call out the general. As always, Jackson answered the challenge.

The portrait was deemed a thorough success.[33] Kellogg departed from the Hermitage well satisfied with his visit, with his host, and with his art. Reportedly, Jackson hated to see his guest leave, but sent him off in his personal carriage as far as Nashville, with three walking sticks specially cut from wood of the estate. Kellogg, too shy to ask the general himself, arranged for Major Donelson to forward a lock of the venerable statesman's white hair.[34]

In Nashville, Kellogg was the special guest of Governor Polk and his wife, a lonely couple who enjoyed having a "trio at the table." At the governor's request, Kellogg allowed his unframed portrait of Jackson to go on public display in the Senate chamber of the Tennessee State House. He also executed a half-size copy for his hosts.[35]

On May 22, 1840, the Democratic citizens of Cincinnati convened to welcome Kellogg. With the presentation of the portrait, testimonials of praise resounded throughout the meeting hall, including the reading of an extract of a letter from Jackson himself. By resolution, the commissioning committee expressed its profound gratitude to Kellogg for the "masterly manner" in which he performed his task.[36]

Figure 155.
Oil on canvas by Miner Kilbourne Kellogg, circa 1840. National Museum of American Art, Smithsonian Institution; transfer from the United States Navy Department

Figure 156.
Oil on canvas by Miner Kilbourne Kellogg, circa 1840. The White House Collection

Figure 157.
Oil on canvas by Miner Kilbourne Kellogg, 1840. Cincinnati Art Museum, gift of Charles H. Kellogg, Sr., 1888

Perhaps for political purposes, Kellogg was allowed temporary possession of the portrait, which he framed and displayed in his studio. In June he journeyed to Washington, stopping in Pittsburgh long enough to exhibit the painting, at the request of city Democrats.[37] The portrait's popularity had been growing with each passing week. In Washington it went on view in the Capitol. President Van Buren, fighting for his political survival in an election year, ordered a copy. So, too, did members of his cabinet: Secretary of War Joel R. Poinsett, Secretary of the Navy James K. Paulding, and Attorney General Henry D. Gilpin. Two of Jackson's old Tennessee friends, Robert Armstrong and John C. McLemore, added their names to the subscription list.[38]

On December 30, 1840, Kellogg thanked Jackson once again for his hospitality of last spring. Kellogg gave an account of himself, explaining that he had spent "*the whole presidential battle,* in placing upon canvas the features of the firm and unflinching defender of the *rights of the People.*" His letter was also one of farewell. At the request of President Van Buren, the artist was presently off to Italy as a diplomatic courier for the State Department.[39]

Assuming that Kellogg completed his standing orders in 1840, he would have painted eight portraits of Old Hickory that year. Records show that at least six paintings did exist. In addition to the original and Polk's smaller version, four other replicas are known to have been in the possession of Martin Van Buren, the War Department, the Navy Department, and the White House. In a letter written to Jackson in May 1841, Van Buren mentioned presenting his portrait to Benjamin Franklin Butler, who was a loyal Jacksonian Democrat and a mutual friend.[40] What became of this portrait is not known. In 1928, in the attic of the old State, War, and Navy Building, another Jackson portrait was discovered, bearing an inscription on the back: "Miner K. Kellogg pxt—1840." This may have been the portrait commissioned by Joel R. Poinsett. It is now in the collection of the State Department. Presumably, the portrait commissioned by James K. Paulding was the one that formerly hung in the anteroom of the secretary of the navy. In 1910 it was transferred to the National Gallery of Art, and in 1967 it came into what is now the National Museum of American Art [Fig. 155].[41]

Records at the White House indicate that a Kellogg portrait of Jackson has been in that collection since the early 1860s [Fig. 156]. This painting hung in Abraham Lincoln's office. In 1864 artist Francis Bicknell Carpenter depicted it hanging over the fireplace mantel in his popular group portrait of Lincoln reading the Emancipation Proclamation to members of his cabinet. The portrait is also barely discernible in Alexander Hay Ritchie's 1866 engraving based on Carpenter's picture. On January 8, 1867, President Andrew Johnson loaned the painting for decoration at the Jackson anniversary banquet held in the dining room of the Metropolitan Hotel. A newspaper account reported that Kellogg, then living in Baltimore, was again about to copy his popular likeness "for the present Hickory [Andrew Johnson] of the Executive Mansion."[42]

Still another *Jackson* by Kellogg is owned by the Cincinnati Art Museum [Fig. 157]. In 1888, a year before the artist's death, his brother, Charles H. Kellogg, presented it to that institution. This is the best of the extant versions, as seen in the detail of Jackson's attire. The likeness is melancholy, as is the one owned by the National Museum of American Art. The White House version is only subtly less so. Although Kellogg replicated Jackson's image faithfully, he made deliberate variations; for instance, the chairs and backgrounds in each portrait are unique. The National Museum of American Art version differs significantly, with the inclusion of drapery and a column, behind which lies a glimpse of some distant shore. Such a seemingly inconsequential detail is interesting, given the provenance of this portrait, which once belonged to the Navy Department. Unfortunately, the original canvas that Kellogg painted at the Hermitage has never been identified. Of the three surviving portraits, the Cincinnati canvas is probably the closest to it, based on the high quality of the execution and the family provenance.[43]

A respectable copy portrait, not by Kellogg, is owned by the Tennessee Historical Society. Currently it hangs in the front lobby of the state capitol. John R. Johnston painted this copy in about 1854 for Granville Stokes, then a member of the Ohio Senate.[44] Johnston, a native of the state, was living in Cincinnati at the time. His portrait is a remarkably accurate copy of the one owned by the Cincinnati Art Museum, as detected in the execution of Jackson's white jabot and collar and, most noticeably, in the design of the chair. Fortunately, Johnston signed this work, which is roughly the same size as all of Kellogg's replicas—about 30 by 25 inches.

IV

When Miner K. Kellogg left the Hermitage in late April of 1840, he believed that he carried with him the last life portrait of Andrew Jackson. Exactly two years later, John Wood Dodge departed under the same false assumption. Given Jackson's advanced age and bad health, their impressions seemed reasonable.[45]

Talk as he might about not sitting for any more portraits, Jackson, coping with a relatively uneventful and solitary retirement after a full and active career of public service, genuinely enjoyed having company. This was especially true since the death of Ralph E. W. Earl in 1838. Like former guests, John Wood Dodge was hospitably welcomed at the Hermitage. He arrived in mid-March of 1842.

Dodge was born in New York City on November 4, 1807. At sixteen, he was apprenticed for four years to a sign and ornamental painter. Soon the greater challenge of portraiture tempted him. He began by borrowing a finely painted miniature on ivory from a friend and proceeding to copy it. Encouraged, he then did portraits of his brothers and sister, and eventually of his friends. Success followed success, in spite of his lack of formal instruction. After about six months of working entirely on his own, Dodge rented a studio and emerged, in his words, a "Miniature Painter."[46]

From the late 1820s and throughout the 1830s, Dodge exhibited at the National Academy of Design. He worked in New York City until age thirty-five when, because of poor health, he began spending winters in such southern locales as Louisville, Lexington, Nashville, Huntsville, and New Orleans.

In 1842 Dodge was in his prime as an artist. In Nashville he was commanding about seventy-five dollars for each miniature set in a locket or case. By the end of the year, his receipts totaled $1,625. His portrait of Jackson was perhaps his most widely touted work. Dodge had his first sitting on March 15, the general's seventy-fifth birthday, and completed the likeness on April 8.[47]

The portrait, a six-inch-square miniature on ivory, was an instant success. On April 14, 1842, the *Nashville Union* reported: *The first glance at the picture impresses the spectator with the idea that he has just entered the apartment of the General who has laid his book upon the table before him, returned his spectacles to their case which is held in his left hand, and is prepared to entertain his friend.*[48]

Figure 158. Above.
Engraving by Moseley Isaac Danforth, after
John Wood Dodge, 1843. National Portrait
Gallery, Smithsonian Institution

Above right: Sword presented to Andrew
Jackson in 1835 by the city of Philadelphia.
The Hermitage: Home of President Andrew
Jackson

Below: President Jackson purchased this
pair of spectacles from John McAllister &
Company of Philadelphia in about 1830. In
retirement, and as his eyesight gradually
worsened, he began wearing a unique pair
of double-lensed glasses whose bifocals
folded back along the inside of the frame.
The Hermitage: Home of President Andrew
Jackson

In the background on the right is a serene landscape; on the left rises a column
upon which hangs a distinctive horse-hilt sword. In January 1835, to mark the
twentieth anniversary of the Battle of New Orleans, a group of Philadelphians
had presented Jackson with this gift made by the city's renowned sword-
maker, Frederick William Widmann.[49] The ornamental scabbard depicts battle
scenes and a portrait of Jackson after the 1824 image by Joseph Wood. The
Bible, lying within easy reach on the table in the foreground, is representative
of the old soldier's state of mind while on the brink of eternity.

Dodge painted this likeness for his own use. In part with an eye toward
publishing it as an engraving, he solicited favorable testimony from among
Jackson's family members and friends. Various newspapers from around the
country echoed the praise.[50]

In May 1842 Dodge carried the miniature to Washington, where he exhibited
it in the Library of Congress, which was then housed in the Capitol. Again
there was praise from Jackson's old acquaintances. By November the artist was
back in New York City advertising his miniature business in the press and
announcing the forthcoming publication of his likeness of General Jackson.
Moseley Isaac Danforth engraved the likeness in the same size as the original
portrait, which was large for a miniature. The finished print, framed by a wide
decorative border that includes vignettes of the United States Capitol and the
Hermitage, evinces Danforth's skill. The *Plebeian* in Kingston, New York,
reported: "As a work of art we are bound to declare that this united work of
Dodge and Danforth is without a rival. There is nothing better or truer than
this triumph of the *burin,* this *chef d'oeuvre* of the pencil."[51]

Danforth's meticulous engraving, which was issued in 1843, has preserved
Dodge's portrait in its entirety [Fig. 158]. In 1844 Dodge exhibited Jackson's
miniature, in addition to one of Henry Clay (executed shortly after the artist
left the Hermitage), at the National Academy of Design. Sometime thereafter
he sold the Jackson portrait to James Robb, a New Orleans banker. For more
than a century, this miniature has been unlocated. Fortunately, Dodge painted
a smaller head-and-shoulders version—without any background or props—for
Jackson's close friend General Robert Armstrong, who assisted him in gaining
the initial sittings [Fig. 159].[52]

Dodge's likeness of Jackson appeared in several engraved versions. It was used
to decorate funeral ribbons, bank notes [Fig. 160], and postage stamps. For
instance, the two-cent "Black Jack" of 1863 proved to be one of the most
popular issues of the United States Post Office [Fig. 161].[53]

Figure 159. Above.
Watercolor on ivory by John Wood Dodge, 1842. Tennessee State Museum

Figure 160. Right.
Five-dollar note with image of Andrew Jackson after John Wood Dodge, issued by the Farmers and Merchants Bank of Cecil County, Maryland, 1863. National Numismatic Collection, National Museum of American History, Smithsonian Institution

Figure 161.
Two-cent "Black Jack" postage stamp, with image of Andrew Jackson after John Wood Dodge, 1863. National Philatelic Collection, National Museum of American History, Smithsonian Institution

V

Typical of the correspondence Jackson had been receiving was the letter of William Henry Brown in August 1843. Brown was soliciting cooperation in the publication of his *Portrait Gallery of Distinguished American Citizens*. He commenced this ambitious undertaking, similar in concept to the illustrated biographical works of Delaplaine and Longacre, as an interesting, practical way of creating public favor for his art. What promised to make Brown's publication different from those of his predecessors was the inclusion of a lithographed sample of each sitter's handwriting, preferably a letter attesting to the accuracy of the artist's cutting skill.

Born in Charleston, South Carolina, in 1808, Brown was America's last great native-born silhouettist. His work compares favorably with that of John Hankes and William J. Hubard, and even rivals the cuttings of the sensational Frenchman Auguste Edouart, who began charming American sitters in 1839. Brown's career commenced in earnest in 1825, when he cut a paper likeness of Lafayette in Philadelphia.

In his letter to Jackson, Brown explained the details of his project: he intended to produce a volume containing between twenty-five and thirty lithographs of notable Americans, based on his original portrait cuttings made in Washington and elsewhere. In 1836 Brown had visited the White House and cut a full-length profile of the President. He had also cut a second profile, depicting Jackson on horseback, which he had presented to him.[54] Although Brown planned on using Jackson's full-length likeness, he suggested, seven years later, that Jackson might wish to submit a written acknowledgment of having received the equestrian portrait silhouette.

Jackson proved impervious to Brown's coaxing. His lack of stamina prevented him from responding to much of his voluminous mail. He dismissed Brown's letter with a sentence scribbled on the envelope: "I am too feeble to comply with the within request." In the end, Brown received a sample of Jackson's handwriting, but apparently it was from James K. Polk.[55]

Brown's *Portrait Gallery* was published in 1845 by E. B. and E. C. Kellogg of Hartford, Connecticut. The silhouette of Jackson depicts him leaning on his cane on the grounds of the Hermitage [Fig. 162]. Although he stood six feet, one inch in his prime, his spare frame made him appear taller. As President he weighed only about 140 pounds but was well proportioned, as depicted by Brown's scissors. Brown in essence corroborated a journal entry made by English actress Fanny Kemble in 1833: "His Excellency Andrew Jackson is very tall and thin, but erect and dignified in his carriage—a good specimen of a fine old well-battered soldier."[56]

Figure 162.
Lithograph by E. B. and E. C. Kellogg
lithography company, after William Henry
Brown, 1843. National Portrait Gallery,
Smithsonian Institution; gift of Wilmarth
Sheldon Lewis

Brown routinely enhanced his silhouettes with paint and brush, whitening hair
and delineating articles of clothing.[57] He placed Jackson's likeness in appropriate surroundings—the Hermitage estate. Although reversed, this setting is
reminiscent of Earl's full-length portrait executed in 1830 and subsequently
engraved by John Henry Bufford.

Neither of Brown's two original paper cuttings of Jackson has been found. In
1861 an adaptation of Brown's full-length silhouette appeared in the second
volume of James Parton's *Life of Andrew Jackson.*

VI

Before the close of 1843, the New Orleans City Council commissioned
another portrait of Andrew Jackson. In 1821 it had purchased a full-length by
Ralph E. W. Earl. More recently, the Whigs of the Second Municipality had

Figure 163.
Oil on canvas by Jacques Amans and
Theodore Sidney Moise, 1844. Gallier Hall,
City of New Orleans

installed likenesses of William Henry Harrison and Henry Clay, both by
Trevor Thomas Fowler, in the council chamber of City Hall. Since the
Democratic rivals were gaining favor, discussion arose as to whether these two
portraits would now be appropriate company for Jackson. Ultimately, it was
decided to ignore party affiliations.

Debate next centered on the nature of the portrait and the amount to be
awarded. The figure of five hundred dollars was at first agreed upon. A
substitute resolution would have allocated one thousand dollars for procuring
Hiram Powers's marble bust. But the majority in council preferred a painting,
and it was decided that the commissioning would take the form of a contest.
The successful artist would execute, within a period of six months, a life-sized
portrait representing Jackson as he looked during the Battle of New Orleans.
The prize offered was one thousand dollars.[58]

In June the city council formally accepted the winning picture, depicting
Jackson astride a chestnut horse while reviewing his troops [Fig. 163]. Two
local portraitists, Jacques Amans and Theodore Sidney Moise, split the award.
Moise, born in Charleston, South Carolina, in 1808, moved to New Orleans
in about 1841. There he worked with a number of artists, including Trevor
Thomas Fowler. Moise's specialty was equestrian art, and the charger upon

which Jackson rides was undoubtedly his work. Amans probably executed the likeness of Jackson. He was the most familiar with him after having done several portraits based on a life sitting. Since his 1840 likeness of a tired, craggy old man would never pass for the hero of New Orleans, Amans painted a younger Jackson, suggestive of Samuel Lovett Waldo's 1819 image.

When the canvas was finished, Amans and Moise had executed the largest oil portrait ever made of Andrew Jackson. Its reception in City Hall was appropriately laudatory. Veterans of Old Hickory's army pronounced the resemblance to be nearly perfect. The general effect, reported the *New Orleans Bee,* was strikingly simple yet animated.[59]

Only time hushed the praise due to these two artists. By the turn of the century, the portrait suffered a series of misattributions, from Waldo to Earl to others. Only in the late 1930s did an art restorer for the Louisiana State Museum rediscover the names of Moise and Amans inscribed in the lower right-hand corner of the canvas.[60]

VII

For more than a decade, Andrew Jackson had been predicting his own imminent death. By the spring of 1845, it seemed as if a kind Providence was seriously willing to consider the matter. But in spite of Jackson's worsening physical condition, his mind was still alert, still responsive to the cares of house and home, and still focused on the great issues of the day. Certain matters demanded his attention. For instance, new debts amassed by Andrew Jackson, Jr., were hounding him. Fortunately, political cronies once again dashed to the general's aid, this time with a loan of $8,000.

That Andrew Jackson remained a voice, if no longer a force, in national affairs was persistently demonstrated that winter and spring in correspondence with the new President. Jackson had peered over the shoulders of his four successors—Martin Van Buren, William Henry Harrison, John Tyler, and now James K. Polk. Van Buren and Polk, both Democrats, received his generous and unsolicited counsel. A current issue that struck at Jackson's political soul was Polk's decision to remove Francis P. Blair as editor of the Washington *Globe.* In 1830 Jackson had breathed life into this newspaper, which became the official organ of his administration. Yet Polk recognized its shortcomings, namely that it did not speak for the entire Democratic platform. For instance, the *Globe* had thoroughly alienated southern Democrats such as John C. Calhoun. The paper's ultimate sale to a Nashville publisher, and reincarnation as the Washington *Daily Union,* spelled the end of an era.[61]

❦

Change was inevitable. At the age of seventy-eight, Jackson realized this better than most people. Yet at the same time, his concern for the future, in part, was to ensure the preservation of the past.

Nothing quite illustrated this link between old and new like the modern art of photography. The daguerreotype process, introduced first in Paris in the late 1830s and shortly thereafter in the United States, was the invention of Louis Jacques Mandé Daguerre. These images were produced when silver-coated copper plates specially treated with chemicals were exposed to sunlight for a regulated period. A mirror image was produced. In the realm of portraiture, one art critic has observed: "The daguerreotype is as near to the living man as we can get. Not even the sensitive paper of the photographic negative intervenes."[62]

Figure 164. Above.
Engraving by Thomas Doney, 1845.
National Portrait Gallery, Smithsonian
Institution

Figure 165. Right.
Lithograph with tintstone by Jean-Baptiste
Adolphe Lafosse, 1856. National Portrait
Gallery, Smithsonian Institution

In the spring of 1845, perhaps even earlier, Andrew Jackson personally experienced this new portrait phenomenon. He was one of the few veterans of the American Revolution to be photographed.[63] At least five plates are extant, depicting three different views and suggesting two separate sittings. No less than four photographers have been associated with one or more of these.

The earliest attribution appeared in the *United States Magazine, and Democratic Review* of September 1845, a little more than two months after Jackson's death. A portrait illustration engraved by Thomas Doney of New York bore the inscription: "From a Daguerreotype by Anthony, Edwards & Co." This image, a three-quarter frontal view, was dated "Hermitage, April 15, 1845" [Fig. 164].[64] In 1842 Edward T. Anthony, a graduate of Columbia and a civil engineer, established in Washington with J. M. Edwards the photographic business that bore their name. Anthony learned the daguerreotype process from the artist-inventor Samuel F. B. Morse and practiced it until 1847, when he entered the supply business. Shortly after Anthony, Edwards & Co. opened its doors, the firm began photographing all of the members of the Senate.[65] In 1843 the company moved to New York City, where in a Broadway studio they opened the National Miniature Gallery. Devoted to exhibiting hundreds of photographic images of prominent Americans, the museum was the first of its kind in the country. Anthony actively built his collection and naturally would have desired an image of Andrew Jackson. Based on a letter dated April 18, 1845, from Alfred Balch of Nashville, a wealthy planter and longtime friend of Jackson, a Mr. Anthony of New York (presumably Edward) was then in Nashville with a "just taken" daguerreotype of the general. Balch considered the remarkable likenesses to be especially expressive of Jackson's almost constant suffering.[66]

Then in 1856 a similar image was published as a large, single-sheet lithograph by Goupil & Co. of New York [Fig. 165]. Jean-Baptiste Adolphe Lafosse, a French lithographer and miniature painter, executed the stone drawing. Information in the bottom margin, however, stated that the image was after a daguerreotype by Mathew Brady. In about 1845, Brady began photography for his *Gallery of Illustrious Americans,* which was published in 1850. Brady, however, made many unfounded claims near the end of his celebrated career. That he arranged to have Jackson's image taken just before his death seems to have been one of them.[67] Yet a Jackson plate—probably a copy—was on display in his New York gallery in December 1850.[68]

In 1897 Charles Henry Hart, in his article "Life Portraits of Andrew Jackson," illustrated a daguerreotype credited to Dan Adams of Nashville, the image of which was identical to those attributed to Anthony, Edwards and Brady. Hart obtained much of his information from Jackson's two surviving grandchildren, Colonel Andrew Jackson III and his sister, Rachel Jackson Lawrence. Colonel Jackson of Cincinnati owned this daguerreotype and was undoubtedly the source for its attribution to Adams. Daniel Adams was born in 1810 in Strabane, northern Ireland, less than seventy-five miles from Carrickfergus, the hometown of Jackson's parents. After immigrating to America, he arrived in Nashville in 1832, where he established himself as an engraver and photographer. Little is known about Adams, who was a resident of the city until his death in 1885.[69]

Rachel Jackson Lawrence recalled her grandfather sitting for this, or a similar image, in his bedroom: "I have a vivid recollection of the arrangement for taking this likeness, in which I was greatly interested. He was much opposed to having it taken and was very feeble at the time. I still have the old plates of some earlier daguerreotypes, but they are entirely faded out."[70]

At the time of the sitting, Rachel and her brother were children, not yet in their teens. Since, in 1897, they were recalling an event of more than fifty years past, it is likely that they remembered the name of Dan Adams, who probably visited the Hermitage, but they may well have confused his work with that of another daguerreotypist.

The small daguerreotype (1⅛ by ¾ inches) once owned by Colonel Jackson is now unlocated. The Library of Congress has in its collection a similar but larger plate, which unfortunately is faded and severely abraded. Jackson's likeness has been reversed, suggesting that it may be a later-generation copy from an original plate. A much clearer plate of this same image was recently discovered wrapped in brown paper tied with twine in the basement of the Mead Art Museum at Amherst College [Fig. 166]. It, too, shows Jackson facing to the right.[71]

A less publicized second view—a profile image—survives in two daguerreotypes, a somewhat faded one in the Library of Congress [Fig. 167] and a sharper one in a private collection [Fig. 168].[72] Based on the similarity of clothing to that in the Anthony, Edwards/Brady/Adams plates, these photographs were probably taken at the same sitting. This second view better evokes Jackson's feebleness. Against the black background he appears suspended in time and space, somewhere between life and death. The pillow behind his back, its striped ticking clearly visible, conveys a sense of convalescence and immobility. In his last weeks Jackson was uncomfortable lying down; thus, he spent his long nights propped up in bed and his longer days in a well-padded chair. His writing materials, Bible, and hymn book were perpetually at reach.[73]

The daguerreotype in private hands provides yet another twist in the attribution puzzle. An inscription on the back of the plate states that it was the work of Langenheim, presumably either of two brothers, William or Frederick,

Figure 166.
Daguerreotype attributed to Anthony, Edwards, & Co., 1845. Mead Art Museum, Amherst College; gift of William Macbeth, Inc.

Figure 167.
Daguerreotype attributed to Anthony, Edwards & Co., 1845. Prints and Photographs Division, Library of Congress

Figure 168. Above.
Daguerreotype attributed to Anthony,
Edwards & Co., or remotely Langenheim
Brothers, Philadelphia, 1845. Private
collection

Figure 169. Right.
Daguerreotype attributed to Daniel Adams,
circa 1845. George Eastman House; gift of
A. Conger Goodyear

whose Philadelphia firm was one of the earliest photographic businesses in the
country. It is not known how this plate became associated with the Langen-
heims; perhaps it is a copy by them. It was, however, owned by a Philadelphian, John K. Kane, a prominent jurist and an avid Jackson supporter. Kane
was one of the commissioners appointed to help settle the French spoliation
claims, and he actively assisted Jackson's war on the Bank of the United
States.[74]

Still a third view of Jackson survives. In this plate the old hero wears his swing-
lens bifocals and faces the camera almost directly [Fig. 169]. Against the dark,
amorphous background, his countenance emerges seemingly from nowhere,
like that of a specter. Yet Jackson looks stronger in this daguerreotype, perhaps
as the result of the slight angling of his head. Then, too, no cushions or props
are visible. That this third, most arresting view represents another sitting
altogether is suggested by Jackson's different attire. Here his white collar
appears to have rounded rather than pointed ends. Also, the jabot no longer
juts out from under his chin, but lays in neat folds upon his chest.

The International Museum of Photography at the George Eastman House in
Rochester owns this daguerreotype, which, judging by its overall superior
quality may be the only original plate now existing.[75] They have attributed it to
Daniel Adams, based on information gleaned from Charles Henry Hart's
article. Curiously, this straightforward likeness is reminiscent of many of
Jackson's caricature images. Perhaps it was about this plate that Jackson
quipped, "Humph! Looks like a monkey!"[76]

❧

Anthony and Edwards, Brady, Langenheim, and Adams have all been associ-
ated in one way or another with original daguerreotypes of Andrew Jackson.
Indicative of the confusing speculation about who actually photographed Old
Hickory, one recent source has suggested that Brady may have sent Anthony

to the Hermitage, since the two men frequently collaborated in daguerreotype undertakings.[77] Based on the plates that have been identified, it is probable that Jackson sat on at least two separate occasions, one of them in the spring of 1845, just before his death. Anthony, Edwards and Daniel Adams seem to be the most likely artists for these sittings, based on the early attribution in the *Democratic Review* and on the combined memories of Jackson's two grand-children.

VIII

By some harbinger of bad news, King Louis-Philippe of France received word that Andrew Jackson, his nemesis from the spoliations controversy, was dying. That spring of 1845 the French monarch demonstrated his continued respect for his old adversary. Louis-Philippe desperately wanted a life portrait of Andrew Jackson to be among those of the American statesmen he was commissioning for the Versailles gallery. To execute this likeness he selected George Peter Alexander Healy and bade him to make haste to the Hermitage, some 5,500 miles away.

Healy was a natural choice. Born in Boston in 1813, he opened an art studio there when he was seventeen. In spite of his lack of formal training, he gradually accrued a following. Encouraged to go to Europe by Thomas Sully and others, Healy sailed for Paris in the spring of 1834. There he studied in the studio of Baron Gros, one of France's leading neoclassical painters. Finally he came to the attention of Louis-Philippe, whose portrait he painted in 1839 for the American minister, Lewis Cass.

In about mid-May of 1845, Healy arrived on the doorstep of the Hermitage, breathless but hopeful. Jackson still lived. The old man received him pleasantly enough, but refused to sit for a portrait on account of his failing health. "Not for all the kings in Christendom," exclaimed Jackson.[78]

Healy retreated to the Nashville home of Judge John Catron, an old friend of Jackson's, to decide his next course of action. In the meantime, he borrowed an Earl portrait belonging to Catron's daughter, Mrs. Marshall, and proceeded to copy it. Having just seen Jackson that day, Healy was struck by a peculiarity in the general's upper face. If only he could get another look at Jackson, he could greatly improve his copy. Toward that end, Judge Catron wrote Jackson's daughter-in-law, Sarah Yorke. Catron emphasized that a formal sitting would not be necessary.

Sarah Yorke was the joy of Jackson's heart and the daughter he never had. At first he resisted her gentle pleadings. When finally she stated her earnest wish that he cooperate, Jackson, eyes wet with emotion, replied, "My child, I will sit."[79]

The following morning, Andrew Jackson, Jr., went to Nashville and summoned Healy. Fate was proving kind to the young painter. What he thought would be a short visit became a stay of several weeks. In that time Healy repeatedly gained access to Jackson in his sickroom. Now Jackson's condition was critical, however. He was swollen from his toes to the crown of his head, and he was in bandages to his hips. On one occasion he lamented, "I wish I could do you greater justice as a sitter, Mr. Healy."[80]

Somehow Healy managed to push his brush a hair's breadth ahead of the Reaper's scythe. Jackson rested more comfortably on Thursday, May 29, having taken some opiates. That day alone, he received and shook hands with more than thirty visitors. Yet having passed a bad night with no sleep, the

Figure 170.
Oil on canvas by George P. A. Healy, 1845.
Musée National de la Coopération Franco-
Américaine, Blérancourt, Cliché Réunion
des Musées Nationaux

Figure 171.
Oil on canvas by George P. A. Healy, 1845.
The Hermitage: Home of President Andrew
Jackson

general was extremely feeble on the morning of May 30. Only an extraordinary effort on Jackson's part allowed Healy to finish the portrait. Upon its
presentation, Jackson examined it for a few minutes before addressing the
artist: "I am satisfied, sir, that you stand at the head of your profession. If I
may be allowed to judge of my own likeness, I can safely concur in the opinion
of my family. This is the best that has been taken."[81]

One houseguest considered the painting a "perfect representation . . . giving
rather the remains of the heroic personage than the full life." It so pleased the
family that they requested Healy to furnish them a copy whenever he returned
to Paris. Healy explained that a copy was never as true as an original and that if
he could be granted just one more sitting, he would paint a second portrait.
Jackson consented and once more Healy made haste with his brush.[82]

Today Healy's two portraits of Jackson hang in appropriate places. The
original, presented to Louis-Philippe before his deposition in 1848, hung for
decades in the Musée Imperial at Versailles. In more recent years it has graced
the walls of the Musée National de Blérancourt near Paris. The painting
depicts Jackson dressed in a dark brown coat and resting against the back of a
green chair [Fig. 170]. Healy's replica hangs in Jackson's bedroom at the
Hermitage [Fig. 171]. It stayed in family hands, passing from Andrew Jackson,
Jr., to his wife, Sarah, and finally to their son, Colonel Andrew Jackson III of
Cincinnati.[83] Although the likeness compares favorably with its French cousin,
Healy's replica is less detailed: the lines beside Jackson's mouth and eyes are
not as defined, and the freely brushed jabot reflects the haste with which the
artist finished his task. The eyes are also telling. In the French version, they are
heavier, evoking a profound melancholy; in the American twin, they are
merely sad.

❦

Before Healy packed up his brushes, Jackson had a favor to ask: would he
linger a little while longer to paint a portrait of his daughter-in-law Sarah?
Although Healy had other commitments from Louis-Philippe, he began work.
Jackson watched his progress intently, hoping to live long enough to see
Sarah's portrait finished. This time Healy's brush was not so fleet.

Early on Sunday morning, June 8, Healy was awakened by the cadenced wails
of the servants, who thought that Jackson had died. In reality, he had only
suffered a fit of fainting. His condition, however, was now perilous. Wishing
not to intrude upon the family, Healy stayed in his own chamber. About 6:00
p.m. he ventured to the sickroom for news. Jackson was breathing so lightly
that it was difficult to know if he was still alive. As Healy later recalled, the
only indication of death was the falling of the general's lower jaw. Andrew
Jackson was finally at peace.[84]

On Tuesday morning, approximately three thousand people converged at the
Hermitage to attend Jackson's funeral. Healy remained on the estate long
enough to finish Sarah's portrait and then returned to Nashville. On June 13,
the *Politician* published a flattering account of Healy's *Jackson,* which had been
on view at the residence of Judge Catron: *It represents him, indeed, as on the
verge of existence—the complexion bloodless—the eye calm, without fire—without
passion—but not altogether without 'speculation'—the form and figure bent and
emaciated—the countenance placid, though much shrunk from its former propor-
tions, which gives to the face a more elongated appearance, and the forehead a little
more of relative elevation than appears in the paintings hitherto made of him.*[85]

❦

Healy's next destination was Ashland, where he would paint a portrait of Henry Clay. Healy spent part of the time in nearby Lexington, in the company of Oliver Frazer and his family. The two painters had been fellow students under Baron Gros in Paris. In the meantime, Frazer had returned to his native state and opened a portrait studio in Lexington. Healy was permitted use of this facility and kept his portrait of Jackson there. Not surprisingly, Frazer made a copy, which was good enough to fool two "coxcombs of the city," recently back from visiting the art capitals of Europe: they mistook Frazer's as the original.[86]

⌀⌀

A full decade after Jackson's death, Healy still retained what he called a study canvas. From his home in Chicago in 1857, he informed a copy artist in Washington that he was fearful of shipping this portrait there, but offered to hand-deliver it in the spring.[87]

Two years later, Healy was painting portraits of the last ten Presidents, commissioned by the United States Congress. By September 1859 he was planning to paint a full-length of Jackson, drawing upon his study portrait. By itself, however, this likeness of a decrepit old man proved inadequate for the task at hand. To assist him, Healy requested and received from Hiram Powers, still in Florence, one of his plaster busts.[88] The outbreak of the Civil War canceled these commissions.

Figure 172.
Oil on canvas by George P. A. Healy, 1845.
Cummer Gallery of Art; gift of Mr. and
Mrs. Algur H. Meadows, 1972

In January 1862 Healy, apparently still intent upon honoring his side of the contract, sent the Jackson portrait to Washington. Before shipping it, he displayed it in his Chicago studio on Lake Street. According to the *Chicago Tribune,* Jackson appeared as he had at the Battle of New Orleans, standing ready to mount a war steed.[89]

What became of Healy's full-length portrait of Jackson remains a mystery. Perhaps it was lost, like many of the artist's works, in the great Chicago fire of 1871. The fate of the smaller study canvas is also uncertain. There is, however, the possibility that this portrait is the one now in the collection of the Cummer Gallery of Art in Jacksonville, Florida [Fig. 172].[90] This portrait, signed "Healy. 1845," is a replica of the one now at Blérancourt, as evinced in the facial lines and folds of the white jabot. Unfortunately missing is a measure of Jackson's vivaciousness, what little of it had been left for Healy to capture.

Still another replica, signed and dated "G. P. A. Healy 1861," is owned by the Corcoran Gallery of Art in Washington, D.C. Healy painted it for Thomas B. Bryan, a Chicago art collector, who on at least one occasion assisted the artist when he was in dire financial need.[91]

⌀⌀

Healy never boasted that he took the last life likeness of Andrew Jackson. At the time he did not need to; the news of Jackson's death quickly spread far and wide. In later years Healy's likeness spoke for itself. How different this image of human frailty was from the crude warrior images of thirty years earlier, or even the romanticized ones of Ralph E. W. Earl and Thomas Sully.

Moreover, Healy's portrait is remarkable as an image of raw courage. A dying Jackson looks posterity squarely in the face. It is little wonder that he still captivates national attention. Even in his own day, great men who had brushed shoulders with Jackson never fully understood him. One was Henry Clay, who, while sitting to Healy, asked the young artist if he considered Jackson to be a sincere man. "I have just come from his death-bed," Healy replied, "and if General Jackson was not sincere, then I do not know the meaning of the word." Clay next gave Healy a look that the artist would never forget. "I see that you, like all who approached that man, were fascinated by him."[92]

Notes

1. Remini, *Andrew Jackson,* vol. 3, pp. 435-36, 440, 444-49; *Correspondence of Jackson,* vol. 5, pp. 571, 573-75.

2. *The Bull Frog* (New Orleans), February 12, 1841; records of the Catalog of American Portraits. Concerning artistic skills, Frances Trollope observed: "From all the conversations on painting, which I listened to in America, I found that the finish of drapery was considered as the highest excellence, and next to this, the resemblance in a portrait." See Trollope, *Domestic Manners,* p. 268.

3. Fortunately, an inscription appears on the back, stating that it was painted by "Thos. J. Jackson" at the Hermitage in June 1838. In 1938 the portrait was discovered among discarded items in a small department store in Abbeville, South Carolina, which was being sold by its elderly owner. The next year the finder of this lost image, a Mr. H. R. Peters of Florida, presented it to the Ladies' Hermitage Association. See records of the Ladies' Hermitage Association.

4. *Nashville Union,* June 9, 1838; Gallatin, Tennessee, *Union,* June 15, 1838. Concerning Jackson's reluctance to sit for portraits, see *Correspondence of Jackson,* vol. 6, p. 416.

5. John Fowler and others to Andrew Jackson, November 6, 1838, Joel Tanner Hart Papers, Durret Collections, University of Chicago.

6. Craven, *Sculpture in America,* p. 197; Price, *Old Masters of the Bluegrass,* pp. 150-53.

7. Jackson to Messrs. Fowler, Ficklin, Hickey, and Cloud, December 24, 1838 (copy), Hart Papers.

8. In 1874 the state legislature authorized $1,700 for the purchase of Hart's busts of Jackson and Henry Clay. An inscription on the back of the *Jackson* states: "The original; modeled at the Hermitage, U.S.A. in Dec. 1838. by J. T. Hart, sclt." This information may well have been inscribed later by someone other than the artist, because technically it is not accurate. The original bust modeled at the Hermitage was a clay version and is now lost. It was owned by the Polytechnic Society of Louisville as late as 1897. In 1902 this organization became the Louisville Public Library. But records dating to 1928 do not show that the bust was then in the library's holdings. See Price, *Old Masters of the Bluegrass,* p. 170; records of the Kentucky Historical Society, Frankfort, and the Louisville Public Library. For record of the bust's purchase by the legislature, see *Acts of the General Assembly of the Commonwealth of Kentucky* (Frankfort, Ky., 1874), p. 81.

9. An accompanying article described an inscription on the back as "J. T. Hart, Ken., Apl., 1838." This has been determined to have been a misinterpretation of Hart's customary script signature, which on the back of the newly discovered *Jackson* reads "J. T. Hart, Sculpt. 1838." At this time it cannot be determined whether this bust was ever owned by the McFerran family, as was the bust recorded in the 1938 newspaper article. I am grateful to Gary Stradling of New York for alerting me to this plaster bust and for furnishing pertinent information and photographs.

10. Remini, *Andrew Jackson,* vol. 3, pp. 454-55.

11. *New-Orleans Commercial Bulletin,* January 10, 1840.

12. *Ibid.; Mississippi Free Trader and Natchez Weekly Gazette,* January 16, 1840 (hereafter cited as *Mississippi Free Trader*).

13. *New-Orleans Commercial Bulletin,* January 10, 1840.

14. Jacques Amans to Jackson, January 10, 1840, Jackson Papers, Library of Congress.

15. *Louisiana Courier,* January 9-10, 1840.

16. Roulhac B. Toledano and W. Joseph Fulton, "Portrait Painting in Colonial and Ante-

bellum New Orleans," *Antiques* 93 (June 1968): 794. When this painting was illustrated, it formed a part of the Felix H. Kuntz collection and was temporarily on loan to the Louisiana State Museum. See *250 Years of Life in New Orleans: The Rosemonde E. and Emile Kuntz Collection and the Felix H. Kuntz Collection* (New Orleans, La., 1968), p. 48.

17. A notice in the Boston *Daily Evening Transcript* in June 1866 reported that Colonel William H. Reynolds had recently presented this painting to Brown University in Providence, Rhode Island. In a note accompanying the gift, Colonel Reynolds explained that the portrait had been given to a former mayor of New Orleans, from whom Reynolds acquired it during the Civil War. At that time the ex-mayor was confined in Fort Jackson on charges of disloyalty to the federal government. Allegedly, Reynolds purchased the painting; sources in New Orleans, however, reported that it had been stolen. In 1981 Brown University sold it to Hirschl & Adler of New York. The portrait's subsequent sale to the Historic New Orleans Collection has returned this handsome work to its place of origin. See *Daily Evening Transcript,* June 22, 1866; records of the Catalog of American Portraits.

18. In 1920 the Chicago Historical Society purchased this portrait from the Charles F. Gunther Collection. This might have been the portrait that General Jean B. Plauché mentioned to Jackson in a letter of January 24, 1844. Plauché, a New Orleans cotton broker, had requested Amans to paint for him a full-length likeness of Jackson. "It is a fine painting," wrote Plauché, "which from its great finish and correct resemblance I consider one of the best in the United States and such appears to be at present the opinion of the best connoisseurs here."

At the time, Jackson was in debt to Plauché, who two years earlier had loaned him six thousand dollars to assist in paying his son's financial obligations. Plauché was one of the few creditors whom Jackson specifically provided for in his will.

In the summer of 1891, the portrait once owned by Plauché was offered for sale, presumably by its owner, Armand Hawkins, a New Orleans publisher and bookseller. A notice in the *Daily Picayune* of July 1 stated erroneously that the portrait was painted in 1839 and was placed upon a platform in the center of the Place d'Armes during the Silver Jubilee. It was then presented to General Plauché by veterans of his former Louisiana command. The *Picayune* purported to be quoting the *Le Courrier* of January 9, 1840. Yet no such account of this portrait or presentation appears in that edition. This should not be surprising, because Amans never requested a sitting until January 10.

The *Picayune* article, however, does list two items of information that are useful in identifying this particular portrait: namely, that the likeness was life-size and that it included a document described as the constitution of the state of Tennessee on the table near Jackson. Of the four versions extant, the only one that fits this description is at the Chicago Historical Society: The life-size canvas at the Historic New Orleans Collection was at the time at Brown University; the smaller version owned by Felix H. Kuntz was not life-size; and the life size version at the Tennessee State Museum does not depict a document resting on the table. Unless Amans painted a fifth version, which has not been discovered, the portrait described in the *Daily Picayune* of July 1, 1891, was probably the one purchased by Charles F. Gunther and subsequently acquired by the Chicago Historical Society.

19. This portrait once hung in the capitol in Nashville. See accession records of the Tennessee State Museum.

20. The resemblance reputedly was so correct that an unidentified French gentleman, the *Bulletin* learned, had ordered a copy. See *Mississippi Free Trader,* January 22, 1840; *New-Orleans Commercial Bulletin,* January 14, 1840.

21. Sometime before Tooley's death in 1844, he presented the piece to his great-grandmother. It descended through the family until 1966, when it was presented to the National Portrait Gallery. See *Mississippi Free Trader,* January 22, 1840; records of the Catalog of American Portraits.

22. Maxwell Whiteman, *Paintings and Sculpture at the Union League of Philadelphia* (Philadelphia, 1978), p. 55.

23. *New-Orleans Commercial Bulletin,* January 14, 1840.

24. Of course, the Union League portrait may itself be a replica. Marchant copied other portraits, such as those of William Henry Harrison and John Quincy Adams. Records of the Union League show that the Jackson portrait was presented by James L. Claghorn through Evan Rogers. Coincidentally, Marchant was a member of the Union League, which owns several of his portraits. Oliver, *Portraits of Adams,* p. 203; *Spirit of the Times,* March 23, 1839; Whiteman, *Paintings and Sculpture at the Union League,* p. 55; *Catalogue of the Collection of Paintings Belonging to the Union League of Philadelphia* (Philadelphia, 1940), pp. 25, 38; records of the Catalog of American Portraits.

25. *Mississippi Free Trader,* January 22, 1840. Prints, portraits, and later photographs were, of course, more common ways of holding on to the past. In contrast to the revealing life portraits taken of Jackson during his visit, the occasion gave rise to a likeness produced from the lithographic press of Jules Lion. Lion was a free black born in France in about 1810. Throughout his career, he dabbled as a painter, lithographer, art teacher, sketch artist, and photographer. Between 1837 and 1866, he was active in New Orleans, winning acclaim for his lithographic series of prominent Louisianians.

In January 1840 Lion produced his lithograph of Jackson. The *Courier* pronounced the image to be a good one, but carefully designated it as only a souvenir. Because Lion published several such lithographs of Jackson, most of which are undated, it is impossible to identify this particular one. See *Louisiana Courier,* January 16, 1840; *Encyclopedia of New Orleans Artists, 1718-1918* (New Orleans, La., 1987), pp. 238-39.

26. *Mississippi Free Trader,* January 22, 1840; Jackson to the Reverend Hardy M. Cryer, February 5, 1840, Jackson Papers, Tennessee State Library and Archives.

27. *Daily Picayune,* February 13, 1842. A label on the back of Fowler's *Jackson* states: "I certify that this portrait is the Original picture for which Genl Jackson sat to me while on board the Steamer Vicksburg on her return to Nashville from this City in Jany 1840. Trevor Tho. Fowler New Orleans *19 Camp St.*" In 1921 this painting was lent by Mrs. William Armistead Lane to the Brooklyn Museum. In 1947 an anonymous donor presented it to the Chicago Historical Society. The National Portrait Gallery owns a replica, which it purchased in 1972 from Kennedy Galleries of New York. See records of the Chicago Historical Society and the Catalog of American Portraits.

28. A photocopy of a written testimonial, dated April 24, 1840, to the excellence of Kellogg's completed portrait is among the records of the Ladies' Hermitage Association. Signed by fourteen of Jackson's friends and colleagues, including Governor James K. Polk, this statement was reproduced in the press. A similar clipping from an unidentified newspaper appears in the Kellogg Papers, Archives of American Art. For a different notice, see *New York Evening Post,* May 11, 1840. See also *Nashville Union,* April 30, 1840.

29. E. P. Richardson, "Archives of American Art Records of Art Collectors and Dealers: I. Miner K. Kellogg," *Art Quarterly* 23 (Autumn 1960): 271-72; Richard J. Boyle, "Miner Kilbourne Kellogg," *Cincinnati Art Museum Bulletin* 8 (February 1966): 17; Miner Kilbourne Kellogg, *M. K. Kellogg's Texas Journal, 1872,* ed. Llerena Friend (Austin, Tex., 1967), pp. 22, 28-32 (hereafter cited as Kellogg, *Texas Journal*); Miner K. Kellogg, "Reminiscences," New Harmony Collection, Indiana Historical Society library, Indianapolis (hereafter cited as Kellogg, "Reminiscences").

30. Kellogg, "Reminiscences"; Samuel G. Heiskell, *Andrew Jackson and Early Tennessee History* (Nashville, Tenn., 1920-1921), vol. 1, p. 620; Jackson to Moses Dawson, April 1, 1840; Kellogg to Dawson, April 17, 1840, Kellogg Letters, Moses Dawson Collection, McDonald Memorial Library, Xavier University, Cincinnati.

31. Kellogg to Elam P. Langdon, April 4, 1840 (transcript), Kellogg Letters, Cincinnati Historical Society; Kellogg to Dawson, April 17, 1840, Moses Dawson Collection.

32. Kellogg, "Reminiscences."

33. Kellogg to Langdon, April 28, 1840, Kellogg Letters, (transcript), Cincinnati Historical Society.

34. Kellogg, "Reminiscences." With regard to the lock of hair, see Andrew Jackson, Jr., to Kellogg, May 5, 1840, Ladies' Hermitage Association.

35. Kellogg, "Reminiscences." Kellogg took advantage of the opportunity to paint a life portrait of the governor, one of the few for which Polk sat. See James K. Polk, *The Diary of James K. Polk During His Presidency, 1845 to 1849,* ed. Milo Milton Quaife (Chicago, 1910), vol. 3, pp. 225, 323.

36. William Burke and others to Kellogg, May 26, 1840, Kellogg Letters, Cincinnati Historical Society. Selected newspaper clippings in the Kellogg Papers, Archives of American Art, make reference to the portrait's reception in Cincinnati.

37. Newspaper clipping in the Kellogg Papers, Archives of American Art; a written testimonial signed by a number of Jacksonians in Pittsburgh is among the records of the Ladies' Hermitage Association.

38. The subscription list is among the records of the Ladies' Hermitage Association.

39. Kellogg to Jackson, December 30, 1840, Jackson Papers, Library of Congress; Kellogg, *Texas Journal,* p. 33; Richardson, "Miner K. Kellogg," pp. 272–74; Boyle, "Miner Kilbourne Kellogg," p. 20.

40. *Correspondence of Jackson,* vol. 6, p. 112; records of the Catalog of American Portraits.

41. Washington *Star,* September 2, 1928; Kellogg portrait file in the curatorial offices of the National Museum of American Art.

42. Newspaper clippings (microfilm) collected in the Kellogg Papers, Archives of American Art.

43. *The Golden Age: Cincinnati Painters of the Nineteenth Century Represented in the Cincinnati Art Museum* (Cincinnati, Ohio, 1979), pp. 76–77.

44. This portrait once belonged to the noted collector of Andrew Jackson memorabilia, Edward J. Hurja of New York City. He may have acquired it there at the Old Print Shop, which advertised it in *Antiques* magazine in August 1937 on p. 84.

45. Concerning Jackson's ill health, see, for example, Jackson to Francis P. Blair, July 17, 1841, Jackson Papers, Library of Congress; Remini, *Andrew Jackson,* vol. 3, pp. 475, 480.

46. Autobiographical letter in the John Wood Dodge Papers, Archives of American Art.

47. *Ibid.*; see also Dodge's account book of miniatures in this collection. Kelly, "Portrait Painting in Tennessee," pp. 218–19; *New York Times,* December 31, 1893.

48. *Nashville Union,* April 14, 1842.

49. For a contemporary newspaper account of this sword, now in the collection of the Ladies' Hermitage Association, see the Washington *Globe,* January 14, 1835.

50. *Nashville Whig,* April 16, 1842; *New York Evening Post,* October 31, 1842, and March 22, 1843; *New York Tribune,* March 28, 1843; *Plebeian* (Kingston, New York), March 30, 1843; *New York Herald,* March 28, 1843; *Marietta Intelligencer* (Ohio), April 13, 1843.

51. *Plebeian,* March 30, 1843; New York *True Sun,* April 4, 1843. For accolades by Jackson and his friends, see Dodge Papers.

52. An inscription penciled on the reverse reads: "Copied by John W. Dodge from his original miniature of General Andrew Jackson April 22nd 1842 for Gen. Armstrong." In 1985 this miniature came to public notice when the Tennessee State Museum purchased it from a private collection in Memphis. Previously, it had been in a private collection in Rye, New York. See Kelly, "Portrait Painting in Tennessee," p. 219; Dodge Papers; *National Academy of Design Exhibition Record, 1826–1860,* vol. 1, p. 126.

In his later years, Dodge painted a number of cabinet-size oil portraits. The National Museum of Racing in Saratoga Springs, New York, owns a 30-by-25-inch oil on canvas portrait of Jackson attributed to Dodge. The image is clearly after the 1842 image but varies significantly in its execution. In this, Jackson appears younger and less fatigued. See records of the Catalog of American Portraits; *Notable Paintings . . . Collection of Mr. & Mrs. Robert W. Lyons* (auction catalogue, Parke-Bernet Galleries, Inc., New York, 1945), p. 44.

53. Craig J. Turner, "Early Engravings of Andrew Jackson," *S.P.A. Journal* 37 (March–April

1975): 421–27.

54. William Henry Brown to Jackson, August 17, 1843, Jackson Papers, Library of Congress; Anna Wells Rutledge, "William Henry Brown of Charleston," *Antiques* 60 (December 1951): 532; "A Relative's Reminiscences of William Henry Brown," *Antiques* 44 (December 1943): 300–301.

55. Brown to Jackson, August 17, 1843, Jackson Papers, Library of Congress. The letter Brown published in his *Portrait Gallery of Distinguished American Citizens* was from Jackson to Polk and was dated December 20, 1840. The contents concerned the death and funeral of a mutual friend, Felix Grundy, a former senator and attorney general of the United States.

56. Frances Anne Butler, *Journal* (London, 1835), vol. 2, p. 131; Reda C. Goff, "A Physical Profile of Andrew Jackson," *Tennessee Historical Quarterly* 28 (Fall 1969): 303–4.

57. "A Relative's Reminiscences of Brown," pp. 300–301.

58. *New Orleans Bee,* June 22, 1844; *Daily Picayune,* July 11, 1844.

59. *New Orleans Bee,* June 22, 1844.

60. Records of the Catalog of American Portraits.

61. Remini, *Andrew Jackson,* vol. 3, pp. 509–11, 515–17.

62. Hart, "Life Portraits," p. 803.

63. Jackson was not, however, the first President to face the camera. Three years before, John Quincy Adams had sat for John Plumbe, Jr., in Boston. Adams recalled the session as being a slow and dull process that put him to sleep. In spite of his breadth of knowledge, he admitted having no conceivable notion of how the impression emerged upon the plate. See Oliver, *Portraits of Adams,* pp. 281–95.

64. *United States Magazine, and Democratic Review* 17 (1845): 161.

65. William Welling, *Photography in America: The Formative Years, 1839–1900* (New York, 1978), pp. 20, 34–36.

66. William and Estelle Marder, *Anthony, the Man, the Company, the Cameras* (n.p., 1982), pp. 25–26. Balch's letter to Anthony is illustrated on p. 32 and is credited to the authors.

67. In an interview with noted Civil War diarist George Alfred Townsend, published in the New York *World* of April 12, 1891, Brady claims to have sent an operative "to the Hermitage and had Andrew Jackson taken barely in time to save his aged lineaments to posterity." This interview has been republished in Beaumont Newhall, ed., *Photography: Essays & Images* (New York, 1980), pp. 45–49.

68. Harold Francis Pfister, *Facing the Light: Historic American Portrait Daguerreotypes* (Washington, D.C., 1978), p. 63.

69. Hart, "Life Portraits," p. 803; Goff, "A Physical Profile of Andrew Jackson," pp. 300–301; Alfred T. Adams to Stanley F. Horn, September 17, 1963, photocopy in the files of the Tennessee State Museum, Nashville. For additional references to Daniel Adams, see the *Nashville Whig,* January 13, 1846, and September 14, 1848.

70. Hart, "Life Portraits," p. 803.

71. The National Portrait Gallery is especially grateful to Marni Sandweiss, director of the Mead Art Museum, for alerting us to this new discovery.

72. Pfister, *Facing the Light,* pp. 63–65.

73. Remini, *Andrew Jackson,* vol. 3, pp. 518–19.

74. Pfister, *Facing the Light,* p. 66; Welling, *Photography in America,* pp. 48–49.

75. A. Conger Goodyear of New York presented this daguerreotype to the Eastman House. In his records he described the image as Andrew Jackson at age seventy-five. If so, this would then date the plate to about 1842. No evidence has been found to substantiate this claim. See Robert Bretz to Stanley F. Horn, February 17, 1967, George Eastman House, Rochester.

76. Horn, *Hermitage,* p. 202.

77. Welling, *Photography in America,* p. 49.

78. Robert J. Evans, *A Catalog of the Paintings by G. P. A. Healy in the Illinois State Museum Collection* (Springfield, Ill., 1974); *A Souvenir of the Exhibition Entitled Healy's Sitters . . . on View at the Virginia Museum of Fine Arts in Richmond* (Richmond, Va., 1950), pp. 8–9; George P. A. Healy, *Reminiscences of a Portrait Painter* (Chicago, 1894), pp. 138–39.

79. *Correspondence of Jackson,* vol. 6, pp. 408–9; John Catron to Sarah Yorke Jackson, May 19, 1845, Jackson Papers, Library of Congress; Healy, *Reminiscences,* pp. 140–42.

80. *Correspondence of Jackson,* vol. 6, p. 408; Healy, *Reminiscences,* p. 142.

81. Quoted in Parton, *Jackson,* vol. 3, pp. 672–73.

82. *Ibid.*; Healy, *Reminiscences,* pp. 142–43; Healy to Martin Van Buren, July 7, 1857, Van Buren Papers, Library of Congress; Healy's diary notes in Healy Papers, Archives of American Art.

83. In 1905 Colonel and Mrs. Jackson accepted an offer from the Ladies' Hermitage Association to buy the painting for $500. The provenance of this portrait, signed "G. P. A. Healy" and dated "May 29th, 1845" (in the background near Jackson's left shoulder), is impeccable. See records of the Ladies' Hermitage Association.

84. Healy to Van Buren, July 7, 1857, Van Buren Papers.

85. Nashville *Politician,* June 13, 1845. The *Politician* added that Healy was copying a portrait by Earl owned by the family of the late Major Rutledge. This may have been the likeness that Earl mentioned as "not finished" in his Memorandum Book for 1817 (Earl Papers), and was probably the same one engraved by Charles C. Torrey in 1826. Healy's copy, assuming that he indeed finished it, may be a portrait now owned by Historic Deerfield.

86. William Barrow Floyd, *Jouett—Bush—Frazer: Early Kentucky Artists* (Lexington, Ky., 1968), pp. 132, 161, 194; Price, *Old Masters of the Bluegrass,* pp. 113–14.

87. Healy to Johnson, August 2, 1857, Healy Papers. Because Healy failed to fully identify this Johnson, he could possibly be Eastman Johnson (1824–1906), or even the less well known David Johnson (1827–1908), a portraitist working in the late 1850s in Washington.

88. Hiram Powers to Theodore Dehon, June 22, 1859; Healy to Powers, September 12, 1859, Powers Papers.

89. *Chicago Tribune,* December 28, 1861; Marie De Mare, *G. P. A. Healy, American Artist: An Intimate Chronicle of the Nineteenth Century* (New York, 1954), pp. 202–4. Healy mentions this painting in his letters to Sarah Madeleine Vinton Goddard in 1861. See George P. A. Healy Papers, Library of Congress.

90. Michaelsen Gallery in New York City advertised this painting for sale in *Antiques* magazine in August 1938, and listed it as coming from the Meeks collection in Lowell, Massachusetts. By 1948 it formed part of the collection of International Business Machines Corporation, which that year loaned it to the State Department for an international tour. IBM disposed of it in 1968, and the following year Hirschl & Adler Galleries sold it to Algur H. Meadows, then chairman of the board of General American Oil Company of Texas. In 1972 he donated it to the Cummer Gallery. See *Antiques* 34 (August 1938): 62; "60 Americans Since 1800," *Art News* 45 (December 1946): pt. 1, 36; records of the Catalog of American Portraits.

91. In 1879 Bryan sold his collection to the Corcoran Gallery. See *A Catalogue of the Collection of American Paintings in the Corcoran Gallery of Art* (Washington, D.C., 1966), vol. 1, pp. 88–89 (hereafter cited as *Catalogue of the Corcoran Collection*).

92. Healy, *Reminiscences,* p. 149.

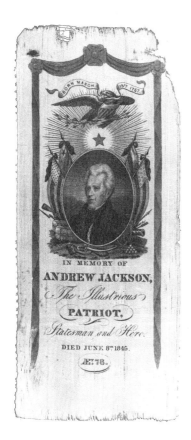

Figure 173.
Silk memorial ribbon, after Ralph E. W. Earl, 1845. Private collection

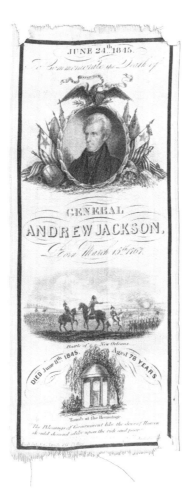

Figure 174.
Silk memorial ribbon, after James B. Longacre, 1845. Private collection

Figure 175.
Silk memorial ribbon, after William James Hubard, 1845. Private collection

Chapter 8

Eternal Glory

Figure 176.
Hand-colored lithograph by Nathaniel
Currier, 1845. National Portrait Gallery,
Smithsonian Institution

I

Three hours after Andrew Jackson died, a coach, pulled at a gallop, whirled through the front gate of the Hermitage and up the dusty drive to the mansion. Out stepped General Sam Houston, his wife, and young son. The onetime governor of Tennessee and former president of the Republic of Texas had hurried to the estate to pay his last respects to his old friend and political mentor. At Jackson's bedside it was already too late for words but not for final impressions. Drawing young Samuel to his side, Houston instructed, "My son, try to remember that you have looked upon the face of Andrew Jackson."[1]

News of Jackson's death rippled throughout the nation. Everywhere flags flew at half mast. Businesses closed. Black suddenly became the national color, as banners of mourning decorated everything from newspaper columns to government edifices. In conversations, almost no one referred to the deceased by his proper name. Somehow such epithets as "Old Hickory" and "Hero of New Orleans" seemed more endearing. In the weeks following, dozens of eulogists recalled his illustrious career as warrior and statesman, rationalizing his shortcomings and glorifying his victories. He was compared with history's most celebrated commanders, from Hannibal to Napoleon, and was deemed superior to them all, save for the immortal Washington.[2]

This nationwide observance of mourning took many forms, including souvenir portraiture. For instance, a bleak array of silk funeral ribbons contained images of Jackson after well-known likenesses by Ralph E. W. Earl [Fig. 173], James B. Longacre [Fig. 174], and William J. Hubard [Fig. 175]. In addition, more than half a dozen hand-colored lithographs depicted his death. Nathaniel Currier alone published at least four such scenes. A typical portrayal was of Jackson lying in bed with his hand resting on an open Bible [Fig. 176]. Watching over him are four figures whose identities can only be surmised. According to Rachel Jackson Lawrence, among those present were her father and mother and Dr. John H. Esselman. Rachel, then twelve years old, stood at the foot of the bed, her eyes fixed on her grandfather's still face.[3]

Even before the end came, there were those who valued Jackson's icon more than ever. President Polk was typical. On May 22, amid the consuming business of Texas's annexation, Polk wrote to Jackson, informing him that he had procured a copy of Thomas Sully's portrait of the general in military costume that had been taken many years earlier. "The contrast between your appearance then and now is very great," observed the President.[4]

Based on Polk's brief description, his copy by an unknown artist was presumably after Sully's 1819 life portrait. In any event, Sully renewed his interest in Andrew Jackson in 1845. With the exception of Ralph E. W. Earl, Sully

Figure 177.
Oil on canvas by Thomas Sully, circa 1824.
National Gallery of Art; Andrew W. Mellon
Collection

executed more images of Jackson than any other artist. His register of paintings listed eleven, three of which he painted during the spring and summer of 1845.[5] Two of these were head-only likenesses, and the third was a dashing full-length, life-size canvas of Jackson on the battlefield at New Orleans, now owned by the Corcoran Gallery of Art. The image of Jackson in all three portraits is virtually the same. Moreover, this image was not new, and it eventually proved to be the inspiration for the twenty-dollar-bill likeness, Jackson's most widely recognized portrait.

According to Sully's register of paintings, he copied his likenesses of 1845 after a study portrait he had done in 1824 [Fig. 177]. Allegedly he presented the study to Jackson, who in turn gave it to Francis P. Blair.[6] Blair always claimed, somewhat mistakenly, that this canvas was Sully's original life portrait, painted when Jackson visited Philadelphia in 1819 [see page 55]. In 1852 Blair loaned the painting to George W. Childs of Philadelphia, who published an engraving by Thomas B. Welch [Fig. 178].[7]

A replica is still owned by a Blair descendant [Fig. 179]. Also extant is a version in the R. W. Norton Art Gallery in Shreveport, Louisiana [Fig. 180]. This likeness is oval in shape and more fully painted in the area of the shoulders.[8]

On July 8, 1845, a month to the day after Jackson died, Sully began his full-

Figure 178. Above.
Engraving by Thomas B. Welch, after
Thomas Sully, 1852. Prints and Photo-
graphs Division, Library of Congress

Figure 179. Above right.
Oil on canvas by Thomas Sully, 1845. Mrs.
Arnold A. Willcox

Figure 180. Right.
Oil on canvas by Thomas Sully, 1845. The
R. W. Norton Art Gallery

Figure 181.
Oil on canvas by Thomas Sully, 1845. The
Corcoran Gallery of Art; gift of William
Wilson Corcoran, 1869

length, life-size portrait [Fig. 181]. When completed on July 31, this portrait, although romanticized, was the most dashing one of Jackson yet. Sully exhibited it that year, along with canvases of Lafayette and Fanny Kemble, at the joint exhibition of the Artists' Fund Society of Philadelphia and the Pennsylvania Academy of the Fine Arts.[9]

Much to Sully's surprise and pleasure, his 1824 study likeness of Old Hickory was to become ubiquitous. On December 22, 1866, Spencer M. Clark, the first head of the United States Bureau of Engraving and Printing, wanted engraved a series of portraits of the former Presidents. To execute these oval portraits, designed for paper currency, he consulted Alfred Sealey, a reputable engraver with the National Bank Note Company of New York. Clark wanted to begin the series with Jackson's image and suggested that Sealey copy an engraving by Moseley Isaac Danforth after Dodge's miniature of 1842. Danforth's popular engraving had been used on state bank notes before the Civil War and on Confederate notes in 1861; in 1863 the United States Post Office selected it for a new two-cent stamp, the "Black Jack."[10]

Inexplicably, the Dodge-Danforth likeness was ultimately rejected. On January 11, 1867, Clark sent Sealey four photographs of Sully's 1824 study image of Jackson. (These could have been either of the actual portrait or Welch's engraving.) Clark specified only that Sealey should continue the form and drapery of Jackson's torso down to the bottom of the oval border. Sealey accomplished this in part by depicting Jackson clutching his cloak in his hand.[11]

Sealey's engraving first appeared in 1869 on the five-dollar United States note [Fig. 182]. Because of the bill's distinctive multicolored design, it was designated the "rainbow series." Although copied by subsequent engravers, the Sealey-Sully likeness of Jackson has decorated a variety of federal notes, including the ten-thousand-dollar bill of 1878, the ten-dollar bill of the early 1900s, and the twenty-dollar bill of today.[12]

II

In 1845, the idea of erecting a grand equestrian statue to one of the nation's foremost patriots was scarcely novel. Yet such a work had never been successfully undertaken in the United States. As early as 1783, the Continental Congress voted to erect an equestrian statue to George Washington. But the all-consuming business of establishing a new and permanent government, compounded by the fledgling state of the arts in America, postponed this endeavor indefinitely.

More than half a century later, the nation still could not boast an equestrian statue to Washington, or to anyone else. Jackson's death, however, rekindled interest in building a national monument to a national hero. An article in the *United States Magazine, and Democratic Review* of July–August 1845 sounded the rallying trumpet: "No mausoleum—no column—no pyramid—a statue alone, is the proper monument which a nation ought to erect to its great dead. . . . A grand, colossal *Equestrian Statue in bronze* . . . is the proper monument for Jackson."[13]

The interest that had been sparked by the *Democratic Review* in July caught fire in Washington in September. The torch bearer was John L. O'Sullivan, the *Democratic Review*'s dynamic editor. On July 10, O'Sullivan, accompanied by Secretary of State James Buchanan, proposed to President Polk the formation of a committee in Washington, "to raise by subscription a sum of $100,000 or more for the erection of a monument, to the memory of Gen'l Jackson." A nonpartisan committee of thirteen was finally selected and invested with organizational and fund-raising authority. Postmaster General Cave Johnson was named chairman. Francis P. Blair, popularly looked upon as the guardian of Jackson's fame, was selected to the all-important post of treasurer. Other able committeemen included John C. Rives, Blair's longtime and trusted financial manager, and Thomas Ritchie, editor of the Washington *Daily Union,* the administration's new organ.

The committee members resolved that Jackson's memorial should be a bronze equestrian statue of the hero of New Orleans, to be erected in Washington, "exhibiting the features, the person, the apparel, the attitude, and almost the action, which belonged to him at the moment of rendering the highest service to his country."[14] A nationwide subscription would fund this statue, whose design would be decided by an open competition.

Coincidentally, at about the same time, the *Daily Evening Transcript* of Boston reported Hiram Powers's interest in sculpting a bronze equestrian statue of Old Hickory, about sixteen feet in height, at a cost of thirty thousand dollars. Powers had been charging some of the highest prices in the art market. Obviously, he was not aware of the gargantuan price tag—more than one hundred thousand dollars—envisioned by optimistic proponents of the subscription process.[15] In comparison, Powers's price seemed a bargain.

Yet as the fund-raising campaign progressed, contributions were proving to be disappointing. Two full years after its inception, the committee was having serious doubts about just what kind of statue its relatively small purse could buy. Perhaps it would have to settle for a pedestrian statue by Powers, similar to his Calhoun monument carved for the city of Charleston in 1845.

Then, in early 1848, Cave Johnson met by chance, one evening in Washington, a young visitor named Clark Mills. He learned that Mills was a sculptor and was about to depart for Europe for further study. Johnson, knowing that he had nothing to lose, invited the young artist to submit a design for the Jackson monument. Mills weighed his relative inexperience with this herculean proposal and at first declined the offer. But then ambition and prospects of future success changed his mind. Mills hurried back home to Charleston and began designing a model.[16]

Clark Mills was an unlikely contestant, who had acquired his artistic skills by chance. Mills was born in Onondaga County, New York, on September 1, 1815. At thirteen, he ran away from home and worked at odd jobs. By the time he reached Charleston, in about 1837, Mills was a jack-of-all-trades. There he found his niche, first as an ornamental plasterer and later as a sculptor.

Mills's sculpted likeness of John C. Calhoun, the favorite son of South Carolina, won him city-wide recognition. In 1845 he carved a marble bust of the statesman principally from memory, with the aid of portraits. Remarkably, this was Mills's first attempt at sculpting. "For his genius," the city council of Charleston presented him with a gold medal.[17]

Mills's reputation quickly spread throughout the state. Technically his works were more studied than inspired, but they pleased his patrons. John S. Preston, a wealthy sugar planter and arts patron, encouraged him to go to Washington. At Preston's expense, Mills was to study the sculpture there and to execute some works for him.[18]

Mills's trip to Washington, and his chance meeting with Cave Johnson, set in motion the sequence of events that would soon win him national acclaim and ultimately a permanent place in the history of American art. However, Mills had never seen his subject, and, as if the challenges facing him were not enough, he conceived an ambitious design. He portrayed Jackson on a rearing horse, in the act of reviewing his troops on the morning of January 8, 1815, just prior to the commencement of the decisive Battle of New Orleans. In acknowledgment of the presentation of arms from his command, Jackson raises his hat according to the military etiquette of the day. His bridle hand is turned down in an attempt to restrain his prancing beast from prematurely dashing down the line.[19]

Mills's dramatic interpretation may have been influenced by engravings of one or more European works, including Jacques-Louis David's renowned painting of Napoleon crossing the Alps. More germane were certain equestrian statues, which underscored the special difficulty of balancing the weight of a mounted horse rearing up on its two hind legs. This feat had never been successfully accomplished before without the aid of some sort of prop, which often appeared awkward.[20]

Meanwhile, back in Charleston, Mills perfected his small plaster model. By the beginning of March 1848, the finished sculpture was winning praises from city residents. Buoyed by this encouragement, Mills carried it to Washington. Approval by the Jackson monument committee would be the equivalent of a national endorsement of Mills's artistic talents. With his future at stake, he had everything to gain by winning the commission and then seeing it through to a successful completion, regardless of the likelihood of exhausting his financial resources.

The committeemen had been able to raise a total of only twelve thousand dollars. Such a modest sum would never have enticed a prominent sculptor like Hiram Powers to undertake an equestrian statue on a scale that was larger than life. But in Mills the committeemen had a willing sculptor. Moreover, they highly approved of his model and entered with him upon a contract— with one special proviso. To alleviate the risk that Mills's inexperience posed, they asked him to put up surety for the successful completion of the work. Mills found ten friends in South Carolina who would back him.[21]

Mills commenced his work on a vacant lot at the corner of Fifteenth Street and Pennsylvania Avenue, near the presidential mansion. He erected a small frame building for a workshop and a residence. Mills approached his art through the modes of science and engineering. For study purposes he purchased a horse, which he trained to assume the rearing stance he desired. Mills also dissected other horses and made plaster casts. From several different breeds he selected the most noble features and combined them all into one perfect specimen.[22]

As work progressed, Mills's studio became a mecca for tourists and interested passersby. Few could appreciate the complexity of his task more than fellow sculptor Henry Kirke Brown, who was himself soon to begin an equestrian statue of George Washington for the city of New York. On May 18, 1849, Brown wrote to his wife about a recent visit to Mills's studio. *We entered a room with one window in it and two doors, one led to the mane [sic] studio, the other to the street. In this little room were two busts, old boots, a few books, fever and ague medicines, a hat full of eggs, his sketches for his great work, and a variety of other articles. . . . He left us a moment to arrange the light in the mane studio, he then showed us in, and wow! an unco sight! this immense horse standing upon his hind legs balancing himself with an enormous tail which could not contain less than a barrel of plaster! But balance the thing did. . . . My eyes wandered around the room. I saw hanging up upon sides of the room casts from dissections of various parts of horses like beef to dry. . . . I saw the boots of the old Hero Jackson. These were partly chopped out of plaster. . . . At the feet of these boots (so to speak) lay the half formed head of the General over which the boots seemed* [to be] *enjoying a temporary triumph. The body too stood aloof from the other members of the same family. . . . These parts are roughed out in plaster and finished separately, and are then to meet on their proper footing.*[23]

Another source reported that Mills examined every detail of the general's military uniform, which was deposited in the Patent Office. "The very sword he wore, and every minutiae of the saddle, holsters, bridle, and even buckles" were faithfully replicated.[24] Yet all that was ever mentioned about the sculpting of Jackson's face was that Mills had studied the best available likenesses. The right profile closely resembles a bust by Powers, whereas the opposite profile and frontal view are reminiscent of the likeness by Ferdinand Pettrich. Coincidentally, Henry Kirke Brown mentioned seeing two busts, presumably of Jackson, in Mills's studio.[25]

Predictably, it was the immense horse, rearing nearly twelve feet high, that stole the show. After experiencing initial awe, visitors studied the great beast of molded plaster more critically, only to discover the real wonder—"that there are no points of contact with the ground, except the hind feet." Moreover, "the artist's weight, 160 lbs., when suspended from the fore feet . . . produces hardly any impression."[26] In balancing the sculpture, Mills discovered that the center of gravity passes through the rider, a principal that had eluded any number of intelligent men before him and was the key to his success.

❧

Still Mills's engineering feat was only half accomplished. The other great obstacle looming before him was the actual casting of the bronze statue. The government furnished the metal, but there was no foundry in the country equipped to do the job. Someone in Pennsylvania offered to build one for twenty thousand dollars, but this was out of the question: Mills had only twelve thousand dollars with which to complete the entire project. As a last resort, Mills built a furnace on his premises, but he had no casting experience whatsoever. Therefore, for practice he melted 1,600 pounds of metal and successfully made four bells.[27]

The casting of the statue progressed by trial and error. The sides of the horse proved to be the most difficult because they involved large one-piece sections. The process was fraught with unforeseen difficulties and accidents. On one occasion Mills's crane broke. A more serious incident occurred while actor Edwin Forrest was marveling at the casting process—as the gates were lifted to let the molten stream of bronze fill the mold, there was an explosion.[28]

For more than two years, Mills persevered. Finally, in October 1852 he completed the casting. The statue lay in ten sections, the horse in four, and the figure in six. In less than three months, Mills assembled the nearly fifteen-ton monument and mounted it upon a white marble pedestal in Lafayette Square, opposite the White House [Fig. 183].

The unveiling was held on January 8, 1853, the anniversary of the Battle of New Orleans. Under bright, crisp skies all of Washington, it seemed, gathered for the occasion; prominent in attendance were the President, members of both houses of Congress, and twenty thousand spectators. When asked to speak, Clark Mills was overwhelmed. Lacking words, he simply lifted his hand toward the statue as it was being unveiled.[29]

Figure 183.
Clark Mills's bronze statue of Andrew
Jackson, dedicated January 8, 1853, in
Lafayette Square

&c/s&

The Jackson monument was the first equestrian statue erected in the United
States. Its successful completion meant everything to Clark Mills. He had
risked his health, reputation, and what little means he possessed. During times
of financial strain, friends had been coming to his assistance. John W. Maury,
a member of the monument committee and the mayor of Washington,
periodically advanced him a sum eventually totaling nearly five thousand
dollars. In addition, committeemen Blair, Rives, and Benjamin B. French
loaned him several hundred dollars each. Ultimately, Congress awarded Mills
twenty thousand dollars for his endeavor and, more important, appropriated
an additional fifty thousand dollars for him to sculpt the long-delayed equestrian statue of Washington.[30]

Notwithstanding his later successes, Clark Mills will always be remembered for
his monument to Andrew Jackson. Although hailed in its day for its naturalistic exuberance, the statue has since been criticized for its naïveté and lack of
artistic inspiration. But, given the physical and technical obstacles that the
artist had overcome, the monument represents an engineering feat as much as
it does a serious sculpture. In pioneering the process of bronze casting in the
United States, Mills refuted the notion that American artists needed European
training to be successful.[31]

In June 1853 Mills exhibited the original plaster and wood model of Jackson
at Railroad Hall in New York City. A fire in Mills's studio in November of the
following year, however, destroyed it as well as the foundry. At the time Mills
was working upon his equestrian statue of Washington. Fortunately, several
castings of the Jackson statue had been placed outside and were saved. As it
happened, Mills still had use for them. During the summer of 1854, he
received an order from the city of New Orleans for a duplicate statue of Old
Hickory. The proposed monument, for which he would be paid thirty-eight
thousand dollars, was to be erected in Jackson Square.[32] On February 9, 1856,
this first replica was unveiled in a citywide ceremony.

Figure 184.
Lithograph with tintstone by Wagner and McGuigan lithography company, 1853. Prints and Photographs Division, Library of Congress

Figure 185.
Pot metal cast by Cornelius and Baker of Philadelphia, after Clark Mills, patented 1855. National Portrait Gallery, Smithsonian Institution; gift of Mr. and Mrs. John L. Sanders in memory of William Monroe Geer

The city of Nashville ordered a second replica, which Mills produced for the same price. Yet by 1875, that locality, still recovering from the devastation it had suffered during the Civil War, had not been able to raise the required sum. Temporarily Mills had a finished statue on his hands, with no buyer. In the end, the Tennessee Historical Society purchased the statue for the city.[33] The monument still enjoys a prominent site in front of the state capitol. Of the three statues, the artist considered this last one to be the most nearly perfect.

❧

Mills's equestrian statue of Jackson inspired any number of photographers and lithographers. In 1853, Blanchard P. Paige of Washington made a daguerreotype, which was copied on stone by B. F. Smith, Jr., and published as a lithograph by Smith and Jenkins of New York City. That same year, Casimir Bohn of Washington had published a similar lithograph by the Philadelphia firm of Wagner and McGuigan [Fig. 184]. Entitled *Mill's Colossean Equestrian Statue of General Andrew Jackson,* this finely executed work depicts three gentlemen whose identities are recognizable grouped directly in front of the monument. In the center stands Franklin Pierce, the newly inaugurated President. (Wagner and McGuigan had produced a similar likeness of Pierce just the year before.) The figure on the left is Francis P. Blair, who points toward the statue and calls attention to the engraved words of Jackson's Jefferson's birthday toast of 1830. The identity of the figure on the right is not certain but resembles Clark Mills.[34]

The popular Jackson monument also inspired replication in the form of statuettes. Today several of these pot metal sculptures are extant [Fig. 185]. Patented on May 15, 1855, they were cast by Cornelius and Baker of Philadelphia. Although the casting of the horse is reasonably accurate, the likeness of Jackson is unrecognizable. At least one bronze version has been identified that is not stamped "Cornelius & Baker"; it may be the work of Mills's own hand.[35]

In 1945, a plaster model, identical in size and shape to the cast statuettes, was presented to the Maryland Historical Society as being the original plaster.[36] If the information is correct, it would mean that the statuettes were really replicas of the plaster model that Mills displayed before the monument committee in mid-1848 for their approval. This may account for the poor likeness of Jackson, since Mills had not yet had a chance to study his portraiture in detail.

❧

Mills's original statue across from the White House has weathered the storms of both nature and politics. Since 1917, on four separate occasions there have been spirited attempts to relocate the monument. The last occurred in 1967, the bicentennial of Jackson's birth.[37] But because the legislators decided to leave well enough alone, Old Hickory still occupies the grassy lawn opposite the executive mansion. No better site could have been selected by the Jackson monument committee or Clark Mills, or even Congress, to pay tribute to the man most responsible for expanding the powers of the presidency.

III

Jackson would always be remembered first and foremost as the hero of New Orleans. In 1859 Christian Schussele underscored this association with grand effect in a group portrait, *General Andrew Jackson Before Judge Hall,* depicting a confrontation that Jackson instigated with civil authorities in New Orleans after his victory of January 8, 1815 [Fig. 186]. The trouble stemmed from Old Hickory's continuation of martial law in the absence of a once-threatening but now defeated British army. Because he insisted on employing every precaution

Figure 186.
Oil on canvas by Christian Schussele, 1859.
The Thomas Gilcrease Institute of
American History and Art

until official word arrived that a treaty ending the War of 1812 had been signed, he caused a furor when he tried to stop local newspapers from spreading rumors of peace.

Meanwhile, relations between Jackson and segments of his army quickly degenerated. By the end of February, the Louisiana militia began talking of mutiny if they were not discharged. Next, Creole soldiers, who decided to register with their consul as French citizens, demanded immediate release from their military commitments. Thereupon Jackson banished them, as well as the consul, from the city. An article in a local French newspaper stated that he had overstepped his bounds, which only enraged him more. The editor was brought before him and forced into revealing the name of the author—Louis Louailler, a member of the legislature. Jackson had him hunted down and thrown into jail. When federal district judge Dominick Augustine Hall intervened, Jackson jailed him for inciting mutiny and then banished him from New Orleans.

Fortunately, on March 13 official word arrived that the peace treaty had been signed, and Jackson promptly ended martial law. Hall now struck back, holding Jackson in contempt of court for refusing to comply with the writ of habeas corpus issued in the Louailler case. Jackson was eventually saddled with a one-thousand-dollar fine for his offense.[38]

ev

Christian Schussele was ideally suited for painting historical genre. Born in French Alsace in 1824, Schussele taught himself portraiture before studying lithography in Strasbourg in 1841. Two years later he ventured to Paris, where he worked under several artists, including historical painters Paul Delaroche and Adolphe Yvon, the latter known for his battle scenes at Versailles. In Yvon's studio Schussele was commissioned to make drawings for elaborate chromolithographic reproductions. Shortly after the revolution of 1848 erupted, he, like many others, fled to the United States.

In Philadelphia, Schussele principally supported himself as a chromolithographer. His real interest, however, lay in painting, and as his reputation and success increased, he abandoned printmaking for the brush. Schussele is best remembered for his group portraits of noted Americans and historical events, including *Franklin Before the Lords in Council* (1856), *Men of Progress* (1857), and *Washington at Valley Forge* (1862).[39]

Schussele's *General Andrew Jackson Before Judge Hall* was commissioned in about 1849 by C. J. Hedenberg, a successful Philadelphia shoe merchant who lived near the artist's studio. Both painter and patron demonstrated great interest in this work, and it is difficult to determine just who exerted more energy toward its successful completion. Hedenberg personally collected reliable portraits of some three dozen gentlemen, whom Schussele then diligently reproduced on the large canvas.[40] Conspicuously centered is the figure of Andrew Jackson. His likeness is a composite taken from unknown portraits. Other prominent figures in the scene, besides Judge Hall, include Jackson's aides-de-camp and counsel, Edward Livingston and Major John Reid. Both men hold documents of defense and flank their celebrated commander.

The actual courtroom drama extended over a period of several days. Based on the painting, Schussele apparently isolated an incident that occurred on March 24, 1815, at the opening session. At 10:00 a.m. Jackson, dressed in civilian clothes and accompanied by his counsel, stepped into the courtroom. Since the termination of martial law, Old Hickory was popular again, and his appearance triggered a spontaneous applause from the full gallery. Sensing Judge Hall's hesitancy to begin the proceedings under circumstances that had suddenly turned adverse, Jackson hushed the assembly with his hand. He then assured Judge Hall that there was no cause for alarm, "the same arm that protected from outrage this city . . . will shield and protect this court, or perish in the effort."[41]

Poised now in his own defense, Jackson and his counsel moved to contest the legality of the proceedings. Unpersuaded, Judge Hall overruled them. Nor would he allow a prepared statement to be read explaining why the general, having acted under the presumed authority of martial law, could not validly be held in contempt.

At a final session the following week, Hall confronted Jackson with nineteen pointed questions concerning his violation of the writ, but Jackson refused to be interrogated. If he could not read his statement defending his conduct, he pleaded that there was nothing further for him to do but to submit to the judge's sentence—a thousand-dollar fine. Jackson wrote a check on the spot and then marched out of the courtroom, still the hero of New Orleans.[42]

Notes

1. Marquis James, *The Raven: A Biography of Sam Houston* (New York, 1929), p. 357.

2. Remini, *Andrew Jackson*, vol. 3, pp. 524-29; Benjamin M. Dusenbery, comp., *Monument to the Memory of General Andrew Jackson: Containing Twenty-Five Eulogies and Sermons Delivered on Occasion of His Death* (Philadelphia, 1846), pp. 69, 325, 332.

3. Roger A. Fischer and Edmund B. Sullivan, *American Political Ribbons and Ribbon Badges, 1825-1981* (Lincoln, Mass., 1985), pp. 22-25; Lawrence, "Jackson at Home," pp. 793-94; Ward, *Symbol for an Age,* p. 203.

4. *Correspondence of Jackson,* vol. 6, p. 407. A copy of Sully's 1819 portrait, smaller than the original and by an unidentified artist, is in the collection of the Ladies' Hermitage Association. It was a gift in 1958 from Mrs. John V. Mershon of Philadelphia. See records of the Ladies' Hermitage Association and the Catalog of American Portraits.

5. Biddle and Fielding, *Sully,* pp. 186-87. Numbers 875 and 876 in the listing of portraits were designs for the device of Jackson's congressional gold medal and not portrait likenesses.

6. Belel Emily Long to Mrs. Lyon Childress, August 3, 1948, copy in the records of the Ladies' Hermitage Association. A replica portrait [see page 209] was also passed down through the Blair family, which the writer of this letter has confused with the study portrait. This study, an oil on canvas, may have been based on a pencil-on-paper sketch that Sully made at about this time. This drawing is now in the Detroit Institute of Arts [see page 57].

7. As a normal business practice for a publisher, Childs sent complimentary engravings of the Jackson portrait to prominent individuals, namely Francis P. Blair, Martin Van Buren, and Senator Lew Cass. In return, he desired laudatory letters of acknowledgment, which could then be published as newspaper notices. See Washington *Daily Union,* January 9, 1853; Blair to Van Buren, November 25, 1852, Van Buren Papers.

This 1824 study portrait was inherited by Blair's only daughter, Elizabeth, who married Captain Samuel Phillips Lee in 1843. The Blair family retained possession of it until 1942, when it was acquired by Andrew W. Mellon for the National Gallery of Art. Biddle and Fielding in *Sully* do not include this study in their list of paintings, although they mention it. In addition, they have incorrectly identified number 884 as the portrait engraved by Welch.

In 1860 George Caleb Bingham, commissioned by the Missouri legislature, painted portraits of Andrew Jackson and Henry Clay for the state capitol. On January 9, while in Washington, he carefully examined Sully's study of Jackson in the home of Captain Lee, with the intention of making a copy. By mid-September, Bingham had completed, in Kansas City, a large equestrian portrait of Jackson, which was lost in a 1911 fire that destroyed the capitol. See John Francis McDermott, *George Caleb Bingham, River Portraitist* (Norman, Okla., 1959), pp. 127-32.

8. The Norton Gallery likeness was previously owned by Frances Fisher Kane, a descendant of Judge John K. Kane, a prominent Philadelphia jurist and Jacksonian. See records of the Catalog of American Portraits; Bruns, *Louisiana Portraits,* p. 143; *Memorial Exhibition of Portraits by Thomas Sully* (Philadelphia, 1922), p. 29.

9. Sully received eight hundred dollars for this painting, whose provenance traces back to Captain Samuel Phillips Lee (see n. 7). Subsequently the portrait passed through the hands of Jacob Thompson, secretary of the interior in James Buchanan's administration, then to John F. Cyle, and finally to William Wilson Corcoran. In 1869 Corcoran donated the painting to the fledgling Washington art gallery named after him. See Biddle and Fielding, *Sully,* p. 187; *Catalogue of the Tenth Annual Exhibition of the Artists' Fund Society of Philadelphia, and the Pennsylvania Academy of the Fine Arts, 1845* (Philadelphia, 1845), pp. 5-6; *Catalogue of the Corcoran Collection,* vol. 1, p. 48.

10. Spencer M. Clark to Alfred Sealey, December 22, 1866 (letters sent), Records of the Bureau of Engraving and Printing, RG 318, National Archives. For examples of currency bearing Jackson's portrait, see Grover C. Criswell, Jr., *North American Currency* (Citra, Fla., 1969).

11. Clark to Sealey, January 11, 1867, RG 318, National Archives. The Bureau of Engraving and Printing recently acquired an oval portrait by an unknown artist that was copied after the Sealey-Sully likeness. See records of the Catalog of American Portraits.

12. Gene Hessler, *The Comprehensive Catalog of U.S. Paper Money* (Port Clinton, Ohio, 1983), pp. 89, 126, 293. On March 15, 1967, the two-hundredth anniversary of Jackson's birth, the United States Post Office, in a ceremony at the Hermitage, issued a ten-cent stamp based on the Sully portrait in the National Gallery of Art. Arthur W. Dintaman engraved the vignette for this small, vertical stamp, which is lavender in color. See unidentified newspaper

clipping in Sully's portrait file in the Catalog of American Portraits.

13. Craven, *Sculpture in America,* pp. 168–69; "Statue to Jackson," *United States Magazine, and Democratic Review* 17 (July–August 1845): 3–4.

14. The resolutions of the monument committee were printed on subscription circulars issued to authorized agents.

15. *Daily Evening Transcript,* September 15, 1845.

16. Washington *Daily Globe,* January 11 and 20, 1853; Washington *Daily Union,* January 18, 1853; Craven, *Sculpture in America,* p. 168.

17. Craven, *Sculpture in America,* pp. 166–68.

18. Preston's brother William was also a great patron of the arts. It was principally his financial backing that enabled Hiram Powers to establish himself in Florence.

19. *Charleston Courier,* March 8, 1848.

20. Andrew S. Keck, "A Toast to the Union: Clark Mills' Equestrian Statue of Andrew Jackson in Lafayette Square," *Records of the Columbia Historical Society* 48 (1971–1972): 293–97; Craven, *Sculpture in America,* pp. 169–70.

21. *Charleston Mercury,* March 27, 1848; Washington *Daily Globe,* January 20, 1853.

22. Washington *Daily Globe,* January 20, 1853; Rosemary B. Hopkins, "Clark Mills: The First Native American Sculptor" (Master's thesis, University of Maryland, 1966), p. 65.

23. Henry Kirke Brown to Lydia Brown, May 18, 1849, Henry Kirke Brown Papers, Archives of American Art.

24. Washington *Daily Globe,* January 20, 1853.

25. Powers had left a few plaster casts of his 1835 bust of Jackson in the care of an uncle in Washington. When he heard that Mills was sculpting Jackson, he warned his uncle not to let any of them out of his possession. Mills probably had free rein with Pettrich's 1836 likeness, as several marble replicas were extant. The influence of Pettrich's likeness may be seen in the apparent elongation of Jackson's face. One source, however, reported that Mills intentionally incorporated this disproportion for visual effect. See *Home Journal* (New York), August 6, 1853. The issue of March 30, 1850, reported, "Jackson never weighed over one hundred forty pounds in his life. His statue resembles a warrior more than double that weight. It would not be so agreeable to the eye unless thus fashioned."

26. *Literary World* (New York), February 10, 1849.

27. Hopkins, "Clark Mills," pp. 61–64; Washington *Daily Globe,* January 20, 1853.

28. *New York Evening Post,* March 24, 1876; Washington *Daily Globe,* January 20, 1853; Craven, *Sculpture in America,* p. 171.

29. Washington *Daily Globe,* January 11 and 20, 1853.

30. *Ibid.,* January 20, 1853; Hopkins, "Clark Mills," pp. 76–77, 80–81.

31. Craven, *Sculpture in America,* p. 174; Hopkins, "Clark Mills," pp. 70–72; James M. Goode, *The Outdoor Sculpture of Washington, D.C.: A Comprehensive Historical Guide* (Washington, D.C., 1974), p. 378.

32. *Daily Evening Transcript,* June 1 and August 11, 1853; July 7, 1854; *Home Journal,* July 22 and November 25, 1854; W. O. Hart, "Clark Mills," *Records of the Columbia Historical Society* 24 (1922): 202; Heiskell, *Jackson and Early Tennessee,* vol. 3, pp. 573–83.

33. The Nashville monument was dedicated in ceremonies held on May 29, 1880. On this occasion, Mills made his last public appearance. He died three years later in Washington. *Daily Evening Transcript,* February 18, 1875; *Daily Evening Bulletin* (San Francisco), March 2, 1875; Hart, "Clark Mills," pp. 202–3.

34. Mills portrait files in the Catalog of American Portraits.

35. This bronze version is now in a private collection. *Ibid.*

36. Mrs. Raymond Hughes of Baltimore presented this statue to the society. According to

Figure 187. Above.
Charcoal and pencil on paper by Christian Schussele, study, 1858. Pennsylvania Academy of the Fine Arts; gift of Mrs. Francis P. Garvan

Figure 188. Right.
Oil on canvas by Christian Schussele, study, circa 1858. Pennsylvania Academy of the Fine Arts; Collections Fund purchase

family tradition, Clark Mills gave it to Mrs. Hughes's uncle, Charles W. Buckingham, a close friend, who had understood that the sculpture was the original plaster model. See records of the Maryland Historical Society, Baltimore.

37. See Goode, *Outdoor Sculpture,* p. 378; *Chattanooga News-Free Press,* March 17, 1967; *Knoxville News-Sentinel,* March 10, 1967; *Kingsport News* (Tennessee), March 9, 1967.

38. Remini, *Andrew Jackson,* vol. 1, pp. 308-15.

39. Michael David Zellman, comp., *American Art Analog* (New York, 1986), vol. 1, p. 207; John Sartain, *The Reminiscences of a Very Old Man, 1808-1897* (New York, 1899), p. 250.

40. Sometime after the portrait's completion, it went on view in Earle & Son's Gallery on Chestnut Street. To accompany the exhibition, Hedenberg published a small pamphlet explaining the portrait and its historical circumstances. Included was a key identifying thirty-six prominent figures. See *Explanation of the Picture of Andrew Jackson before Judge Hall, at New Orleans, 1815 . . . Painted by C. Schussele, of Philadelphia* (Philadelphia, 1919). A copy is on microfilm in the papers of Christian Schussele, Archives of American Art.

In 1866 *General Andrew Jackson Before Judge Hall* was exhibited at the Pennsylvania Academy of the Fine Arts. From 1868 until his death in 1879, Schussele held an honorary chair of drawing and painting at the academy. Given his close association, it is appropriate that that institution owns his two study sketches, both curiously drawn in the reverse of his grand canvas. A charcoal sketch [Fig. 187] was a gift in 1976 from Mrs. Francis P. Garvan. The academy purchased an oil sketch [Fig. 188] in 1957 from Sotheby Parke-Bernet of New York City. This painting had previously formed part of the Colyer Collection at the Bennington Museum in Vermont. See Pennsylvania Academy of the Fine Arts, *The Last 3 Years—A Selection of Recent Acquisitions* (Philadelphia, 1978), p. 21; Rutledge, *PAFA Exhibition Record,* p. 199; Ruth Levin to James Barber, May 8, 1989, Schussele portrait file, Catalog of American Portraits; Sotheby Parke-Bernet auction catalogue 1761, for May 17, 1957, no. 45.

General Andrew Jackson Before Judge Hall is now owned by the Thomas Gilcrease Institute of American History and Art in Tulsa, Oklahoma. In 1950 Mr. Gilcrease purchased it from the Knoedler Gallery in New York City. Before 1946, the painting had belonged to the Walker Art Center in Minneapolis. When that institution began refocusing its collection on contemporary art, it disposed of many historical works, including Schussele's dramatic courtroom sketch of Andrew Jackson. See Gertrude F. Sierk to Anna Wells Rutledge, February 12, 1945; Debra Christensen to James Barber, May 11, 1989, Schussele portrait file, Catalog of American Portraits.

41. Remini, *Andrew Jackson,* vol. 1, p. 314.

42. In 1844, Jackson's friends in Congress successfully passed a bill, signed by the President, that restored to him his fine, with interest—a total of $2,732.90. See Remini, *Andrew Jackson,* vol. 3, pp. 490-91.

Figure 189.
Rachel Jackson. Oil on canvas by Ralph
E. W. Earl, circa 1825. The Hermitage:
Home of President Andrew Jackson

Figure 190.
Oil on canvas by Ralph E. W. Earl, circa
1825. The Hermitage: Home of President
Andrew Jackson

Chapter 9

Postscript: Portraits of Rachel

I

The depth of Jackson's affection for his wife Rachel Donelson Robards was evident in the value he placed upon her portraits. Anyone visiting the Hermitage in the years after his death was reminded of this strong attachment by Uncle Alfred, one of Jackson's last servants, who enjoyed giving impromptu tours through the mansion. In the general's bedroom, Alfred's finger would weave here and there, capturing his audience's attention in the invisible web his voice and gestures spun of Jackson's long life. Invariably he would point to the portrait of Rachel over the mantel, opposite the bed where Jackson died, and tell how every morning the general would kneel before it and thank God for sparing his life one more night so that he could look upon her face.[1]

~

Others besides Uncle Alfred remembered intimate encounters between Jackson and his deceased beloved through the medium of portraiture. One evening while Jackson, then President, was vacationing at the Rip Raps, Virginia, his private secretary, Nicholas P. Trist, had to disturb him about some small but pressing business just before the President retired to bed. Trist discovered Jackson, dressed in his night clothes, seated in his room at a little table with his wife's prayer book open before him and a large miniature of her propped up against some books. Later Trist learned that this was Jackson's nightly routine. Moreover, it was widely known among his friends that he wore Rachel's miniature next to his heart, suspended by a strong black cord.[2]

The practice was an old one, as indicated by a letter Jackson had written to Rachel many years earlier. On a cold winter's night in early 1813 the general was in Nashville awaiting a shipment of arms before embarking with his Tennessee volunteers for duty in New Orleans. In the letter, dated January 8 (two years to the day before his glorious victory), he penned his love to Rachel before he went to bed.[3] He related that Dinwiddie, the family's old servant and keeper of the stables, had delivered her letter and miniature that evening. "I shall wear it near my boosam [*sic*]," he confided, but then added that this was unnecessary because his memory never failed to conjure up her likeness.

What became of that miniature is not known. In 1842 Jackson admitted that he had no likeness of either his wife or himself from their early years. Perhaps it, like many family treasures, was lost in the 1834 Hermitage fire.

II

The Ladies' Hermitage Association now owns several portraits of Rachel. The earliest appears to be the one once owned by General John Coffee, Jackson's former business partner, cavalry lieutenant, and devout friend who married Rachel's niece, Mary Donelson.[4] Tradition in the Coffee family always held that the portraits of Rachel and Andrew [Figs. 189 and 190] were painted in 1825. Both would have been fifty-eight years old, which the likenesses seem to corroborate.

Rachel's likeness has undergone heavy repainting, perhaps because of damage suffered in the fire that destroyed the Coffee homestead, Hickory Hill, in Florence, Alabama, during the Civil War. The woman who emerges from under a fluted white bonnet is double chinned, stout, and robust. A pearl necklace and earrings soften the image of this gentle matron of the Hermitage, who on one occasion, after lighting her pipe and taking a few puffs, handed it to a guest with the friendly enjoinder, "Honey, wont you take a smoke?"[5]

ᙯ

Allegedly, Rachel was almost attractive in her youth. In maturity she stretched her skin to the fullest, as was said discreetly in New Orleans during her visit in 1815.[6] When accompanied by her tall, lean, angular husband the contrast was great, as noted by a young girl who recalled years later: *Side by side with him stands a coarse-looking, stout, little old woman, whom you might easily mistake for his washerwoman, were it not for the marked attention he pays her, and the love and admiration she manifests for him. Her eyes are bright, and express great kindness of heart; her face is rather broad, her features plain; her complexion so dark as almost to suggest a mingling of races. . . . But, withal, her face is so good-natured and motherly, that you immediately feel at ease with her, however shy you may be of the stately person by her side. Her figure is rather full, but loosely and carelessly dressed, so that when she is seated she seems to settle into herself in a manner that is neither graceful nor elegant. . . . This is Mrs. Jackson.[7]*

ᙯ

Figure 191.
Rachel Jackson. Oil on canvas by Ralph E. W. Earl, circa 1827. The Hermitage: Home of President Andrew Jackson

The portrait that probably comes closest to being a true representation of Rachel is also in the Hermitage collection. It was originally owned by General Richard K. Call and his wife, Mary, who in their early years were great admirers of Jackson.[8] In 1826 they requested that Andrew and Rachel sit to Ralph E. W. Earl for their portraits. The Calls, however, were not satisfied with the general's likeness and requested another.[9] The portrait of Rachel was more successful [Fig. 191].

Although far from being a copy of the Coffee likeness, the Call painting is similar in its overall design. Rachel is seated in a chair and wears a bonnet from which a lace mantilla cascades onto her shoulders. A double collar of lace and a sprinkling of jewelry distinguish this painting from the others, as does the introduction of Rachel's left hand, clutching purse strings, in the bottom center of the canvas. Her face is a little thinner, but a double chin is still prominent.

Records reveal that Earl approved highly of this likeness. In the spring of 1830 Jackson had been President for a little more than a year and a widower since December 1828. Jackson desired a miniature of Rachel painted after one of Earl's portraits. Curiously, he did not specify which one he preferred. Earl, writing from Fairfield, Tennessee, in April, apprised his friend of the arrangements he was making. The only portrait, Earl stated, "which I would wish to send forth to the world as a correct representation of that good and pious woman is in the possession of General Call."[10]

For his own purposes Earl wanted an engraving made from this portrait as well. Therefore, he arranged with Call to ship the painting from his home in

Tallahassee to James Barton Longacre in Philadelphia. In 1826 Earl and Longacre had collaborated successfully in publishing an engraving of Jackson, so Longacre was an obvious candidate to undertake this new endeavor. What followed, however, was a year's delay in shipping the portrait; it finally arrived in Philadelphia in June 1830. By now Longacre was justifiably perplexed and wanted to know if Earl still desired him to proceed with the engraving.[11]

Apparently, plans had changed. President Jackson was suddenly in earnest about obtaining a miniature likeness from the Call portrait now in Longacre's care. That, seemingly, was the first priority; the engraving would have to be postponed still further. Yet in all probability it was never undertaken, because no such engraving of Rachel by Longacre has ever been found.

Instead, Longacre painted his own miniature of Rachel, which he sent to the presidential mansion in May 1831 with instructions to return it if it did not please the President. Jackson was not satisfied. Earl delivered this news to Longacre in a hasty note, enclosing the miniature, which Andrew Jackson, Jr., was entrusted to carry. Earl seconded the President's opinion that the miniature was not a "correct copy from the original painting, which is an exact likeness of the late Mrs. Jackson."[12] The President's son, wrote Earl, would explain the particulars.

This rejection of Longacre's work was a telling pronouncement on his artistic skills, particularly as a painter. He was only partly successful in capturing Andrew Jackson's likeness from life in 1829. The two watercolor portraits believed to be products of that sitting are stilted [see pages 108 and 109].[13] The instrument of Longacre's success was principally the engraver's burin.

Figure 192.
Rachel Jackson. Oil on canvas attributed to Washington Bogart Cooper, after Ralph E. W. Earl, circa 1830. Tennessee State Museum

III

Meanwhile, thoughts of Rachel encroached on the President's executive concerns and carried Jackson in spirit, if not in body, back to the Hermitage, where a portrait of his beloved hung with one of his own. Just that October of 1830, Jackson had returned from a visit to his estate. Sometime during his respite, he had agreed to let a portraitist from Nashville make copy likenesses of Rachel and himself. It was his understanding that this artist, now unidentified, would cart his brushes and paints to the Hermitage. Jackson, however, was aghast when he learned that the artist, claiming he could not work at the Hermitage, arranged to copy the portraits in Nashville.[14] The portraits were returned safely; nevertheless, Jackson was furious. No one had consulted him about this change of plans. Anything having to do with the memory of Rachel was sacred ground and dangerous to trespassers.

The offending artist could have been Washington Bogart Cooper. A copy portrait of Rachel attributed to him is in the collection of the Tennessee State Museum [Fig. 192]. Cooper was born in 1802 near Jonesboro, Tennessee. Together with his younger brother William, Cooper taught himself the rudiments of drawing, sometimes sketching people and animals on barn doors and stables. Allegedly he received a little formal instruction in Murfreesboro, and later he studied briefly with Thomas Sully and Henry Inman in Philadelphia. In any event, Cooper was in Nashville about 1830, plying his trade as a portraitist.[15] His portrait of Rachel, found years ago in the tower of the State House among a collection of Cooper's unfinished works, evokes folk traits in both sitter and artist.[16] Although this homely likeness in no way resembles the portraits formerly owned by the Coffee and Call families, in some respects it fits the description of still another painting, now lost.

"There is a portrait of Mrs. Jackson," wrote biographer James Parton, "in white satin, topaz jewelry, low neck and short sleeves; fat, forty, but not fair."[17] Parton researched his *Life of Andrew Jackson,* published in 1861, more than a decade after his subject's death. He personally interviewed dozens of Jackson's contemporaries and inspected many of the general's old haunts. Naturally, the Hermitage was one of them, where Parton noted Rachel's picture still hanging in the parlor. By his own account, the topaz jewelry he referred to was a gift from the ladies of the city of New Orleans.[18] In the copy portrait attributed to Cooper, this yellow jewelry contrasts vividly against a black dress, a drastic change of color from the white one described by Parton. Rachel's death no doubt influenced the copyist to make this alteration.

A portrait similar to Cooper's copy appears as an illustration in the third and last volume of Samuel G. Heiskell's *Andrew Jackson and Early Tennessee History.* The execution of this work, no longer extant, exceeds all others in crudity. Curiously, Rachel is depicted wearing a light-colored dress. Whether it was indeed white satin, as described by Parton, cannot be determined from an aged black-and-white illustration.[19]

IV

On May 15, 1889, the Ladies' Hermitage Association was officially organized to preserve and restore the home of Andrew Jackson. After the death of Jackson's daughter-in-law, Sarah Yorke, in 1887, the general's grandson, Colonel Andrew Jackson III, and his wife, Amy Rich, lived on the property as custodians. In 1893 they moved to Cincinnati, taking with them what remained of the family possessions. Suddenly bereft of furniture and furnishings, the association eventually arranged to purchase the family furniture, one room at a time. In 1897 it commenced with restoration of Jackson's bedroom. For one thousand dollars, Colonel Jackson sold miscellaneous furniture, Jackson's last life portrait by Healy, and a portrait of Rachel. With the help of a granddaughter, Rachel Jackson Lawrence, and Uncle Alfred, both of whom remembered how the house looked in 1845, the room was arranged as it had been at the time of Jackson's death.[20] Thus, Rachel's likeness was returned to a familiar patch of wallpaper above the mantelpiece, where it hangs today.

This was the picture the ex-President gazed upon first thing every morning. Understandably, it was the portrait he most treasured [Fig. 193]. The likeness, an idealized copy by Earl of the Call painting, was executed from fond memories instead of stark realities. Rachel's dark eyes shine with a new luminance; no longer do they reflect the concerns of family and household that were so much a part of her existence.[21] She now holds a red rose, a subtle reminder of life's beauty and fragility. To the old man's dying day, Rachel was the personification of both.

Because accurate records of Earl's work do not survive, the circumstances of his painting this portrait can only be surmised. He may have done it at his studio in the presidential mansion in April 1831. It was at this time, in the midst of the cabinet resignations, that Francis P. Blair recorded a poignant incident: *Let me tell you a fact to make you sensible of the deep-rooted, affectionate attachment of which the rough bosom of a war-worn veteran is susceptible. Earl has a few days ago received from the Hermitage Mrs. Jackson's portrait. He did not intend that the President should see it, but he stepped in by accident when Earl was copying from it. He stood and gazed at it for a few moments with some fortitude, until as the association rose in his mind he began to weep, and his sobs became so deep that Earl carried the picture away to relieve him.*[22]

Figure 193.
Rachel Jackson. Oil on canvas by Ralph E. W. Earl, circa 1831. The Hermitage: Home of President Andrew Jackson

Figure 194.
Rachel Jackson. Oil on canvas by Howard Chandler Christy, after Ralph E. W. Earl, 1941. The White House Collection; gift of the State of Tennessee

Figure 195.
Rachel Jackson. Watercolor on ivory by Louisa Catherine Strobel, after Ralph E. W. Earl, circa 1831. The Hermitage: Home of President Andrew Jackson

Figure 196.
Rachel Jackson. Engraving by John Chester Buttre, after Louisa Catherine Strobel, after Ralph E. W. Earl, not dated. National Portrait Gallery, Smithsonian Institution

Blair may have been in error about Earl receiving the portrait of Rachel from the Hermitage. It was at this time that James B. Longacre sent the miniature that so dissatisfied Jackson. With it, he probably returned to Earl the Call portrait from which he had worked. It bears restating that this was the only image Earl considered worthy of replication.

The portrait of Rachel that was hung almost permanently over the mantelpiece in Jackson's bedroom was itself the model for two copy versions. A fairly faithful one, by an unidentified artist, possibly W. B. Cooper, is in the Tennessee State Museum.[23] A more contemporary and spirited version, painted by Howard Chandler Christy, was presented by the state of Tennessee to the White House in 1941 [Fig. 194].[24] This later work, however, resembles more the glamorous MGM movie star Norma Shearer than it does Rachel Jackson.

V

Early on Monday morning, June 2, 1845, the last week of Jackson's life, he surrendered a personal memento that would become a treasured heirloom. The occasion was the customary visit of his twelve-year-old granddaughter, "Little Rachel," who would come into his bedroom every day to kiss and bid him goodbye before going off to school in Nashville. Calling her by a favorite name, Jackson said, "Wait a moment, my baby," detaining her just long enough to slip from a vest pocket his wife's miniature. Together with the guard he then removed it from around his neck and presented it to her. "Wear it," he enjoined, "for Grandpa's sake."[25]

Undoubtedly this was the large-scale miniature that Nicholas Trist saw Jackson admiring late one night at the Rip Raps. The President's urgent request for such a likeness, about which he consulted Earl in 1830 and then refused from Longacre the next year, may have been finally fulfilled by an amateur artist, Louisa Catherine Strobel. Born in England in 1803 of American parents, Strobel spent much of her youth in Bordeaux, France, where her father was the American consul.[26] There she developed her interest in miniature painting. Having visited the United States as a child, she returned there to live in 1830. Her introduction to Andrew Jackson was most likely the result of her father's diplomatic connection to the administration.

Strobel's watercolor-on-ivory miniature, an altered version of the Call likeness, is signed "L. C. Strobel" along the right edge and may date as early as 1830 [Fig. 195]. It was engraved probably in the late 1840s or 1850s by John Chester Buttre of New York [Fig. 196]. Notwithstanding the subtle yet legible signature on the front, Strobel's work suffered a long misattribution to Anna Claypoole Peale.[27] In January 1819 Anna painted a miniature from life of Andrew Jackson in Washington. Rachel, however, did not accompany him on that trip and probably never met Miss Peale on any other occasion.

At the age of twenty, Jackson's granddaughter Rachel married Dr. John Marshall Lawrence. As an adult she apparently lived up to her grandfather's request. In a portrait of her, painted when she was in her sixties by Edith Flisher, she is depicted wearing the miniature of her namesake.[28]

Notes

1. Remini, *Andrew Jackson,* vol. 2, p. 152; Mary C. Dorris, *Preservation of the Hermitage, 1889-1915: Annals, History, and Stories* (Nashville, Tenn., circa 1915), p. 140.

2. Parton, *Jackson,* vol. 3, pp. 601-2; Dusenbery, *Monument to the Memory,* p. 74.

3. Jackson, *Papers of Jackson,* vol. 2, p. 353.

4. In 1901 Coffee's son, Alexander Donelson Coffee, presented the portrait to the Hermitage along with likenesses of Andrew Jackson, General and Mrs. John Coffee, and Colonel and Mrs. John Donelson, who were the parents of Mrs. Coffee. See Mary Coffee Campbell to Mary C. Dorris, April 19, 1901, Coffee portrait file, Ladies' Hermitage Association. Also in this file is a typescript of a wire service clipping from Florence, Alabama, April 23, 1901, and printed in an unknown newspaper, reporting this gift.

5. This necklace and the earrings may be the jewelry that Jackson presented to his new daughter-in-law, Sarah Yorke Jackson, before she went to live at the Hermitage in April 1832. See Remini, *Andrew Jackson,* vol. 2, p. 354. For the quotation from Rachel, see Parton, *Jackson,* vol. 3, p. 162. For another reference to Rachel's predilection for a pipe, this one from Andrew Jackson himself, see *Correspondence of Jackson,* vol. 3, p. 271.

6. James, *Life of Jackson,* p. 257. According to one biographer, the anti-Jackson party published a caricature at the time, "in which the short and stout Mrs. Jackson was represented standing upon a table, while Mrs. [Edward] Livingston was employed in lacing her stays, struggling to make a waist where a waist had been, but was not." See Parton, *Jackson,* vol. 2, p. 323.

7. Parton, *Jackson,* vol. 3, pp. 160-61.

8. This friendship disintegrated in 1836 when General Call, the newly appointed governor of the Florida Territory, pestered President Jackson for a military command to quell the Seminole uprising and then bungled the campaign, inciting Jackson's ire. See Remini, *Andrew Jackson,* vol. 3, pp. 309-10.

Rachel's portrait was donated in 1895 by Mrs. Ellen Call Long, the Calls' daughter.

9. *Correspondence of Jackson,* vol. 6, p. 483; Robert Butler to Jackson, April 23, 1828, Jackson Papers, Library of Congress; Jackson to Call, May 12, 1828, Jackson Papers, Library of Congress.

10. Ralph E. W. Earl to Jackson, April 3, 1830, Jackson Papers, Library of Congress. This letter appears in *Correspondence of Jackson,* vol. 4, pp. 132-33, but is dated April 5.

11. James B. Longacre to Earl, June 23, 1830, Earl Papers.

12. Earl to Longacre, May 15, 1831, Longacre Papers.

13. These are in the collection of the National Portrait Gallery.

14. *Correspondence of Jackson,* vol. 4, pp. 218-19.

15. Kelly, "Portrait Painting in Tennessee," p. 212.

16. Based on accession records in the Tennessee State Museum, this portrait was a gift of Mrs. Paralee Haskell, State Librarian, to the State Library.

17. Parton, *Jackson,* vol. 2, p. 650.

18. *Ibid.,* pp. 323-24.

19. A visitor to the Hermitage, probably in the 1870s, noticed a portrait of Rachel in a white satin embroidered dress hanging above the mantelpiece in Jackson's bedroom. See clipping from unidentified newspaper in the Andrew Jackson Donelson Papers.

20. Horn, *Hermitage,* pp. 46, 53-56.

21. One visitor to the Hermitage recorded the following account after viewing an unidentified portrait of Rachel: "I had just looked upon her likeness, fresh as yesterday—on features handsome in youth and marked in age by amiability and benevolence, telling not of talents, nor accomplishments, but of the every day duties and common place realities of life." See *Hartford Times,* September 23, 1833.

22. Blair to Mrs. Benjamin Gratz, August 20, 1831, in Thomas H. Clay, "Two Years with Old Hickory," *Atlantic Monthly* 60 (August 1887): 193.

23. Accession records, Tennessee State Museum.

24. *New York Times,* October 27, 1941.

25. Hart, "Life Portraits," p. 804.

26. John M. Belohlavek, *"Let the Eagle Soar!" The Foreign Policy of Andrew Jackson* (Lincoln, Nebr., 1985), p. 35.

27. This discovery of the signature was made by Richard K. Doud, keeper of the Catalog of American Portraits, during a survey of the Hermitage collection in 1975. See Strobel portrait file in Catalog of American Portraits. Still another miniature of Rachel, now unlocated, has been misattributed to Anna Peale. In 1941, Fanny O. Walton offered this piece, given to her by her cousin, John Marshall Lawrence (son of Rachel Jackson Lawrence), to the Ladies' Hermitage Association for two hundred dollars. At the time, the association believed that it already owned a miniature by Peale and refused it. See letter of Walton to the Ladies' Hermitage Association, November 28, 1941, Ladies' Hermitage Association.

28. This portrait remained in her family's possession until 1925 when her granddaughter, Rachel Jackson Smith, sold it to the Ladies' Hermitage Association. See records of the Ladies' Hermitage Association; Catalog of American Portraits.

Appendix

The Jackson portraits illustrated here are representative of Ralph E. W. Earl's extensive work during the eight years he lived in the presidential mansion. They have been arranged in approximate chronological order and reveal how Jackson's image evolved through the artist's eye. Because of the great demand for his paintings, Earl used a formula approach in producing them in haste. His ability to copy accurately is evident not only in the facial reproductions, but also in certain background props. For instance, the chair depicted in Figure 197 is recognizable as one of a set made by the noted French cabinet-maker Pierre Antoine Bellangé, and purchased by President James Monroe in 1817. The likeness of Jackson in Figure 198 is identical to an original Earl portrait once owned by Vice President Martin Van Buren. About 1833, John W. Casilear, a student of Asher B. Durand, engraved Van Buren's *Jackson* for George P. Morris's *New York Mirror*.[1] The engraving was titled *The Presidents of the United States* [Fig. 199]. Designer Robert W. Weir may have reversed Jackson's image so that it would face that of John Quincy Adams.

Figure 197. Top.
Oil on canvas by Ralph E. W. Earl, circa 1830–1832. The Daughters of the American Revolution Museum; gift of Mrs. Cyrus Griffith Martin

Figure 198. Right.
Oil on panel by Ralph E. W. Earl, circa 1830–1832. North Carolina Museum of Art, purchased with funds from the state of North Carolina

Figure 199. Far right.
Engraving by John W. Casilear, 1834. The Historical Society of Pennsylvania

1. For replicas of the unidentified *Jackson* once owned by Van Buren, in addition to other portraits of Jackson by Earl, see Catalog of American Portraits. Concerning the engraving of Van Buren's *Jackson,* see Thomas W. Harman to Asher B. Durand, August 5, 1833; George P. Morris to Durand, August 8, 1833, Durand Papers. I am grateful to Professor Noble E. Cunningham, Jr., of the University of Missouri for bringing these letters to my attention.

Figure 200.
Oil on canvas by Ralph E. W. Earl, circa 1833. Private collection

Figure 201.
Oil on canvas attributed to Ralph E. W. Earl, circa 1833. The Hermitage: Home of President Andrew Jackson

Figure 202.
Oil on canvas by Ralph E. W. Earl, not dated. Washington County Museum of Fine Arts, Maryland

Figure 203.
Oil on canvas by Ralph E. W. Earl, circa 1834 or after. The Museum of Fine Arts, Houston, the Bayou Bend Collection; gift of Miss Ima Hogg

Figure 204.
Oil on canvas by Ralph E. W. Earl, circa 1834 or after. Pennsylvania Academy of the Fine Arts; John Frederick Lewis Memorial Collection

Figure 205.
Oil on canvas by Ralph E. W. Earl, circa 1834 or after. Friends of Linden Place

Figure 206.
Oil on canvas by Ralph E. W. Earl, circa 1834 or after. The Hermitage: Home of President Andrew Jackson

Figure 207.
Oil on canvas by Ralph E. W. Earl, circa 1834 or after. Tennessee Historical Society Collection, Tennessee State Museum

Figure 208.
Oil on canvas by Ralph E. W. Earl, circa 1834 or after. The White House Collection; gift of the White House Historical Association, 1977

Figure 209.
Oil on canvas by Ralph E. W. Earl, circa 1834 or after. Mabel Brady Garvan Collection, Yale University Art Gallery

Selected Bibliography

Manuscript Collections

Brown, Henry Kirke. Papers. Archives of American Art, Smithsonian Institution, Washington, D.C.

Dodge, John Wood. Papers. Archives of American Art, Smithsonian Institution, Washington, D.C.

Donelson, Andrew Jackson. Papers. Library of Congress, Washington, D.C.

Earl, Ralph E. W. Letters. Tennessee State Library and Archives, Nashville.

———. Papers. American Antiquarian Society, Worcester, Massachusetts.

Frazee, John. Papers. Archives of American Art, Smithsonian Institution, Washington, D.C.

Garlick, Theodatus. Autobiography (typescript). The Western Reserve Historical Society, Cleveland, Ohio.

Hart, Joel Tanner. Papers. Durret Collections. University of Chicago, Illinois.

Healy, George P. A. Papers. Archives of American Art, Smithsonian Institution, Washington, D.C.

Jackson, Andrew. Papers. Library of Congress, Washington, D.C.

———. Papers. Tennessee Historical Society, Nashville.

———. Papers. Tennessee State Library and Archives, Nashville.

Kellogg, Miner Kilbourne. Letters. Cincinnati Historical Society, Ohio.

———. Letters. Moses Dawson Collection. Xavier University, Cincinnati, Ohio.

———. Papers. Archives of American Art, Smithsonian Institution, Washington, D.C.

———. Reminiscences. New Harmony Collection. Indiana Historical Society, Indianapolis.

Livingston, Edward. Papers. Princeton University Library, Princeton, New Jersey.

Longacre, James Barton. Papers. Archives of American Art, Smithsonian Institution, Washington, D.C.

Peale-Sellers Papers. American Philosophical Society, Philadelphia, Pennsylvania.

Powers, Hiram. Papers. Archives of American Art, Smithsonian Institution, Washington, D.C.

Purviance, John H. Papers. William R. Perkins Library, Duke University, Durham, North Carolina.

Records of the Bureau of Engraving and Printing. Record Group 318. National Archives, Washington, D.C.

Records of the Bureau of Indian Affairs. Record Group 75. National Archives, Washington, D.C.

Records of the Department of State. Territorial Papers: Mississippi. Record Group 59. National Archives, Washington, D.C.

Records of the General Accounting Office. Record Group 217. National Archives, Washington, D.C.

Sully, Thomas. Papers. Archives of American Art, Smithsonian Institution, Washington, D.C.

Van Buren, Martin. Papers. Library of Congress, Washington, D.C.

Vanderlyn, John. Papers. Archives of American Art, Smithsonian Institution, Washington, D.C.

———. Papers. Roswell Randall Hoes Collection, Senate House Museum, Kingston, New York.

Ward, Aaron. Papers. Boston Public Library, Massachusetts.

Unpublished Sources

Averill, Louise Hunt. "John Vanderlyn, American Painter (1775–1852)." Ph.D. diss., Yale University, 1949.

Davison, Nancy Reynolds. "E. W. Clay: American Political Caricaturist of the Jacksonian Era." Ph.D. diss., University of Michigan, 1980.

Hopkins, Rosemary B. "Clark Mills: The First Native American Sculptor." Master's thesis, University of Maryland, 1966.

Reynolds, Donald Martin. "Hiram Powers and His Ideal Sculpture." Ph.D. diss., Columbia University, 1975.

Symonds, Susan Clover. "Portraits of Andrew Jackson: 1815–1845." Master's thesis, University of Delaware, 1968.

Wunder, Richard P. "Hiram Powers, Vermont Sculptor, 1805–1873." Manuscript in curatorial files, National Museum of American Art, Smithsonian Institution, 1978.

Newspapers and Journals

Baltimore *American and Commercial Daily Advertiser*
Baltimore *Niles' Weekly Register*
Boston *Daily Evening Transcript*
Boston Statesman
Charleston Courier
Charleston Mercury
Charles Town, [West] Virginia, *Farmers' Repository*
Cincinnati Advertiser
Cincinnati Daily Gazette
Cincinnati *Liberty Hall and Cincinnati Gazette*
Hartford *Connecticut Courant*
Nashville *National Banner and Nashville Whig*
Nashville *Politician*
Nashville Republican
Nashville Union
Nashville Whig
Nashville Whig and Tennessee Advertiser
Natchez *Mississippi Free Trader and Natchez Weekly Gazette*
New Orleans Bee
New-Orleans Commercial Bulletin
New Orleans *Daily Delta*
New Orleans *Daily Picayune*
New Orleans *Le Courrier de la Louisiane*
New Orleans *Louisiana Courier*
New Orleans *Louisiana Gazette*
New York Evening Post
New York *Home Journal*
New York *National Advocate*
New York *Spirit of the Times*
Philadelphia *Democratic Press*
United States Magazine, and Democratic Review

Washington *Daily Globe*
Washington *Daily Union*
Washington *Globe*
Washington *National Intelligencer*
Washington *United States Telegraph*

Books and Articles

Ackerman, Donald. "Dating Jackson Historical China." *APIC Keynoter* 87 (Spring 1987): 27–29.

Adams, John Quincy. *Memoirs of John Quincy Adams, Comprising Portions of His Diary from 1795 to 1848*. Edited by Charles Francis Adams. 12 vols. Philadelphia, 1874–1877.

———. *The Diary of John Quincy Adams, 1794–1845*. Edited by Allan Nevins. New York, 1951.

An Album of American Battle Art, 1755–1918. Washington, D.C., 1947.

Alexander, Constance Grosvenor, comp. *Francesca Alexander: Memories*. Cambridge, Mass., 1927.

Arthur, Stanley Clisby. *Audubon: An Intimate Life of the American Woodsman*. New Orleans, La., 1937.

Ashton, John. *English Caricature and Satire on Napoleon I*. New York, 1968.

Audubon, John James. *Journal of John James Audubon, Made During His Trip to New Orleans in 1820–1821*. Edited by Howard Corning. Cambridge, Mass., 1929.

Barber, James, and Frederick Voss. *The Godlike Black Dan: A Selection of Portraits from Life in Commemoration of the Two Hundredth Anniversary of the Birth of Daniel Webster*. Washington, D.C., 1982.

Bassett, John Spencer. *The Life of Andrew Jackson*. Hamden, Conn., 1967.

Bellows, Henry W. "Seven Sittings with Powers, the Sculptor." *Appleton's Journal of Literature, Science, and Art* 1 and 2 (1869).

Belohlavek, John M. *"Let the Eagle Soar!": The Foreign Policy of Andrew Jackson*. Lincoln, Nebr., 1985.

Benton, Thomas Hart. *Thirty Years View; or, A History of the Working of the American Government for Thirty Years, from 1820 to 1850*. 2 vols. New York, 1856.

Biddle, Edward, and Mantle Fielding. *The Life and Works of Thomas Sully (1783–1872)*. Philadelphia, 1921.

Binns, John. *Recollections of the Life of John Binns: Twenty-nine Years in Europe and Fifty-three Years in the United States*. Philadelphia, 1854.

Black Hawk. *Black Hawk, an Autobiography*. Edited by Donald Jackson. Urbana, Ill., 1964.

Blaisdell, Thomas C., Jr., *et al. The American Presidency in Political Cartoons, 1776–1976*. Berkeley, Calif., 1976.

Bolton, Theodore. *Early American Portrait Painters in Miniature*. New York, 1921.

Boyle, Richard J. "Miner Kilbourne Kellogg." *Cincinnati Art Museum Bulletin* 8 (February 1966): 17–23.

Brady, Cyrus Townsend. *The True Andrew Jackson*. Philadelphia, 1906.

Bridaham, Lester Burbank. "Pierre Joseph Landry, Louisiana Woodcarver." *Antiques* 72 (August 1957): 157–59.

Brown, William Henry. *Portrait Gallery of Distinguished American Citizens, with Biographical Sketches, and Fac-Similes of Original Letters*. Hartford, Conn., 1845.

Bruns, Mrs. Thomas Nelson Carter, comp. *Louisiana Portraits*. New Orleans, La., 1975.

Bumgardner, Georgia Brady. "Political Portraiture: Two Prints of Andrew Jackson." *American Art Journal* 18 (1986): 84–95.

Bush, Alfred L. *The Life Portraits of Thomas Jefferson*. Charlottesville, Va., 1962.

Butler, Frances Anne. *Journal*. 2 vols. London, 1835.

Butler, William Allen. *A Retrospect of Forty Years, 1825–1865*. New York, 1911.

Calhoun, John C. *The Papers of John C. Calhoun*. Edited by W. Edwin Hemphill *et al*. 15 vols. Columbia, S.C., 1959–1983.

Callow, James T. *Kindred Spirits, Knickerbocker Writers and American Artists, 1807–1855*. Chapel Hill, N.C., 1967.

Canfield, Frederick A. "The Figure Head of Jackson." *Proceedings of the New Jersey Historical Society* 7 (July 1922): 221–23.

Carrick, Alice Van Leer. "Silhouettes, the Cut and Gilded Type." *Antiques* 8 (December 1925): 341–44.

Catalogue of Robert Street's Exhibition, of Upwards of 200 Oil Paintings. . . . Philadelphia, 1840.

A Catalogue of the Collection of American Paintings in the Corcoran Gallery of Art. Washington, D.C., 1966.

Catalogue of the Collection of Paintings Belonging to the Union League of Philadelphia. Philadelphia, 1940.

Clay, Thomas H. "Two Years with Old Hickory." *Atlantic Monthly* 60 (August 1887): 187–99.

Cline, Isaac Monroe. *Art and Artists in New Orleans During the Last Century*. New Orleans, La., 1922.

Compilation of Works of Art and Other Objects in the United States Capitol. Washington, D.C., 1965.

Cook, William C. "The Early Iconography of the Battle of New Orleans, 1815–1819." *Tennessee Historical Quarterly* 48 (Winter 1989): 218–37.

"Corcoran Investigates What Washington Collects." *Art Digest* 26 (February 1952): 9.

Cosentino, Andrew F. *The Paintings of Charles Bird King (1785–1862)*. Washington, D.C., 1977.

Craven, Wayne. *Sculpture in America*. Newark, Del., 1968.

———. "Asher B. Durand's Career as an Engraver." *American Art Journal* 3 (Spring 1971): 39–57.

Criswell, Grover C., Jr. *North American Currency*. Citra, Fla., 1969.

Curtis, James C. *Andrew Jackson and the Search for Vindication*. Boston, 1976.

Davison, Nancy R. "Andrew Jackson in Cartoon and Caricature." *American Printmaking Before 1876: Fact, Fiction, and Fantasy*. Washington, D.C., 1975.

Delaplaine, Joseph. *Delaplaine's Repository of the Lives and Portraits of Distinguished American Characters*. Philadelphia, 1815.

De Mare, Marie. *G. P. A. Healy, American Artist: An Intimate Chronicle of the Nineteenth Century*. New York, 1954.

Dickson, Harold E. *John Wesley Jarvis, American Painter, 1780–1840*. New York, 1949.

Dorris, Mary C. *Preservation of the Hermitage, 1889–1915: Annals, History, and Stories*. Nashville, Tenn., circa 1915.

Drepperd, Carl W. "Three Battles of New Orleans." *Antiques* 14 (August 1928): 129–31.

———. "Selling Jackson's Great Victory." *Antiques* 38 (November 1940): 220–21.

Dunlap, William. *A History of the Rise and Progress of the Arts of Design in the United States*. 3 vols. New York, 1834.

Durand, John. *The Life and Times of A. B. Durand*. New York, 1894.

Dusenbery, Benjamin M., comp. *Monument to the Memory of General Andrew Jackson: Containing Twenty-Five Eulogies and Sermons Delivered on Occasion of His Death*. Philadelphia, 1846.

Dwight, Edward H. "Aaron Houghton Corwine: Cincinnati Artist." *Antiques* 67 (June 1955): 502–4.

Ellis, David M., *et al. A History of New York State.* Ithaca, N.Y., 1957.

Encyclopedia of New Orleans Artists, 1718–1918. New Orleans, La., 1987.

Evans, Robert J. *A Catalog of the Paintings by G. P. A. Healy in the Illinois State Museum Collection.* Springfield, Ill., 1974.

Explanation of the Picture of Andrew Jackson before Judge Hall, at New Orleans, 1815 . . . Painted by C. Schussele, of Philadelphia. Philadelphia, 1919.

Fabian, Monroe H. *Mr. Sully, Portrait Painter: The Works of Thomas Sully (1783–1872).* Washington, D.C., 1983.

Fischer, Roger A., and Edmund B. Sullivan. *American Political Ribbons and Ribbon Badges, 1825–1981.* Lincoln, Mass., 1985.

Floyd, William Barrow. *Jouett—Bush—Frazer: Early Kentucky Artists.* Lexington, Ky., 1968.

French, Henry W. *Art and Artists in Connecticut.* Boston, 1879.

Goff, Reda C. "A Physical Profile of Andrew Jackson." *Tennessee Historical Quarterly* 28 (Fall 1969): 297–309.

The Golden Age: Cincinnati Painters of the Nineteenth Century Represented in the Cincinnati Art Museum. Cincinnati, Ohio, 1979.

Goode, James M. *The Outdoor Sculpture of Washington, D.C.: A Comprehensive Historical Guide.* Washington, D.C., 1974.

Green, Fletcher M. "On Tour with President Andrew Jackson." *New England Quarterly* 36 (June 1963): 209–28.

Groce, George C., Jr. "The First Catalogue of the Work of Joseph Wood." *Art Quarterly* 3 (supplement) (1940): 393–400.

Groce, George C., Jr., and David H. Wallace. *The New-York Historical Society's Dictionary of Artists in America, 1564–1860.* New Haven, Conn., 1975.

Groce, George C., Jr., and J. T. Chase Willet. "Joseph Wood: A Brief Account of His Life and the First Catalogue of His Work." *Art Quarterly* 3 (Spring 1940): 149–61.

Hamilton, Thomas. *Men and Manners in America.* Edinburgh, 1843.

Harris, Charles E. "Figureheads of the 'Constitution.'" *Antiques* 30 (July 1936): 10–13.

Hart, Charles Henry. "Life Portraits of Andrew Jackson." *McClure's Magazine* 9 (July 1897): 795–804.

Hart, W. O. "Clark Mills." *Records of the Columbia Historical Society* 24 (1922): 200–203.

Healy, George P. A. *Reminiscences of a Portrait Painter.* Chicago, 1894.

Heiskell, Samuel G. *Andrew Jackson and Early Tennessee History.* 3 vols. Nashville, Tenn., 1920–1921.

The Hermitage: A History and Guide. Hermitage, Tenn., 1965.

Hess, Stephen, and Milton Kaplan. *The Ungentlemanly Art: A History of American Political Cartoons.* New York, 1975.

Hessler, Gene. *The Comprehensive Catalog of U. S. Paper Money.* Port Clinton, Ohio, 1983.

Hone, Philip. *The Diary of Philip Hone, 1828–1851.* Edited by Allan Nevins. 2 vols. New York, 1927.

Horn, Stanley F. *The Hermitage, Home of Old Hickory.* Richmond, Va., 1938.

Hunt, Charles Havens. *The Life of Edward Livingston.* New York, 1864.

Hunt, Louise Livingston. *Memoir of Mrs. Edward Livingston with Letters Hitherto Unpublished.* New York, 1886.

Hunter, Wilbur Harvey. *The Story of America's Oldest Museum Building.* Baltimore, Md., 1964.

Jackson, Andrew. *Correspondence of Andrew Jackson.* Edited by John Spencer Bassett. 7 vols. Washington, D.C., 1926–1935.

———. *The Papers of Andrew Jackson.* Edited by Harold D. Moser *et al.* 2 vols. to date. Knoxville, Tenn., 1980–.

Jackson, Carlton. "Another Time, Another Place—The Attempted Assassination of President Andrew Jackson." *Tennessee Historical Quarterly* 26 (Summer 1967): 184–90.

James, Marquis. *The Raven: A Biography of Sam Houston.* New York, 1929.

———. *The Life of Andrew Jackson, Complete in One Volume.* Indianapolis, Ind., 1938.

Jordan, George E. "New Orleans Masterpieces: The Jackson Portraits." *New Orleans Art Review* 2 (January–February 1983): 13–14.

Julian, R. W. *Medals of the United States Mint: The First Century, 1792–1892.* Edited by N. Neil Harris. El Cajon, Calif., circa 1977.

Keck, Andrew S. "A Toast to the Union: Clark Mills' Equestrian Statue of Andrew Jackson in Lafayette Square." *Records of the Columbia Historical Society* 48 (1971–1972): 289–313.

Kellogg, Miner Kilbourne. *Kellogg's Texas Journal, 1872.* Edited by Llerena Friend. Austin, Tex., 1967.

Kelly, James C. "Portrait Painting in Tennessee." *Tennessee Historical Quarterly* 46 (Winter 1987): 193–276.

Kip, William Ingraham. "Recollections of John Vanderlyn, the Artist." *Atlantic Monthly* 19 (February 1867): 228–35.

Kloss, William. *Treasures from the National Museum of American Art.* Washington, D.C., 1985.

Latour, Arsène Lacarrière. *Historical Memoir of the War in West Florida and Louisiana in 1814–15, with an Atlas.* Facsimile of 1816 edition with an introduction by Jane Lucas de Grummond. Gainesville, Fla., 1964.

Lawrence, Rachel Jackson. "Andrew Jackson at Home." *McClure's Magazine* 9 (September 1897): 792–94.

Lester, C. Edwards. *The Artist, the Merchant, and the Statesman, of the Age of the Medici, and of Our Own Times.* 2 vols. New York, 1845.

"Letters from Andrew Jackson to R. K. Call." *Virginia Magazine of History and Biography* 29 (April 1921): 191–92.

The Life of John James Audubon, the Naturalist. New York, 1901.

Loubat, Joseph F. *The Medallic History of the United States of America, 1776–1876.* New Milford, Conn., 1976.

MacBeth, Jerome R. "Portraits by Ralph E. W. Earl," *Antiques* 100 (September 1971): 390–93.

McCormack, Helen G. "The Hubard Gallery Duplicate Book." *Antiques* 45 (February 1944): 68–69.

McDermott, John Francis. *George Caleb Bingham, River Portraitist.* Norman, Okla., 1959.

Marceau, Henri. *William Rush, 1756–1833: The First Native American Sculptor.* Philadelphia, 1937.

Mearns, David C. *The Story Up to Now: The Library of Congress, 1800–1946.* Washington, D.C., 1947.

Memorial Exhibition of Portraits by Thomas Sully. Philadelphia, 1922.

Meschutt, David. "The Peale Portraits of Andrew Jackson." *Tennessee Historical Quarterly* 46 (Spring 1987): 3–9.

Minutes of the Common Council of the City of New York, 1784–1831. 19 vols. New York, 1917.

Mondello, Salvatore. "John Vanderlyn." *The New-York Historical Society Quarterly* 52 (April 1968): 161–83.

Morrissey, Eleanor Fleming, comp. *Portraits in Tennessee Painted Before 1866.* N.p., 1964.

Murrell, William. *A History of American Graphic Humor.* 2 vols. New York, 1933–1938.

Naeve, Milo M. "William Rush's Terracotta and Plaster Busts of General Andrew Jackson." *American Art Journal* 21 (1989): 18–39.

National Academy of Design Exhibition Record, 1826–1860. 2 vols. New York, 1943.

National Society of the Colonial Dames in the State of Alabama, *Alabama Portraits Prior to 1870.* Mobile, Ala., 1969.

Nevins, Allan, and Frank Weitenkampf. *A Century of Political Cartoons: Caricature in the United States from 1800 to 1900.* New York, 1975.

Newhall, Beaumont, ed. *Photography: Essays & Images.* New York, 1980.

The Official Catalogue of the Tennessee Centennial and International Exposition, Nashville, Tennessee, U.S.A., May 1st to October 31st, 1897. Nashville, Tenn., 1897.

Ogden, H. A., and Henry Loomis Nelson. *Uniforms of the United States Army.* New York, 1959.

Oliver, Andrew. *Portraits of John Quincy Adams and His Wife.* Cambridge, Mass., 1970.

Parton, James. *Life of Andrew Jackson.* 3 vols. New York, 1861.

———. *Caricature and Other Comic Art, in All Times and Many Lands.* New York, 1877.

Pennington, Estill Curtis. *William Edward West, 1788–1857: Kentucky Painter.* Washington, D.C., 1985.

Pennsylvania Academy of the Fine Arts. *The Last 3 Years—A Selection of Recent Acquisitions.* Philadelphia, 1978.

Pfister, Harold Francis. *Facing the Light: Historic American Portrait Daguerreotypes.* Washington, D.C., 1978.

Pierce, Catharine W. "Francis Alexander." *Old-Time New England* 44 (October–December 1953): 29–44.

———. "Further Notes on Francis Alexander." *Old-Time New England* 56 (October–December 1965): 35–44.

Pintard, John. *Letters from John Pintard to His Daughter, Eliza Noel Pintard Davidson, 1816–1833.* 4 vols. New York, 1940–1941.

Poesch, Jessie J. "A Precise View of Peale's Museum." *Antiques* 78 (October 1960): 343–45.

Polk, James K. *The Diary of James K. Polk, During His Presidency, 1845 to 1849.* Edited by Milo Milton Quaife. 4 vols. Chicago, 1910.

Poorc, Bcnjamin Pcrlcy. *Perley's Reminiscences of Sixty Years in the National Metropolis.* 2 vols. Philadelphia, 1886.

Price, Samuel Woodson. *The Old Masters of the Bluegrass: Jouett, Bush, Grimes, Frazer, Morgan, Hart.* Louisville, Ky., 1902.

Prucha, Francis Paul. *Indian Peace Medals in American History.* Lincoln, Nebr., 1971.

Pyatt, Joseph O. *Memoir of Albert Newsam.* Philadelphia, 1868.

Quincy, Josiah. *Figures of the Past.* Boston, 1883.

Reaves, Wendy Wick, ed. *American Portrait Prints.* Charlottesville, Va., 1984.

Reid, John, and John Henry Eaton. *The Life of Andrew Jackson.* Philadelphia, 1817.

Remini, Robert V. *Andrew Jackson and the Course of American Empire, 1767–1821; American Freedom, 1822–1832; American Democracy, 1833–1845.* 3 vols. New York, 1977–1984.

Richardson, E. P. "Archives of American Art Records of Art Collectors and Dealers: I. Miner K. Kellogg." *Art Quarterly* 23 (Autumn 1960): 271–77.

Rutledge, Anna Wells. *Catalogue of Paintings in the Council Chamber, City Hall, Charleston, South Carolina.* Charleston, S.C., 1943.

———. "Early Painter Rediscovered: William Wilson." *American Collector* 15 (April 1946): 8–21.

———. "William Henry Brown of Charleston." *Antiques* 60 (December 1951): 532–33.

———. "Paintings in the Council Chamber of Charleston's City Hall." *Antiques* 98 (November 1970): 794–99.

———, comp. *Cumulative Record of Exhibition Catalogues: The Pennsylvania Academy of the Fine Arts, 1807–1870.* Philadelphia, 1955.

Sartain, John. *The Reminiscences of a Very Old Man, 1808–1897.* New York, 1899.

Schlesinger, Arthur M., Jr. *The Age of Jackson.* Boston, 1945.

Scott, Emma Look. "Ralph Earl: Painter to Andrew Jackson." *Taylor-Trotwood Magazine* 7 (April 1908): 29–34.

Sellers, Charles Coleman. *Charles Willson Peale.* 2 vols. Philadelphia, 1939–1947.

Sherman, Frederick Fairchild. "Samuel L. Waldo and William Jewett, Portrait Painters." *Art in America and Elsewhere* 18 (February 1930): 81–86.

"60 Americans Since 1800." *Art News* 45 (December 1946): 30–39.

Smith, Seba. *Letters Written During the President's Tour, 'Down East,' by Myself, Major Jack Downing, of Downingville.* Cincinnati, Ohio, 1833.

A Souvenir of the Exhibition Entitled Healy's Sitters . . . on View at the Virginia Museum of Fine Arts in Richmond. Richmond, Va., 1950.

"Statue to Jackson." *United States Magazine, and Democratic Review* 17 (July–August 1845): 3–4.

Stauffer, David McNeely, and Mantle Fielding. *American Engravers upon Copper and Steel.* 3 vols. New York, 1907–1917.

Stehle, R. L. "Ferdinand Pettrich in America." *Pennsylvania History* 33 (October 1966): 389–411.

Stephens, Stephen DeWitt. *The Mavericks, American Engravers.* New Brunswick, N.J., 1950.

Stuart, James. *Three Years in North America.* 2 vols. Edinburgh, 1833.

Sullivan, Edmund B. *American Political Badges and Medalets, 1789–1892.* Lawrence, Mass., 1981.

Swan, Mabel M. "Master Hubard, Profilist and Painter." *Antiques* 15 (June 1929): 496–500.

———. "A Neglected Aspect of Hubard." *Antiques* 20 (October 1931): 222–23.

Swett, Lucia Gray, comp. *John Ruskin's Letters to Francesca and Memoirs of the Alexanders.* Boston, 1931.

Thorpe, Russell Walton. "The Waldo Portraits: Of Our Seventh President." *Antiques* 53 (May 1948): 364–65.

Toledano, Roulhac B., and W. Joseph Fulton. "Portrait Painting in Colonial and Ante-bellum New Orleans." *Antiques* 93 (June 1968): 788–95.

Trollope, Frances. *Domestic Manners of the Americans.* Edited by Donald Smalley. New York, 1949.

Tudor, Henry. *Narrative of a Tour in North America.* 2 vols. London, 1834.

Turner, Craig J. "Early Engravings of Andrew Jackson." *S.P.A. Journal* 37 (March–April 1975): 421–509.

Van Buren, Martin. *Annual Report of the American Historical Association for the Year 1918 . . . Autobiography of Martin Van Buren.* Edited by John C. Fitzpatrick. Vol. 2. Washington, D.C., 1920.

Voss, Frederick S. *John Frazee, 1790–1852, Sculptor.* Washington, D.C., 1986.

Ward, John William. *Andrew Jackson, Symbol for An Age.* New York, 1962.

Welling, William. *Photography in America: The Formative Years, 1839–1900.* New York, 1978.

Wharton, Anne Hollingsworth. *Social Life in the Early Republic.* Philadelphia, 1902.

Whiteman, Maxwell. *Paintings and Sculpture at the Union League of Philadelphia.* Philadelphia, 1978.

Wikoff, Henry. *The Reminiscences of an Idler.* New York, 1880.

William James Hubard, 1807–1862: A Concurrent Study and Exhibition, January, 1948. Exhibition catalogue. Valentine Museum. Richmond, Va., 1948.

William Rush, American Sculptor. Exhibition catalogue. Pennsylvania Academy of the Fine Arts. Philadelphia, 1982.

Zellman, Michael David, comp. *American Art Analog.* 3 vols. New York, 1986.

Index

Italicized page numbers refer to illustrations.

Clay, Henry, 53, 75, 78, 81, 85, 153, 154,
156, 157, 158, 159, 161, 170, 171,
199–200; portraits of, 53, 123, 126,
131, 182, 189, 192, 199, 200, 219
Claypoole, James, 53
Clevenger, Shobal, 88
Coffee, John, 43, 45, 125, 223–24, 225
Coffee, John Donelson, 125
Coffee, Mary Donelson, 224
Coffin handbills, 153, *154,* 162
Compromise Tariff of 1833, 115
Connecticut: artists in, 102, 110, 116;
Jackson in, 115, 163
Constitution, USS, 164–65, 166
Cooper, Washington Bogart, 225, 226, 227
Cooper, William (artist), 225
Cooper, William (merchant), 57
Cornelius and Baker, 216
Corwine, Aaron: portrait of Jackson after,
98; portrait of Jackson by, 74, 85, *86,*
87, 124
Crawford, William H., 53, 77, 85, 152
Creek Indians, 27, 28, 32
Creek War, 75, 92, 125, 153
Currier, Nathaniel: lithograph of Jackson
by, *207*

Dacre, Henry: caricature of Jackson by, *173*
Daguerre, Louis Jacques Mandé, 193
Dallas, Alexander J., 41
Danforth, Moseley Isaac: engraving of
Jackson by, 176, *189,* 211
Dasha, R., 96
David, Jacques-Louis, 79, 213
Davis, Charles Augustus, 123
Davis, E. S., 93
Davis, Warren R., 167
Debucourt, Philibert-Louis, 34
Decker, John, 89
Delaplaine, Joseph, 34, 45, 54, 190
Delaroche, Paul, 218
Dewey, Samuel W., 166
Dickens, Charles, 111
Dickerson, Mahlon, 166
Dickinson, Charles, 32, 76
Dinwiddie (Jackson servant), 223
Distribution Bill, 169–70
Dodge, Jeremiah, & Son, 166
Dodge, John Wood: engraving of Jackson
after, *189,* 211; likenesses of Jackson
after, *190;* miniatures of Jackson by,
176, 188–89, *190*
Donelson, Andrew Jackson, 54, 113, 120,
136, 167, 179, 186
Donelson, Emily, 119, 136, 155
Doney, Thomas: engraving of Jackson by,
194
Drake, Joseph Rodman, 62
Durand, Asher B., 230; engraving of
Jackson by, *67;* portraits of Jackson by,
102, 123, *124, 125,* 180
Durant, Charles Ferson, 164

Earl, Jane Caffery, 43, 45
Earl, Ralph, 42
Earl, Ralph E. W., 28, 42–46, 55, 96, 109,
114, 115, 126, 134, 135–47, 152, 176,

177, 188, 193, 226–227; engravings of
Jackson after, 74, *91,* 106, *139, 141,
206,* 207; portrait of Jackson attributed
to, *48;* portraits of Jackson by, 28, 29,
32, 43, *44, 45,* 46, 64, *88, 89, 90,* 91,
92–93, 94, 134, 135, *136, 137,* 138,
139, 140, 141, *142, 143, 144, 145,*
146–47, 183, 191, 197, 199, *222,* 224–
25, *230, 231, 232*
Earle, James, 55, 87
Eaton, Charles J. M., 122
Eaton, John Henry, 39, 41, 42, 77, 78, 82,
83, 84, 96, 103, 110, 138, 139–40, 155,
156
Eaton, Margaret O'Neale (Peggy), 110,
138, 150, 155, 156
Eckfeldt, Adam, 104
Eckstein, Frederick, 119, 185; bust of
Jackson by, 74, 87–88
Eckstein, Johann, 87–88
Edouart, Auguste, 190
Edwards, J. M., 194. *See also* Anthony,
Edwards & Co.
Edwin, David, 56; engraving of Jackson by,
38, *39,* 41
Elliott, Jesse D., 164–65, 166
Endicott, George, 157, 163, 167
Esselman, Dr. John H., 207
Etter, David Rent: portrait of Jackson by,
102, *125*

Fairman, Gideon, 83, 96
Flisher, Edith, 227
Florida, 28, 32, 50, 51, 53, 66, 69, 74, 75,
89, 138, 151
Force Bill, 115
Forrest, Edwin, 214
Forsyth, John, 126
Fowler, Trevor Thomas, 192; portraits of
Jackson by, 176, 184, *185*
France: artists in, 197, 198; spoliations
claims against, 123, 150, 167–69, 196
Frazee, John: busts of Jackson by, 102, 117,
118, 119
Frazee, Lydia, 117
Frazer, Oliver, 199
French, Benjamin B., 215
Fürst, Moritz: medals of Jackson by, 42, 76,
77, 102, *103, 104*

Gallatin, Albert, 27
Garlick, Theodatus: sculpture of Jackson
by, 102, 118–19
Geddes, John, 79
Georgia: artists in, 42, 43, 79
Gevelot, Nicholas: bust of Jackson by, 29
Gilpin, Henry D., 187
Gimbrede, Thomas: engraving of Jackson
by, 38, *39*
Goupil & Co., 195
Green, Duff, 96
Greenough, Horatio, 122, 126
Gros, Baron, 197, 199

Hall, Dominick Augustine, 32, 162, 217,
218
Hall, Henry B.: engraving of Jackson by,
141

Hankes, John, 94–95, 190
Harding, Chester, 98
Harrison, William, Jr.: engraving of Jackson
by, *84*
Harrison, William Henry, 170, 171, 183,
192, 193
Hart, Charles Henry, 60, 141, 195, 196
Hart, Joel Tanner: busts of Jackson by, 176,
178, 179
Hayne, Robert, 109
Healy, George P. A., 200; portraits of
Jackson by, 89, 122, 176, 197, *198,
199,* 226
Hedenberg, C. J., 218
Hemphill, Joseph, 139
Hermitage, 28, 32, 43, 44, 50, 76, 77, 85,
96, 102, 114, 119, 128, 134, 135, 136,
139, 140–41, 146, 176, 177, 178, 179,
185, 186, 188, 189, 191, 195, 197, 198,
207, 223, 225, 226
Herring, James, 108
Hervieu, Auguste: lithograph of Jackson
after, *106;* portrait of Jackson by, 102,
104, *105,* 106
Hewins, Philip: portrait of Jackson by, 102,
115, *116*
Hoffy, Alfred M.: caricature of Jackson by,
159, *160,* 161
Holmes, David, 28
Hone, Philip, 26, 115
Hopkinson, Joseph, 41, 76, 77
Horseshoe Bend, Mississippi Territory, 27,
32
Houdon, Jean-Antoine, 59, 119
Houston, Sam, 78, 91, 207
Hubard, William James, 190; likeness of
Jackson after, *206,* 207; lithographs of
Jackson after, 102, 111, *112, 113;*
portrait of Jackson by, 102, 111;
silhouette of Jackson attributed to, *94,*
95

Illman, Thomas: engraving of Jackson by,
115
Imbert, Anthony, 166, 167
Indian Removal Bill, 102, 103, 104
Indians, 27, 28, 103–4, 151, 163–64. *See
also* Black Hawk; Chickasaw Indians;
Creek Indians; Creek War; Indian
Removal Bill; Seminole War
Ingham, Samuel D., 156
Inman, Henry, 41, 184, 225
Italy: artists in, 106, 111, 121, 122, 199

Jackson, Amy Rich, 226
Jackson, Andrew: attempted assassination,
122–23, 150, 166–67; as congressman,
27, 32, 37; death, 198; early years, 26–
28; election of 1824, 46, 74, 85; health,
33, 69, 76, 87, 96, 115, 116, 120, 123,
178, 179, 184, 185, 188, 190, 193, 194,
195, 197–98; military career, 26, 27, 28,
33–34, 37, 43–44, 50, 51, 54, 69, 75,
151, 162; physical description, 27, 28,
37, 42, 60–61, 62, 75, 76, 111, 120,
124, 138, 144, 179, 180, 186, 190, 198;
as President, 74, 75, 96, 102, 103, 110,
114, 115, 119, 123, 125, 135–36, 138,

❧
Photography Credits

Jan White Brantley: Figures 7, 147, 148, 163
Brenwasser: Figure 180
June Dorman: Figures 47, 59, 60, 108, 112, 118, 134, 150, 159, 192, and page 141 (beaver hat)
Fouts Commercial Photography: Figure 53
Jim Frank: Figures 25, 26
Helga Photo Studio: Figure 97
Tom Liddell: Figures 3, 15, 40, 48, 54, 64, 65, 68, 76, 77, 88, 98, 102, 103, 106, 136, 144, 171, 189, 190, 191, 193, 195, 206, and pages 91 (subscription list), 141 (cane), and 189 (sword and spectacles)
McLaughlin Studios & Associates: Figure 92
Thomas Moulin, Moulin Studios: Figure 93
J. Nathan Prichard: Figure 145
Joseph Szaszfai: Figure 20
Warolin: Figure 197
Rolland White: Figures 4, 5, 8, 10, 14, 22, 23, 29, 32, 36, 43, 44, 45, 52, 55, 70, 71, 74, 75, 78, 94, 95, 99, 113, 114, 152, 154, 157, 158, 162, 164, 165, 173, 174, 175, 176, 183, 185, 196

❧
Andrew Jackson: A Portrait Study

Edited by Frances K. Stevenson and Dru Dowdy

Designed by Polly Sexton, Washington, D.C., and electronically typeset in Adobe Garamond by Unicorn Graphics, Washington, D.C.

Printed on eighty-pound Warren's Lustro Offset Enamel White with Strathmore Grandee Ivory endsheets by Collins Lithographing and Printing Company Inc., Baltimore, Maryland